WRITING

A GUIDE FOR BUSINESS PROFESSIONALS

WRITING

A GUIDE FOR BUSINESS PROFESSIONALS

C. W. GRIFFIN
Virginia Commonwealth University

HARCOURT BRACE JOVANOVICH, PUBLISHERS

San Diego New York Chicago Austin Washington, D.C.
London Sydney Tokyo Toronto

To
Dick, *who got me started*
Hanna, *who helped along the way*
Barbara, *who saw it through with me*

ISBN: 0-15-597676-1

Library of Congress Catalog Card Number: 86-81624

Printed in the United States of America

Copyrights and Acknowledgments **pp. 79–80** Copyright © 1980 by The New York Times Company. Reprinted by permission. **p. 89** Reprinted by permission of James J. Kilpatrick. **pp. 278–82** Reprinted from "How to Keep Your Honda Car Alive," with permission of John Muir Publications, Santa Fe, NM 87504. **pp. 375–77** Reprinted by permission of the *Northwestern Endicott Report*, published by The Placement Center, Northwestern University, Evanston, IL.

PREFACE

The goal of this book is to teach students to write well on the job. It draws on recent research in the field of business writing, uses examples drawn from actual documents, and involves students in realistic writing situations to show them how to write on-the-job documents clearly, interestingly, and persuasively.

Part 1, "The Writing Process," shows students how to analyze a writing situation by clarifying their goals, understanding their readers , and deciding on the appropriate voice to use. Then it helps them become aware of the informational, organizational, stylistic, and design choices they can make in a particular writing situation.

Part 2, "Letters and Memos," begins by familiarizing students with the standard formats for letters and memos, with their methods of production in a modern office, and with the various contexts in which they can be written. Then it presents strategies for informing and persuading readers in letters and memos—what to say and what not to say, how to organize ideas, what style is appropriate to use, and how to design letters and memos for quick reading.

Part 3, "Long Documents," focuses on reports, proposals, manuals, and oral presentations. It begins with two preparatory chapters: The first chapter explains how to plan a long document—how to clarify goals, adapt to multiple audiences, identify the kind of information needed, find that information, and make an outline. The second chapter shows how graphics—tables, charts, and graphs—can be employed in longer documents.

Each of the subsequent chapters—on reports, proposals, and manuals—addresses a specific problem in writing longer documents. The chapter on reports teaches students how to organize facts, opinions, and recommendations in order to present information clearly. The chapter on proposals explains how to adapt the material to the degree of resistance expected from readers. Finally, the chapter on manuals shows students how to explain complex procedures and systems in concise, straightforward terms.

Part 4, "Your Job Campaign," is more detailed than is usual in texts of this type. Most students in a business writing course are preparing to look for a job. "Your Job Campaign" discusses how the research and writing techniques described earlier may be applied to the tasks of identifying a fulfilling career (Chapter 15), designing a résumé, writing a cover letter, and preparing for an interview (Chapter 16).

Part 5, "Editing Your Writing," is based on a careful study of the kinds of mistakes students actually make when learning to write on the job. After showing students how important it is to follow the conventions of standard English, Part 5 gives strategies for locating and solving problems of grammar, punctuation, spelling, and mechanics.

"Easy writing's curst hard reading," said the Irish playwright Richard Brinsley Sheridan. Writing this book has *not* been easy. I have examined thousands of documents, talked with hundreds of writers at work, studied current research in the field, and followed the advice of a number of colleagues. But I hope the result will be easy to understand and easy to use. I also hope it will prove to be a helpful tool for instructors and a practical guide for students.

Thanks go to many people in the business and academic worlds, including colleagues Jim Kinney, Dorothy Scura, and Ann Woodlief at Virginia Commonwealth University and Barbara Walvoord at Loyola College in Maryland, all of whom encouraged me during the early stages of this project. Thanks also go to those who reviewed the manuscript in various stages, including Deborah Andreen, University of Delaware; Larry Bush, Virginia Commonwealth University; Michael Connaughton, St. Cloud State University; Robert Gieselman, University of Illinois at Urbana-Champaign; Janet Kotler, University of Richmond; Dick Leatherman, International Training Consultants; Jeanette Morgan, University of Houston-University Park; Richard Ramsey, Indiana University at Fort Wayne; and Jim Suchan, University of Alabama. Warmest thanks to Susan Wiseman, an editor so capable as to be often a co-author. And finally, thanks to Marlane Agriesti, Debbie Hardin, and others at Harcourt Brace Jovanovich who gave me their support, encouragement, and good advice.

C. W. GRIFFIN

CONTENTS

WRITING

A GUIDE FOR BUSINESS PROFESSIONALS

PART

1

The Writing Process

CHAPTER

1

Analyzing Writing Situations

This chapter will show you some of the challenges you will face when writing at work. Then it will help you cope with these challenges by understanding the process of writing.

A Writing Situation

A strip-mining operator applies for a permit to mine coal in a small valley. Almost immediately, the families living there protest to their state representative that strip-mining will deface their land and ruin thousands of acres of good crop land. The representative writes to the governor, demanding that the permit not be granted.

The governor is in a quandary. He wants to support the coal mining industry in his state, but he does not want to take any action that will alienate the representative and his constituency. To resolve his dilemma, the governor instructs one of his cabinet secretaries to study the problem and determine whether or not the permit should be granted. He wants a brief report recommending the action he should take, accompanied by two letters giving his response to the mining operator and to the representative. He will then send the letters out with his signature.

As is typical in any large organization, the problem is passed down the chain of command—from the cabinet secretary to a division director, to a project manager, and finally, to the people who will actually write the report and letters. Here is what happens.

The cabinet secretary turns the assignment over to the director of the Division of Labor and Natural Resources, the agency responsible for such matters. She instructs the director to prepare a report studying alternative solutions and recommending the best one. She also tells him to draft the letters of response to the mining operator and the representative. The division director then gives the task to the appropriate project manager within the agency, who in turn assigns it to her staff to complete by the fifteenth of the month.

The staff sets to work on the problem. Their study goes well and they agree on the substance of the report. But they almost miss the deadline because they cannot agree on the report's organization and style. Finally, they agree to set it up as a technical report, beginning with a statement of the problem, followed by detailed discussions of each alternative they studied, and concluding with the alternative they recommend. To minimize arguments about style, they assign the best writer in the group to draft the report and the governor's two letters, which the group will then critique and revise. This efficient process produces, in the shortest amount of time, a final draft that reflects the best thinking of the group.

Now the documents start back up the chain of command. First, they are submitted to the project manager. Because she is familiar with the methodology and terminology used by her staff, she understands the report quickly and approves it. She does ask that they justify their recommended solution in more detail by discussing several additional studies that support it. Since she does not know how a letter from the governor should sound, she ignores the drafts of the governor's two letters.

After the project manager receives the revised report, she submits it to her division director. The director approves its substance, but is disturbed by its language and organization. "You've got to remember," he tells the project manager, "the cabinet secretary and the governor are not specialists in this field. They won't understand the technical language used in this report. And they're not going to take the time to read to the end to get to the solution you recommend. Start by describing the problem and your solution, so they can get to these quickly. Then follow with detailed discussions of all the solutions you studied. Also, cut out this detailed rationale (the very material the project manager had told her staff to include a week earlier). They won't care about all this."

The report is sent back to the staff and the revisions are made. The division director then submits the materials to the cabinet secretary, who approves the report, but does not like the sound of the letters. "You're making the governor sound too distant and formal," she says. "Get rid of some of those big words and stuffy expressions. Make him sound like a human being so people will like him and want to accept his recommendations." So the division director revises the letters. Finally, the materials reach the governor, who skims the report for its main ideas, accepts its recommendation, and signs the letters after scanning them hurriedly.

WRITING ON THE JOB—FACING COMPLEX CHALLENGES

Writing at work often means facing complex challenges. Situations like the one you just read about are *not* uncommon. The writers in this situation coped with a number of challenges.

- The writers had to adapt their writing to readers with different interests and expectations. Their project manager was particularly concerned that they support their arguments with enough evidence. On the other hand, the agency director assumed that their evidence was sound and was more concerned that the report be written simply and directly, so that a nontechnical reader could understand it easily. Much writing done on the job is subject to such differing demands and pressures.
- The writers had to make sure that the report was organized so that busy readers like the governor and his cabinet secretary could pick up the main points quickly. This meant that they had to realize that the major goal of the report was to resolve the governor's dilemma by recommending the best solution, not to give him detailed discussions of each alternative. This solution was then highlighted at the beginning of the report.
- The writers even had to be concerned about the tone of voice of their letters, making sure they sounded the way the governor would want to sound.
- Other problems the writers faced are typical of those that confront writers at work. They had to learn to write efficiently as a group, to accept the criticism of multiple readers, and to be willing to continue revising their documents until they had satisfied everyone.

Although you won't always have to write in a group or satisfy the different needs of so many readers, writing on the job will pose similar challenges for you. Over the course of your career, you will have to write a variety of documents: letters, memos, and reports certainly, and probably also proposals and manuals.

Some of your writing situations will be fairly simple ones. You may have to write a letter to a client confirming an order, a memo to employees summarizing vacation schedules, a report on the results of a trip, or a proposal to add an inexpensive piece of equipment. But some will be more complex. You may have to write a memo to employees that explains why their working hours have to be cut back, a letter to a client that diplomatically explains that the breakdown of a system was his fault, or a proposal convincing management to adopt a new and expensive system.

ANALYZING WRITING SITUATIONS

This book will prepare you to cope with the challenges of writing on the job by giving you a way to *think* about the writing you do. Writing is a process of making *decisions* and *choices*. For example, when writing a research report, you decide to include some of the information you have found but to leave out other information. You decide to organize your report in a certain way, perhaps beginning with a statement of your major goal. And you constantly make word and sentence choices—rejecting one word for another and shortening one sentence while you lengthen another.

But what are these decisions and choices based on? They are based on your analysis of a writing situation—what you want to accomplish with your reader, who your reader is, and how you want to sound in the document. In a research report, you begin with a statement of your major *goal* because you want your reader to understand it right away. You include some information because you think your *reader* will be interested in it, and exclude other information that he or she already knows. And you revise a sentence to make it clearer or choose one word over another because it makes you *sound* better.

In this book, you will learn how to use this process to write effective letters, memos, reports, proposals, and manuals. The rest of this chapter will give you an overview of the process. You will see how to analyze each writing situation you face by clarifying the goals you want to achieve, understanding the needs and expectations of your readers, and deciding on the appropriate voice you want to use. Let's look more closely at the three steps in analyzing your writing situation.

Your Goals

The report writers in our coal mining example had to reorganize their report because they didn't realize that their major goal was to recommend the best solution to the governor's dilemma, not to provide him with detailed discussions of every alternative. In this book, you will learn to clarify your goals in each writing situation. Sometimes, your major goal will be obvious. You'll know right away that you are writing a memo to warn someone about a problem, or a letter to answer someone's question about a policy. But at other times, you'll have to think hard to clarify your goals. There will be times when you realize that you have more than one goal—you may want to announce a change in vacation policy but also make sure that employees accept the new policy willingly. You'll also see that your goals can change over the course of writing a document, especially if it's a long one. For example, a letter that begins as an attempt to answer a client's complaint may turn into an attempt to persuade her to continue with your product in spite of current problems.

Your Readers

In light of your goals, you will learn to analyze your readers' needs and expectations. Nontechnical readers will need simple and concise explanations of technical subjects, while more technical readers may want precise and detailed discussions of the same subjects. A busy executive may not take the time to read all the way to the end of a report to find your recommendations—he will want to see them at the beginning. (Remember how the division director in the coal mining example required his writers to reorganize their report for the governor, putting their recommended solution at the beginning.) And an angry client may care little for an explanation of why a problem occurred, but will want to know right away what you are going to do about it.

Your Voice

As you read this book, you are hearing the sound of someone talking to you. This sound is called the *voice* of a piece of writing. I hope the voice you are hearing at the moment sounds helpful and friendly—that's my intention. But the original letters written for the governor's signature sounded anything but friendly. In fact, his cabinet secretary was so bothered by their formal and distant sound that she had them revised so they sounded more appropriate for the situation. You will also have to shift your voice to fit your writing situation. Sometimes, you will want to sound more formal—a report to top managers should certainly reflect your respect for their position in the organization. But other occasions will require different voices—a memo to a co-worker or a letter to a client can be less formal and more friendly.

MAKING DECISIONS AND CHOICES

Your analysis of each writing situation—the way you clarify your goals, understand your readers, and decide on your voice—will lead you to make certain *decisions and choices* as you write and revise. Our coal mining situation is a good example of how this process works, although the decisions and choices were made not by the original group of writers but by their superiors. Remember that their project manager decided they needed to add more technical information to the report at one point. Of course, their division director later decided to take it out. The director also decided that the report should be organized differently and that the writers should use simpler language. Then the cabinet secretary suggested that they change the wording of the letters to make the governor seem less distant and formal.

The decisions and choices you make in each writing situation will be drawn from four broad categories.

Your Information

You will make certain information choices, deciding *what* to say in a particular memo, report, or proposal. In a report, for instance, you may choose to discuss both sides of a question to enable your readers to make the best decision possible. Or, to make a proposal more convincing, you may choose to describe the advantages of a proposed new system in great detail.

Your Organization

You will also decide *how* to organize your document, grouping facts and ideas in certain ways and locating main ideas in certain places. For example, in order to convince your manager to buy a new piece of equipment, you may organize your memo around the *problem* that the old equipment is creating and the *solution* that the new equipment would provide. Writing a report to busy decision makers, you may decide to summarize your major recommendations right at the beginning to let them know what you think they should do. But in a proposal suggesting a change to someone who has continually opposed it, you may decide to begin with your most convincing arguments before you make the actual proposal.

Your Design

On the basis of your analysis of a writing situation, you will decide how to design or lay out your document on the page. For a memo to employees to be posted on the bulletin board, you will probably try to write in short paragraphs that can be read and understood quickly. In a letter responding to someone's questions, you might break up answers into separate paragraphs, using a different heading for each one. And when writing user manuals that explain how to operate a complex system, you will probably use a variety of design techniques, such as headings, listings, and highlighting with different type styles.

Your Style

Your stylistic choices—the kinds of words you use and the types of sentences you put them in—will grow principally out of the voice you decide to use. At times, you will choose such formal words as "accumulate," "avoid," or "ascend." At other times, you may choose their more informal equivalents, "collect," "stay away from," or "climb up." You will also choose to cast your sentences in certain ways, varying their length, structure, and emphasis.

The following diagram illustrates this process of analyzing the writing situation at work.

You analyze a writing situation to	Clarify your goals Understand your readers Decide on your voice
This understanding leads you to make decisions and choices about your	Information Organization Design Style

But don't let this discussion of the writing process mislead you. Some real, on-the-job writing situations are going to be a lot less complicated than I've indicated. Many of the letters, memos, and reports you write will be so routine that you will hardly need to analyze your writing situation at all. Because you have written these documents so many times before, you will already have worked out your decisions about goals, readers, and voice. In these situations, words, sentences, and even whole paragraphs may come to you without much effort at all.

This discussion also makes the whole process seem much more orderly and rational than it really is. Your own experience tells you that writing isn't just a mechanical, step-by-step process in which you first clarify goals, understand readers, and decide on your voice, then painstakingly make decisions about what information to include or how to organize it. Rather, you will find yourself focusing at different times on different concerns. At one point, you may have to clarify the major goal of a report so you will know how to organize it. At another point in that report, you may be more concerned about whether using a particular word will express just the personality you want to project.

And you will often circle back and forth when writing a document—making, remaking, and making yet again a decision about what to say or how to say it. You may change your mind three or four times about the major goal of a proposal, begin a letter again and again until you have found just the right voice, or revise a paragraph or shift it around to improve your organization.

In other words, this discussion of how to analyze a writing situation is not a complete description of your writing process. Nor is it a system or set of procedures that you can follow step by step. Writing is just too complicated to be boiled down to one model or a set of rules or formulas. But when you *are* having problems in a particular situation—wondering what word to use, what idea to put first, or whether to include a particular fact—this approach will help you to analyze the situation and solve your problems.

The best way to understand this approach is to see it in action. The next section of this chapter will show you how one group of writers analyzes a writing situation in order to improve an important memo. You will see how their decision about what voice to use leads them to certain word choices, how their clarification of their major goal leads them to reorganize the memo, and how their understanding of the needs of their readers leads them to omit information and change words and sentences.

A Writing Situation

Cathy McCleney, vice-president of a small manufacturing company, has a tricky memo to write. About a month ago, her company decided to adopt a flextime work schedule, a system that allows employees to choose the hours they will work. Most people in the company endorsed the new system, but some were skeptical and a few were downright negative.

Cathy must now tell employees when flextime will be implemented, explain how the system will work, and persuade them to accept the new system. After pacing the floor, she prepares a rough outline and then dictates her draft into a tape recorder for her secretary, Sam. A little later, he keys the memo into his word processor, inserting a few needed punctuation marks and checking spelling with the word processing program's spelling checker.

"Well, what do you think of it?" Cathy asks Sam when he brings her the completed memo.

MEMORANDUM

TO: All Employees
FROM: Catherine McCleney
SUBJECT: Flextime Procedures
DATE: February 4, 19--

The company's innovative flextime system will be implemented beginning March 1, 19--. Beginning on this date, employees will work successive shifts. The first shift will begin at 7:30 a.m. and finish at 3:30 p.m.; the next will begin at 8:00 and finish at 4:00; the next will begin at 8:30 and finish at 4:30; and the final one will begin at 9:00 and finish at 5:00.

It is necessary that all employees in each division meet with their department managers to design their work schedules in such a manner that all assignments are performed to their fullest and in a timely manner. Department managers must insure that enough personnel are present in each department to carry out its functions. All phones in customer service must be manned at all times, personnel must be at each station on the production line, and invoice processing must be done expeditiously.

With the cooperation of all employees, this system can be made to succeed.

"To tell you the truth, Ms. McCleney, I'm just not sure," says Sam tactfully. "Frankly, the memo seems a little confusing to me. Is there any way you could make it seem less complicated?"

"This thing needs a little more work," responds Cathy. "Maybe I'd better get some help on it."

Later that morning, at the meeting of her three division directors, Cathy says, "I've written that flextime memo, but I'm having some problems. I want to get it right because I'm worried about the way people are going to react to this new system. You remember how touchy some were when we first brought it up."

Rich O'Brien, director of customer relations, is the first to skim the memo. "You know," he says, "there's nothing really wrong with this memo. But I do see some ways to improve it. For one thing, it's a little too authoritarian. Your tone of voice will get some people even more upset than they already are."

"Why don't you personalize the style a little and maybe simplify the language? You could substitute 'Cathy' for 'Catherine' in your From line, change 'The company's' to 'Our' in the first line to make everyone feel included, and substitute 'start' for 'implemented.'"

Cathy starts to interrupt, but before she can, Rich continues. "And if you personalize the first paragraph, you've got to personalize the second one too. Begin it by saying that you need people's assistance. That seems less formal and distant than 'It is necessary that. . . .' You might *ask* people to meet with their department managers rather than order them to, and you could substitute 'Your cooperation' for 'With the cooperation of' in that last sentence."

Cathy is a little taken aback by all these suggestions, but finally has Sam make the changes on the word processor. Turn to page 12 to see how the revised memo looks.

"Those changes do improve the memo," Cathy admits, a little grudgingly. "Anybody got any others?"

"You're right, it's much better," chimes in Thelma Johnson from finance. "But I see another problem.

"If you're just trying to tell people when the new flextime system begins, then that first sentence is fine. People want to know when it will start and you're telling them. But remember how reluctant some people were about this new system. Aren't you also trying to persuade people to accept the system? If that's true, why not begin with its benefits? Maybe these will convince them to give it a try. Then you can get to other particulars. Also, I don't think you need to spell out every little detail of the shifts in the first paragraph. Let the department managers do that."

After Thelma suggests some other changes, the memo is prepared again. Look on page 13.

"This is looking better all the time," says Vince Pacelli, director of operations. "But it still looks a little too cluttered to me. Why not divide the first paragraph up into two? And simplify some of those

MEMORANDUM

TO: All Employees
FROM: Cathy McCleney
SUBJECT: Flextime Procedures
DATE: February 4, 19--

Our new flextime system will start on March 1. Beginning on this date, employees will work successive shifts. The first shift will begin at 7:30 a.m. and finish at 3:30 p.m.; the next will begin at 8:00 and finish at 4:00; the next will begin at 8:30 and finish at 4:30; and the final one will begin at 9:00 and finish at 5:00.

We need your assistance to operate this system successfully. Please meet with your department manager to design work schedules in such a manner that all assignments are performed to their fullest and in a timely manner. Department managers must insure that enough personnel are present in each department to carry out its functions. All phones in customer service must be manned at all times, personnel must be at each station on the production line, and invoice processing must be done expeditiously.

Your cooperation will make this program a success and benefit everyone.

words and sentences. Our people in operations hate to read complicated memos!

"In that second paragraph, you could change 'assistance' to 'help.' And if you change that, you ought to simplify 'to operate' too. What about substituting 'to make' instead? And shorten that second sentence! That whole thing could read something like, 'Please meet with your department manager to schedule work so that all assignments are performed fully and efficiently.'

"For that matter, most people don't even need that sentence or the rest of this paragraph. That information should be given just to

MEMORANDUM

TO: All Employees
FROM: Cathy McCleney
SUBJECT: Flextime Procedures
DATE: February 4, 19--

After March 1, you will be able to design your own working day. This is the date that our new flextime procedure goes into effect. You can come in as early as 7:30 a.m. and leave at 3:30 p.m., or you can arrive as late as 9:00 a.m. and stay until 5:00 p.m. If you have children, you can get them off to school before coming to work. If you like to do things in the afternoon, you can come in early and leave early.

But we need your assistance to operate this system successfully. Please meet with your department manager to design your work schedule in such a manner that all assignments are performed to their fullest and in a timely manner. Department managers must insure that enough personnel are present in each department to carry out its functions. All phones in customer service must be manned at all times, personnel must be at each station on the production line, and invoice processing must be done expeditiously.

Your cooperation will make this program a success and benefit everyone.

department managers anyway. Why not leave the rest of the paragraph out and announce it to the managers at this afternoon's meeting? Then you could just end the memo by reminding people that they will be meeting with their managers soon to work out schedules."

Look on page 14 to see how Vince's revisions turned out. A memo that was dull, unclear, and unpersuasive has become interesting, clear, and convincing. As a result, employees may be more willing to accept the flextime system and more ready to help make it work.

MEMORANDUM

TO: All Employees
FROM: Cathy McCleney
SUBJECT: Flextime Procedures
DATE: February 4, 19--

After March 1, you will be able to design your own working day. This is the date that our new flextime procedure goes into effect. You can come in as early as 7:30 and leave at 3:30, or you can arrive as late as 9:00 and stay until 5:00.

This system should make all our lives a little easier. If you have children, you can get them off to school before coming to work. And if you like to do things in the afternoon, you can come in early and leave early.

But your department manager will need your help to make this system a success. He or she will be meeting with you shortly to work out schedules.

Your cooperation will make this program a success and benefit everyone.

How did Cathy's group do it? They analyzed their writing situation—their goals, readers, and voice—and therefore made some basic changes in the way the memo was written.

- They decided that the voice should be more personal and therefore chose less formal language.
- They realized that their major goal was to persuade people to accept the change, not just to tell them about it. They therefore reorganized the memo so that it began with how the new system would benefit employees.

- They considered the needs of their readers carefully and therefore made the memo more readable by simplifying words, shortening sentences and paragraphs, and leaving out unnecessary information.

APPROACHING THE WRITING PROCESS

The situation just described is a kind of dramatic model of the way you will write and revise at work. Obviously, you won't always write in a group and get the help of others. But you can approach your writing problems in the same way. If you are wondering how to begin planning an important proposal for a client, start by clarifying your major goal. Ask yourself, "Exactly what do I want to accomplish?" If you are trying to decide whether to include a particular section in a proposal or report, ask yourself, "Do my readers need to know this?" And if you are trying to decide whether to begin a letter or memo with the more formal "Enclosed are the . . ." or the more everyday "Here are the . . .," recognize this as a voice problem and ask yourself what voice would be more appropriate.

You know that writing is not a simple process—following a few rules won't produce a good letter or memo. But there *is* a way to think about the process, a way to analyze each writing situation you will face. The goal of this book is to familiarize you with the kinds of writing situations you will face at work and to show you how to analyze them so you can write most effectively. The next chapter will show you in detail how to go about clarifying your goals, analyzing your readers, and deciding on the most appropriate voice to use. Chapters three and four will demonstrate the range of information, organization, design, and stylistic choices you can make and show you how these can grow out of your analysis of a writing situation. The rest of the book will show you how to use the approach you have learned to write the letters, memos, reports, proposals, manuals, and other documents you will have to write on the job.

SUMMARY

1. To write well on the job, you will have to cope with complex challenges.
2. To cope with these challenges, analyze each writing situation—clarifying goals, understanding readers, and deciding on an appropriate voice.
3. This analysis will lead you to make the most appropriate information, organization, design, and stylistic choices.
4. As you develop the ability to approach the writing process in this manner, the documents you write will become more interesting, clear, and convincing.

APPLICATIONS

1. To examine how you go about the process of writing, choose two very different pieces of writing you have done in the past. You might choose from some of the following examples:

   - a letter, memo, or report written at work
   - a paper written for a class
   - a journal kept over a period of time
   - a letter to a relative or friend
   - a résumé or a letter applying for a job
   - an article written for a school paper

   Now analyze the important decisions you made as you wrote each piece by answering the following questions:

   a. What *goals* did you have for each piece? Were you trying to explain something, tell about experiences you had had, or persuade someone to do something?
   b. Who were your *readers*? Were their needs and expectations different? Did they expect you to use technical language, for example? Did they expect you to know your subject well? Did they expect you to prove your points? How important were correct grammar and punctuation?
   c. What *voice* did you use in each piece? Was one voice more serious than the other? Was one more formal?

2. To find out how people write on the job, interview four or five people in different jobs. You might choose friends, relatives, as well as other people you know. Focus your questions on the following areas:

   a. What kinds of writing do you do? Is it mostly letters, memos, and reports, or do you write other kinds of documents as well? Are there any kinds of documents you have to write periodically?
   b. Are you aware of your goals when writing a particular document? Describe the major goal you were trying to accomplish in one document. Do the readers you write for have different needs and expectations? How would you describe these? Are you aware of varying your voice in the documents you write? Why do you do this?
   c. What kinds of special problems do you face as you write? Do you ever have to write a document for someone else to sign? Do you ever have to write and revise in a group? Do you ever have to write the same document for multiple readers who have different backgrounds, needs, and expectations? How do you adapt your writing to these different readers?

3. Imagine that the editor of a popular teen magazine has asked you to write a brief article (400–600 words) describing your career or intended career. Your article will appear along with 15 others in a special issue of the magazine devoted to introducing young people to a variety of different careers. You are advised that subscribers to the magazine are mostly 16–18 years old.

   Before writing the article, gather a group of four or five people to plan your approach together. Answer the following questions:

   a. Who are your *readers*? What are some of their important interests and values that you will want to appeal to in the article? Based on this analysis, what kind of information about your career will you include? What information might you omit? What kind of language will you use—how technical or difficult will your language be, for instance?
   b. What sort of *purpose or goal* will you have in mind as you plan and write the article? Will you simply describe your career for your readers or will you try to convince them that it would be an appealing one for them? On the basis of this decision, jot down a brief outline of your article. Note in particular how you will begin it, and list the major ideas you will include.
   c. How do you want your *voice* to sound in the article? Do you want to be relatively formal or informal? On the basis of your voice decision, list some words that you might *not* use in the article. In general, what kinds of words will you use? How long or short will your sentences be?

   After planning your approach, have each member of the group write his or her own article and then compare the results. How similar or different are they? Can you explain the similarities and differences?

4. People have legitimate disagreements about how to write a particular document. Often these arise because of the different ways they analyze a writing situation. You may, for instance, have disagreed with some of the decisions and choices made in the flextime memo discussed in this chapter. If you did, what were some of your disagreements? What other decisions and choices would you have made? Discuss your decisions and choices with others and then rewrite the memo according to your conclusions.

5. Working with a group of three or four others, find some examples of ineffective writing. These could be letters, memos, reports, student papers, articles in scholarly journals, and so forth. Using the approach to writing described in

this chapter, discuss how you would revise these documents. Would you include or omit information, reorganize the information, use a different style, or design the documents differently? Why would you make these changes? Would your concern be more with accomplishing a certain goal, fulfilling the needs and expectations of readers, or using a certain voice? After your discussion, have each member of your group revise one of the documents and then explain the revisions to the rest of the group.

CHAPTER

2

Your Goals, Readers, and Voices

Whether you are writing a two-paragraph memo or a two-hundred-page report, your questions will always be the same—what is my goal, who is my reader, and how should I sound? This chapter will help you answer these questions.

In the last chapter, you saw that to write well on the job, you have to analyze each writing situation carefully. Your analysis then guides you in writing an effective memo, letter, report, proposal, or other document. The purpose of this chapter is to show you in detail how to analyze a writing situation: how to clarify your major goal, analyze your readers' needs and expectations in light of this goal, and decide on the appropriate voice to use.

YOUR GOALS

A Writing Situation

Some people call the memo that follows the billion dollar memo. Why? Because it was one link in a chain of mistakes and miscommunications that contributed to the 1979 accident at Three Mile Island, a nuclear facility located in Pennsylvania. The accident occurred because the water surrounding the nuclear core fell so low that the core was uncovered and began to heat up. Meltdown, a disaster of staggering potential, was only narrowly avoided. Costs to repair the resulting damages have been estimated at one billion dollars.

Actually, some people in the company that had built the facility knew months before the accident that unless certain procedures were changed, the possibility of uncovering the core existed. Yet

BABCOCK & WILCOX COMPANY
POWER GENERATION GROUP

TO: Manager, Plant Integration
FROM: Manager, Plant Performance Services Section (2149)

SUBJECT: Operator Interruption of High Pressure Injection (HPI)
DATE: August 3, 1978

References: (1) . . . to . . . , same subject, February 9, 1978
(2) . . . to . . . , same subject, February 16, 1978

References 1 and 2 (attached) recommend a change in B&W's philosophy for HPI system use during low-pressure transients. Basically, they recommend leaving the HPI pumps on, once HPI has been initiated, until it can be determined that the hot leg temperature is more than 50° F below T_{sat} for the RCS pressure.

Nuclear Service believes this mode can cause the RCS (including the pressurizer) to go solid. The pressurizer reliefs will lift, with a water surge through the discharge piping into the quench tank.

[continued]

because of faulty communications and bureaucratic slip-ups, the procedures were not changed. After you read the memo, you will understand why. Since its subject is a technical one, you may need the following summary to understand it:

- *Paragraph 1.* This paragraph states that the attached references recommend changing a particular procedure.
- *Paragraph 2.* Nuclear Service, the department in the section that sent the memo, believes that such a change may result in problems.
- *Paragraph 3.* Therefore, it sets forth two questions that should be answered before the procedure is changed.
- *Paragraph 4.* The author of the memo notes that the attached

```
We believe the following incidents should be
evaluated:

1. If the pressurizer goes solid with one or
   more HPI pumps continuing to operate,
   would there be a pressure spike before the
   reliefs open which could cause damage to
   the RCS?

2. What damage would the water surge through
   the relief valve discharge piping and
   quench tank cause?

To date, Nuclear Service has not notified our
operating plants to change HPI policy
consistent with References 1 and 2 because of
our above-stated questions. Yet, the
references suggest the possibility of
uncovering the core if present HPI policy is
continued.

We request that Integration resolve the issue
of how the HPI system should be used. We are
available to help as needed.[1]
```

references *do* suggest that the core may be uncovered if present procedure is not changed.

- *Paragraph 5.* The author asks that the Plant Integration Unit resolve the issue.

Now imagine that you are the Plant Integration manager who receives this memo in the morning's mail. Read it quickly, just as the manager did, and see whether you can understand what the writer wants you to do.

[1]Stanley M. Gorinson and Kevin P. Kane, *Staff Report to the President's Commission on the Accident at Three Mile Island: The Role of the Managing Utility and Its Suppliers* (Washington, D.C.: U.S. Government Printing Office, 1979) 227.

The writer's major goal was to request that the Plant Integration manager resolve the question of whether procedures needed to be changed. Yet the manager didn't do it. In fact, apparently he didn't even notice the request. When he testified before the Nuclear Regulatory Commission after the accident had occurred, here is what he said about reading the memo.

> I don't recall ever really feeling the significance of what [he] was trying to communicate. It seemed to me that it was a routine matter; Nuclear Service was asking . . . two questions, and I sent it on, two of the questions [to be] answered in a rather routine manner.[2]

The important request to determine whether to change current procedures came at the end of the memo instead of the beginning. The Plant Integration manager therefore overlooked its significance and focused instead on the two questions in the middle.

The Complexity of Clarifying Your Goal

The Babcock & Wilcox memo is a classic example of the kind of misunderstanding that can occur when a writer's major goal is not clear to his or her reader. But before we condemn its writer too harshly, we might speculate about the complexity of the situation he faced. He may, in fact, have had conflicting goals. On the one hand, he probably wanted to tell his reader about the recommended change in procedure and describe his reservations. On the other hand, he wanted to request that the manager decide whether the procedures should be changed and warn of the possible consequences of not changing them. He may never have decided which of these goals was the most important and which should therefore have been highlighted. The result was this confusing and costly memo.

You will have to deal with similar problems when you write on the job. You may hardly have the time to focus on your goal, especially if you have to get a report out in half a day. Or you may be interrupted and distracted by the telephone or by people dropping in with important questions. And some of your writing projects may be so complicated that you won't be able to clarify your major goal easily. You may even face a situation like the one just described, in which you have conflicting goals. Or you may begin a letter with one goal—perhaps to answer a client's question about a new system—and realize before you finish that your goal is really to persuade your client to buy the system.

How to Choose Your Goal

Considering these kinds of constraints, how can you focus clearly on your major goal so that you can be sure of accomplishing it in any

[2]Gorinson and Kane, 135.

memo, letter, or report you write?[3] One way is to think of your major goal as the bridge between you and your readers. Your goal is how you want to affect your readers—what you want to happen to them as a result of what you have written. You may want them to feel good about a job well done, to be aware of a new company policy, to understand why a change was made, to be able to operate a new system, to buy a new piece of equipment, or to make a crucial decision.

Another way to picture your major goal in a particular situation is to see it as the "so that" of your writing—you are writing a memo *so that* your staff will follow a new procedure, a letter *so that* your client will be persuaded that you can solve his problem, a report *so that* your manager will understand exactly what's wrong with an antiquated system, or a manual *so that* an operator will be able to use a new system effectively. If you think about your major goal in this fashion, then you will have a way of continually clarifying it for yourself. Even if you lose sight of it because you become deeply involved in your subject, or if it changes as you progress through a document, or if you begin to sense that you are facing conflicting goals, you can always stop and say to yourself: "I am writing this document *so that* my reader will [be affected in this way]."

The Effects of Your Goal on Content and Organization

When you learn how to write particular documents later in this book, you'll see how a precise definition of your major goal can be particularly helpful as you decide what information to include and what to leave out. If, for instance, your major goal in a memo is to show an operator how to run a new system, you may decide not to bother to describe the system in great technical detail, since your reader doesn't need to know this. But if your major goal is to show a technician how to repair that same system, then you will have to give details.

You'll also see how a clear understanding of your major goal can affect the way you organize a document. If you are writing a memo to inform your staff about some new office procedures, you will probably organize your memo in a top-down pattern, putting the most important procedures at the beginning and then following with others. But if you realize that your goal is also to persuade your staff to adopt the new procedures readily, you may decide to begin the memo by describing how people will benefit from the new procedures before getting to the procedures themselves. For instance, when the writers revising the memo in Chapter 1 finally decided that their major goal in the flextime memo was to persuade

[3] By the way, when I use the term "goal," I mean the same thing someone else might mean by "purpose" or "intention." If you are more comfortable with one of these words, substitute it as you read.

employees to accept the new system, they put the system's benefits first.

Think, Think, Think— The Key to Effective Writing

If you were totally systematic and worked in an ideal world, you would begin every new writing task by carefully thinking about the major goal you wanted to accomplish. Unfortunately, you won't always be so systematic—you'll dash off a letter sometimes without thinking twice, and you'll probably begin some reports without knowing where you will end up or what you are really trying to do. And the world of work is far from ideal—you'll be interrupted as you write, have to meet impossible deadlines, and have a manager on your back if you don't write something in a certain way.

But if you can discipline yourself to clarify your major goal for a writing project (ideally when you begin but certainly before you finish), you will write more effectively. Get in the habit of thinking to yourself, "I am writing this document *so that* my reader will [be affected in this way]."

What would have happened if the writer of the Three Mile Island memo had read his memo over and decided to clarify his major goal? He might have said to himself, "I am writing this memo *so that* my reader will decide whether to change procedures or not. Since that's my major goal, I'd better begin with it." He might then have revised the first part as the memo on the right shows (changes are underlined), and the Three Mile Island accident might have been prevented.

YOUR READERS

A Writing Situation

Imagine, if you will, the following situation. You have become convinced that buying a new data processing system can save your organization thousands of dollars. You research the system carefully, reading available technical materials and talking with salesmen and technicians. Then you organize your proposal into three major sections—a technical description of the system, a recommendation that the organization adopt it as soon as possible, and a rationale explaining why.

As you write, you devote most of your time to the detailed technical description because your research has made you so familiar with it. In fact, you spend so much time on this first section that you have to rush through the final rationale section. And you neglect completely to mention the problems that have arisen with the present costly system, which were the reasons why you began looking for a new system in the first place.

Your manager reads your proposal and likes it. Since his field is

BABCOCK & WILCOX COMPANY
POWER GENERATION GROUP

TO: Manager, Plant Integration
FROM: Manager, Plant Performance
Services Section (2149)
SUBJECT: Proper Use of HPI System
DATE: August 3, 1978

References: (1) B. M. Dunn to J. Taylor, same subject, February 9, 1978
(2) B. M. Dunn to J. Taylor, same subject, February 16, 1978

This is to request that Plant Integration decide the important question of how the HPI system should be used. The attached references suggest the possibility of uncovering the core if present HPI policy is continued.

References 1 and 2 (attached) recommend a change in B&W's philosophy for HPI system use during low-pressure transients. Basically, they recommend leaving the HPI pumps on, once HPI has been initiated, until it can be determined that the hot leg temperature is more than 50° F below T_{sat} for the RCS pressure. . . .

data processing, he understands and even appreciates your technical discussion. And since you and he have talked so many times about the problems with the present system, he doesn't even notice that you have neglected to write about these. In fact, he is so pleased with the proposal that he submits it for approval at the next meeting of the division heads.

Shortly after, he calls you in and says disappointedly, "The division heads just didn't seem to go for your proposal. I got the impression they hadn't even taken the time to read most of it closely. Two grumbled about all the technical discussion they couldn't understand, and they all complained that they didn't know what was wrong with the present system or how the one you propose would benefit us. They kept asking how much money your new system would save.

"But this is too good an idea to give up on yet," he continues. "What about revising the proposal to make it more acceptable to the division heads? If you can finish by Tuesday, I'll take it back to their next meeting."

You set to work. Getting out the company directory, you first list the names of the division heads, just to make sure you know who they all are. As you make this list, you begin to visualize two you are already acquainted with. You see Jean Grayson, Director of Sales, who has only been with the company about six months, and Harry Sullivan, Director of Plant Operations, who began as a foreman 20 years ago and worked his way up the ladder. You don't know the other division heads, those in charge of employee relations, finance, and engineering, but you resolve to find out as much as you can about them.

In the next few days, you talk with your manager and a few friends scattered throughout the organization to learn all you can about the division heads. You try to find out what experience each has had with data processing systems and also how each feels about using them. In addition, you remember what your manager said about their reactions to your original proposal, especially their impatience with your detailed technical discussion and their desire to know the problems with the present system and the benefits of yours. On the basis of what you have learned, you develop the following rough outline for the revised proposal:

1. Problem with old system
2. Solution—new system
3. Rationale—cost benefits
4. Discussion—technicalities

Now you rewrite the proposal on the basis of your outline, trying to make the whole thing sound as nontechnical as possible. You begin with a statement of the "Problem"—that the antiquated system currently in use wastes thousands of dollars annually. Then you follow immediately with a "Solution" section that briefly describes the system you recommend, and then a "Rationale" section listing the cost benefits of the new system. Finally, you close with a "Discussion" section, setting forth the technical features of your system and methods for implementing it. And before you do your final draft, you get some friends outside your department to critique your style, just to make sure you are writing in a way that people outside the field of data processing can understand.

Your proposal is finished by Tuesday morning, just in time for your manager to approve it and get copies ready for the meeting. "This is a good revision," he says. "It will appeal directly to the division heads. They will understand the problem, will be motivated to read your proposed solution, and should be convinced by your description of benefits. And now that your technical discussion comes at the end of the proposal, each can read as much or as little as he or she wants. I'll bet the heads will approve the proposal."

Understand Your Readers

As the preceding example indicates, you've got to know who your readers are and understand their needs and expectations in order to accomplish your goals. But from ancient times when people first wrote on clay tablets until this moment when I am keying this sentence into my word processor, the problem of all writers has been the same: How can we understand people we can't see or talk to? Many times, we don't even know who all our readers are. And even when we do, we don't have the kind of feedback that we get in conversation, when someone can ask for more information, nod if she likes our ideas, or scowl if she doesn't.

Since you can't often bring your readers into your physical presence while you write, you'll have to make them present in some other fashion. The best way to do this is to ask yourself these five questions about your readers.

1. Who are my readers?
2. How will they use this document?
3. What do they already know about this subject?
4. What is important to them about this subject?
5. How will they react to this subject?

But wait a minute before you become overwhelmed by all these questions. The fact is that you won't necessarily have to answer all five for every writing situation. In fact, when writing a routine letter or memo, you may hardly have to be conscious of any of them, since you will have thought about them before. Even when writing a new document, you will sometimes have to focus on only one or two. But learning how to answer *all* the questions will prepare you to analyze your readers' needs and expectations in any writing situation, whether you are doing a one-page memo or a 25-page proposal. Therefore, we'll discuss each one in detail.

Who Are My Readers?

It's important to train yourself to *identify* your readers, especially since they may vary so widely from one document to another. At one time, they may be people in a field office trying to understand your memo announcing a new policy or procedure. At another time, they may be division managers reading a report you have written or deciding on a proposal you have made. At still another, they may be clients trying to decide whether or not to buy a product or service you have described in a letter.

One consideration that will help you make appropriate writing choices will be your *relationship* to your readers. If they are clients or others outside your organization, you will have to be careful to portray yourself and the organization in the best possible light. If they are above you in the organizational hierarchy, you will have to remember that they are usually busy and preoccupied with their own problems and responsibilities; therefore, you will have to make sure not to waste their time with unnecessary information. But if they are on your level or below you, you will have to make sure to give them all the information they need.

How Will They Use This Document?

Once you've identified your readers, your next step is to *visualize* them reading the document you have written. Seeing your readers actually using your document will help you make the best writing choices. If you are writing a report on a project, you might picture your manager getting ready to read it. She is sitting at her desk at 7:45 on a Friday morning. She was up a little too late the night before and is tired, but she has to study your report, along with two others, so she can present her recommendations about all three projects at an 11:00 meeting. If you want her to digest your report, you'd better keep it short and put your important points at the beginning, where she can find them easily.

If you are writing an article on your pet project for the company newsletter, you might visualize a fellow employee from another division in the organization, sitting over lunch and glancing through the newsletter to find something interesting. If you begin your article with a long technical description of the project, you know he'll turn the page to something more interesting. Instead, you've got to get his attention with a snappy lead, something that tells him right away what you're doing and how it will benefit him and the organization. Of course, if you are writing another kind of document, say a set of procedures for a technician who must operate a system you have developed, then you'd better forget the snappy lead and the benefits and get right to what the technician will have to do and how he'll do it.

Once you have identified and visualized your intended readers, you will have to understand their particular needs and expectations in order to fulfill them as you write. You may be tempted to picture your readers' minds as empty buckets into which you merely pour information. This is simply not true. Readers' minds are much more like wells than buckets—rich reservoirs of facts, feelings, and ideas. You will have to know what's already in your readers' mental reservoirs about a subject in order to understand what they need in a given document. In particular, you will need to understand what knowledge, values, and feelings your readers will bring to your document. To do this, answer the next three questions.

What Do My Readers Already Know About This Subject?

The classic mistake of writers on the job is to write as if their readers know as much as they do about a subject. For example, because he didn't stop to think about what his readers did and didn't know about the subject, the writer of the data processing proposal discussed earlier spent too much time on technical details and none on the problem his new system would solve. Once he realized that his readers weren't even aware of the problem, he knew he had to describe it at the very beginning of his proposal.

Most writers (especially those with technical backgrounds) have been trained to present information as accurately and in as much detail as possible. But because they fail to realize that many of their readers don't know as much as they do, they often end up writing in a style that is too technical for their readers to understand. Here, for instance, is an economist trying to explain a method for estimating costs to top managers in a public utility.

This report estimates production costs, specifically fuel expenses, using a probabilistic simulation of a utility's generating system for predicting the costs of meeting forecasted load curves. Its purpose is twofold: (1) to provide an instructional example to show how one mechanically estimates equivalent load duration curves needed to calculate expected energy output on a generating unit basis; (2) to propose two methods of treating storage hydro units when using the equivalent load duration curve method of estimating energy output by generating unit.

Another public utility economist would have the background to understand this technical language. But most managers will not *and cannot* be familiar with such technicalities. Their job is not to know everything; it's to be able to draw on the knowledge of others in order to make the best decisions.

If you are a specialist, you will have to learn to translate what you know into language that nonspecialists will understand. If you are an engineer, you may have to describe your project in a memo that can be understood by people in marketing, data processing, and operations, as well as in a technical report for other engineers. If you are an accountant, economist, or attorney, you may have to explain a concept you understand well to decision makers who don't understand it at all. And if you work in a government agency or a complex field such as health care or insurance, you may have to write manuals that translate highly technical information into language that the general public will understand. You will learn more about how to do this in chapter four, which shows you how to choose a style that is adapted to your reader's level of knowledge.

What Is Important To My Readers About This Subject?

Authorities on writing say, "Don't tell your readers too much! But then again, don't tell them too little either!" But how do you know how much is too much—or too little? Primarily by deciding what is important to your readers. As you've seen, few people in top management will want to know all you know about the subject of a proposal. And readers of a procedures manual will usually not need a detailed description of the policies behind particular procedures. In fact, most readers will want to know *less* than you can tell them.

On the other hand, a reader may return a report or proposal and say he wants more. "What do you mean, more?" you grumble. "I thought you wanted me to be concise!" What your reader wants is not more words, but more information—about the new plant site you are recommending, about the benefits of the new system you wish to implement, or about the factors to consider in making an important decision. Your readers want you to be concise, but they want sufficient detail too.

Your analysis of what is important to your readers will not only tell you how much information they need, but it will also help you organize that information. A letter to place an order, for example, should begin with a detailed description of your order and its amount. But a letter to confirm a previously telephoned order should begin with a reference to the call and the date and time of your order. In each case, you are leading with the information your reader most wants to know. If your manager has asked you to write a report analyzing several alternatives and recommending the best one, you should begin by describing the alternative you recommend, since this is what is most important to her. Then continue with a discussion of the strengths and weaknesses of each alternative.

Knowing what is important to your readers can even affect the way you lay out or design a document. Writing a brochure describing personnel policies for new employees, you may decide to present policies in the form of questions and answers for quick reference, beginning with important questions about salary and promotion procedures, then following with questions about insurance, sick leaves, vacations, etc. Your readers can then skim the brochure, going immediately to the sections that most concern them. To guide them, you might number questions, use headings between major sections, and separate them with white space.

A Writing Situation

Often people write to readers to whom very different kinds of things are important. In these cases, they have to adapt what they say and how they say it to the interests of their intended readers. Watch how David T. Lykken, a professor of psychology and psychiatry, adapts what he says about lie detection to different kinds of readers.[4] This first excerpt comes from an article published in *Psychology Today*. Lykken assumes that readers of that magazine will be most interested in how lie detectors are used, so he gives a simple explanation.

> A polygraph can be used in two ways; [*sic*] to detect lies or to find out whether someone knows something. To uncover a liar, an examiner simply hooks the person up to the machine and asks him a question: "Did you kill John Doe?" The polygrapher evaluates the subject's answer by comparing the accompanying changes in his breathing, heart rate, and skin resistance with his physiological responses to irrelevant questions that also are supposed to produce emotional responses. When a person lies, his autonomic responses are stronger than when he tells the truth. Most polygraphic examinations are lie-detector tests. [From "Guilty-Knowledge Test: The Right Way to Use a Lie Detector," *Psychology Today* 8.10 March 1975: 58.]

Now here is an excerpt from another article by Lykken on lie detection, but this time published in *Modern Medicine*, a journal read primarily by physicians. This time, he talks about a distinction that is important to them, that the lie detector is a psychological rather than a physiological test.

> And the polygraph test, in all of its several forms and variants, *is* a psychologic test; don't let the fancy apparatus mislead you. Measurements of certain physiologic responses—the changes in heart rate and respiration and the electric resistance of the palmar skin—are substituted for the verbal responses or behavioral observations more commonly employed in psychologic diagnosis or assessment. There is no pattern of physiologic response that is pathognomonic of lying, no unique reaction that all people involuntarily display when they attempt to deceive but not when they are merely upset, frightened, or angry. [From "The Lie Detector Industry: Just Nine Years More to 1984," *Modern Medicine* October 1975: 60.]

In this third excerpt, from an article published in *American Psychologist*, Lykken discusses something of interest to psychologists—the kind of training that people who administer the test should have.

> It is clear that polygraphic interrogation *is* an area of applied psychology because the lie detector clearly is a psychological test. If persons

[4]Articles from which excerpts are taken are collected in Martin Steinman, *Words in Action* (New York: Harcourt Brace Jovanovich, 1979) 387–410.

> who administer and evaluate Stanford-Binets or Rorschachs or MMPIs are psychometrists, then the polygrapher is a psychometrist also, and one basic science that should underlie his art is the science of psychological assessment. Since the polygraph test involves the study of autonomic (rather than verbal or other operant) responses to psychological stimuli, a second basic science area which is directly relevant to polygraphy is psychophysiology. [From "Psychology and the Lie Detector Industry," *American Psychologist* 29 October 1974: 725.]

Not only does Lykken adapt what he says about his subject to the interests of his readers; note how he adapts his *style* (how he says it) to their backgrounds and level of knowledge.

- In the first excerpt, addressed to readers who have only a general knowledge of the subject, Lykken keeps his sentences short—average sentence length is fourteen words. Also, his words are simple—layman's terms such as "breathing, heart rate, and skin resistance" are used.
- In the second excerpt, addressed to physicians, Lykken's sentences are much longer—average sentence length is now 24 words. Nor does he hesitate to use medical terms such as the "electric resistance of the palmar skin," "physiologic" or "pathognomonic."
- In the third excerpt, addressed to readers who bring a psychological background to the subject, Lykken's sentences are still longer—average length is now 29 words. And his vocabulary is even more specialized. He now refers to tests such as "Stanford-Binets," "Rorschachs," and "MMPIs," and uses words such as "psychometrists" and "psychophysiology."

Like Lykken, you will probably have to adapt to the needs of different kinds of readers in different documents. But you may also have to mediate between the needs of different kinds of readers in the same document. You may have to address a policy and procedures manual both to managers in the home office, who want accurate general statements of policy, and to agents in the field, who need this policy translated into straightforward statements of procedure. In this case, you will have to walk a kind of linguistic tightrope, generalizing clearly for managers while specifying exactly for people in the field.

Or you may have to direct a technical report to engineers, for whom technical data and methodology are important, and to executives, who don't care about detailed technical information, but who want very much to know about how the new product or system will benefit the organization. In this situation, you'll probably have to write different parts of the report for different groups of readers. You can direct the summary, introduction, and list of action recommendations more to executives, and the conclusions, technical discussion, and appendices more to other engineers.

The reason why insurance policies and mortgage contracts are so confusing to most of us is that the same policy or contract is written for two groups of readers, to whom very different things are important. The first group, attorneys, require that the language be legally correct and properly detailed. Yet this language confuses the second group, the general public, who want the terms of their mortgage or insurance explained in the most simple and direct way possible. "Plain English" legislation, passed now by a number of states, requires that writers of such documents make them comprehensible to the general public by using short sentences, nontechnical language, abundant personal references, and concrete illustrations. Also, these documents must be laid out in a clear, direct manner with no "fine print." You will learn all these techniques later in this book.

How Will My Readers React To This Subject?

Will they be positive, neutral, skeptical, or possibly downright negative?

A Writing Situation

Imagine someone writing a memo to all state school principals announcing an annual conference. Since the writer doesn't know how his readers will react, he assumes the worst—that they will be reluctant to attend the conference. Therefore he must persuade them. To do this, he chooses to attract readers by describing interesting conference topics and well-known speakers in his first paragraphs.

The theme for this year's Conference of Massachusetts Secondary School Principals is "Planning for the Challenges of the 80s." Sessions will cover such topics as computers in the classroom, stress management for administrators and teachers, and preparing students more effectively for competency tests.

Featured speakers are J. Harrison Coleman, Attorney General; Dr. Ronald Chapman, President, Northeastern University; and Dr. William H. Seewall, Professor of Administration and Supervision, University of Massachusetts. They will talk, respectively, on the legal issues involved in teacher evaluation, new trends in teacher education, and the pros and cons of master teacher and merit pay plans.

Once he has hooked readers with major attractions of the conference, the writer continues with details of time and place.

The conference will be held at the Sheraton Motor Inn in Boston, June 24–26. It will begin with the keynote speech by Attorney General Coleman at 10:00 a.m. Wednesday and close on Friday afternoon at 3:00 p.m.

Please fill out the form below to indicate your interest in attending. The enclosed brochure gives additional details.

Later, after the writer knows who will be attending the conference, he decides to send a short reminder. Since his readers this time are only those who have responded positively to his first memo, he knows that the information they now need consists of meeting arrangements—time, place, lodging, and travel arrangements. Just as he led with attractions in his first memo to persuade reluctant readers to attend, he will now lead with this information.

In both of the preceding cases, the writer adapted his information and his organization to the *anticipated reactions* of his readers. You will frequently have to do this. Writing a memo that proposes something your readers will favor, you can lead with your recommendations. But if you know your readers are especially negative, you might do well to begin with the ways your recommendation will save money. When we get to chapters on how to write particular documents, we'll discuss in more detail how to adapt your organization to the reactions you anticipate from your readers.

Sometimes, the most practical way to answer the five questions discussed in this section will be to talk to your readers in person, finding out, for example, what they want to know in a monthly project report. Or maybe you can call your principal reader on the phone, asking him how much information he needs in a report and how he wants that information organized. If you can't talk to your readers, you can try getting someone else to read your document. Just watching others read what you have written and hearing them respond can keep your writer's feet planted firmly on the ground. You might even ask someone to play the role of your intended reader, asking all the questions that he or she might ask.

The questions in this section won't give you a complete profile of your readers, but they will help you focus on their important characteristics. The diagram here, called an "audience wheel," summarizes the questions.

You Can Develop a Profile of Your Readers by Asking Yourself These Five Questions.

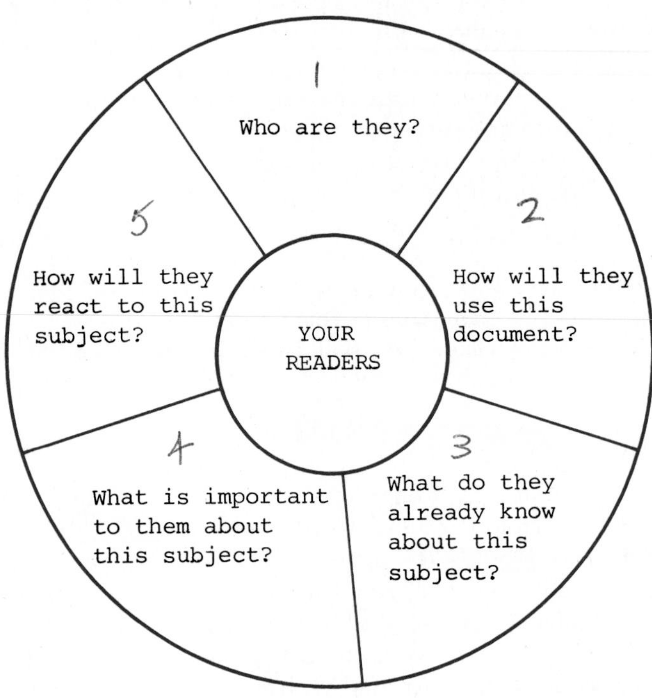

YOUR VOICE

> If you really want to hear about it, the first thing you'll probably want to know is where I was born, and what my lousy childhood was like, and how my parents were occupied and all before they had me, and all that David Copperfield kind of crap, but I don't feel like going into it, if you want to know the truth.

Describe the person who uttered these words. Don't worry about the book they came from or the author of that book—just think about the speaker. What kind of person is he? He is young, isn't he? He is probably an adolescent, and a hostile one at that, to judge by words such as "lousy" and "crap." And he is rebellious—he refuses to begin his life's story by telling us about his birthplace, childhood, and parents' occupation the way a traditional author such as Charles Dickens might have done. You can even sense his antagonism in his sentence structure—his words tumble out, strung together in one long, almost disconnected sentence.

You don't need to know that these words are spoken by Holden Caulfield, the young hero of J. D. Salinger's *The Catcher in the Rye* (New York: Modern Library, 1951) 3, to understand this much about him. Why? The answer is that the words and sentences he uses create a *voice,* they project a personality, and on the basis of this voice and personality, you draw conclusions about the kind of person he is.

Professional writers, especially fiction writers, are continually choosing words and sentences that create distinctive voices in their writing. At the opening of *Adventures of Huckleberry Finn* (Boston: Houghton Mifflin, 1958) 3, for instance, Mark Twain introduces us to his hero, Huck, as follows:

> You don't know about me, without you have read a book by the name of "The Adventures of Tom Sawyer," but that ain't no matter. That book was made by Mr. Mark Twain, and he told the truth, mainly. There was things which he stretched, but mainly he told the truth.

This is the voice of an adolescent again, just a few years younger than Holden Caulfield, but these words project a very different personality. For one thing, the speaker is not nearly so well-educated as Holden. Note words such as "without," "ain't," "made," and "stretched," for example. And you don't sense the kind of hostility here that you sense in Holden, partly because the speaker's balanced clauses and short sentences indicate that he has himself well under control. Couple these ideas with the fact that the speaker seems very concerned with what is true and what is not (note that he uses the word "truth" twice and is careful to say that Twain "stretched" the truth somewhat in *The Adventures of Tom Sawyer*), and you have someone who is so young and unsophisticated that he sees things with childlike clarity and tells the truth about what he sees. This is just the kind of person Twain needs to tell his story about the corrupt South.[5]

Fiction is not the only type of writing that has voice. The documents you write on the job—your letters, memos, reports, and proposals—will have distinctive voices also. The voice decision you make for any document can be a crucial one, for it will determine two important things—how you present yourself to your readers and what relationship you establish with them.

Your Professional Voice

Depending on the kind of work you do, you will probably have to develop a professional voice in your writing. Economists sound like economists and doctors sound like doctors—each discipline has its characteristic language. Note these two particular professional voices in the following excerpts.

[5] I am indebted to Walker Gibson's excellent *Persona: A Style Study for Readers and Writers* (New York: Random House, 1969) for the concept of voice and for some of this discussion.

Because trends in the monetary aggregates have been distorted by deposit innovations and regulatory reform, we have departed from rigid monetarism.

Measuring amniotic fluid phospholipid levels can help determine fetal maturity and thereby lower perinatal mortality and morbidity associated with this complication of pregnancy.

There is nothing wrong with using a characteristic professional voice. The passages above, for instance, are clearly written, and would be perfectly understandable to their intended readers, other specialists in their fields.

How to Adapt Your Voice to Writing Situations

The key to choosing your voice is to be able to adapt your voice to your writing situation. If you are talking to other professionals, then sound professional by using the language that they will understand. Appropriate use of technical language will make your readers feel comfortable and help them understand your points quickly and easily. But if you are talking to people who are not insiders, then you must shift your voice by making different word and sentence choices.

Look, for instance, at how an attorney might describe an antitrust suit in a memo to a company executive.

MEMORANDUM

TO: George Higuerra
FROM: Amy Slosberg
SUBJECT: TVA Antitrust Suit
DATE: April 1, 19--

The Tennessee Valley Authority is bringing suit in federal district courts in New York, Colorado, and Tennessee against ten foreign and three domestic uranium producers, charging them with eight major violations of the antitrust act. TVA alleges that the uranium producers, holding secret meetings in various countries to divide the world uranium market, have (among other things). . . .

Now watch how the same writer uses quotations, shorter sentences, and different words to shift from a legal to a journalistic voice so that he can interest a variety of readers of a company newsletter in the same information.

TVA Posse Pursues Uranium Producers

"We've had enough," TVA has finally said. "We're not going to let uranium producers overcharge us or victimize us with any antitrust violations."

Thus, TVA, faced with a staggering uranium bill, is suing uranium producers, charging them with nearly every transgression in the antitrust textbook. Among other things, uranium producers have. . . .

Here is another example of how a writer can shift voice with situation. First, you hear the enthusiastic voice of a sales representative, trying to generate interest in a new training session.

TO: Friends and Clients
FROM: Jessica Leatherman

About a year ago, a client asked me if we had a course in "letter writing." "You have got to be kidding," I told him. "Me? Teach <u>letter writing</u>!" In my letters, I ramble, stumble, hang long sentences together, misspell, and in short, generally do a lousy job of organizing.

I did nothing about the first request. Six weeks ago, another client also asked about letter writing. You know me! I sensed a need in the marketplace looking for a solution, and if it's training, that's my job.

Now note the voice of the same sales representative when making a formal proposal for a training session to a particular client.

Dear Bob:

Recently, you asked about our new letter writing course. Here is the essential information: the course meets for four sessions, each three and one half hours long. The trainer, whose background is in professional writing and editing, will show participants how to write letters and memos that are clear and interesting to read.

Focusing on the actual writing of workshop participants, she will show them how to choose words that really communicate their message, sentences that are easy to understand, and organizational formats that are clear to the reader.

Notice how the writer shifted from the more intimate, informal voice of the sales letter, full of personal pronouns, short sentences, quotations, and exclamations, to the quiet, more formal voice of the proposal, created by more complex words and longer sentences. In each case, she made the appropriate voice decision and then chose the words and sentence patterns that would create that voice.

Avoid the *Pompous Professional* Voice

There is one voice you should avoid in writing, the voice of the *pompous professional*. This is the voice of the writer who feels that it is the professional's job to sound as pompous and stuffy as possible. For example, listen to the voice of this bureaucratic writer:

We are now approaching the season when electrical demand is at peak, largely because of the use of air conditioning. With the approach of this critical air-conditioning season, we must direct our efforts to reduce consumption of electricity, which costs $650,000 annually in this organization. Accordingly, I have directed the Director of Installation Services to delay operation of this equipment, including window type units, until seasonal temperatures are such that inside temperatures consistently exceed 78–80 degrees F.

This writer is simply saying,

In order to save electricity, installation service will not turn on any air-conditioning equipment until temperatures inside go above 78–80 degrees F.

Students preparing to join the ranks of a profession are tempted to write in this pompous voice. Here is a student writing about her internship with a law firm:

Observations such as the aforementioned proved very enlightening, and the termination of my internship arrived much too soon. Now when I am assailed with the same questions concerning my possible career in law, my answers have a certain structure. My conception of what a legal career actually entails has increased tenfold. My expectations, therefore, have become much more realistic. I feel I have an inkling of the potential problems I may encounter.

When asked why she wrote in such an artificial voice (much unlike the voice she had used in other papers), this student replied that she was simply trying to sound "professional."

The Ideal Voice

Is there an ideal voice to strive for in writing? One that cuts across professional lines? I think so. No matter how technical or specialized your field, you ought to resolve to present as natural a self as possible to the reader, to sound like a real person talking on paper to other real people. This is *not* to say, "Write as you talk!" No one wants to read anything that is full of the pauses and "uhms" of speech. But it *is* to say that good writing sounds like good talking—that a good writer can create the illusion that he or she is sitting at your elbow, conversing clearly, interestingly, and persuasively. Here, for instance, is the beginning of a book on structural aluminum design written by an engineer. See if you don't agree that the voice you hear is natural and conversational:

> This is a book that grew from a practicing designer's notebook. It is both a reference book and a text. The title, "Structural Aluminum Design," could perhaps better be "Designing with Aluminum Alloys," because the scope and application of the book goes beyond load-carrying structures. Aluminum's greatest fields of application are generally those requiring lightness and strength. . . .[6]

This passage presents the reader with a person who thinks clearly, expresses himself well, and is interested in what he is doing—a truly professional voice.

[6]Karl Angermayer, *Structural Aluminum Design* (Richmond: Reynolds Metals, 1968) 3.

Create a Relationship with Your Reader

The voice you use also creates a relationship with your reader. This relationship can be a formal and distant one or an informal and therefore closer one. In fact, you can locate different voices on a spectrum, moving from very formal through informal to colloquial:

Formal/Distant — Informal — Colloquial/Intimate

Think of the different kinds of voices you might use in a letter sending someone information. Here are some different beginnings for such a letter. Note how they move across the relationship spectrum.

Formal	Per your request As you requested
Informal	As you asked Here is the information Here's the information
Colloquial	Hey, you wanted to know about OK, Bill, here's the info

Note how the voice of the following letter changes as the writer shifts his relationship with his reader. In the first version, the writer keeps his distance from the reader by using a formal voice.

Dear Sir:

In reference to your request of September 14, 19--, the proposal formulated for the valves and valve controls is attached. Also included is a schematic and bill of materials, as well as copies of catalog cuts on the items quoted.

Please notify us when you wish to order.

Sincerely yours,

Thomas Hodges

Now suppose the writer chooses to bring himself and his reader closer. He might use a more personal, informal voice by revising the salutation and the stilted phrase "In reference to your request. . . ."; replacing the participle "formulated" with the more personal verb phrase "we formulated"; replacing "is attached" with the less formal "here is"; substituting the active "I have included" for the passive "included"; and so forth.

Dear Mr. Levinson:

In answer to your request of September 14, 19––, here is the proposal we formulated for the valves and valve controls. I have also included a schematic and bill of materials, as well as copies of catalog cuts on the items quoted.

Please let us know when you wish to order.

Sincerely,

Tom Hodges

Imagine now that Hodges wishes to bring himself still closer to Levinson because their relationship is a personal as well as a professional one. He might add some personal details, substitute the more personal "I promised" for "we formulated," use a word such as "putting" rather than "included," change a few other words, and use some contractions. The result would be this letter:

Dear Sam:

Ann and I certainly enjoyed your visit to Detroit last month, especially that fine dinner at the Flying Cloud. And congratulations on your promotion. Your new job sounds like a challenge.

Here's the proposal for the valves and valve controls I promised you. I'm also putting in a schematic and bill of materials, plus copies of catalog cuts on the items quoted.

Let me know when you want to order. And, by all means, do come see us again soon.

Cordially,

Tom Hodges

Choose Among Formal and Informal Voices

To write well, you have to be sensitive enough to your writing situation to know how much psychological distance you want between you and your reader, to decide on this basis how formal or informal you want to be, and then to choose the appropriate words and sentence patterns. In general, familiar words, personal pronouns, active verbs, and short sentences create a more intimate, informal voice. Their opposites—less familiar words, impersonal references, passive verbs, and longer sentences—create a more formal and distanced one.

This concept of the writer's voice can answer a number of the following questions that vex business and professional writers.

- Should I use personal pronouns in my writing?
- Should I use contractions?
- Can I begin sentences with such words as "and" and "but"?

And the answer is, "Sure!" if you want your voice to sound personal and informal. However, if the voice is to be more formal and distant, other choices should be made. The question is not so much whether such usages are correct or incorrect; the question is whether they are appropriate to your writing situation.

SUMMARY

In this chapter, we've discussed how to analyze your writing situation. To do this, you should

- clarify your major goals
- identify your readers and understand their needs and expectations
- decide on the appropriate voice

Notice that I've not numbered these. That's because I don't want you to think about this as a step-by-step procedure to be applied mechanically to every writing situation. Rather, internalize this approach so much that it becomes the way you naturally think about writing. Then you really will clarify your goals, understand your readers, and decide on your voice.

APPLICATIONS

1. *Your Goal:* List four or five pieces of writing you have done recently and briefly describe the major goal of each. You might reread the "so that" discussion at the beginning of this chapter and use this phrase in each description.

NOTICE FROM PAYROLL ACCOUNTING

Due to the increased interest in direct deposit with the company credit union, certain savings and loans, as well as certain Phoenix area banks, we are currently conducting a survey to determine the feasibility of making direct deposit to these institutions. Our decision will be based on the amount of interest expressed and the willingness of the institution in question to accept necessary terms of deposit.

You will be notified in writing by August 26, 19--, if the institution you are interested in will not participate in the direct deposit system. Otherwise, direct deposit will begin with your September 15, 19-- paycheck with the institution named below.

Please complete the attached form and mail directly to the Corporate Salary Payroll Department no later than July 29, 19--.

TO: Corporate Payroll Accounting
SUBJECT: Direct Deposit of Salary Paycheck

Effective with the September 15, 19-- pay period, I request that my paychecks be sent

2. *Your Goal:* Look at the notice beginning on page 44 that was distributed to all the employees of a large organization. Read it carefully, as though you were one of the employees, to see whether you can discern the writer's goals. One way to do this is to ask yourself, "What's going to happen to me because of this?" Now rewrite the notice so that its goal is clear to your readers.

3. *Your Readers:* Analyze the reader of a document you have written lately. Begin with a paragraph in which you first identify the reader by name and occupational position, and then describe that person in the act of reading your document. Then write two or three more paragraphs in which you describe what the person already knows about your subject,

directly to the institution named below. I understand that this will automatically be done unless I am notified by August 26 to the contrary. Pertinent information is as follows:

Employee's Name: ______________________

S.S. Number: ______________________

Location: ______________________

Phone Number: ______________________

Name of Institution: ______________________

Your Account Number: ______________________

____
Signature and Date

what is important to him or her about your subject, and how he or she will probably react to it. Finally, explain briefly how the characteristics you have described affected (or should have affected) the way you wrote to that person—the information you gave to him or her, the way you organized it, the voice you chose, and the way you designed your document.

4. *Your Readers:* Read the following excerpts[7] from three different documents, all on the subject of undersea exploration. Then discuss how each writer has adapted his information, organization, and style to his readers. The first is addressed to the lay or popular reader, the second to executives, and the third to scientists:

To Laymen:

The sea is "water" only in the sense that water is the dominant substance present. Actually, it is a solution of gases and salts in addition to vast numbers of living organisms, the majority of which are quite minute. Since the beginning, materials in solution and in suspension, carried by rivers, have been deposited in the oceans and seas of the world. It is to the wealth related directly and indirectly to these materials that this article is directed, rather than pirate treasure. [From J. W. Chanslor, "Treasure from the Sea," *Science and the Sea* (Washington, D.C.: U.S. Naval Oceanographic Office, 1967) 9.]

To Executives:

One day last month, a crowd of government officials, Naval officers, and civilians gathered at New London, Connecticut for the launching of General Dynamics' new Star II and Star III submarines. But while GD is famous for its military undersea craft, the two Stars were not fighting subs. Inside their thin skins was packed industry's most advanced and sophisticated electronic equipment, designed to make the subs the latest giant step in one of the fastest growing research and development programs in the world today.

Its ultimate aim is nothing less than to discover all the wealth that lies in and beneath the sea. Financed by both the federal government and industry, the ambitious project has turned the ocean into a huge market, one that needs both a variety of services and a wealth of equipment and goods. [From George J. Berkwitt, "Profits Under the Sea," *Dun's Review and Modern Industry* (June 1966): 32.]

[7]These excerpts are taken from three articles collected in Thomas E. Pearsall, *Audience Analysis for Technical Writing* (Beverly Hills: Glencoe Press, 1969) 3, 15, 21.

To Scientists:

During August, September, and October, 1965, the U.S. Navy's Special Projects Office and Office of Naval Research conducted Project Sealab II off La Jolla, California. The main purpose of the project was to evaluate the performance of men and equipment in a high-pressure, underwater environment (1). *Sealab II*, an underwater habitat, was placed on the bottom for 45 days. Three ten-man teams lived in *Sealab II* for about 2 weeks each. The men lived at ambient pressure for the entire period and had access to the surrounding water through an open entryway in the bottom of *Sealab II*. [From Thomas A. Clarke, Arthur O. Flechsig, and Richard W. Grigg, "Ecological Studies During Project Sealab II," *Science* 157 (1967): 1381.]

5. *Your Readers:* To practice adapting to your readers' values, write two advertisements for the same automobile, the first for the magazine *Road and Track*, a favorite of car and racing buffs, and the second for a popular magazine such as *Time* or *Newsweek*. Now describe how you adapted each ad to the values and interests of your readers.

6. *Your Voice:* Collect some passages written in very different voices from novels, stories, magazines, or newspapers. Then compare the voices by noting some of the word and sentence choices that make them different. You might look at novelists such as William Faulkner, Ernest Hemingway, or Tom Wolfe, or newspaper columnists such as William Buckley and Art Buchwald. You might look in pocket romances, historical or spy novels, newspaper editorials, or specialty magazines.

7. How would you explain the concept of voice to someone else? What voice would you advise a new college student to use in his or her writing? What about someone just entering a particular organization?

8. Practice writing in different voices by doing some of the following:
   - **a.** Write a letter from Annamaria Gonzalez, an engineer at General Dynamics, in three different voices requesting information about how a jet engine works. Try to make your voices range from very formal through informal to colloquial.
   - **b.** Write a memo asking employees to comply with a new expense-reporting policy. First request it, then require it, and finally demand it.

c. Write a brief summary of your accomplishments during college as part of an application for membership in an honor society to which you have been invited to apply. Now revise your summary for inclusion in the college yearbook.

CHAPTER

3

Your Information, Organization, and Design

"What exactly should I say in this memo about the new overtime policy?" "How should I begin this report?" "How can I lay out this manual so it will be easy to read?" This chapter will help you answer questions like these—questions of information, organization, and design.

To understand such a complex process as writing, it helps to look at it from different perspectives. In the last chapter, we focused on how to analyze a writing situation by clarifying your goals, understanding the needs and expectations of your readers, and deciding on the appropriate voice to use. You saw how this analysis can help determine the decisions and choices you make when writing—the information you include, the way you organize that information, the style you choose, and the way you design your document.

The next two chapters focus more directly on these major choices and discuss them in detail. You will become familiar with the variety of choices at your command and learn some ways to make the best ones. In particular, you will learn how to answer four questions.

1. What information should I include in this particular document?
2. How should I organize this information?
3. How should I design/lay out this document?
4. What style should I use?

YOUR INFORMATION

An ancient parable illustrates a classic problem in communication. There are many versions, but one goes like this.

> All the inhabitants of an ancient village were blind. One day an elephant arrived just outside the village. In order to learn what the elephant was, the villagers sent some of their brave fellows out to touch various parts of the animal.
>
> When the men returned, here is what they reported.
>
> The first, who had felt the elephant's broad side, said, "This must be a palace with wide, high walls."
>
> The second, who had felt its squirming trunk, said, "No, this is not a palace. It's a giant snake."
>
> Another, who had touched the elephant's leg, said, "This is not a palace and neither is it a snake. Instead, it must be a giant tree."
>
> And so it went. Other blind men had touched the elephant's tusk, tail, and ear. But the more the villagers were told about the elephant, the more confused they became. They never knew what the elephant was really like.

The inhabitants of the village were misled because they only received partial information. Readers of your documents are like the villagers in this story—they depend on you for the information they receive. Your document is like the eyes of your readers—they see whatever subject you are talking about through these eyes. If you don't want to mislead readers the way the blind men did their fellow villagers, then you must give them the information they need in the quantity in which they need it by answering the following two questions.

What Do I Say?

On first thought, you may think that the information you can give someone about a subject is fixed. If someone asks you to help solve a problem or report on a project, you simply tell him what there is to know about the subject. Of course, this is not true. Subjects may be fixed—that is, problems and projects do exist. But you have to *select* the information you give someone about a subject. In the story above, the elephant was there, but the blind men selected (too partially, as it turned out) what they told people about it.

Therefore, one of your jobs as a writer is to select the information you will give to your reader about a subject. Where do you get this information? When writing papers in school, your major problem may have been finding something to say. But ordinarily, this won't be the case when you're on the job, especially when you write memos, letters, and short reports. Because you will likely write about some aspect of your job—the subject you know best—you will usually have plenty of information for your document. Of course, for longer projects like formal reports, proposals, and manuals, you may have to consult external sources such as experts and printed materials. We'll talk about how to do this in section three.

But even though you will usually know the information you need to write a short document, you will have to call it up out of memory.

In these situations, there are three brainstorming techniques that may help you—*listing*, *free writing*, and *questioning*. To see how these might help you probe your memory for information, imagine a fairly typical on-the-job writing situation, such as the one that follows.

A Writing Situation

Over the past few years, the subject of health and fitness has become a kind of hobby with you. You have read a good deal about the subject, and you try to keep yourself in pretty good shape. Several times, you have suggested that a fitness program be organized at your company, but the response has always been that there's no money to finance the project.

One Tuesday morning, however, your manager approaches you and says, "You know, we just might be able to find some money for your fitness program. The budget people have told us we have a surplus in our operating account of about $7,500. But if we don't allocate it by the end of this fiscal year, we'll lose it, and the fiscal year ends a week from today. Think you could give me a two-page memo on your ideas by tomorrow afternoon? I'll submit it to division heads for their approval. They'll be getting other requests, of course, so make yours good." (By the way, you'll find that it's not unusual to get such a project dumped on your desk at the last minute. When writing on the job, you have to do the best you can in the time you've got, no matter how short.)

Anyway, here's your big chance to get your pet program funded, so naturally you drop everything else to concentrate on the memo. Since there's no time to get information about other programs, you'll have to rely on what you already know about such programs. You begin by—

Listing

This method for tapping the deeper wells of your memory just requires that you list ideas about your subject as fast as they come to mind. After a few minutes, your list looks like this.

- Fitness is a fad right now—everyone's aware of it
- Not enough people stay fit—too tired at night when they go home to do much
- Can be costly—use lots of expensive equipment
- Can be cheap—all really need is exercise rug
- Lots of different activities to do—appropriate for different people
- Jogging really hurts some people
- Need some place to do it
- May have to motivate people to come
- Can't expect all to come—but will get a lot

- Need money to buy lots of equipment—weights, balls, rackets
- Need a track, basketball courts, pool—not for $7,500
- Be modest
- Got to have a facility though—some place to go
- Try that empty warehouse on Fourth Street

By the end of your listing session, you've got quite a few facts and ideas, but you still need more. So you decide to try another technique called—

Freewriting

This is another form of brainstorming. But the difference between it and the free association list you made above is that when freewriting, you try to talk to yourself on paper by writing nonstop for a certain period of time. Work as fast as you can for five or ten minutes, writing down everything that comes to mind. If you don't think you have enough material from your first free-write, you can do it again. Here's the way your first five-minute free-write on fitness might look.

Don't have much time for this memo. Got to get started quick, or I'll never finish on time. But don't know enough yet. So, what do I need to know? First, got to visualize the program--see where it'll be and how many people will be there. What'll they be doing, anyway? Some will be in aerobic dance classes or exercising --others will be playing sports--no, no sports. Those don't work for a serious fitness program. Emphasis won't be on play, but on getting in shape.

But then they'll hate the program. OK, guess I'll have to have some games, but will go for the ones that really do make you fit--basketball, racquetball, etc. Maybe I could schedule different activities on different nights--two nights a week for games, two for aerobics. But don't want to segregate men and women. Lots of fun doing things together--everything will be coed--that'll put emphasis on fun and fitness, not on competition . . . hey, fun and fitness might be a good title--or have fun with fitness.

Need to think too about what they'll be doing, what kinds of equipment they'll use . . .

By now, you've got lots of information, but before you sit down to organize it, you decide to try one last discovery technique called—

Asking questions

This is a favorite technique of newspaper reporters researching a story. In fact, they even have a customary set of questions to ask.

- ***Who*** are the people involved in this story?
- ***What*** happened, anyway?
- ***Where*** did this happen?
- ***When*** did this happen?
- ***Why*** did this happen?
- ***How*** did this happen?

You're not writing a newspaper story, but you decide to try the questions anyway, just to see if they'll give you any additional information.

Who? Everyone I can motivate to participate in the program. Will try to get cross-section; higher management as well as subordinates. In fact, if I can get some upper management to take part first, that'll motivate others.

What? Program will be divided into two segments: sports activities—basketball, racquetball, volleyball; fitness activities—Nautilus, aerobic dancing, exercise classes.

Where? Try for the old warehouse over on Fourth Street. Can fix it up for a little money—big expense is to install large court with goals and nets and a set of smaller ones for racquetball. Problem—three blocks away from plant and executive offices. Solution—none. Only building around.

When? Four nights a week—Mondays/Wednesdays for sports activities and Tuesdays/Thursdays for exercise/dance classes.

Why? Easy—purpose is to give people the chance to be more healthy and fit. Studies show this leads not only to reduced sickness and absence from job, but increased productivity also. Bring to work that big study I read so I can quote from it.

How? Already answered for the program. But what about for the memo? Let's see—why not begin with the purpose, then activities, etc.

You haven't got your ideas completely organized by any means, but you do have enough information to begin planning the actual memo. And when you used that last technique of questioning, you really did begin to see an organizational pattern emerge. (We'll return to this situation when we get to the organization section of this chapter.)

How much do I say?

As I've said, the information you need for most letters, memos, and short reports will be at your mental fingertips. Or, at least, not too far away. In fact, often your major problem will be that you know too much rather than too little. Knowing too much can work against you in two ways.

Sometimes, knowing too much will cause you *not to give your reader enough information*. For example, when writing instructions, you may omit steps because the procedure comes so easily to you that you are not even aware of all the steps that *should* be included. Or, in writing a memo about a training workshop, you may describe its time and place, but neglect to explain fully what the topic of the workshop will be. Why? Because you are so aware of what the workshop is about that you forget your reader is not.

Even more likely, your detailed knowledge of your subject can cause you *to give your reader too much information* instead of too little. Rather than just focusing on the outcome of a trip you took to solve a problem, you'll be tempted to overload your report with unnecessary details—when each meeting took place, how long each lasted, what the subject was, and so on. But all your reader wants to know is whether you solved the problem and how you did it (very briefly!). This tendency to fill something full of extraneous details shows up sometimes when people write procedures manuals. They are tempted to put in everything they know, rather than just what their readers need to know. Here's an example from a manual used in a state agency.

Any person licensed to practice medicine or any of the medicinal arts, any hospital resident or intern, any nursing professional, any person employed as a social worker, any probation officer, any teacher or other person employed in a public or private school, kindergarten, or nursery school, any person who provides full or part-time child care for pay on

```
a regularly planned basis, any mental health
professional and any law enforcement officer, in
his professional or official capacity, and any
professional staff person, not previously enumerated,
employed by a private or State-operated hospital,
institution, or facility which children have been
committed to or placed in for care and treatment who
has reason to suspect that a child is an abused or
neglected child, shall report the matter immediately.
```

What the reader of the manual needs to know can be summarized in one short sentence.

```
Anyone who works with children in a professional
capacity must report suspected child abuse or neglect
immediately.
```

Focus on Your Readers' Needs

To select what kind of and how much information your reader needs, try to focus not on what you know about a particular subject, but on what your *reader* needs to know. Don't think like this.

- "I've got to write that memo about the upcoming workshop."
- "I've got to write that trip report."
- "I've got to write that long clause about child abuse and neglect."

But rather, specify your *goal* for each document, like this.

- "I'm writing that memo *so that* people will know when and where that workshop is and what it's about."
- "I'm writing that trip report *so that* my manager will know how we solved the problem."
- "I'm writing that clause about child abuse *so that* my reader will know when to report it."

A specific goal statement will usually direct you to the information your reader needs.

YOUR ORGANIZATION

We human beings understand our experiences by organizing them into patterns. We remember what we did on a given day by recalling it in chronological patterns. For example, first I got up, then I got dressed, etc. When we look at a room, we perceive spatial patterns; first a green rug, then a large easy chair, then a shiny brass lamp, etc. In attempting to understand more complicated experiences, we simply use more complex patterns. To understand the political inclinations of our friends, for example, we might classify them, dividing them into such groups as liberal, moderate, or conservative. And to understand a sport we're not familiar with, we might analyze it, breaking it down into its rules, number and types of players, equipment, goals, etc.

Choosing Your Organizational Pattern

When you write at work, you'll use the same sorts of patterns to organize your information. You may narrate the events of a meeting in chronological order; spatially arrange the physical details of a machine in order to describe it; compare people; contrast alternative solutions; analyze causes and effects of problems; or classify programs and issues being discussed.

There will be times when you will hardly have to pause a moment to decide on the most appropriate organizational pattern, especially when writing fairly simple documents. A short, routine memo, letter, or report can often be organized as fast as you write it. For example, you might organize a simple request by stating your request and your deadline.

Michelle:

Please assemble 300 McCook Plant Training Manuals. We'll need these by Tuesday, September 28.

Or you might organize a response to a request for information by referring to the request, giving the information, and then closing politely.

Dear Dr. Ackley:

We have received your recent inquiry regarding a dental expense insurance claim submitted on behalf of the above-named person.

Benefits have been allowed and a payment was made to the provider on March 30, 19--, in the amount of $77.75.

We hope this has satisfactorily answered your questions. If we can be of further help, please contact us.

You might write a brief transmittal letter to accompany some documents to be sent to someone by referring to the documents in one paragraph and then identifying them in the next.

Dear Mr. Wilson:

Enclosed are the policies you requested for use in your insurance seminar.

Form #11919 is the old policy. Form #11996 is the more recent version.

Hope these can be of use to you.

Even some short reports will be fairly easy to organize. Note how the writer of the following status report begins with a paragraph summarizing his major activities, and then describes each in more detail in the succeeding paragraphs.

Attached is my August Status Report. I was able to accomplish a great deal. My major areas of effort during this period were Quality Reporting, Louisville; AccuTest, Indianapolis; and Internal Audit, Richmond. Among my most noteworthy accomplishments were the following:

- Installation and initial testing of the Quality Reporting System software.
- Continued testing to identify and correct AccuTest, Indianapolis, response time problems.
- Identification and cleanup of disk space on the Internal Audit Richmond system.

Attached is a detailed discussion of each of these areas.

You will write many other routine letters, memos, and reports, possibly thanking someone for a job well done, making arrangements for a conference, acknowledging receipt of some documents, or changing simple procedures.

Your Organizational Pattern Should Enhance Your Goal

But even when writing such routine documents, you may have to make a conscious choice of the most appropriate organizational pattern. Should you, for instance, begin a memo about a training workshop by telling your readers what the arrangements and schedule will be, or by giving them the purpose and goals of the training? And how do you give bad news to your reader—do you begin by giving your reader the bad news that you don't have the money to buy some software she wants, or by explaining why? These choices will have an impact on how your reader understands and reacts to what you have to say.

In more complicated writing situations, you must be even more careful to choose the best organizational pattern. But you must also remember that these patterns are not artificially applied from the outside. Rather, like the information you give the reader, these patterns arise naturally from your writing situation. As you carefully think through each situation, ask yourself, "What's my goal in writing this letter, memo, report—what is the effect I want to have on my reader as a result of this?" By keeping your goal in mind, you will discover the most appropriate organizational pattern. For example,

- If you want readers to know about the changes to be made in a policy manual, the benefits of a new insurance policy, or the arrangements for a meeting, you will probably organize main points by *listing* them.
- If you want readers to understand a complex project (for instance, how you plan to organize an advertising campaign for a new product), you might *analyze* the campaign into parts: (1) Planning Phase; (2) Mass Media Phase—TV, magazines, newspapers; (3) Evaluation Phase.
- If you want readers to help you solve a problem, you might *describe* the problem, *illustrate it*, and suggest a *solution*.
- If you want readers to agree to a proposal, you might *state* the proposal and then *give your reasons* for it.

By the time you finish this book, you will be familiar with the major organizational patterns you can use in writing on the job, both those mentioned above and others discussed later. What's important, though, is not that you know the name of each pattern, but that you know how to arrive at the appropriate organizational pattern for each document you write. To do this, you will need to draw up an outline or *plan*, essentially a sketch, of your main ideas.

Methods for Planning Short Documents

In school, you learned to use the traditional outline for planning, with Roman numerals, letters, Arabic numerals, and so forth. We'll review this method when we get to section three, where we'll discuss different ways to organize ideas for long documents. Here, we're going to focus on three methods for organizing short documents like letters, memos, and short reports. These methods are *jot-listing, nutshelling,* and *reader-questioning*. They will help you accomplish the same purpose as the formal outline, but each is more flexible and easier to use. But as we discuss these, remember that a successful plan grows out of a clear goal. No plan will work unless you know what your goal is.

Jot-Listing

This method, simply listing your major points, works best when you have a few points or when they should be arranged chronologically. In a letter to persuade a client to buy a new product or system, you might list the following main points:

1. Product description
2. Advantages of using
3. Cost

To inform your manager about the results of a trip you took to check on quality control procedures at a number of plants, you might plan your report by listing the stops you made and noting beside each stop how well procedures were being followed.

Or you might quickly plan a monthly status report by listing the major projects you were engaged in.

1. Studied cost control system
2. Completed performance appraisals
3. Attended workshop
4. Miscellaneous activities

More and more frequently now, managers are dictating their reports for someone in a word processing center to type. Because it is such a quick and easy method for planning a document, jot-listing is an ideal planning tool in such situations. Before you pick up the telephone or turn the tape recorder on to dictate, make a jot list of your major points, adding additional notes if you need to. Then you will have a kind of script to follow as you dictate. Thus, rather than searching for your next major point, you can devote yourself to choosing just the right language to say something.

Nutshelling

This planning method works especially well when you are planning a complicated piece of writing and need to boil your main ideas down to their essentials. To use it, imagine yourself talking to your reader and begin by saying: "In a nutshell. . . ."; then follow with a short summary of your main ideas. The conversational phrase "In a nutshell" will force you to focus just on main ideas.

I could have used this method to plan this chapter by saying, "In a nutshell, I'm going to. . . . ," until I had finally come up with a statement that forms the plan for the chapter: "In a nutshell, I'm going to show you how to go about selecting your information, organizing that information, and designing your document." Needless to say, nutshelling (or any other planning method for that matter) doesn't take all the pain out of writing—I spent weeks on this chapter—researching, thinking, writing bits and pieces—before I was ready to come up with my nutshell statement. But once I could nutshell my ideas, they were crystallized for me.[1]

To see how this method works, imagine someone writing a memo to inform plant personnel about a new set of complicated safety regulations just announced by a federal agency in a letter that was three pages long. The writer knows that people in the plant must understand the procedures thoroughly, but she also knows that they will read any such memo hurriedly. So she needs to set forth the essential parts of the new regulations in quick, readable form. She might say to herself, "In a nutshell, I want to tell them three things—what safety clothing to wear, what procedures to follow when operating machinery, and what to do in case of an accident." Under each of these major sections, she can then set forth the specific items that her readers need to know.

Reader-Questioning

One way to think about writing is to see it as an attempt to answer readers' questions, either expressed or implied. Therefore, one way to plan a piece of writing is simply to ask yourself, "What are the questions my readers need answered in this report, memo, letter, manual, etc.?" Your questions become the plan for the main sections of the document and your answers become your main points. The advantage of this questioning technique is that it focuses your attention not on what you know and may want to say about a document, but on what your *reader* needs to know. Thus, it helps you decide on your main points and present them in a sequence that corresponds to your reader's needs.

Because reader-questioning forces you to stand in your reader's shoes and build your plan around his or her needs, it's an excellent way to plan a manual that guides someone through a procedure. The writers of a state commission planning a consumer's manual on auto insurance used the following questions to organize their material:

1. Why buy auto insurance?
2. What types of insurance am I required to buy?

[1]The technique of *nutshelling* was first suggested by Linda Flower in her excellent book, *Problem-Solving Strategies for Writing* (New York: Harcourt Brace Jovanovich, 1985) 94–95.

3. What types of insurance are available in addition to the required coverages?
4. How much insurance do I need?
5. How do I shop for insurance?
6. How do accidents and violations affect my rates?
7. When should I buy insurance?
8. How do I register complaints about my insurance company?

These questions provided a guide for the writers, showing them what information to include, what to exclude, and how best to arrange that information. Incidentally, these writers actually used the questions as headings for different sections of their manual. Thus, the questions guided readers quickly to the sections they needed to read.

These three planning methods can be used interchangeably. Each is an efficient procedure for helping you plan your writing so that you give readers the information they need in the way that will be most helpful to them. Jot-listing and nutshelling will probably be more helpful in planning short documents; reader-questioning can be used with a document of any length.

A Writing Situation

Let's see how you might use these methods to plan the fitness memo discussed on pages 51–54 of this chapter. After quickly reviewing that discussion, imagine you're now ready to try to organize all the information you generated earlier. After rereading your notes, you begin with a *jot-list* of the major points you might make in the memo. Actually, the answers to the journalist's questions you asked earlier form a kind of jot-list in themselves. From them, you are quickly able to make the following list:

1. Participants
2. Program activities
3. Time/location
4. Purpose

This jot-list is a beginning, but it's just not enough. Even if its categories are the right ones to use, they're not arranged logically, because surely the purpose of the program should come before the others. You decide to try *nutshelling* to refine your organization further. "In a nutshell," you say to yourself, "I want to tell my readers about this program—who'll participate, what they'll do, where it will be, its purpose, and its costs." Not much more help. So you decide to try *reader-questioning*. "What's the first question my readers will have?" you ask yourself. "They'll probably want to know why I'm writing this memo in the first place." Then it hits you! You haven't yet really clarified your goal for the memo.

You think back over what your boss said when she told you to write it and realize she didn't give you a goal either. She just told you to write a memo. But, of course, your goal was implicit in what she said—she wanted you to propose to division heads that the extra funds in the budget be used to set up the fitness program. Now you can formulate your specific goal: "I'm writing this memo *so that* division heads will use the extra funds to set up a fitness program."

You are now ready to list the questions your readers will have.

QUESTION	ANSWER
Why are you writing this memo, anyway?	Goal: To persuade you to fund this fitness program.
What program?	Brief Program Description: participants/activities/time/place
What's the purpose of such a program?	Promote health/fitness in order to reduce absenteeism and increase productivity
How much will it cost?	Brief budget amounting to around $6,000 for equipment, place, promotion, etc.

You've now organized the main points of your proposal. Of course, you haven't finished yet. You've still got to write a draft, get your manager to critique it, and then revise. When she does, you're probably going to find that you have spent too much time describing the program and its purpose (after all, that's what you thought about the most) before answering the bottom line question of the division heads, "How much will it cost?" But considering the groundwork you have already laid in discovering and organizing your ideas, your proposal probably stands a good chance of being approved.

YOUR DESIGN

Most people don't worry much about how to design or lay out their documents. Once they've selected their information and organized it, they usually feel ready to write. Sometimes the result is that ideas that are well organized and even well expressed are not understood because a document looks too complicated to bother reading. The following memo, announcing a major division reorganization, is an example. See if you can grasp its details on first reading.

MEMORANDUM

TO: All Employees
FROM: Warren Jamison
SUBJECT: Consumer Affairs Division
DATE: December 16, 19--

In order to provide more services to consumers, this agency will create a new Consumer Affairs Division. By combining several existing departments into this division, we hope to cut costs of unnecessary duplication of services. This new division will enable us to provide consumers with up-to-date information on new products and services as well as respond to questions and complaints in a timely manner. In addition, it will give us the capacity to predict future demand trends through consumer research.

This reorganization will be effective on July 15 of this year. By that time, offices will be centralized, clerical staff will either be reassigned from another division or hired, and new managers will be in place. All staff who will be affected by this reorganization have already been notified. Meetings with appropriate managers will be held on April 30 to explain applicable details.

In the meantime, we are announcing the following departmental and managerial shifts so that this process may be completed as expeditiously and easily as possible. The Publications and Communications Departments will form the nucleus of the new division, being joined by the newly created Consumer Research Department. Mary Tau will remain as chief of publications; a new position, deputy chief, will be created to provide her with assistance. Additional staff will be added as necessary. Mark Boone will replace Joan Terry as new chief of consumer communications; he will be joined by Marguerite Jarvis, who will be the new deputy chief of that department. Joan Terry will become chief of the new division. She will be joined by Jerry Carver as her deputy chief. Joan will be interviewing prospective staff for the new division in the near future. We will announce additional managerial changes as they occur.

We hope that all employees will give the new division and its personnel their full support and cooperation.

How did you do? Not very well, if you are like most readers. In fact, you'd probably have to reread the memo several times in order to follow its details. The writer needs to redesign the memo so that readers can glean essential information quickly and easily. To do this, the writer can draw on some frequently used design devices. These are *Separators, Enumerators,* and *Illustrators*. First look at the memo below and its continuation on the next page to see how they are listed. These devices are listed for you on pages 65–66.

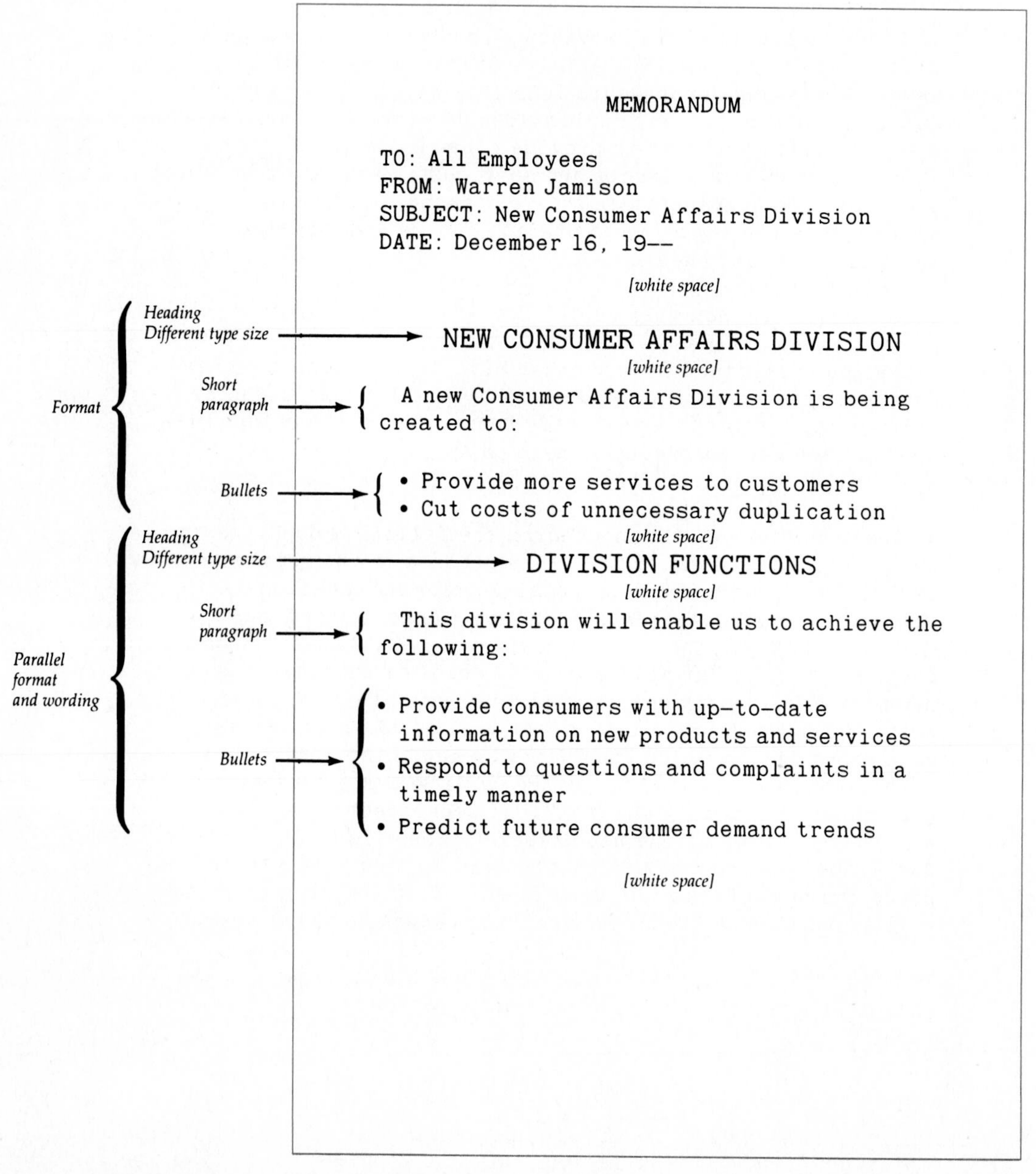

MEMORANDUM

TO: All Employees
FROM: Warren Jamison
SUBJECT: New Consumer Affairs Division
DATE: December 16, 19--

NEW CONSUMER AFFAIRS DIVISION

A new Consumer Affairs Division is being created to:

- Provide more services to customers
- Cut costs of unnecessary duplication

DIVISION FUNCTIONS

This division will enable us to achieve the following:

- Provide consumers with up-to-date information on new products and services
- Respond to questions and complaints in a timely manner
- Predict future consumer demand trends

1. **Separators**
   a. Headings
   b. Short paragraphs
   c. White space between paragraphs
   d. Parallels
   e. Different type sizes
2. **Enumerators**
   a. Numbers

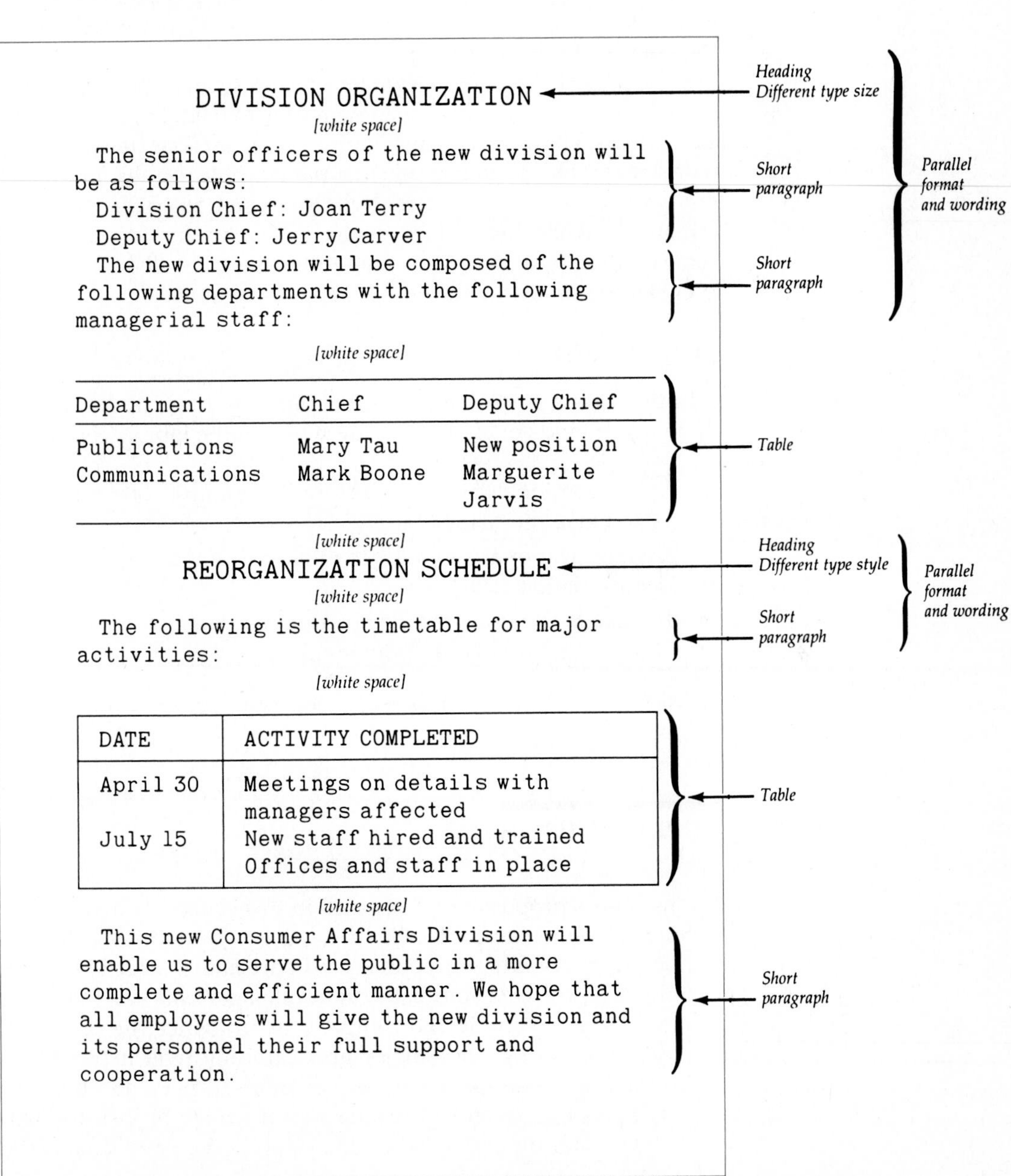
DIVISION ORGANIZATION

[white space]

The senior officers of the new division will be as follows:

Division Chief: Joan Terry
Deputy Chief: Jerry Carver

The new division will be composed of the following departments with the following managerial staff:

[white space]

Department	Chief	Deputy Chief
Publications	Mary Tau	New position
Communications	Mark Boone	Marguerite Jarvis

[white space]

REORGANIZATION SCHEDULE

[white space]

The following is the timetable for major activities:

[white space]

DATE	ACTIVITY COMPLETED
April 30	Meetings on details with managers affected
July 15	New staff hired and trained Offices and staff in place

[white space]

This new Consumer Affairs Division will enable us to serve the public in a more complete and efficient manner. We hope that all employees will give the new division and its personnel their full support and cooperation.

   b. Letters
   c. Bullets, asterisks, etc.
3. **Illustrators**
   a. Tables
   b. Charts
   c. Graphs

The best way to understand how these design devices work is to see how they can simplify such a complicated document as the memo you tried to read above. The devices are labeled for you on the example on pages 64–65.

You can see how using design techniques such as these can make even the most complicated document easy to read. Separators such as headings, short paragraphs, white space, parallels, and different type sizes break up information into manageable chunks. Enumerators such as numbers, letters, bullets (•), and asterisks (*) list information, while illustrators depict it graphically. We'll discuss some of these design devices more fully, especially illustrators, in a later chapter on using graphics in long documents.

SUMMARY

In this chapter, we have talked about how to go about making three major kinds of choices as you write on the job.

1. Informational choices—the type and quantity of information you give the reader.
2. Organizational choices—the patterns you use to make that information clear.
3. Design choices—the layout devices you use to make the information easy to understand.

Practice making some of these choices in the applications that follow.

APPLICATIONS

1. The fitness proposal we discussed in this chapter has now been approved and the project is ready to go. Equipment has been bought, the building prepared, and part-time instructors hired. Since the project is your baby, your manager asks you to write a memo to everyone in the company to announce the program. After considering your major goal carefully (will it be just to inform people about the project or more to persuade them to participate?), plan and write the announcement. Since most people read such announcements fast, pay particular attention to the

way you select the information you include, the way you organize it, and the way you design the memo.

2. Teachers in a school system received the following confusing letter one spring. As you read it, you might remember that some teachers have temporary (one-year) contracts. Each spring, they want to know whether they will be rehired. Of course, all teachers want to know what their raise will be.

Dear Colleagues:

I am writing to all teachers to inform them concerning the status of promotions and salaries. It is the policy of the Barber County School Board to follow the procedures given in our State Employees Handbook as to dates of notification of employees who will not be continued. Since the latest possible such date has passed, any employees who have not received such notification are assured of continuation.

It is not clear, as you know, whether the funds will be available for salary increases for this second year in the biennium, depending on the county treasurer's assessment of state finances to be made sometime in August, on rulings by the Board of Supervisors as to whether money may be shifted from one budget category to another in order to fund increases, and on other aspects of the funding situation.

Salary notification letters must, therefore, be delayed until these funding determinations can be made.

In light of what you have learned about informational and organizational choices in this chapter, analyze the major problems of this letter. Now decide on the major goal of the letter, and make a brief plan for correcting the problems, using one of the planning methods suggested in this chapter. Following your plan, rewrite the letter.

3. Following is a memo that was sent to employees in a bank. It is fairly well organized, but poorly designed. Too much information comes at you too fast. Using some of the design devices we

MEMORANDUM

TO: All Employees
FROM: Marlane James, Training Director
SUBJECT: Update on Procedures
DATE: February 18, 19--

There have been some questions concerning the bank's system that have not been answered in the information that our employees have received to date. One question concerns those customers who have, or open, only a savings account with our bank. The question is, "Can these customers receive a bank system card?" The answer is "yes"; they can request one through the branches. The form to be used in ordering the savings account is Card Request Form 189. By checking the first box, filling in the customer's signature and address, and then forwarding the form to the ATM PROCESSING CLERK at the Operations Center, savings customers will receive a system card that they can use to access their savings account.

Another question that has been brought up is, "Can customers change their URS number if they would prefer to use a 3-digit number they already know?" The answer is "no." If customers wish to have their URS changed to protect themselves (e.g., someone who should

discussed in this chapter, redesign this memo. Try to use the following techniques: headings, short paragraphs, white space, parallels, different size type, and some form of enumeration. As you revise, also delete any unnecessary information.

4. Because the number of 18-year-olds applying to college is smaller than it was a few years ago, colleges are scrambling for students. One way most colleges attract new students is through brochures advertising the school.

   Although many of these brochures are done by professional advertising firms, the head of admissions at your school has decided to go a different route. She wants a brochure produced

```
not, knows their URS) a randomly generated URS
will be reassigned to their bank system card.
However, we do not have the capability to let
customers change the number. They must accept
the number generated by the computer.

Besides these questions, one operational
procedure should be emphasized. Joan Amato
has requested that all employees be informed
that any Security Validation Request Forms
received through the branch are to be
forwarded to SECURITIES VERIFICATION. The
customers are receiving this form in the mass
mailing packet, and some are returning it to
the branch instead of returning it by mail in
the envelope provided. This is fine as long as
the employee taking the Validation Request
Form forwards it to SECURITIES VERIFICATION.
```

by in-house staff. After all, they should know the strengths of the school better than anyone else. And perhaps they'll come up with some unique ways of presenting these strengths to prospective students.

Since you are currently working in the admissions office, you and four others have been asked to draw up the brochure. Working with the group, write the brochure. Begin by setting your major goal; then collect information through the discovery techniques we discussed, organize that information, and write the brochure. As your group drafts and revises the brochure, pay particular attention to voice and design, since the brochure should appeal to 18-year-old readers.

CHAPTER

4

Your Style: Words and Sentences

To write simply and directly is the desire of every good writer. This chapter will show you how to develop such a style through word choice and sentence structure.

In chapter three, we discussed your information, organization, and design choices. In this chapter, we'll focus on your stylistic choices. People use the word style to apply to many things—they talk about a person's style of dress, the styling of an automobile, and even someone's lifestyle. In all these instances, style seems to be a way of doing something. We are going to define style in writing as *the way a writer uses words*—actually, the way he or she *chooses* words and sentences.

An event that occurred in 1973 illustrates the theme of this chapter. In that year, officials at Citibank of New York City made a pioneering decision. As part of a campaign to change their corporate image, they decided to rewrite their consumer loan agreement so that it could actually be understood by ordinary people who wanted to make a loan. People who borrow money from a bank or other lending institution sign such an agreement, promising to pay the money back in a certain way within a certain period of time. But until recently, most consumers who signed such agreements couldn't understand what they said. Why? Because they were written in complex, legal language that no one but attorneys could follow.

Following is part of one provision from the original Citibank agreement. Its goal is to explain when a borrower is in default. Not only did consumers have trouble understanding such language, but lawyers, judges, and even Citibank's own lending officers found some of it incomprehensible.

```
In the event of default in the payment of this or any
other Obligation or the performance or observance of
any term or covenant contained herein or in any note
or other contract or agreement evidencing or relating
to any Obligation or any Collateral on the Borrower's
part to be performed or observed; or the undersigned
Borrower shall die; or any of the undersigned become
insolvent or make an assignment for the benefit of
creditors; or a petition shall be filed by or against
any of the undersigned under any provision of the
Bankruptcy Act; or any money, securities or
properties of the undersigned now or hereafter on
deposit with or in the possession or under the control
of the Bank shall be attached or become subject to
distraint proceedings or any order or process of any
court; or the bank shall deem itself to be
insecure. . . .
```

When the same provision appeared in the revised agreement, it looked like this.

```
I'll be in default:
  1. If I don't pay an installment on time; or
  2. If any other creditor tries by legal process to
     take any money of mine in your possession.
```

Changes like this one didn't come easily. Even though a marketing executive might have considered that most of the original provision was unnecessary, someone whose job was to collect unpaid loans might have wanted to keep the original language to protect the bank. But the change was finally made. And if you remember the discussion from the previous chapter, you'll see that changes were made in the information, organization, and design of the provision. Much detailed information was deleted; the main idea, "I'll be in default," was put at the beginning; and numbers and indentations were used to make the provision particularly easy to read.

But the major change was the *style* of the provision, its words and sentence structure. Words that are unfamiliar, legal sounding, and impersonal were replaced by words that are simple and down-to-earth. And instead of a convoluted sentence, full of tortuous twists and turns, we now have a straightforward one, composed of three easily readable parts. This chapter is about how to write in such a readable style—by understanding the variety of word and sentence choices at your command, and by knowing which choices to make in a particular writing situation.[1]

YOUR WORDS

To write in an appropriate style, you first need to be aware of the important word choices you can make. We'll discuss these on the following pages.

Choose Between Simple and Complex Words

When writing at work, you will use words that range from simple to complex. Most of the time, you will use simple words: these are short, frequently used, and often derived from Anglo-Saxon, the primitive Germanic language that was the parent of modern English. But sometimes you will use more complex words: these are longer, less frequently used, and often derived from Latin, a sophisticated language that strongly influenced English during the Middle Ages and the Renaissance. Often, you will find both simple and complex synonyms for something you want to say. For example, you may choose to replace complex words such as "commence," "insufficient," "enumerate," or "residence" with more simple words such as "start," "not enough," "count," or "home."

Complex words will create a more formal voice, while simpler words will seem less formal. If you want to distance yourself from a reader, you might say more formally, "We *acquired* the product." To be less formal, you might say, "We *got* the product." To be more formal you might say, "We *effected* the change," rather than the less formal, "We *brought* the change *about*," or even the simpler, "We *changed* it."

Some writers at work, probably laboring under the illusion that they sound more professional, will always choose the complex over the simple word. They feel that they have to write "ascertain" or "determine" rather than "find out"; "endeavor" rather than "try"; "personnel" rather than "people"; or "subsequent" rather than "later." They don't realize that true professionals choose the word most appropriate to their writing situation. Whether that word seems long or short, simple or complex, impressive or not, makes no difference in and of itself.

Here, for example, is a sentence full of complex words about aluminum manufacture.

```
While it consumes substantial amounts of energy in its
initial manufacturing processes, the amount of energy
it conserves in recycling processes and in its ulti-
```

[1]If you want to read more about the Citibank case and about other situations in which organizations revised documents to make them more readable, take a look at *How Plain English Works for Business: Twelve Case Studies* (Washington, D.C.: U.S. Department of Commerce, Office of Consumer Affairs, 1984).

```
mate applications more than offsets the original
energy input.
```

Such words as "consumes," "substantial," "manufacturing," and "processes" might make this sentence sound appropriate for a formal report on aluminum manufacture. But the sentence didn't appear in such a report; instead, it appeared in a brochure designed to encourage the general public to recycle aluminum cans. These words are just too complex and formal for such a document. The following simpler words would have been much more appropriate:

```
Although it takes large amounts of energy to make
aluminum in the first place, the energy saved through
use and recycling more than offsets this.
```

There is no question that complex words will sometimes be more precise than their simpler counterparts. Words such as "assent," "constitutes," and "analyze" can give you shades of meaning that synonyms such as "agreed to," "make up," or "examine" cannot. But because complex words are less familiar to many readers, they won't understand them as easily or as quickly as they will the simpler ones. In fact, you will often find yourself walking a tightrope between the accuracy of complex words and the readability of simple ones. You will have to assess each writing situation, and make the best decision you can.

Choose Between Concrete and Abstract Words

Suppose someone said to you, "Raising the mayor's salary will have serious political consequences." What could this sentence mean? It's impossible to tell. The person could mean that taxpayers will be mad as hornets over the higher taxes they will now have to pay; or that the vice mayor and the other members of city council will demand the same raise; or that the higher salary will attract a better candidate, perhaps someone who will beat the incumbent mayor in the next election.

Why can we interpret this statement in so many different ways? Obviously, it is because the word "significance" can be taken in different ways. The reason is that "significance" is so abstract that it can apply to many instances of the same thing. On the other hand, the ideas that taxpayers will be mad as hornets, that other members of the council will demand the same raise, or that a better candidate will beat the old mayor are all expressed in concrete terms. These words *show* us what the speaker means.

This distinction between *abstract* and *concrete* words is an important one to know when writing on the job, for there will be times when one kind of word will be more appropriate than another. Abstract words are words that have been generalized from particular instances—"economy," "environment," "personnel," and "communication" are examples. Particular instances of these abstractions are expressed in concrete words—you might refer to the 15 dollars in your pocketbook right now (economy); to three old and twisted oak trees in your front yard (environment); to the five supervisors in your plant (personnel); or to what you told someone last night (communication).

Abstract words work particularly well when you are summarizing something. The summary, purpose statement, and conclusions of a long report; the recommendations of a proposal; and the conclusions of a position paper should usually be expressed in abstract language, for you are trying to pull things together for your reader. Thus, the following statement might be appropriate as the conclusion of a long discussion:

> We had made significant progress toward this goal by process improvements, reduced energy consumption, and environmental improvements; however, we had not yet attempted to increase the level of productivity on a plant-wide basis.

But if such a statement appears near the beginning of a report, as this one did, then it will not work because readers will not understand the general phrases without some concrete explanation. "What is significant progress?" they may ask. "What kinds of process improvements have been made?" "How much did you reduce energy consumption?" "What kinds of environmental improvements did you make?" To show them what you mean, you will need to use concrete language like the following:

> Our goal was to save $165,000 per year. We had accomplished 45% of this goal by doing the following: replacing all line cutters older than five years; reducing the amount of electricity used in the plant by 30%; and replacing all dust traps. But we had not made a plant-wide effort to increase our line operators' productivity.

In an admirable effort to be more concise, writers at work will sometimes use abstract language. But they must realize that if they don't use concrete words that show what they mean, then readers must slow down and interpret abstractions for themselves. Look at the following statements, for instance, and pick out the abstract words and phrases.

- A number of the items received from that supplier contained imperfections.
- It will be noted that considerable savings have been accomplished through initiation of improved purchasing methods.

Did you identify "number," "items," "imperfections," "considerable savings," and "improved purchasing methods" as abstractions? Your readers will know more concretely what you are talking about if you tell them, in these cases, that "five TVs" were "scratched," and that "$3,330" was saved because of the improved purchasing methods of "competitive bidding" and "buying in lots of 100."

Choose Between Personal and Impersonal Words

Human life is a drama. People are constantly doing—talking, laughing, thinking, feeling. Yet the central actors in the drama often sink beneath the surface of the writing done on the job. That is, we tend to emphasize not the actors themselves, but the outcomes of what they have done—their ideas, activities, products, and results. For instance, look at the following sentences.

- The bureau has gathered statistics regarding the new installations.
- The department maintains direct supervision of all services.
- Subsidized adoption has been designed as a resource to facilitate legal adoption of individuals with special needs.
- A study was conducted to determine whether the company's accident record was higher than normal.
- It has been recommended that the company implement that policy.

Somewhere in these sentences are people. *Someone* collected those statistics referred to in the first sentence; *someone* in the department is supervising someone else; *someone* helps children with special needs to be adopted; *someone* has studied accidents; and *someone* else has recommended something. But here, because people are left out, these sentences are dull and indirect.

There may be times when you will not want to use personal words in writing on the job. On certain occasions, for instance, you may want to maintain a more impersonal voice, particularly when you have to establish your authority in a situation or when you are writing a formal, public document. And when writing a report, you may decide that your readers are more interested in what is being recommended than in the people making the recommendations. Also, if you are speaking for your whole organization, you may decide that personal references are inappropriate.

But whenever you can, make your writing as personal as possible. Notice how using some personal words in the sentences quoted earlier results in more direct and concise sentences.

- *We* have gathered statistics regarding the new installations.
- *Field representatives* directly supervise all services.
- Subsidized adoption is meant to help *people* adopt *children* with special needs.

- *They* have tried to find out whether the company's accident record was higher than normal.
- *The operations group* recommended that the company implement that policy.

Sometimes, people may tell you that personal words are not appropriate when writing on the job. If this was ever true, it is certainly not true today. Some of the country's most successful executives advocate that their employees write personally. And most scholars and scientists now debunk the argument that an impersonal style insures objectivity; they know that objectivity lies in their treatment and presentation of facts more than in their style. Even the style of scientific journals is becoming more personal; some editors actually tell scholars to use personal words.

Using personal words, especially personal pronouns, often has the effect of planting your stylistic feet on the ground, and therefore making what you have to say easier for the reader to understand. Here is an unnecessarily complicated introduction to a book on aluminum engineering.

> Advances in the knowledge of the structural behaviour of aluminum assemblies have necessitated some revisions in this fourth edition of "Strength of Aluminum." Of principal interest is an introduction to design using the plastic approach as it applies to beams, plates, shells, and local loads on extrusions.
>
> To facilitate the choice of a suitable alloy, only the alloys, products, and tempers most widely used in structures have been included. . . .[2]

Now watch what happens when we rewrite the three sentences by including some personal pronouns as subjects.

> We now know more about the structural behaviour of aluminum assemblies; therefore, we have revised this fourth edition of Strength of Aluminum. You will be most interested in the introduction to design, which uses the plastic approach as it applies to beams, plates, and local loads on extrusions. To help you choose a suitable alloy, we have included only the alloys, products, and tempers most widely used in structures.

Some writers may fear that such an introduction would seem overly egocentric. You will have to make that decision for yourself. I suspect that most readers will so appreciate the clarity and simplicity of the style that they won't even notice the personal pronouns.

[2]*Strength of Aluminum* (Ontario, Canada: ALCAN Products LTD, April 1973) 1.

Choose Between Active and Passive Words

When you don't use personal words, you are often thrown into the passive voice. You will write, "A study of the causes of that accident is being conducted by us"; rather than "We are conducting a study of the causes of that accident"; or better yet, "We are studying the causes of that accident." Not only are the last two versions more direct and concise, they are also easier to read. Studies have shown that it takes readers longer to process information that is written in the passive voice.

What is the difference between active and passive voice? Let me explain the grammatical differences first. Imagine that you have just written a report. There are two ways you can communicate this to someone else. You can either say, "I just wrote that report," or "That report was just written by me." The first sentence is in the active voice because the subject of the sentence is active—he or she has actually done something. But in the second sentence, the subject is the passive "report" rather than the person who wrote it. When you write in the active voice, you usually put the person who acted at the beginning of the sentence—you put him or her in charge. But when you use the passive, you relegate the actor to the end of the sentence or leave the actor out completely. You lose the central character in the drama.

Sometimes, you will want to use the passive voice. If, for instance, the actor in a particular situation is not as important as what was done, you may wish to change a sentence such as "*I* performed that experiment recently," to "*That experiment* was performed recently." And if you want to take the personal sting out of an implied criticism, you may want to say,

"Production quotas should be met as soon as possible";

rather than the more direct and accusatory,

"You should meet production quotas as soon as possible"; or "I want you to meet production quotas as soon as possible."

But don't slip into the habit of many business and technical writers and overuse the passive. If you can say something in the active voice, you will make your statement a little easier for your reader to understand.

If you are prohibited by a manager or an organizational policy from using personal pronouns, one solution is to *personify* the subject of the sentence instead of using the passive. Thus, rather than saying, "The experiment was performed," you could say, "The experiment revealed that. . . ." Or rather than saying, "All programs are supervised by the department," you could say, "The department supervises all programs."

Choose Between Abstract Nouns and More Concrete Verbs

When writers on the job focus on the results of human actions rather than on the actors themselves, they tend to smother concrete verbs in unnecessarily abstract nouns. They write the more abstract,

"Our *intention* was to examine the process carefully" rather than "We *intended* to examine the process carefully"; "We rendered *assistance* to those who needed it" rather than "We assisted those who needed us"; and "We could not ascertain the *location* of the flaws," rather than "We could not *locate (or find)* the flaws."

After a while, some writers on the job get into the habit of smothering verbs, perhaps because their voice sounds more inflated and seemingly impressive. By adding such endings as -ion, -tion, -ment, -ance, and -ence to verbs, writers change "consume" to "consumption," "illustrate" to "illustration," and "announce" to "announcement." But this style becomes dull and difficult to understand because their sentences are built around abstract nouns connected by prepositions and weak verbs. For example, noun + preposition + noun + verb + noun + preposition + preposition + noun, and so on. The result is a sentence in a government manual like, "Protection to children involves the immediate investigation of all complaints of child abuse and neglect." A more simple and direct way of writing this sentence is, "To protect children, immediately investigate all complaints of child abuse and neglect."

Choose Between Technical and Nontechnical Words

Often, specialists within a field communicate best by using specialized, technical language, sometimes called *jargon*. The jargon of people in data processing is made up of such words as "input," "output," "interface," "bit," "byte," and "batch." Physicians communicate with words such as "congenital," "tract," "anticoagulant," "abdominal," and "hemorrhage." Engineers use words such as "metallurgical," "casting," "alloy," and "heat treat quench chamber." When specialists talk to each other, such technical language is a familiar shorthand that enables them to communicate quickly and efficiently. These words all substitute for less concise ways of saying something. For instance, it would be a waste of time for a specialist in computers to say "that which is put into a system" rather than "input."

Here is an example of technical jargon used effectively to describe an experiment.

> Water content was determined by drying for 24 hr. at 70 C. in vacuo. Nitrogen in fresh and dried products was measured by Kjeldahl analysis. Lipid content of the dried samples was determined by gravimetric analysis of material extracted with chloroform, methanol, and water by the procedure of Bligh and Dyer (1). Samples were ashed in a muffle furnace at 450 C. for about 16 hr.[3]

[3]J. Miller, Y.-Y. D. Wang, and L. R. Beuchat, "Protein Quality of Several Multi-Component, Commercially Prepared Foods," *Journal of The American Dietetic Association* 75 (September 1979): 262–64.

But here are examples of another kind of jargon that is not effective at all.

- The status attainment process of the target group is a subject of continued study.
- An ambulatory encounter is defined in this manual as a visit to a physician or health or medical worker.
- The precise nature of the causal factors of the caries experience has evaded investigators until this point in time.
- In order to communicate in a manner which is meaningful to an alter, one must first discern the alter's cognitive state.

Although they may sound technical at first, words such as "status attainment process," "target group," "ambulatory encounter," "caries experience," and "alter's cognitive state" are more aptly called *buzzwords*—they have little meaning to anyone. Rather than serving as a simple shorthand for complex concepts, these words do the opposite—they complicate simple concepts.

This kind of jargon has been so often parodied that it is a wonder that it has not self-destructed in embarrassment. A passage from the famous speech that Winston Churchill delivered to Parliament just after the British retreat at Dunkirk has been jargonized as follows:

> We shall oppose the aggressors through the optimal mobilization and implementation of all existing defense-oriented modalities.

This is what Churchill's original sentence looked like.

> We shall defend our island, whatever the cost may be. We shall fight on the beaches. We shall fight on the landing grounds. We shall fight in the fields and in the streets. We shall fight in the hills. We shall never surrender.

Russell Baker, a nationally syndicated columnist, has translated the story of "Little Red Riding Hood" into jargon. It begins like this.

> Once upon a point in time, a small person named Little Red Riding Hood initiated plans for the preparation, delivery, and transportation of foodstuffs to her grandmother, a senior citizen residing at a place of residence in a forest of indeterminate dimension.
>
> In the process of implementing this program, her incursion into the forest was in midtransportation process when it attained interface with an alleged perpetrator. This individual, a wolf, made inquiry as to the whereabouts of Little Red Riding Hood's goal, as

well as inferring that he was desirous of ascertaining the contents of Little Red Riding Hood's foodstuffs basket, and all that.[4]

When should you use technical language? When you are communicating with another specialist in your field who will understand it. Then such language is a kind of shorthand that will help you communicate efficiently. But when you are communicating with nonspecialists, use the nontechnical language they will understand. And don't use technical language simply to impress readers or to make yourself feel more a part of a particular group. Most of all, don't succumb to the temptation to overuse technical language. Don't refer to suggestions or contributions to a discussion as "input," as in, "Would you *input* to this discussion." Don't refer to every response as "feedback," as in "Would you give me your *feedback* on this." And find synonyms for words such as "model" and "parameters," so that you don't overuse these.

SENTENCES

Suppose you've had an accident at work. You have filed for benefits under workmen's compensation, but your organization is disputing your right to payment. You wonder whether your employee accident insurance will pay your bill, so you look up the appropriate provision in your policy. You find this.

If you are otherwise entitled to sickness and accident benefits and there is a dispute as to your entitlement to payments for which you are making claim pursuant to any Workmen's Compensation or occupational disease law or other similar applicable law, the sickness and accident benefits shall be paid in full if satisfactory arrangements are made to assure that any overpayment of sickness and accident benefits which may result by virtue of your success in pursuing such claim shall be reimbursed by you.

Now that you've read it, do you understand it? If so, how many times did you have to read it? Did you find yourself reading and rereading? For that matter, did you ever understand it? Now read the following revision.

The following situation may arise:
Suppose you claim sickness and accident benefits

[4]Russell Baker, "Little Red Riding Hood Revisited," *The New York Times* 13 January 1980.

```
from a source such as Workmen's Compensation or under
an occupational disease law. But your claim is being
disputed.
  Until the dispute is settled, can you collect the
benefits under this policy?
  The answer is yes, but you must arrange to repay
these benefits if you ever collect them from the other
source.
```

Why is the second version so much easier to read? Partly it is because I used some of the techniques suggested in the first part of this chapter. Assuming that most readers would not be familiar with the complicated language of insurance policies, I substituted simpler for more complex words, got rid of the technical language, changed some nouns to verbs, and kept the personal pronouns. But notice that I did some other things as well: I divided the one long sentence into four shorter ones, varied the sentence patterns, and then tied sentences together by repeating words such as "claim" and "dispute." The rest of this chapter will discuss these and other ways to make sentences clear to your reader.

Use Sentence Lengths That Suit Your Reader

The major reason why the original sentence from the insurance policy above is so difficult to read is that it's just too long. But to understand why it's too long, you need to understand how readers process information.

When we read something, we hardly even see letters; for that matter, we usually don't even notice words. Rather, we tend to read in phrases or what psychologists call "chunks" of information. As we read these chunks, we store them in our short-term memory (which lasts about twelve seconds) until we reach the end of the sentence. Once we have reached the end of the sentence, we decide what all the chunks together mean and then go on to the next sentence. In the insurance policy sentence, for instance, most of us would read in chunks like the following:

```
  [If you are] [otherwise entitled] [to sickness and
accident benefits] [and there is] [a dispute] [as to
your entitlement] [to payments] [for which you are]
[making claim] [pursuant to any Workmen's
Compensation] [or occupational disease law] [or other
similar applicable law,] [the sickness and accident
benefits] [shall be paid in full] [if satisfactory
arrangements are made] [to assure that any
overpayment] [of sickness and accident benefits]
[which may result] [by virtue of your success] [in
pursuing such claim] [shall be reimbursed by you.]
```

But there is one problem with our capacity to process information. Our short-term memory is limited to approximately seven chunks of information. If we don't reach the end of a sentence by the time we have processed this number, we will probably forget some of the chunks before we can combine them into a whole meaning. The problem with the insurance sentence is that it is composed of 21 chunks. If you are like most readers, you probably lost the meaning somewhere around chunk seven, after "payments" in the third line. Yet you still have 14 chunks to go before the end of the sentence. No wonder most readers get lost in this sentence.

I do need to qualify the discussion above in two ways. First, different readers will "chunk" different words into phrases. Therefore, your chunks might not be the same as someone else's. More importantly, readers who are familiar with the subject of a document can combine more words into one chunk than others. Thus, it is conceivable that an insurance agent might read this whole sentence and, because he is so familiar with what it says, divide it into only five or six chunks.

Once you understand how readers process the sentences you write, you realize that there is no one ideal sentence length of 15 words, 25 words, or 30 words. Rather, the length of your sentences will vary with your readers. Sentences in newspapers and magazines are typically short, 10 to 22 words, because they are addressed to general readers. But sentences in scholarly journals, written for specialists who will be familiar with the subject matter, can be much longer, even 40 to 50 words, and still be understood. You will have to gauge the familiarity of your readers with your subject matter and then decide how long your sentences should be.

In school, your writing teachers may sometimes have asked you to combine overly short sentences into longer, more complex ones. On the job, your problem will usually be just the opposite—how to shorten and simplify sentences so your reader can comprehend them easily. Here are three ways to do this.

Reduce Stock Phrases

Business and professional writing is full of stock phrases that can be shortened. Writers say, "A difference of opinion exists regarding that"; when they could simply say, "We disagree about that." Or they say, "It is the purpose of this paper"; when they could say, "My purpose is to. . . ." When you can, reduce phrases such as the following to their one-word substitutes:

- a considerable amount of (much)
- for the purpose of (to)
- a decreased number of (fewer)
- has been engaged in a study of (has studied)
- a large number of (many)
- in sufficient quantities (enough)

- at a time when (when)
- at the present time (now)
- in the not too distant future (soon)
- come to the conclusion (conclude)

Cut the Deadwood

There is no use making your readers process information that they don't need. To prevent this, cut any unnecessary words. If you have difficulty cutting words, you can use the following key word technique to help.[5] Suppose you have written this sentence.

```
It must definitely be recognized that quite often the
addition of a particular word may actually weaken a
sentence rather than adding very much to its meaning.
```

Now you decide it's too long and you want to cut it down to its essential meaning. To do this, you underline the key words, as follows:

> It must definitely be <u>recognized that</u> quite <u>often</u> the <u>addition</u> of <u>a</u> particular <u>word may weaken a sentence</u> rather than adding very much to its meaning.

Next, you rewrite the sentence around these key words.

```
Recognize that adding a word may often weaken a
sentence.
```

To practice, try this key word technique on the following sentence:

```
It is the responsibility of each and every department
head to properly arrange the activities of the
department in such a manner that all employees,
including the department head, will receive the
full vacation to which they are duly entitled.
```

Did you come up with something like the following revision?

```
Each department head must arrange the department's
schedule so that all employees receive their full
vacation.
```

Why do writers clutter their sentences with so many unnecessary words? Perhaps they wish to inflate them just a little, as this writer did by writing, "A great deal of progress has been made toward accomplishing this objective"; when all he meant was, "We have

[5]This technique was first suggested by Linda Flower in *Problem-Solving Strategies for Writing* (New York: Harcourt Brace Jovanovich, 1985) 193–95.

made a great deal of progress." Or maybe writers on the job feel they have to protect themselves by writing overly qualified sentences like the following:

> Basically, it is realized that the use of aluminum conduit (or other structural member) for masts would be, of course, related to a function of the size materials involved and strengths required.

This writer could have saved fifteen words and said, "Whether we use aluminum conduit for masts will depend on the size of materials and their strength."

Sometimes, people on the job write sentences that spell out too much, probably in an attempt to be as precise and accurate as possible. But the result is often a sentence that is longer than necessary. For example,

> The local department shall be the public agency responsible for receiving and investigating complaints and reports of child abuse and neglect.

This writer could have said,

> The local department shall receive and investigate all reports of child abuse and neglect.

Or how about this one.

> It is recognized that certain extracurricular activities contribute significantly to the educational objectives of the school. Those that do not contribute or that interfere with the educational objectives of the school should be reorganized or eliminated.

All this writer needed to say was,

> Extracurricular activities that do not contribute significantly to educational objectives should be reorganized or eliminated.

Split Up Long Sentences

In order to know how to take sentences apart, you simply have to know how they are put together. Luckily, there are only about six major ways to combine sentences in English. Imagine that you have written the following two short sentences and you want to combine them:

We wrote the report.   We delivered it.

1. You might connect them with a coordinating conjunction such as "and" or "but."
   We wrote the report, *and* we delivered it.
2. You might connect them with a semicolon and a conjunctive adverb such as "therefore" or "then."
   We wrote the report; *then* we delivered it.
3. You could use a relative pronoun such as "which," "that," "who," or "whom."
   We delivered the report *that* we had written.
4. You might use a subordinating conjunction such as "before" or "after."
   We delivered the report *after* we wrote it. We wrote the report *before* we delivered it.
5. Frequently writers reverse the parts of the sentence in #4.
   After we wrote the report, we delivered it.
6. You might connect them by reducing one of the sentences to a verb phrase.
   After writing the report, we delivered it.
   Before delivering the report, we wrote it.
   We wrote the report *to deliver it* on time.

There are other ways to connect sentences, but these are the major ones.

Now that you know how sentences are put together, you can take them apart. If you want to split two sentences, simply look for the words or punctuation marks that connect them and divide them there. Try this method on the following sentence:

```
We have noted with pleasure that for the past several
years you have made all payments ahead of time, and
the thought has occurred to us that you might be
interested in shifting to a regular account, which
would save you substantial amounts of interest
charges.
```

If you split this sentence around its connectives, "that," "and," "that," and "which," and revise a few words, you could get:

```
We are pleased. For the past several years you have
made all payments ahead of time. A thought has
occurred to us. You might be interested in shifting to
a regular account. This would save you substantial
amounts of interest charges.
```

But you probably wouldn't want to divide this sentence quite so much. In fact, if the first sentence sounded like a slightly stuffy banker talking, our version now makes the banker sound like a slick loan shark. In this case, you might settle on dividing the sentence into two or three shorter ones. How short or long your sentences are is partly a voice decision. The main thing is to develop the ability to split sentences when you want to.

Try this technique again by applying it to the following long sentences:

> Because hospital administration is such a varied occupation, which involves working with complex equipment, intricate systems, and numbers of people, we think that any person interested in such a career should have a rich background in the humanities, the sciences, and in business administration.

Dividing this sentence at its connective points and adding the word "therefore" to emphasize the causal relationship, you would get:

> Hospital administration is a varied occupation. It involves working with complex equipment, intricate systems, and numbers of people. Therefore, we think that any person interested in such a career should have a rich background in the humanities, the sciences, and in business administration.

The following sentence may appear more complicated:

> The company's "Durogrip" adhesive system is a family of two-part urethane structural adhesives that bond extremely well to reinforced plastics, so we have specified them for all reinforced plastic bonding because plastic surfaces need only be wiped with a primer prior to bonding.

But if you note the "which" in the third line, the "so that" in the fourth line, and the "because" at the end of the fifth line, you might revise it as follows:

> The company's "Durogrip" adhesive system is a family of two-part urethane structural adhesives. We have specified them for all reinforced plastic bonding for two reasons: (1) they bond extremely well to reinforced plastics; and (2) the plastic surfaces need only be wiped with a primer prior to bonding.

And even though the following long sentence doesn't contain any connectors such as "that" and "which" to mark junction points, it can still be divided.

> The goal of the <u>Fundamentals of Supervision</u> training program is to provide each participant with the basic

```
supervisory knowledge, skills, and abilities needed
to perform the duties and carry out the
responsibilities of a supervisor within the corporate
structure of the bank in a positive, productive
manner.
```

Restoring the omitted subject of the second sentence and changing the infinitive "to perform" to a verb, you would get:

```
The goal of the Fundamentals of Supervision training
program is to provide each participant with basic
supervisory knowledge, skills, and abilities. These
will enable him or her to perform the duties and carry
out the responsibilities of a supervisor within the
corporate structure of the bank in a positive,
productive manner.
```

The length of your sentences will depend partly on how familiar your readers are with your subject. The less familiar they are, the shorter your sentences should be.

Control Your Long Sentences

Long sentences in themselves do not create problems for a reader. For instance, the following 46-word sentence is easy to understand because its writer has controlled it so well:

```
When all the bureaucratic, corporate structures are
reduced to their minimum constituents; when all the
office or shop equipment is removed; when the
paperwork, production schedules, deadlines, and all
the major and minor corporate complexities are
reduced to their lowest common denominator; what
remains is people.
```

Note how the writer has controlled his sentence by using the connector "when" to signal the major relationship in the sentence and the semicolon to control its length.

You can use the same sorts of devices to keep your own long sentences from sprawling. To signal logical relationships, use the types of connectors we talked about earlier in the discussion of sentence length: coordinating conjunctions such as "and/but"; conjunctive adverbs such as "therefore/however"; relative pronouns such as "that/which/who"; and subordinating conjunctions such as "after/if/when." (If all these grammatical terms confuse you, simply think of these as "and" connectors, "therefore" connectors, "that/which" connectors, and "after/when" connectors.) And to signal closure to your readers, so they can catch a mental breath before proceeding, use punctuation marks such as semicolons, colons, and dashes.

Now that you know some ways to control long sentences, see whether you can use connectors and punctuation marks to bring the following 88-word monster, taken from a state code, under control:

> If any common carrier authorized to do business in this State shall employ any person in any position of trust in this State, and shall apply to any surety company for security for the faithful performance of duty by such employee, or for any form of fidelity insurance, and such surety company shall refuse to become responsible for such employee, or, having become responsible for such employee, shall thereafter cancel such responsibility, such surety company shall furnish to such employee a statement in writing of the reasons therefore. . . .

Actually, the sentence goes on for another 200 words, but I won't bore you with any more of it. One way to revise this sentence is as follows:

> If the following conditions occur: (1) a common carrier authorized to do business in this State employs a person in a position of trust; (2) that carrier applies to a surety company for security for the faithful performance of duty by that employee or for any form of fidelity insurance; (3) the surety company either refuses to become responsible for the employee or later cancels such responsibility; then the surety company must furnish to the employee a written explanation of its reasons for refusing.

The sentence is still long—no doubt about that. But now it is at least clear.

Placement is another device you can use to control longer sentences. Generally speaking, readers look for your most important ideas at the ends of sentences rather than at the beginning. Therefore, put them there when you can. Rather than saying, "We must locate the cause of that trouble *in the first place*," say, "*In the first place*, we must locate the cause of that trouble." And revise a sentence such as, "The lack of quality control in the packaging department is *the next problem we must deal with*," to, "*The next problem we must deal with* is the lack of quality control in the packaging department."

By the way, there is another reason why transitional phrases such as "in the first place" and "the next problem" are usually better placed at the beginning of sentences. Generally speaking, sentences are easier to understand if they present *old* information (something your reader is already familiar with) before giving *new* information.

One way to do this is to use a transitional expression to refer to your previous discussion in some way. We'll talk more about this *old/new* principle in the section on paragraphing in Chapter 16.

Vary Your Sentences to Maintain Your Readers' Interest

If you don't limit the length of your sentences and control them carefully, your meanings may not be clear to your reader. But if clarity is your *only* concern, your sentences will be dull and monotonous. To keep your reader's interest, vary your sentences. Instead of writing all subject–verb sentences, for instance, vary the types of sentences you write. For example, ask some questions: "What is the next step in this procedure?" "How well do you understand the concept of quality control?" Or give a command: "Let's take a look at. . . ." "Inspect these machines carefully because. . . ." Use an interjection: "Well!" "No!" Even use an occasional sentence fragment: "Why don't people cooperate on this issue? *Because they don't really want to.*"

And vary the length of your sentences. Look at the varied length of sentences in the following paragraphs from an article by James Kilpatrick, the well-known TV commentator and columnist.[6] Kilpatrick has just returned from a convention of managing editors and is relating their complaints about the writing abilities of young reporters.

> APME stands for Associated Press Managing Editors. Most of the members are old geezers getting a little long in the tooth, relics of the glorious days of green eyeshades and rimfire Underwoods, but some of them are young bucks who prattle on about the marvels of video terminals and computerized typesetting. They share a common affliction: Their faces bare marks of suffering that even the best gin will never smooth away. And their anguish, to hear them tell it, gets worse with every passing year.
>
> The pain emerges from the copy they are called upon to edit day by day. Young reporters, it is said, arrive in their city rooms ill-equipped for the job at hand. Their sentences wander off in all directions; their spelling is only so-so; their sense of organization is seldom very keen. And it is not only the neophytes who cause despair; many experienced reporters also are stuck in pedestrian paths of prose composition.

[6]James J. Kilpatrick, "To Write Well, Mix Short Sentences with Dash or Period," *Richmond News Leader*, 5 Nov. 1978.

Notice Kilpatrick's different sentence lengths. In the first paragraph, his first sentence has seven words; his second has 44; his third has five (I'm counting the words before the colon as a separate sentence); his fourth has 15; and his fifth has 14. The average sentence length is only 17 words, but more importantly, he has composed the paragraph of two very short sentences, two of average length, and one very long one.

And note how Kilpatrick uses a strong punctuation mark, the colon, to close his third sentence quickly. Most writers on the job are afraid of colons and semicolons because they have forgotten how to use them. But Kilpatrick uses both effectively. In the second paragraph, he uses semicolons to break up two longer sentences. The third sentence is 20 words long, but by the time Kilpatrick finishes splitting it with semicolons, he has three sentences with seven, five, and eight words, respectively. And note that a semicolon divides the next 22-word sentence into shorter sentences of ten and twelve words apiece.

Finally, vary sentence structure when you can. Note how this paragraph, actually the last paragraph in the same article by Kilpatrick, uses a variety of structures.

> Organization, precision, clarity—these are three virtues of readable prose. To these one might add a sense of cadence, a sense of imagery, a feeling for simile and metaphor. Writing is hard work, but it is not as tough as it often is made out to be. The path toward better writing lies chiefly in a love of the language. Without that abiding affection, a reporter's task is mere drudgery. If the AP's managing editors will cultivate an appreciation of the good sentence--the one, good, muscular sentence--in time their city room troubles will cure themselves.[7]

In this one short paragraph, Kilpatrick has managed to vary the structure of almost every sentence. He inverts the normal pattern in the first sentence by beginning with three complements, "organization, precision, clarity," which would ordinarily follow the verb. He begins the second sentence with a prepositional phrase, "to these" and ends with the series, "sense of cadence, a sense of imagery, a feeling for simile and metaphor." The third sentence contains an "as . . . as" construction, the fifth begins with the prepositional phrase "without that . . . ," the sixth with the clause, "if the . . . ," and contains the inserted phrase "the one, good, muscular sentence." Such writing ability is developed only after years of practice, but you can begin to train yourself by being aware of some of the devices professionals like Kilpatrick use.

[7]Kilpatrick.

SUMMARY

In this chapter, we have discussed your stylistic choices.

1. Your word choices can range from simple to complex, concrete to abstract, personal to impersonal, and technical to nontechnical. You will also choose between nouns and verbs and active and passive verbs.
2. Your sentence choices can be based on length, degree of control, and the amount of variety you want.

APPLICATIONS

1. Revise some of the following passages taken from actual memos, letters, reports, etc., so they are clear to a typical reader you know. Try to stick as closely as you can to the meaning of the passage.
   a. It is a reasonably simple task to demonstrate that nursing today is, in all respects, a profession. What is perhaps more difficult is to argue with decisive effectiveness that the people who actively pursue nursing as a vocation constitute a body of professionals, in every regard. It is not enough to say that simply because an individual is legally and duly conferred acceptance into a profession that he or she automatically becomes a professional. (*Hint:* Begin by getting rid of all the deadwood phrases.)
   b. The term "independent study" shall be interpreted to include only those instances when such study is limited to those students who have demonstrated the maturity and ability requisite for this type of learning experience and when the supervising teacher provides for appropriate direction, a means of accountability, and student evaluation. Supervised study hall is not interpreted as independent study. (*Hint:* Begin by dividing the first sentence into two main parts.)
   c. As Commission experience with the use of automated systems expands and matures, certain situations occur that require new expressions of policy in order to properly and consistently respond to them. What in the course of development and initial use can be handled informally often grows to dimensions that if handled casually can result in loss of control as similar situations reoccur. (*Hint:* Simplify words and try using more personal words.)
   d. The company is experiencing the loss of hundreds of thousands of cash dollars each and every year because of unchecked corrosion. The occurrence of this corrosion

comes about as a direct or indirect result of improper preparation for the handling, the shipping, and the storage of in-process and finished aluminum products. While we are cognizant of the fact that the accumulated loss is extremely expensive, it is very unlikely that any individual can confirm exactly how costly the total loss is or what it accumulates to in terms of delayed or unacceptable deliveries and the loss of quality customers who will not bother to investigate our record at a future date so never come back. (*Hint:* Try getting rid of unnecessary words, changing some nouns to verbs, simplifying words, and splitting sentences.)

e. Many times when pursuing the solutions to ever-increasing numbers of ever more complex problems there is a propensity to lose sight of certain basic operating procedures such as the maintenance of safe work areas and the implementation of safe operating practices. (*Hint:* Simplify words and use more concrete words.)

f. The process begins with someone in an organization perceiving a need or desire for a new information system, or major enhancement of an existing system, and communicating that perception to someone who can analyze the situation and develop a specification of what is most appropriate for satisfying the need for information. This specification of user requirements is then used to design a data processing system by selecting components and arranging them in a manner so that their interaction will result in the specified information being accurate, timely, appropriately detailed and cost justified by its usefulness. (*Hint:* Translate this impersonal, abstract language into language that is more personal and concrete.)

g. Corporate policy is modified to permit the substitution of CASH (coin/currency), with proper written and current documented authorization on file at the operating office/branch, as reimbursement for FIRST PARTY checks made payable to the banks MERCHANT DEPOSITOR who, during their normal course of business, CASHES checks for their customers. (*Hint:* Try finding key words and rewriting shorter sentences around these. *Warning:* This one may be impossible!)

2. Find a complicated paragraph written to specialists in your field, perhaps from an article or textbook. Now translate it into language that is simple enough to be understood by someone just entering the field. Afterwards, describe what you had to do to translate it.

3. Locate some definitions of concepts central to a particular field. You will probably see that while the definitions are precise, they

are also technical and abstract. Using simple, nontechnical, and concrete language, rewrite these definitions for the reader of a popular magazine.

4. Get two or three paragraphs you have written lately and analyze their style. If you think the style is effective, explain why, using concepts discussed in this chapter. Perhaps you will find that the words are appropriately simple and personal and that the sentences are well-controlled and varied. If you don't think the style is effective, rewrite the paragraphs and then explain what you did, again using concepts from this chapter.

PART

2

Letters and Memos

CHAPTER

5

Letters and Memos: An Introduction

When you get ready to write a letter or memo, all sorts of questions may occur to you. Should I even write in this situation? Won't a quick phone call do just as well? If I do write, what format style should I use? How do I use dictation equipment? When do I have to be afraid of the legal consequences of what I say? This chapter will help you answer these questions.

The world of work is a world of communication. And it's not only people in sales or public relations who have to communicate with each other. Even if you are in data processing, accounting, or engineering, you're going to find that you are continually required to communicate with others, both in talking or in writing. You may—

- Write a brief memo to your boss about a project.
  "The Maxwell project is going fine. We should be finished by the 30th of the month."
- Phone someone from another organization to ask for help.
  "Look, John, I need your advice on the problem, I just can't seem to crack it by myself."
- Persuade someone in a letter to agree with you.
  "Although I understand what you mean, I feel that we ought to. . . ."
- Evaluate an employee in a personal conference.
  "Bill, your sales performance has dropped off during the past few months. You're just not meeting your quotas. . . ."

- Explain something in a manual to a client.
  "To delete a line in this program, simply place the cursor at the beginning of the line and. . . ."
- Commend someone in person for a job well done.
  "Congratulations, you did a fine job. In fact, that's the first time that I've seen it done so well!"

SHOULD I TALK OR WRITE?

Sometimes, it's better to communicate orally than it is to write. Making a quick phone call to find out the status of a project or dropping by someone's office to get some important advice is a lot quicker and less expensive than writing a letter or memo to get the same information. And if you want to commend someone for a job well done or have to reprimand someone else for not doing a job well, you should probably do it face to face, to take advantage of the more immediate and personal qualities of oral communication. In short, talking is often the best way to communicate at work.

But remember the Three Mile Island memo we discussed in Chapter 2, the memo that should have warned readers of the disaster before it happened. When the writer of that memo didn't get any response from the manager to whom he had written, he contacted him orally several times to find out when some action would be taken. He never got a satisfactory answer, even when he asked him about it in a face-to-face meeting. Here is a situation when the writer should probably have followed up with a strongly worded memo, both to impress the manager with the seriousness of his request and to have a formal record of the communication.

The major difference between talking and writing is an obvious one—writing is more permanent. Therefore, whenever a record is needed, write a letter or memo. If you are describing a product or service to clients, do it in a letter so they will have something to refer to later. For the same reason, put a set of instructions about how to operate a complicated system in a memo. Even if you place an order or give instructions over the phone, you may well want to confirm the conversation in writing. And after you commend or reprimand someone orally, you should probably follow up with a letter or memo as a record for you and for your readers. In short, when what you have to say is important or complicated, you'd better put it in writing.

But even though writing is different from talking, you will find yourself saying the same sorts of things—reporting, asking, persuading, evaluating, explaining, commending—in a letter or memo as you would in speaking. In fact, letters and memos are simply the way people at work talk to each other on paper. The next three chapters are about how to write them effectively. This chapter will show you their formats, explain how they are produced in modern offices, describe the different circumstances within which they are written, and explain how they function. The next two chapters will then describe the typical letter and memo situations you will face during your career and show you how to produce the best letter or memo in each situation.

WHAT ARE THE DIFFERENT FORMATS FOR LETTERS AND MEMOS?

Letters

As you rise through the ranks in your career, you may get a secretary, administrative assistant, or word processing center to format and type your letters. But at first, you may have to type your own. Because of this, you should be familiar with the basic format styles of letters. A concern with such conventions may seem trivial until you realize that most readers of your letters will expect them to be laid out in one of these ways. If you deviate from these conventions, you run the risk of leading your reader to pay more attention to the letter itself than to its message.

Over the years, three major letter styles have developed—block, modified block, and semi-block style. You will find that authors of different textbooks will describe them in slightly different ways, but look on pages 100–102 to see the way they generally appear.

Memos

A memo is most often used for interoffice communication. The conventional format for a memo is just about as widely accepted as those for letters, but there is only one and it is much simpler. On the right is a typical looking memo.

HOW ARE LETTERS AND MEMOS PRODUCED?

If you had walked into an office of a hundred years ago, you'd probably have encountered a group of clerks seated at high desks, updating ledgers and drafting documents. While you were there, a messenger, perhaps tired and dusty from his long journey, might have arrived to deliver a bundle of important letters. Walk into offices today and you'll be greeted by dramatically different sights—in one office you may see people drafting letters or reports with pencil and yellow pad or working at their own typewriters. At others, you will see secretaries busily producing letters on electric or electronic typewriters. At still others you'll see people, perhaps both secretaries and administrators, staring at the screens of their computer terminals. In some offices, you'll even notice an electronic printer whirring out a message from a distant city.

Unlike writers a hundred years ago, who just had to be proficient

MEMORANDUM

TO: Students in Business Communications
FROM: C. W. Griffin, Associate Professor of Business
SUBJECT: Typical Memo Format
DATE: October 15, 19--

Typically, a memo begins with the headings "To," "From," "Subject," and "Date," although the placement of these can vary from one organization to another. You will quickly get used to the particular format of your organization.

The subject line is probably the most important line because it identifies the major topic of the memo. Therefore, you should try to specify your subject as precisely as possible. To do this, use a short phrase consisting of a noun ("Format" in the example above) plus adjectives like "Typical Memo."

Paragraphs may be either blocked at the margin, as these are, or indented.

You may sign a memo if you wish, but sign it at the top after your name, not at the bottom. Many people use initials only.

jw

with ink and quill pen, you will have to prepare yourself to produce documents in a number of ways. But the basis of all modern methods of document production and transmission is the ability to type, fast and correctly. Once you have learned basic typing skills, you can make use of a modern typewriter, a word processor, and even dictation equipment.

Typewriters, Electric and Electronic

The electric typewriter, which enabled a typist to work fast and efficiently, was long the centerpiece of modern offices. Over time, electric typewriters became more sophisticated and convenient to use, even giving operators the ability to correct mistakes as they typed. A recent development is the electronic typewriter, which

VIRGINIA COMMONWEALTH UNIVERSITY

Telephone • (208) 109-8765

block Style

Dateline → October 15, 19--

Operate return 4 times to leave 3 blank line spaces

Inside address → John Smith, Student
Business Communications
Virginia Commonwealth University
Richmond, VA 23284

Double space

Salutation → Dear Mr. Smith:

Double space

Body of letter

This sample letter illustrates the block style. Its main feature is that all parts of the letter--dateline, inside address, salutation, and complimentary close--begin at the left margin. The parts of the letter and the appropriate spacing around the parts are noted for you.

Double space

Some people prefer its crisp, business-like appearance. Others feel that it looks somewhat cold.

Double space

I am using what is called the mixed style of punctuation, with a colon after the salutation and a comma after the complimentary close.

Double space

Complimentary close → Sincerely, Respectfully

Operate return 4 times

Name and title → C. W. Griffin, Associate Professor

Department or division → Department of English

Double space

Processor's initials → jr

Double space

Enclosure notation → Enclosure

VIRGINIA COMMONWEALTH UNIVERSITY

Telephone • (208) 109-8765

Tab to center for dateline placement October 15, 19--

Jane Smith, Student
Business Communications
Virginia Commonwealth University
Richmond, VA 23284

(DS)

Dear Ms. Smith:

(DS)

Subject line Subject: Modified Block Style Letter

(DS)

The modified block style is probably the most popular of the three letter styles. As you can see, the only difference between it and the block style is that the dateline and complimentary close begin at the center of the page.

You'll note that the salutation is appropriate this time for a woman when you don't know whether she's married or not. If you are writing to one person, other appropriate salutations might use a title (Dear Dr. Jones), a last name (Dear Mrs. Jacobs), or a first name (Dear John).

This time, the complimentary close is "Sincerely yours," which is just as popular a close as the equally informal "Sincerely" that I used in the block letter. "Cordially" and "Cordially yours" usually indicate a personal or professional friendship, while "Respectfully" and "Respectfully yours" are used to show special respect. The close "Yours truly" is now considered to be a little old-fashioned.

Note also that I included a subject line to give the reader the subject of the letter right away. This may aid in reading or filing the letter, and is optional with all three styles. The subject may also be shown simply in capital letters at the left margin.

Tab to center for closing placement Sincerely yours,

C. W. Griffin, Associate Professor
Department of English

VIRGINIA COMMONWEALTH UNIVERSITY

Telephone (208) 109-8765

October 15, 19--

Business Writing Students
Business Communications
Virginia Commonwealth University
Richmond, VA 23284
(DS)
Attention: John Smith, Student
(DS)
Ladies and Gentlemen

This letter illustrates the semi-block style, which is exactly like the modified block style except that each paragraph is indented.

Some readers may think of this as conservative and old-fashioned, while others may find the indented paragraphs a help to quick reading.

You'll note that this time I addressed the letter to the whole class. There may be times when you want to address a letter to a whole organization and use an attention line under the inside address to direct it to a particular person as I did.

Whether or not you use an attention line, you can use a salutation such as "Ladies and Gentlemen." "Dear Sir or Madam" is not used very often now.

You will note that I am using what is called the open style of punctuation in this letter, with no punctuation after either the salutation or the complimentary close.

Cordially

Bill Griffin, Associate Professor
Department of English

enables a typist to perform a number of operations. Using an electronic, for instance, you can instantly correct the part of your document that appears on the screen. In addition, you can store a document and retrieve it for later typing, as well as switch from one typestyle to another and set margins automatically. Some electronics even have programs that will check spelling for you.

Word Processors

The heart of many modern office systems is the computer, composed basically of a keyboard that puts information into a processing unit, which can then store it, manipulate it in various ways, display it on a video screen, or print it out on a high speed printer. As a writer, you will be most concerned with the computer used as a word processor to produce letters, memos, reports, or other documents.

If you work for a small organization or do a lot of writing, you may well have access to your own word processor; in fact, there may be a system located in your office. You will find that such a system has the capacity to save you hours of time wasted in writing or typing rough drafts, conferring with typists, editing drafts, and having them retyped again and again. To see how such a system works—

A Writing Situation

Imagine that you are a systems consultant who studies a client's needs for data processing equipment and then recommends a system tailored to those needs. You are halfway through such a study for a client when you are asked for a letter giving a brief progress report on your work. You begin by calling up from your word processor's memory the notes you had been keeping as the study progressed. After studying these, you key in a brief plan for your report, basically a jot-list of your major points, which you will leave on the screen as you write the letter. Then right under this plan on the screen, you begin your letter.

Since you just wrote your client last month, you save time by calling up the date, inside address, and salutation from the previous letter in your word processor's memory, and then updating it simply by changing the date. Then following your plan, you begin keying in the actual letter. You proceed just as you would on an ordinary typewriter, drafting sentences, paragraphing where appropriate, underlining, entering punctuation marks, capitalizing letters, and so forth.

But because you can see the letter on the screen, you can also revise as you type. For instance, when you notice that you have left an important point out of a paragraph, you simply insert it with another sentence. When you need a table that is already in your notes, you call it up from the word processor's memory and insert it where needed. You even move an important paragraph closer to the beginning of the letter, so your client will see it quicker. When you have finished drafting the letter, you edit it on the screen, changing inappropriate words and phrases, and you proofread, adding punctuation marks where needed and using the automatic checker to check your spelling. After you have finished, you simply press the "Print" key and print a clean copy, with margins perfectly justified (even right and left), ready to be signed and mailed.

As you can see, the system of word processing just described gives you enormous freedom and flexibility in writing. No longer do you have to write out a draft in longhand or on the typewriter, negotiate for a typist's time, revise again and again, or correct mistakes on the typewriter. Depending on the complexity of your system and your own experience, you can spend anywhere from a day to a few weeks mastering a particular word processing system. But once you do, you will never want to write in any other way.

Word Processing Centers

But now imagine that you are a data processing consultant for a large organization. Let's say this time that you are an in-house consultant—you travel from city to city for your organization, analyzing the data processing needs of various units. To save money, your organization has centralized all word processing functions. That is, instead of each manager having to write in longhand, use a typewriter, dictate to a secretary, or even type on a word processor, your organization has created a word processing center.

When you have a letter, memo, or report to write, you simply pick up the phone, dial the center, which is open 24 hours a day, and begin dictating your document into recording equipment. Later, a transcriptionist keys your document into the word processing system, making whatever changes are necessary. Then your document is printed and returned to you either for signing or revision. If you revise, you return the document to the center with revision notations, changes are made, and a final copy is printed for your signature.

To see how such a system actually works, let's replay the writing situation we discussed above, only this time you'll dictate your letter to the word processing center.

A Writing Situation

You begin by reviewing the notes you've been keeping as your project progressed, which you had previously dictated to and had typed by your center. Then you make a plan for the letter. Because it will be the only visual guide you will have as you dictate (no screen to look at this time), your plan is more elaborate than the jot-list you did before, with your main points spelled out, necessary facts and figures penciled in, and even a few key phrases written out.

Now you begin to dictate. Here is what your transcriptionist will hear. Messages for the transcriptionist are in brackets.

```
March 10, 19--. [This is Lee Corder with a one-page
letter for Rene Burton. R-e-n-e Burton. You can get
her inside address from my letter to her dated
February 18. I'll need a copy to revise and would like
a copy of the final version to go to Roger Tomlin,
Director of Systems Planning.] Dear Rene [colon]:
Here is my progress report on your data processing
needs [period]. [New paragraph] Phase [initial cap]
One [comma], [initial cap] Assessment [comma], has
now been completed [period]. In our study [comma], we
interviewed five employees in each of your accounting
[comma], personnel [comma], operations [comma], and
traffic departments [period]. In addition [comma], we
observed the work flow in these departments for three
days each [comma], as well as studying documents
produced during the last six months [period].
```

Dictation

cost + time

When you first try to dictate documents to a word processing center, the procedure may be more difficult than writing in longhand, typing yourself, or even keying the letter into a word processor yourself. After all, not only do you have to write the letter aloud now, without seeing what you've already written on paper or a screen, but you also have to include spelling, punctuation, and other instructions for the transcriptionist. And pausing to figure out what you're going to say next will probably feel awkward, not to mention the tricky business of switching the machine on and off, moving the tape back and forth as you review what you've already written, and then finding your place so you can continue.

It is true that learning the techniques of this kind of dictation will take some practice. But if your organization doesn't already have such a system, it will probably institute one in the future. Studies have shown that machine dictation is six times faster than longhand and twice as fast as shorthand. Given the rising salaries of secretaries today, most organizations can't afford *not* to make use of such systems. And learning how to use a central word processing system will not be as hard as you think. Begin by thinking of your writing process as occurring in the three stages outlined below and described in detail in the appendix at the end of this chapter.

1. *Advance planning*. "Your dictation can never be better than your preparation," says one experienced dictator, who knows that advance planning is the most crucial step in dictation. Since you won't be able to visualize what you're writing, you need to prepare carefully for your dictation, reviewing relevant notes and materials and making a fairly detailed plan of the entire document.
2. *Dictating*. The key at this stage is to be aware that you are addressing two audiences—the reader(s) of your document *and also* the transcriptionist who will be typing the document. You'll need to give the transcriptionist necessary typing instructions, which are listed in the appendix. Don't worry about pausing (even experienced dictators do) to choose a word, find a phrase, or plan a sentence or two ahead. And you will quickly learn to operate the recorder in order to review what you've already said or move forward to continue dictating.
3. *Revision and editing*. If your memo or letter is short and therefore first-time-final (you don't want to see it except to sign), then you can review and revise auditorily by replaying your tape. But if your document is long or complicated, you'll probably want to see a printed draft to revise (add or take out information, reorganize main points, etc.), edit (change words or phrases), and proofread (find and correct errors).

Study the appendix on dictation at the end of this chapter to learn the detailed steps you should follow. With practice, you'll quickly get to the point where you will be able to dictate letters, memos, and even short reports quickly. Thus, you will enable your organization to take further advantage of a centralized word processing center, with its ability to produce flawless copies, file electronically all documents transcribed, and send them out over an electronic mailing system, if one is available.

Electronic Mailing Systems

Another outgrowth of computer-based word processing is the electronic mail terminal. Large organizations now have terminals that can send and receive documents electronically. You can sit at a terminal, key in a document, and send it to any other terminal connected to yours. With such a system, you can send and receive messages instantly. As soon as you arrive at the office in the morning, you can switch on your terminal, press a key, call up all your electronic mail, and answer it as needed. To use such a system, you only have to have the ability to use a keyboard that is exactly like a typewriter. Such systems will likely become more popular in the next few years.

WHAT WILL BE THE DIFFERENT SITUATIONAL CONTEXTS FOR MY LETTERS AND MEMOS?

The letters and memos you write on the job will be done in different situational contexts; that is, in different sets of circumstances. Sometimes, you will write to people within your organization, subordinates or perhaps managers; at other times, to people outside, perhaps clients or members of the general public. Maybe you will write to people from a foreign country. The purpose of this section is to help you understand these various contexts so you will know how to write in a particular situation.

Writing Within Your Organization

Usually, an "inside" communication, from someone within an organization to someone else in the same organization, is written in the form of a memo. At times, you'll have to be aware of the consequences a memo may have on your own career. A short memo to your immediate supervisor about the subject of a phone call may carry little weight, so you can dash it off fast and informally.

```
Dave:
  Finally got around to that computer service call.
They promised to come tomorrow to work on Jane's
system. I'm betting they won't make it till next week.
```

But a memo reporting on your monthly activities, even a short one, may be used as part of your next evaluation for a promotion or a raise. In writing such a memo, you'll have to consider very carefully what to say and how to say it, especially if you have not made as much progress as you hoped on a couple of projects.

Because memos flow along established lines of communication and relationships within a hierarchy, you should follow certain codes and conventions when writing them. You'll quickly learn these once you begin working for an organization. You'll learn to document a point with upper management but not to waste their time with too many details; to omit a sentence that may unnecessarily anger a colleague; and to be sensitive to the feelings of those who work under you, even when you must write a memo evaluating their job performance.

You'll also learn that your memos frequently represent not just you but your whole department or division. Thus, you can't always be as blunt and direct as you may feel like being. You'll even learn how important it is to address your memo to the most appropriate person and to make a careful decision about who should receive copies. You'd be foolish to address a suggestion for a change in departmental procedures to a division chief if that meant ignoring your own department head. And if you address a memo to a colleague asking that a project be completed sooner, you'd better realize that he'll interpret your sending a copy to his manager as pretty heavy pressure.

Generally, the practice that has developed over the years is to use memos for informal communications and to reserve letters for special occasions, such as an announcement of a promotion or raise, a commendation for a job well done, or a termination notice. Because letters are thought to be more formal and "official" than memos, the circumstances surrounding them can be even more delicate than those surrounding memos. While it may be easy to write an employee a commendation letter for doing an outstanding job, it may be very difficult to write a letter that reprimands someone for poor performance. In this situation, you'll need to choose words that do not hurt the person unduly, but that leave no room for misunderstanding. Otherwise, you may later wind up in litigation with the employee or with his union.

In general, remember that whenever you write a letter or memo to someone within your organization, what you write can have important consequences. Be aware of these consequences and prepare for them as much as you can.

Writing Outside Your Organization

If they like and respect you, people will be more inclined to do what you want them to do—buy goods and services, obey regulations, agree to a new procedure, or whatever. Therefore, when writing to readers outside your organization, try to earn and keep their goodwill. To do this, write in as warm and as pleasant a voice as possible (without being oily, of course). For example, it would be professional suicide to refuse a request with a curt "Your request has been denied," if you could say more sympathetically, "We are sorry, but we are unable to approve your request at this time."

And avoid the cold, stock phrases that some writers use to start their letters.

INSTEAD OF SAYING	TRY SAYING
Enclosed please find the copy	Enclosed is the copy
Attached please find the copy	Attached is the copy
Per your request	As you requested (or asked)
In reference to our telephone conversation	I enjoyed talking with you
With regard to your request	In response to your request

People who have to read letters beginning with such "automatics" must feel a little like automatons themselves. Speaking of automatics, use form letters with discretion and sensitivity. Because they save so much time and money, you will have to use them in some situations. But when possible, take the time to adapt the form letter to each particular situation. With the advent of word processing, you can do this easily.

One other way to earn readers' goodwill is to put them at the center stage of your communication rather than yourself. You can do this by using pronouns like "you" and "your" rather than "I" or "my." Rather than saying, "I am writing to respond to your request of September 25 for . . . ," you might say, "On September 25, you requested that we send you . . . ; I am happy to do so." And instead of beginning a letter of commendation with, "I'd like to congratulate you on . . . ," simply begin with, "Congratulations."

Of course, you are going to encounter some sticky situations when writing to people outside your organization. You may have to write a letter to a client explaining how to solve a problem, without ever acknowledging that he is the one who caused the problem in the first place. To write such a letter effectively, you will have to choose your words carefully so as not to anger him and thereby lose his business. And even if a shipment you need is unduly late, you may find that if you complain too caustically, your angry vendor may not make an extra effort later on just when you need it the most. In short, every letter you write creates a special relationship with someone. You'll have to be as aware of the overtones of this relationship as you would if you were talking with him or her in person.

Writing to Someone from Another Country

You don't need to look any farther than the highways you drive to see how heavily the United States is involved in international commerce. At any moment, you're likely to find yourself beside a Japanese Honda, Isuzu, Mazda, or Nissan; a German Audi, Mercedes, or Volkswagen; not to mention a French Peugeot or Renault, an Italian Ferrari or Fiat, a Swedish Saab, or even a classic British MG. What's true in the automotive industry is also true in the chemical, computer, steel, and oil industries, as well as in businesses such as finance and publishing. We work in an international economy.

And whether you work in business, industry, government, or one of the professions, it's more and more likely that you will be involved in this world economy in some way. If you don't actually work abroad, you may well have to travel to foreign countries or work with foreign nationals who have come to this country. Therefore, you should have at least an elementary idea of what it's going to be like to communicate in this international context.

Because so few of us have traveled to a foreign country, we Americans may not realize how different people in other cultures are from us and from each other. And not just in the obvious ways, such as language or dress. They can be different in other, less tangible ways. If you were to work in Latin America, for instance, where people are relaxed about time, a client might be as much as an hour late without being disrespectful. In Germany, on the other hand, where people are much more precise, you'll rarely have to wait for someone to keep an appointment. And if you were to travel in a variety of foreign countries, you'd find that people differ in how close they will stand to you, in the way they greet you (with a handshake, hug, or nod of the head), and in what they consider good manners at meals.

It's not surprising that such cultural differences carry over into the way people from different cultures write memos and letters. For example, you may find that people at work in other cultures just don't write as much as we do in America. The Japanese, for example, tend to communicate about business matters either by telephone or face-to-face. Even when communicating abroad, they are more likely to use the telex than a letter. Letters in Japan are used primarily for matters of confirmation, courtesy, or questions of very high policy. In Japan, it is often considered to be more polite to make a personal call than it is to write a letter.

Also, the way documents are written in foreign countries can be very different from the way they are written in America. An American reader might find a memo report written in a German organization to be tiresomely detailed and precise, while the same report written in Chinese might seem too general and vague. And writers in different cultures will organize information differently from the way we do. One study found that while American writers tend to move through a subject in a linear fashion, from point to point, Oriental writers will view a subject from different tangents, progressing in a series of circular movements; Arabic writers will develop ideas through a series of parallels, both positive and negative; and French and Spanish writers will tend to digress from the immediate subject, introducing what looks like extraneous information.[1]

People from different cultures can also write in different styles. For example, Germans tend to be direct, while writers from Spanish cultures will be more flowery, as in, "I offer you my heartfelt thanks for . . . ," or "Standing ready to attend further instructions, I remain your sure servant."

Letter-writing practices of the Japanese, a people with whom we shall have to communicate more and more, differ dramatically from our own. A letter written in Japan will usually not begin with the main message. Rather, it may begin with a remark or two about the season or the weather; followed by an inquiry about the receiver's health or by congratulations; this in turn followed by thanks for a gift or some other kindness shown. Only after all these remarks will the writer get to the main idea. In addition, the letter will probably be very formal and polite, and follow strict rules in the salutation

[1]Robert B. Kaplan, "Cultural Thought Patterns in Inter-Cultural Education," *Readings on English as a Second Language for Teachers and Teacher Trainers*, ed. Kenneth Croft (Boston: Little Brown, 1980) 339–428.

and use of pronouns, rules that depend on the relative status of the sender and the receiver.[2]

The Japanese are especially indirect when it comes to saying no. One communications consultant for a large aircraft company tells about the time he read a two-page letter from Japan, written in very good English. Yet at the end, the reader didn't know what the writer was talking about. Only later that afternoon did he realize that the writer was saying no—very politely.

Given these differences in the ways people in different countries conceive of and write letters, how can you write effective letters to them? You might feel (and look) foolish if you try to be as flowery as someone writing in Spanish or as indirect and ambiguous as the Japanese. But if you keep differences in culture in mind, you can at least make sure that your voice is *diplomatic* and your style is *clear*. For the sake of diplomacy, you might begin a letter to a Japanese reader with a compliment; one to a Spanish-speaking reader with an elaborate, "It is my honor to . . ."; and a letter to a German with the more direct, "Last week, you asked about the possibility of. . . ." In general, it's probably a good idea to be a bit more formal to any foreign reader than you might be to an American one. And to make sure that your foreign readers understand exactly what you are saying, write in a style that is as readable as possible; in other words, use simple, unidiomatic, nontechnical words, and sentences that are fairly short and uncomplicated.

If you do find yourself in a job that requires regular correspondence with someone in a foreign country, then learn everything you can about that person's culture. Read studies of the culture; obtain handbooks and brochures that describe the country and its customs; or sign up for one of the short courses in culture and languages offered by many universities. And by all means, prepare yourself to function effectively in the world economy by studying at least one foreign language while you are still in college. No matter what language you study, you'll learn to spot some of the important ways in which another culture differs from your own and learn to be sensitive to how people from another culture think, live, and act.

WHAT WILL BE THE LEGAL CONTEXT FOR MY LETTERS AND MEMOS?

Whatever you do at work, like whatever you do anywhere else, is subject to the law. While legal issues vary from one kind of work to another, you will quickly learn which are the most sensitive in your industry. Generally speaking, if you write truthfully and accurately, you won't have problems. But there are a few situations when you will have to be particularly aware of the legal implications of what you do. The next few paragraphs will alert you to two of these. As

[2]Saburo Haneda and Hirosuke Shima, "Japanese Communication Behavior as Reflected in Letter Writing," *The Journal of Business Communication* 19.1 (1982): 19–32.

you read them, remember that you are reading a layman's description of the law. If you have any questions or doubts in an individual situation, consult a qualified attorney.

Evaluating the Work of Other People

One of the toughest tasks you'll face over the years is evaluating the work of others. But you will have to do it. You will have to assess the performance of people working under you, and you will be asked to recommend others—subordinates, colleagues, friends, and even managers—for particular jobs.

When evaluating the work of others, you should be aware of two legal constraints. First, you cannot discriminate against anyone on the basis of sex, age, race, religion, or national origin. Second, if you make a false or derogatory statement that injures someone's character or reputation, you could be held liable for *defamation*. Oral defamation is called *slander*; if it is in writing, it is called *libel*.

In order to be held liable for defamation, you must have *published*, that is, communicated your comments about someone to a third party. In other words, if you tell someone that you consider her to be lazy or incompetent (not advisable if this is a person you must work with), you are within your legal rights. But if you communicate this information to another person who is not privileged to have this information, you can be liable for defamation. The concept of *privilege*, which means that you can make a statement that might otherwise be considered defamatory to certain people in certain circumstances, is a further protection. But the concept is complex, open to judicial interpretation, and may vary from state to state. It's best to assume that your readers are not privileged, and therefore not make any statements that could be considered defamatory.

In light of these legal constraints and protections, how can you best write documents that evaluate people, especially if you have something negative to say about them? Performance evaluations won't present much of a problem because in most such situations you will use a form that requires you to rate employees numerically in categories such as job knowledge, dependability, quantity of work, quality of work, and so forth. But you may have to document a rating in a brief narrative statement. To do this in a way that will help the employee the most and at the same time protect yourself, don't make sweeping negative generalizations such as "This person doesn't understand her job, is undependable, and uncooperative."

Rather, remember that your major goal when writing a negative comment in a performance evaluation is to provide information so the person can improve his or her performance. Therefore, describe specifically what was expected and then describe factually how well the person has met the expectation. Let's say, for example, that you have given someone an "average" rating in the category, "Does work on time," because he habitually submits his weekly progress reports late. To document this rating, you might write the following narrative comment:

```
Peter Hamilton is responsible for submitting a
weekly status report by 4:00 p.m. each Friday. Five
times in the last six months he has submitted these
reports late, sometimes as much as a week late.
```

Not only will your specific comment protect you from charges of libel (you didn't accuse Peter of being lazy or sloppy in his work habits), but it shows him what he needs to do to improve in the category—just get his reports in every Friday by 4:00 p.m.

If you have to make negative comments about a person in a letter of recommendation, you are facing a tougher situation. After all, when writing negative comments in a performance evaluation, you can at least comfort yourself by saying that your goal is not to hurt the person, but to help him or her improve behavior. But your primary goal in a letter of recommendation is not to help the person you are evaluating, at least not directly; it's to help your reader predict how well that person will be able to do a job. And you are legally responsible for giving your reader accurate information; in fact, if your letter is false or misleading, your reader may have cause for legal action against you. Since you would probably hate to be the cause of someone's not getting a job, what do you do if you must communicate some unfavorable information? In other words, how do you protect yourself and the person you are evaluating at the same time?

If someone has asked you to write a letter of recommendation, one way out of the dilemma is to let the person know that your comments cannot be entirely favorable. Frequently, in such situations, the person will find someone else to write the letter. You might even suggest this. Such a suggestion might be momentarily painful for the person and awkward for you, but you have protected him or her from unfavorable comments.

However, there will still be times when you must make unfavorable comments in a letter of recommendation. If your comments are not very negative, you can try casting them in a positive context; for example, "So-and-so has had a few problems relating to others, but has worked hard to overcome them." If your comments are more negative, protect yourself and the other person by focusing on facts of behavior ("In the past year, so-and-so's error rate has risen by approximately ten percent"), and responding only to questions asked and topics suggested. In other words, don't offer negative judgments unless you absolutely have to. Finally, ask that your evaluation be kept confidential.

Describing a Product or Service

Even if you are not in marketing or advertising, you may still have to describe a product your organization makes or a service it performs in a letter, brochure, manual, or proposal. You should therefore have some familiarity with the laws governing such descriptions. Generally speaking, if you take the precaution to be truthful and accurate in your descriptions, you won't run into any trouble. If you are truthful, for example, you will never be guilty of *fraud*, the intentional misrepresentation of a fact that causes harm to another person. (For your own protection, you should know that advertising claims, even if exaggerated, are usually not considered to be fraudulent, because the courts assume that adults can make judgments about the relative value of such claims.)

A more likely danger is the possibility that something you say about a product or service may inadvertently become a *contract* that obligates you. Most of us think that contracts are written documents with lots of fine print and complicated provisions. This is not necessarily so. A contract is simply based on an offer and an acceptance of that offer. And it need not be in writing. If you offer to maintain my lawn for $15 per week and I accept, we have a contract.

When you write a letter, brochure, or manual, you will need to be careful that it does not form the basis of a contract. If, for example, you say in a letter to a client, "We will have 12,000 reams of 20-weight, fan-fold paper ready for delivery by March 15," you may have a contract to fulfill. And if your client in turn makes an obligation on the basis of your offer, you may face a suit if you breach that contract.

Statements made in brochures and handbooks can also become bases of contracts. Suppose, for instance, that in trying to demonstrate in a handbook how much your organization cares for employees, you make the statement that "No one working for us can be dismissed without proper cause." Later, you have to dismiss some employees because gross revenues have fallen dramatically. These dismissed employees would have an issue on which they could bring suit, the question of whether you dismissed them for "proper cause." It's best to have an attorney check such documents to make sure you are not making such an inadvertent offer.

The concept of *warranty* is another reason why you should be careful about what you say in describing a product or service. A warranty is a promise that a product or service will perform in a certain way. An *express warranty* is an explicit statement that a product is of a certain quality or will perform in a certain way. If an automobile salesman tells you, for example, that the car you are buying is this year's model and it turns out to be last year's model, you have cause to sue for breach of warranty. Products and services also carry *implied warranties*. Some warranties that are usually implied are that the seller has title to what he is selling, that goods will match the samples shown you, that products or services are well suited to the purposes and safe for the uses for which they are sold.

When describing a product or service, you need to be careful that you do not inadvertently imply a warranty. Don't say in a brochure, for example, that this product is guaranteed against all defects, unless your attorney has checked such a statement. And be careful in describing the services you will provide to someone. In describing a training session, say, "This two-day session will show participants a variety of techniques for using the new Data Line processing system." But don't say, "At the end of this two-day session, all participants will be able to use the Data Line processing system effectively." If you do, you may have made an implied warranty that you have to fulfill. Also, when describing a product or service, be careful not to use someone's name, picture, or likeness in a sales letter or advertisement without that person's permission. If you do, you could be guilty of *invasion of privacy*. *Privacy* is the right of a person to be let alone and free from unwarranted publicity.

We'll end this discussion of the legal context within which you write with the same advice that began it. If you write accurately and honestly on the job, you won't often run the risk of getting into legal trouble. But since whatever you do is governed by the law, there are a few writing situations in which you will have to exercise more than usual care. If you are ever in doubt about the legal consequences of what you are doing, consult a qualified attorney.

AM I INFORMING OR PERSUADING?

Letters and memos are written in hundreds of different situations. You might write a letter to notify an employee of a promotion; to transmit some important documents to a client; to request that a client pay an overdue bill; to respond to someone's question about an insurance policy; or to persuade someone to buy a new system from you. Or you might write a memo to notify employees about a change in policy or procedure; to explain to someone how to operate a new system; to report on the progress of a project; or to persuade your manager to replace a piece of obsolete equipment.

But what all these situations have in common is that your goal is always to affect readers in a particular way—you want something to happen to them. You may want to make them feel good about a job well done, to be aware of a new policy, to understand why a change was made, to be able to operate a new system, to buy a new piece of equipment, or whatever. The key to writing an effective letter or memo then, as we've discussed before, is to decide what your major goal is; that is, to decide what you want to make happen to your readers. You can then make the writing choices that will help you accomplish this goal.

Informative Situations

Often, you can accomplish your goal simply by giving readers the information they need. In other words, whatever you want to happen to your readers will happen just because they understand your subject clearly. For example, if you want your readers to know about a change in company policy, a memo announcing this change will be enough to accomplish your goal. If you want to remind people about the dates and agenda for a meeting, a letter giving this information would suffice. And if you want someone to understand how to operate a new machine or follow a new procedure, an instructional memo will be enough.

We're going to call these situations *informative situations*—those occasions when just making your subject clear will accomplish your goal. You will find that your major concern in such situations will be making your subject as accessible to your readers as possible—making sure that you give just the information readers need, that you organize it so they can understand it easily, and that you use a clear style and an appropriate design.

Persuasive Situations

But often, just making your subject clear to readers won't be enough to accomplish your goal. In order to have the effect on them that you want, you're going to have to motivate them toward your goal. For example, if you want subordinates to attend a 7:00 a.m. meeting and be ready to work, you may have to motivate them by explaining why you set it at such an early time. If you want your manager to buy a new piece of equipment or adopt a new data processing system, you'll have to prove that it will benefit the organization in some way. If you want a client to buy a product or adopt a service, you're going to have to convince the client to do it. And if you want someone to pay an overdue bill, you may have to bring pressure to bear to force the person to do it.

We're going to call these *persuasive situations*. Here your concerns will go beyond just making your subject accessible to a reader. In these situations, not only will you have to present your subject clearly, you will also have to present it convincingly. Thus, you will choose the information, organization, style, and design that will predispose your reader to your point of view. In essence, in a persuasive situation, you're going to have to write in such a way that you *move* your reader toward your goal.

Sometimes, you may be uncertain whether your situation is an informative or persuasive one. After all, if you are writing a memo describing your organization's training programs for the year, you want to inform people about the programs, but you also want to persuade them to attend. And if you are writing a memo to your manager informing him about a new idea, you certainly want to persuade him to accept it. In such cases, you may have to be aware that you are trying to accomplish two goals at the same time, and will therefore use both informative and persuasive techniques to accomplish them.

The next two chapters are about how to write letters and memos in typical informative and persuasive situations. Chapter 6 will discuss letters and memos that inform and Chapter 7 those that persuade. But you will see that the techniques discussed are not engraved in stone, nor are they just to be applied to one type of letter or memo. In every writing situation, you will need to figure out your major goal as best you can and then make use of the techniques that will help you accomplish this goal.

SUMMARY

In this introductory chapter, we've talked about the following topics:

1. Whether it's better to talk or write in a given situation.
2. What formats are used when writing letters and memos.
3. How letters and memos are produced in the modern office.
4. The important contexts in which letters and memos are written—organizational, public, international, and legal.
5. Whether a writing situation is informative or persuasive.

APPENDIX: A CHECKLIST OF DICTATION STEPS

Here are the steps to follow in dictating a letter or memo. You will have to adapt them to the system you use.

1. *Advance Planning*

   Materials. Collect all relevant materials, including the letter or memo you are answering, necessary files, notes, etc.

   Writing situation. Analyze the writing situation by clarifying your goals, understanding your readers, and deciding on the voice you will use.

   Plan. Make some sort of plan to follow, which may be as simple as a few notes you've jotted in the margins of the memo or letter you're answering, a jot-list of main points, or a more detailed outline.

2. *Dictating*

   Preliminaries. Give date, your name, type of document (letter, memo, etc.), type of copy (first-time final or draft), approximate length, type of stationery, number of copies, letter and punctuation style, and priority for processing (routine or rush).

   Inside address and salutation. Give receiver's name (spell it), address, and the appropriate salutation.

   Instructions. Dictate document, giving special instructions for—

   - spelling—proper names and unusual words
   - mechanics—capitals, underlining
   - punctuation—unusual marks
   - format—paragraph indentions, special headings, etc.

Closing information. Give complimentary close, your name and title, distribution of copies, and filing information.

3. *Revision and Editing*

   Revise organization, style, or format, if necessary.

   Edit, looking especially for the following:

   - faulty sentence structure—words omitted, phrases that don't make sense, etc.
   - inaccurate pronoun references
   - inappropriate shifts in verb tense
   - errors in word choice
   - incorrect punctuation marks and misspellings

APPLICATIONS

1. You have been asked to recommend someone you know for a job. Your friend is bright, capable, and gets along well with others. But you have noticed that your friend tends to put things off to the last minute and is occasionally late for appointments. Do three things.
   a. Prepare to give a short recommendation over the phone. To do this, make a jot-list of the points you will cover.
   b. Write a follow-up letter, giving your recommendation in more detail. If you have access to tape recording equipment, dictate the letter just as you would to a company word processing center.
   c. Using at least two of the format styles discussed in this chapter, write the letter.

2. Write a short letter thanking a prospective employer for giving you an appointment for a job interview and confirming its time and place. In writing the letter, you want to convince the employer that you are the kind of bright, enthusiastic person who should be hired.

3. Using one of the letter styles described in this chapter, write a letter that commends a subordinate for instituting a new, more efficient filing system. In such a letter, it's customary both to commend the person and to describe what the person did in some detail.

4. Someone from another country is coming to work for your organization or to attend your school. This person has written, asking for information about housing in the area. Write the letter that responds to this request, remembering that you want to encourage the person as much as possible.

5. Imagine that the person who interviewed you for the job in Application 2 has asked to see three samples of your writing. Using one of the letter styles described in this chapter, write a letter in which you transmit three pieces of your writing—a report, a proposal, and a business memo.

6. Your instructor has asked you to write a memo evaluating your progress so far in this class. You are to focus *as concretely as possible* on both positives and negatives—strengths you've developed and weaknesses you still have. At the end of the memo, recommend any changes that might improve the class for you.

CHAPTER

6

Letters and Memos that Inform

This chapter will show you how to write memos and letters that tell people what they need to know. You will learn to give information simply, clearly, and logically.

"Ours is an information society," people are fond of saying. Nowhere is this more true than in the world of work. People at work are constantly communicating information—

- *telling* someone about a change in procedure or the schedule of a training session;
- *asking* whether a particular objective can be accomplished or how soon a task will be completed;
- *responding* to requests for the dates of a meeting or for the production schedule for next month;
- and *instructing* someone how to operate a system or what to do in an emergency.

In the last chapter, we called these *informative situations*—situations in which you can accomplish your goal by making your subject as accessible to your readers as possible. In this chapter, you're going to learn how to write letters and memos in these four typical informative situations—telling, asking, responding, and instructing. These are not the only informative situations you will encounter during your career, but because they are typical ones, what you learn about them will transfer easily to others.

In this chapter, we'll discuss each of these four situations to give you a *feel* for the way good writers make decisions and choices in any informative situation. Sometimes we'll focus more on what kind of and how much information to give readers; at others, we will focus more on how to organize this information; at still others, on the style and design to use. Gradually, you will become aware of a set of principles or guidelines that you can apply to any informative situation. At the end of the chapter, we'll review these principles by applying them to a particular writing situation.

TELLING PEOPLE SOMETHING

Many times on the job, you will need to give people information. You may, for example, want to notify them about a change in work schedules for the following week, announce that new quality controls will be instituted in a plant, or inform them about the progress of plant construction. Many of these writing situations will be routine and fairly simple. You will hardly need to pause for a moment, for instance, to decide how you are going to tell prospective participants about the scheduling arrangements for a training seminar. You can make a mental jot list—location, date, and time—from which you can write the following memo:

```
MEMORANDUM

TO: Participants in Effective Speaking
    Seminar
FROM: Eric Smithfield
SUBJECT: Time/Date of Seminar
DATE: August 7, 19--

The seminar on effective speaking will be held
in the second floor conference room on April
12 and 13, from 9:00 to 4:30. You'll have an
hour for lunch.
```

And it wouldn't take you long to write a short memo notifying people of a change in the time of a meeting.

```
MEMORANDUM

TO: All Division Heads
FROM: Rosa Martinez
SUBJECT: Change in Meeting Time
DATE: June 6, 19--

Tomorrow's meeting will be in the conference
room on the fourth floor of the executive
office building. We'll begin at 9:00 and hope
to finish by 10:30. Be sure to bring your
notes from the last meeting.
```

To Organize Ideas, Determine Your Major Goal

But there are going to be times when you will have to write about more complicated subjects, possibly to a wide variety of people. In these situations, one of your major problems will be to decide how to organize your information. The following confusing memo about health insurance is a good example of what happens when a writer doesn't organize information very well. As you read it, imagine that you are an employee in this organization, and ask yourself the question anyone would ask in such a situation: "What in the world is this memo about?"

MEMORANDUM

TO: All Faculty and Staff
FROM: Kanisha Adkins
SUBJECT: Changes in Health Insurance
DATE: March 15, 19--

May is traditionally the month for health care open enrollment. This period allows you to pick up family coverage or to switch health care plans without the usual additional cost. These changes become effective July 1.

Last fall, the State Department of Personnel put the health care contract out to bid. Because of this lengthy process, the state health care contract has not yet been awarded. We may not receive all information until mid-May, and we are concerned about providing information to our less than 12-month faculty and staff. If you are less than 12-month faculty or staff, please make sure that your correct summer home address is on file in the personnel department so that health care and summer payment information can be mailed to your home.

Because of this year's delay, the open enrollment period will be extended from May 1 until June 15. Important information detailing a new health care option, new rates, and other significant changes will be distributed as soon as it is released. A schedule of general meetings will be listed in an insert with May 1 paychecks.

Why is this memo so confusing? Because it doesn't make any sense until you realize that this writer's major goal is to tell you how to change your health insurance coverage—when to change it and what changes can be made. You have to wade through two paragraphs before you get to the first part of this idea, that "the open enrollment period will be extended from May 1 until June 15."

This writer needed to plan her memo, defining her major goal more precisely, so she could focus on her goal first and then on other information you may need to know. She might have accomplished this simply by talking to herself, trying to describe her goals as clearly as possible. Her conversation might have gone like this:

What's the main thing I'm trying to tell people? That May is the traditional period for health care enrollment. No, that's just background explanation.

Try again. What's the main idea? That during this period they can change coverage. Right, that's part of it. But not all.

What else? I've got it! When is the enrollment period this year? Then I can tell them all those other things--why we extended the period, that I'll be sending them some other information, and that they should leave their summer address with me if they plan to be away.

Or she might have made a jot-list of her main points, trying to separate her major goal from her others. After several tries, it might have looked like this:

Major goal: tell them about changing health insurance--when/how
Other goals: tell them--

- what changes they can make
- why enrollment period is different
- that other info will come
- that they need to leave summer address before they go

But the method that would have led her most quickly to her major goal would have been to imagine a kind of question and answer session with her readers, essentially, the reader-questioning method we discussed in Chapter 3. Starting with her readers' most important question, it might go like this:

READERS	WRITER
When can we make changes in our health insurance?	During the period from May 1 until June 15.
What kinds of changes can we make?	You can pick up family coverage or switch health care plans without additional cost.
Why has the period been changed this year?	We've extended it because lengthy contract negotiations have kept us from completing all arrangements.
When will we know more about changes?	Before May 1, you'll receive information about new changes you can make.
In the meantime, what should we do?	Make sure we have your summer address if you plan to be away.

Any of these planning techniques should have resulted in the improved version of the memo to the right. Note that the main ideas have been reorganized and unnecessary information has been omitted.

This revision puts main ideas—when you can make changes in your health insurance and what changes can be made—in the first paragraph where they belong. Once you understand these, you are ready to understand the rest of the memo. Of course, the writer made other changes to make information more accessible. She cut out some unnecessary information, especially the too-lengthy explanation about contract negotiations as well as much of the confusing information about 12-month faculty and staff. And she redesigned the memo so that all its paragraphs are short and quickly read. We'll discuss changes like these later in the chapter. Right now we will focus on organizing an informative letter or memo so that your information is immediately clear to your reader.

Follow a *Priority Pattern* of Organization

Often you can organize an informative document most clearly by following a *priority pattern*—putting your main idea at the beginning, then following with your next most important idea, etc. This is essentially what the writer of the health insurance memo did. Here is an example of a warning memo to supervisors of labs in a large

MEMORANDUM

TO: All Faculty and Staff
FROM: Kanisha Adkinson
SUBJECT: Changes in Health Insurance
DATE: March 15, 19--

This year, the open enrollment period on your health insurance will extend from May 1 until June 15. During this time, you may pick up family coverage or switch health care plans without the usual additional cost.

Although our usual open enrollment period is May 1 to May 31, we have had to extend the period this year because all new contract arrangements are not yet complete.

Before May 1, you will receive information describing a new health care option, new rates, and other significant changes that result from our new contract.

If you plan to be away from the college during this period, please be sure the personnel department has your correct summer address so we can send this important information to you.

research center that should follow this pattern, but doesn't. Notice how the warning is buried in the middle of the first paragraph:

On January 20, 19--, the Analoy Company issued a recall of all HB-4 Aluminum Centrifuge Rotors with Serial Numbers 7554102 through 7754746. After extensive usage, these rotors may become potentially destructive. When used with the Pace RC-2 and RC-2B Centrifuge, these rotors may become particularly hazardous.

Please notify your internal safety personnel and all laboratory users of this recall and hazard alert. For

```
additional information, we recommend that you contact
Ms. Verna Hairing, Analoy Co. She may be reached by
telephone at (203) 326-5897, Ext. 302.
```

This writer thought he was being logical as he wrote this first draft, because he was following the sequence of events just as they had occurred to him. First he had received a notice from Analoy recalling a certain group of rotors because they could be potentially destructive. Then he had decided to warn lab supervisors and instruct them to notify the appropriate people. But as he revised the memo and rethought its primary goal, he realized that he was following writer's logic rather than reader's logic.

He saw that what had occurred to him second in the sequence—that people needed to be warned about the problem—should have come first in the memo, since this was the most important information for his readers. He then rewrote the memo, leading with his warning and following with the necessary explanation. Note also that this time he explained exactly *why* supervisors were to contact Ms. Hairing—in order to return the rotors.

```
  Warning! HB-4 Aluminum Centrifuge Rotors, Serial
Numbers 7554102 through 7754746, may become
potentially destructive after extensive usage.
  When used with the Pace RC-2 and RC-2B Centrifuge,
these rotors may become particularly hazardous.
  Analoy has issued a recall of all these rotors.
Please notify your internal safety personnel and all
laboratory users of this recall and hazard alert.
  If any equipment in your lab has one of these rotors,
please call Ms. Verna Hairing, Analoy, to find out how
to return them to the company. She may be reached at
(203) 326-5897, Ext. 302.
```

Readers tend to process information from the top down, looking for the most important ideas at the beginning of a document. Once they understand these, they have a framework for understanding the rest of the document. This is the reason why most of us have been taught to begin an academic paper with a thesis and a paragraph with a topic sentence. This is good advice when clarity is your major concern. You can follow this priority pattern (diagrammed on the next page) when writing informative letters and memos.

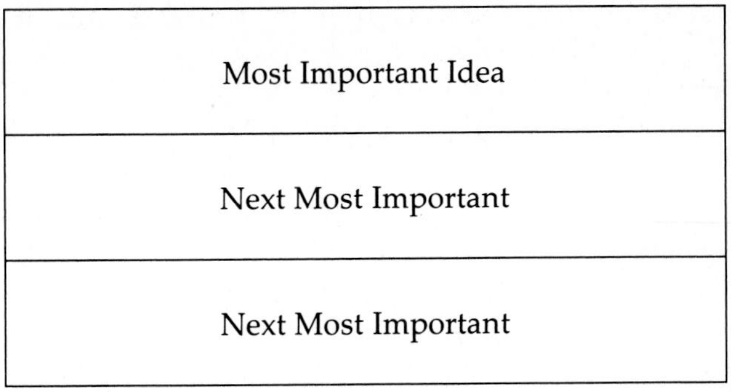

Most Important Idea
Next Most Important
Next Most Important

Notice how easy it is to read the following memo about the status of a loan because the auditor begins each paragraph with his most important idea (underlined):

On this examination, I discovered that our manager had been adding credits on our Collateral Reports rather than subtracting them. This was not an intentional error to inflate collateral loan value, rather a failure to communicate between our two field agents. I reversed these transactions in the amount of $43,559.20 on Collateral Report #0085. This corrected the collateral overstatement.

I also found that none of the deposits had been applied to the loan. This was due to a new note teller handling the transactions. She was advancing funds as requested on the Collateral Reports, but not curtailing the loan as requested. Greg Mills and I reconciled the Grid Note to the loan outstanding on our Collateral Reports. The Account had not been using a cash collateral account to this point. Greg established this account in order that future receipts can be deposited to that account.

Even though you may not understand all the technical language of the memo, you can quickly see that the auditor's major discoveries were that the manager had been adding credits instead of subtracting them and that none of the deposits had been applied to the loan.

Use Organizational Patterns that Fit the Writing Situation

Of course, in writing informative letters and memos, you will have to use other organizational patterns also. You may have to define a problem and discuss its causes or effects, analyze a situation by breaking it down into parts, or arrange information into categories. Here, for instance, is part of a memo informing readers of changes in their retirement insurance. Since the information is complicated, the writer has decided to organize it into categories:

The Tax Equity and Fiscal Responsibility Act of 19-- (TEFRA) requires significant changes in the forms of benefits that are payable under employee benefit plans in the United States, including our retirement plan. The changes are effective January 1, 19--.

Survivorships--At retirement, a member may elect a survivorship benefit only in favor of a surviving spouse. Also, the pop-up modification of the survivorship benefit might be ruled out under TEFRA; final regulations of the IRS will clarify this point.

Guaranteed payments--A member will continue to be able to name a spouse or a person other than a spouse as the beneficiary under a retirement plan pension guaranteed for a period of years. Because of a plan amendment effective January 1, the period will be extended to that permitted under TEFRA, with a maximum of 20 years.

Lump sum death benefit--The lump sum death benefit will no longer be permitted. This benefit, which is paid on the member's death during retirement in amounts elected by the member, has been provided by the member by a reduction in pension.

Active service death benefit--A member during active service may name a spouse or a person other than a spouse to receive the active service death benefit (equal to one year's salary) under the Retirement Plan.

While the writer of this memo could still clarify her meaning by using less technical language, the major categories are easy for readers to follow.

ASKING PEOPLE FOR INFORMATION

You will also find yourself in another typical informative situation—asking someone for information. You may want to know, for example, how soon a project will be completed, whether a meeting should be held to discuss an issue, or what advice someone can give you about a problem.

Follow a Priority Pattern of Organization

Whenever your goal is to ask someone for information, you should try to follow the priority pattern we discussed in the last section—locating your request at the beginning of your document and then following it with any necessary explanation. Most writers of requests are tempted to do just the opposite, leading with long explanations that only confuse their readers. It's also a good idea to highlight your request by putting it in a paragraph by itself. A request should be organized like this:

Your Request
Your Explanation

The following request, written by someone in a welfare agency, is confusing because its writer didn't follow this pattern. As you read it, see whether you can find the actual request.

The State Office on the Elderly wants some information on elderly people in the work force in this state. To do this, they have constructed a survey which they want to send to our agency directors, requesting that they in turn distribute the survey to staff who work with the elderly.

Eighteen local agencies have been randomly selected. Attached is a listing of those agencies. SOE will be responsible for supplying the needed number of questionnaires.

What has not been worked out are the mechanics of dissemination of the questionnaire to the selected agencies and the return of the questionnaire to the State Office on the Elderly. I have not received any specific direction regarding the Department's cost of postage in sending out and returning the questionnaire. As this questionnaire is to be sent to local welfare agencies, would you tell me how much it would cost to send it out through the RPS courier service?

As the State Office on the Elderly is planning to send out the questionnaire in early April, I would appreciate feedback to the postage issue as soon as possible.

Did you finally locate the request at the end of the third paragraph: " . . . would you tell me how much it would cost to send it out through the RPS courier service?" If the writer had followed the priority pattern, the letter would have begun with this request and followed with the necessary background explanation.

Limit Your Information to What the Reader Needs to Know

There is a second problem with this request. The writer has told readers *much* more than they need. How much background would you need in order to respond to this request? All you really need to know is that there is a questionnaire to be distributed to 25 agency directors. You don't need to know that the directors will distribute it to their staff, that the agencies have been randomly selected, that the State Office on the Elderly will supply the questionnaires, that the mechanics of dissemination have not been worked out, and that the writer has not received any instructions as to cost. In other words, the writer could have eliminated most of this information, writing a short memo like the following:

Would you please find out how much it would cost to have the attached questionnaire sent out and returned through the RPS courier service?

This questionnaire has been prepared by the State Office on the Elderly to be distributed to the directors of eighteen local agencies. A list of their names and addresses is attached.

Since the SOE wants to distribute the questionnaire in early April, let me know your answer as soon as possible.

Now I have reorganized the letter, locating the request in the first paragraph by itself so the reader will understand it quickly. And I have also eliminated much of the unnecessary information—information that the reader doesn't need in order to respond to the request.

Use Lists to Clarify Complicated Requests

Of course, there will be times when your requests are more complicated than the one above, either because you have a number of requests or a request with multiple parts. In this situation, a list can be an effective method for clarifying various parts of the request. For instance, even though you may not understand the content of the following request, you can still see how easy it is to read, because the writer has led with the request and then itemized important parts.

Please verify the following selection and processing criteria used in the development of the Consumer and Packaging output interface.

You'll need to respond as soon as possible so that changes can be made and test files can be created and forwarded to the appropriate divisions using this data.

- Only GI Account Number 6964 is selected (this includes both budget and posting records for Consumer and Packaging).
- Only Control Entity 0290 is selected.
- Fields selected include cost center, expense suffix, monthly budgeted amount, yearly budgeted amount, and the difference between monthly budgeted amount and monthly posted amount.
- The expense suffix field will be expanded to five positions (from four positions).

Use a Friendly Voice

One other point about writing requests for information. Some writers are tempted to use an impersonal and even curt voice when making a request. This seems especially true of requests from regulatory agencies, which often read more like demands than requests.

It will be appreciated if you will furnish us with a copy of the aforementioned report, with an original certificate attached.

We request that the ten notes be addressed in proper form according to statement instructions and be submitted for attachment to the annual statement.

Pursuant to Section 20.60 of the state code, it is requested that your company file quarterly statements until further notice.

In Chapter 2, you learned that the voice you use creates a relationship with your reader. Even when you are in a position of power or authority over someone, don't make your reader feel powerless by using an unnecessarily cold and distant voice. Remember, you want your reader's *help* in answering your request.

Mrs. Janice D. Saunders
1141 Florence Street
South Hill, OH 43107

Dear Mrs. Saunders:

Per your request of April 15, 19--, concerning the facilities charge of $6.00 in the rate schedule of the A & N Electric Cooperative.

This is to advise you that the facilities charge is designed to offset some of the fixed costs of providing electric service which are experienced by the utility whether the customer makes use of any electricity or not. For instance, the utility has an investment in facilities to provide service such as the meter, service drop, and a portion of its distribution facilities and transformer capacity which are sized to supply power when the customer wants it. In addition, the utility has the expense of bill preparation, postage to mail the bill, and accounting involved in maintaining the customer account records. These expenses are borne by the utility whether the customer uses any electricity or not.

RESPONDING TO REQUESTS FOR INFORMATION

Limit Your Information to What the Reader Needs to Know

Your biggest problem in responding to requests for information will be deciding just how much information to include in your response. Because you will usually know so much about the subject, you may be tempted to give your reader more information than is really needed. Beginning on the preceding page is a response from a utility company to a customer who wrote to ask why a facilities charge of $6.00 had suddenly appeared on her electric bill. As you read it, imagine that you are the customer who has asked the question.

Traditionally, in the past, the charges for electricity were much higher in the first steps of the rate schedule to offset the fixed costs. A & N's rate schedule prior to the present one charged 10.1 cents per kilowatt-hour for the first 50 kwh and 7.1 cents per kilowatt-hour for the next 100 kwh. The present rate schedule charges 5.2 cents per kilowatt-hour for the first 500 kwh. Consequently, when the flat charge of $6.00 per customer per month was authorized, the first steps of the rate were lowered.

Under the old rate schedule, those customers who utilized only a few kilowatt-hours in a month did not contribute their part toward the fixed costs of serving them, but now each customer is required to pay $6.00 no matter whether any electricity was used that month or not.

Thank you for your letter. I hope we have explained this charge to you satisfactorily.

Did you get lost quickly and stop reading this letter? I suspect the utility customer did. The problem is that the writer has overloaded the customer's information circuits. She asked a simple question and received too much information in too technical a style. All the writer really needed to do was to explain that the new $6.00 charge covered certain fixed costs incurred by the utility whether the customer used the service or not. Something like the following short letter would have sufficed:

Mrs. Janice D. Saunders
1141 Florence Street
South Hill, OH 43107

Dear Mrs. Saunders:

We are happy to explain the new facilities charge of $6.00 that appeared on your bill from us last month.

This $6.00 charge covers certain fixed costs, such as meters, lines, transformers, and billing procedures, which must be borne by a utility whether a customer uses any electricity that month or not.

Until now, customers who used only a little electricity did not pay their share of the fixed costs. This new system makes the rates fairer by requiring that all customers pay a proportion of the fixed costs, since we have these expenses whether the customer uses a large or small amount of electricity.

We hope this explanation is helpful to you. Please contact us if you have further questions.

This time, we've told the customer only what she needs to know in order to understand why her bill went up—that the increased charge covers fixed costs and that now she must pay her share of these costs. Note that a response will also follow the priority pattern we have been discussing.

Reference to Request, if Necessary
Response to Request
Further Explanation

Close + Build goodwill

Use a Natural Style and Language that Suits the Situation and the Reader

Let's look at another reason why the original "facilities charge" letter was so hard to understand. Read the original letter again, this time focusing on its style, especially the words and phrases the writer uses. Did you notice how impersonal and technical the style is? The stilted phrases, "Per your request" and "This is to advise," make the writer sound like a robot. As we said in the last chapter, avoid using "automatic" phrases like these and others such as—

- We are in receipt of your request
- Please be advised
- Enclosed please find
- We regret to inform you

For these kinds of phrases, substitute the more human:

- In response (or in answer) to your request
- We have received your request
- Here is the information you requested
- Enclosed is the
- We are sorry to have to tell you

When writing responses, try to resist talking in a too impersonal voice. It is true that some organizations don't allow their employees to use the personal pronoun "I" in certain situations. The purpose of this policy is to protect individual employees from being held liable for statements they might make. Thus, if you were responding to a letter from a disgruntled customer, you might not be able to say,

```
I can assure you that. . . .
```

But you could say,

```
We can assure you that. . . .
The company can assure you that. . . .
United Technologies can assure you that. . . .
```

But however you phrase a response, don't sound like an automaton. Write as naturally as your situation will allow.

Another stylistic problem in the response above is that the writer has sometimes chosen language that is just too specific and precise for an ordinary customer. For example, most people certainly wouldn't understand and probably wouldn't care about the complicated explanation of the rate schedules in the third paragraph:

```
 A & N's rate schedule prior to the present one
charged 10.1 cents per kilowatt-hour for the first
50 kwh and 7.1 cents per kilowatt-hour for the next
100 kwh . . . .
```

If this letter were to another expert in the field, the writer might need to be this precise. But in this situation, what the customer wants is a general explanation for the rate increase. In other words, the writer must translate technical knowledge into language that the reader can understand.

INSTRUCTING PEOPLE ON HOW TO DO SOMETHING

Over the next few years, the world of work will become more and more complex. Because of this, you will no doubt have to write letters and memos giving people instructions—perhaps telling someone how to set up a new office system, how to revise the procedures for a data processing system, or how to use a complex piece of equipment. In fact, writing clear instructions is so important that a whole chapter in Part Three will be devoted to how to write good instructional manuals. Here we will focus on the major problem you will face when writing instructional letters and memos.

Give Appropriate Information and Organize It Sequentially

Read the following set of instructions. Even though you may not be familiar with some of the language, you will get the gist of the message, because the writer has given readers the appropriate information and organized it sequentially.

MEMORANDUM

TO: All Machine Operators and Mechanics
FROM: Reuben Brownlee, Supervisor
SUBJECT: Safety Procedures
DATE: March 10, 19--

Whenever it becomes necessary to jump out, bypass, or disconnect switches, oil pumps, or any safety devices that protect people or machinery, the following procedure will be used:

1. The person performing the work will fill out two danger tags indicating exactly what has been jumped out, disconnected, or bypassed. These tags will be signed and dated.

2. One tag is to be attached to the device on which the work was performed; the other tag

is to be attached to the operating console of the equipment.

3. The shop log book will be filled out giving complete information on the safety device.

4. The person placing the device back in operation will be responsible for checking for proper operation, returning the danger tags to the shop, and recording work performed in the shop log book.

Use a Design that Facilitates Understanding

Now compare the instructions you just read with this next set addressed to some employees of a bank. Here again, the information is appropriate, it is organized sequentially, and the style is clear. Why, then, are the following instructions so difficult to understand?

MEMORANDUM

TO: All Team Instructors
FROM: Sue Jenkins, Training Coordinator
SUBJECT: New Financial Services Procedure
DATE: May 9, 19--

In our meeting of September 12, we discussed the problems associated with the latest regulation regarding interest payment periodicity for National Fund customers. It has been decided that the Financial Services Department will notify these customers by phone of the lesser rates associated with the greater frequency of interest payment periodicity. These customers will be given any additional information they require concerning how the new regulation affects their accounts when they are called. After the customer has been notified and in turn has decided how they want their interest paid, they will be mailed an S-RFA which reflects their decision. A copy of this will then be kept on file in the Operations Center.

The answer is obvious. The memo has been so poorly *designed* that it is almost impossible to see where one step ends and another begins. How much easier these instructions would be to follow if the writer would redesign her memo, listing each item separately, as I did in the following revision:

At the meeting of September 12, we decided on the following procedure for Financial Services to use in notifying our National Fund customers about the new regulation regarding their interest payments:

1. Notify these customers by phone of the fact that they will receive less interest if they want to receive their payments more frequently.
2. When you call, give these customers any additional information they require about how the new regulation affects their account.
3. After customers have decided how they want interest paid, mail them a prepared S-RFA reflecting their decision.
4. Keep a copy of this S-RFA on file in the Operations Center.

The model I followed in designing these instructions can be diagrammed as follows:

Introduction with Necessary Background Explanation
Step 1:
Step 2:
Step 3:
Step 4:

Address Your Reader Directly

In addition to redesigning the memo, I did make one major stylistic change to simplify it. The writer of the original must have felt that she could not use any personal pronouns in her instructions. For this reason, she uses such wordy and awkward passive phrases as "It has been decided . . . "; "These customers will be given . . . "; and "After the customer has been notified. . . ." To cut the number of words and simplify the instructions, I used personal pronouns ("you" is often understood) to refer to the people who must follow the instructions. The old injunction against using personal pronouns in business writing has caused more than one writer of instructions to confuse his or her readers.

The simple and natural way to write instructions is to address your reader directly, using "you" if you need to. Often, of course, the "you" will be understood. Look again, for instance, at the rewritten instructions to the electricians discussed at the beginning of this section and see how using a few pronouns can simplify and personalize them. Words that can now be deleted are in brackets.

Whenever [it becomes necessary] you have to jump out, bypass, or disconnect switches, oil pumps, or any safety devices that protect people or machinery, follow this procedure:

1. [The person performing the work will] Fill out two danger tags indicating exactly what has been jumped out, disconnected, or bypassed. Then, sign and date these tags [will be signed and dated].
2. [One tag is to be attached] Attach one tag to the device on which the work was performed; attach the other tag [is to be attached] to the operating console of the equipment.
3. [The shop log book will be filled out] Fill out the shop log book, giving complete information on the safety device.
4. [The person placing] Whoever places the device back in operation [will be responsible for checking] should check for proper operation, return the danger tags to the shop, and record work performed in the shop log book.

Note how using this direct voice focuses on the actual work to be performed by highlighting actions; for example, "fill out" and "attach."

SUMMARY

You've seen that when you write informative letters and memos, you'll often find yourself in one of four typical situations—giving readers information, asking someone for information, responding to someone's need for information, and telling someone how to do something. (There will be other informative situations, but these are the major ones.)

You've seen also that your writing problems will vary with the situation. In one situation, your major concern may be organizing your information so your reader understands it quickly. In another, you may be more concerned with limiting the amount of information you give a reader. In yet another, using a style that is simple enough for a reader to understand may be your biggest concern.

But your general goal in any informative situation will always be the same—to make a subject that you know well as accessible to your reader as possible. To accomplish this, follow the principles of information, organization, style, and design applied in this chapter. In a nutshell, they are as follows:

1. Give your readers only the information they need—no more, no less.
2. Organize your document for easy reading—frequently, this means following the priority pattern appropriate to the writing situation.
3. Use a style that is as simple, down-to-earth, and as personal as possible.
4. Design your document so that it can be read quickly and easily.

Now let's see how you might apply these principles in a typical nformative writing situation.

A Writing Situation

You work for the human resources division of a large bank. Six months ago, the vice-president in charge of your division decided that the bank needed to develop a recruitment and development training program for management trainees. In the past, the bank had only an informal system, with each department hiring and training its own management trainees. Your VP wanted to develop a more formal program to enable the bank to choose the most promising trainees for management and then teach them the essentials of the banking business. You were given the job of researching existing programs in other large banks and then proposing the system that your bank should adopt.

You found a wide variety of programs. Some banks recruit almost exclusively from undergraduate schools of business. They fill specific positions with students who have been trained in management, accounting, marketing, finance, etc. Other banks lean more heavily on graduate programs in business, preferring to hire people who are completing MBAs, often in the field of finance. Still others are more like your bank, with no systematic program.

After studying these results, you propose to your VP that your bank should recruit students from a wide variety of backgrounds; some with MBAs in finance, others with undergraduate degrees in accounting, marketing, management, and data processing, but still others with more general training in history, foreign languages, and even the sciences. Your reasoning is that these specialists and generalists will learn from each other over the years, and the resulting managers will have a broad perspective that will enable them to adapt to changes in the years ahead.

But you also recommend an extended training program, in most cases lasting about a year, in which all management trainees will be oriented to bank policies and procedures by working for a short period of time in a number of different jobs—serving as tellers, handling customer complaints, working in the consumer loan department, the trust department, and so forth. Also during this training period, trainees who need them will take short courses in basic finance, in accounting, in oral and written communications, and in management theory. In short, through courses and on-the-job training, your bank will provide trainees with a year's education in banking.

Your VP likes your proposal and convinces the bank's board of directors to approve a pilot program to test your ideas. And you are asked to direct the task force that will implement the pilot program. You have asked five people from different departments—including commercial, international, personnel, trust, and operations—to be on the task force. All have agreed. But two have asked for a background memo on the project in preparation for the first planning meeting of the group. You agree, thinking it won't be much trouble to dash off a quick summary of the project. Besides, it'll help prepare you for the meeting.

A week before the meeting, you begin to draft a memo describing the project. You start by telling how your VP approached you about a program; then you describe the various kinds of programs you researched; and finally you explain the program that was approved by the board. Your memo begins like this:

This is to inform you about the background of the bank's new recruitment and management training program. In January of this year, Melinda Price approached me about the bank's lack of any formalized training program for management trainees. She asked me to conduct a study of various programs and propose

```
a systematic program that we might adopt. The purpose
of such a program would be to recruit and train
prospective managers for the bank. After being
presented to the board of directors and approved,
the program would be implemented as expeditiously
as possible.
  In my research, I found a number of different
systems in use around the country. Some banks
recruited more from. . . .
```

At this point in your draft, you are interrupted by a phone call. When you finally get back to your memo, you begin by rereading it. "Good Heavens," you say to yourself, "this sounds awful! If I got this memo, I'd pitch it in file 13 before I finished the first paragraph. What's wrong with it, anyway?"

As you read and reread the memo, you become aware of some of its problems. For one thing, your voice is too cold—a memo that should make people feel good about being part of an interesting project begins with the distant, "This is to inform. . . ." And you begin to wonder whether people need to know all the details you're telling them—do they really even care that the VP approached you, that you researched a number of alternative programs, or that the proposal was finally approved? As you think about the memo, you realize that *you're* not even clear about your goal.

"Why am I writing this thing, anyway?" you ask yourself. "These people don't want a history of how the project developed. All they really want to know is what has been proposed and what they're supposed to do." Gradually, you clarify your goal even more. You realize that part of the goal of this first memo to the task force should be to make them feel a part of an interesting and challenging project. (This is a persuasive goal, but many times you will find that a situation that begins informatively will turn out to be persuasive also.)

In order to accomplish this part of your goal, you decide to write a letter rather than a memo. You feel that a letter addressed to each member of the task force will make him or her feel that this is a special and important project. And to further motivate task force members to do an especially good job, you ask your VP to write a short letter, thanking them for participating in the project and emphasizing its importance.

As you continue to plan, you are also able to clarify your informative goal. Rather than just give the task force general background information on the project, you finally decide that your particular goal should be to give them information that will prepare them for the first planning meeting.

"Now, what do they need to know to begin planning this project?" you ask yourself. In answer, you begin listing the questions members might have.

- What exactly is this project, anyway?
- What's its purpose?
- What part do you want me to play in this project? What do you want me to do?
- What's our time frame? What do we need to accomplish and how soon?

With these questions in mind, you begin all over again to draft your letter.

We won't chronicle the rest of the painful process by which you produce your final draft; instead, we'll skip ahead and examine it to see what kinds of choices you finally settled on. Each member of your task force receives a personally addressed copy of this letter.

Dear ---:

Welcome to the new Task Force on Recruitment and Training of new Managers. Thank you for being willing to help us get this challenging program started. The purpose of this letter is to help you prepare for our first planning meeting at 9:00 a.m. on the 16th of August in the fourth floor conference room.

Purpose of the program. We hope to create a program that will enable us to recruit and train talented young people for management positions. We want to develop in these people the management skills to meet the challenges and changes that lie ahead of us in the next 20 years.

Suggested content of the program. This first pilot program will recruit 25 graduates of colleges around the country. This group will be composed of people from a variety of backgrounds.

- Some will be graduates of business programs with majors in accounting, data processing, and finance.
- Others will be graduates of respected MBA programs with specializations in banking and finance.
- Still others will have degrees in liberal arts and the sciences.

During the year, each of these trainees will be assigned to a number of departments throughout the bank. In addition, they will take courses in areas in which they need training--accounting, communications, management theory, etc. Some of these courses could be taught in-house; others could be taught at local universities.

At the end of the year, we'll evaluate the program to measure its successes and strengthen its weaknesses.

Activities schedule. If we are to be ready for recruiting early this spring, we need to accomplish the following objectives at our first planning meeting:

1. Decide on the departments within which our trainees will work and draw up a schedule of work for the first year.
2. Decide how to involve the managers of these departments so they will understand our goals and participate willingly.
3. Decide on the kinds of courses trainees will probably need and determine how best to implement the training.
4. Discuss ways to publicize the program, both within the bank and at colleges and universities.

I'm sure other areas of discussion will occur to you as you prepare for our first meeting. Thanks again for participating in this exciting project. See you at 9:00 on the 16th.

This letter will accomplish its goals—it will make members of the task force pleased to be a part of the project and give them the information they need to prepare for a productive discussion at your first meeting. Its personal and down-to-earth style creates a warm and welcoming voice, while it communicates clearly essential information about the project. Its information is complete—telling task force members about the purpose of the project, describing how it will work, and setting forth suggested items for discussion at your first meeting. But it doesn't overwhelm readers with information about the project's development that would mean little to them. It is organized clearly, moving from purpose through program content to the discussion schedule. Finally, its design encourages easily readability—paragraphs are short and manageable, headings are used, and facts are itemized where possible.

No letter is ever perfect. But this letter, growing out of a clear analysis of the situation and following the informative principles discussed in this chapter, will be a success.

APPLICATIONS

1. You work in the employee relations department of a large corporation and have been put in charge of implementing an employee fitness program. The company has furnished one room as a gym with a universal weight machine and other exercise equipment. A small outdoor jogging track has also been prepared. In addition, there will be aerobic dancing and exercise sessions, as well as classes on special subjects such as preventing heart attacks, the dangers of smoking, and the effects of alcohol.

Write a memo to everyone in the company, from hourly people to executives, telling them about the program and its various components. Your goal is to inform people about the new program *and* to convince them to take part. You will need to be fairly detailed—in length about the equivalent of a typed page—but don't overwhelm your readers. Be sure to put your main point at the beginning, and since you have so many parts to describe, design your memo for easy reading. Use a jot-list to plan this memo and include it when you hand in your memo.

2. Use your current job or a past job experience to do the following tasks:

a. Write a letter asking someone for information that you need to complete a task.

b. Write a letter or memo giving someone information that has been requested.

c. Write a memo giving someone instructions on how to do something.

3. You are interested in attending a summer program offered by a university abroad. Write a letter requesting information about the program. You will have to describe exactly what you want to know so your reader will know how to respond.

4. You have seen an advertisement for a "hiring and firing" training seminar that interests you. Write to request more information about the seminar. Be sure to specify exactly what information you want to know in order to decide whether you want to attend.

5. Six months ago, you lost your glasses and received money for another pair from your employee group vision insurance plan. This month, you broke this pair and wrote the insurance company, asking for enough money to buy another pair. Here is the reply you received:

Dear ---:

We are in receipt of your recent inquiry regarding a Vision Expense Insurance claim.

Under the present provisions of our Group Vision Care Expense Insurance Plan, payment of benefits for lenses shall be limited to one such lens, or set of lenses, for you and each dependent in any period of 24 consecutive months, except that if a subsequent lens or set of lenses is received during such 24-month period by reason of prescription change and the new lens or set of lenses differs from the most recent ones by an axis change of 20 degrees, or by a .50 diopter sphere or cylinder change such new lens or set of lenses shall be considered a covered Vision Care Expense. Unfortunately, this clause does not apply in your particular situation and our benefit determination is therefore negative.

What problems do you find in this letter? After discussing them with others in your class, rewrite the letter to correct these problems.

CHAPTER

7

Letters and Memos that Persuade

How do you persuade people to make a change—either in the way they think or the way they do something? You overcome their resistance *to the change. This chapter will show you how to write letters and memos that accomplish this goal.*

As you saw in Chapter 6, business, industry, government, and the professions thrive on information. But they depend on change. This chapter is about how to persuade people to make a change, whether it is changing their minds, their feelings, or their actions. It will help you to write memos that persuade your personnel department to authorize a new position, your manager to purchase a new machine, or employees to join a new health insurance plan. And it will help you write letters that persuade a client to buy a new computer, a supplier to change a shipping schedule, or a buyer to pay an overdue bill.

Most writers on the job are probably not aware how often they write persuasive letters and memos. They may know that a long memo proposing that their organization adopt a new data processing system is persuasive. But they may not realize that a letter responding to a client's request for product information or a memo announcing a new flextime system (remember this example from Chapter 1) can have strong persuasive components also. And as you saw in the memo to the bank task force at the end of the last chapter, a situation that looks informative may turn out to be persuasive as well. To see how easily this can happen, look at the example of the first informative memo we discussed at the beginning of Chapter 6. Remember that the goal of this memo was simply to give prospective workshop participants scheduling arrangements.

MEMORANDUM

TO: Participants in Effective
    Speaking Seminar
FROM: Eric Smithfield
SUBJECT: Time/Date of Seminar
DATE: August 7, 19--

The seminar on effective speaking will be held in the second floor conference room on April 12 and 13, from 9:00 to 4:30. You'll have an hour for lunch.

But now let's change the situation just a little. Imagine that two people who originally signed up for the seminar had dropped out just before this memo was written. In order to keep others from dropping out, the writer might have added the following persuasive paragraphs, which appeal to the desire of employees for practical training and at the same time alleviate their fears about performing in front of groups.

MEMORANDUM

TO: Participants in Effective
    Speaking Seminar
FROM: Eric Smithfield
SUBJECT: Time/Date of Seminar
DATE: August 7, 19--

The seminar on effective speaking will be held in the second floor conference room on April 12 and 13, from 9:00 to 4:30. You'll have an hour for lunch.

This seminar promises to be very practical. In addition to focusing on how to make oral presentations to large groups, you will discuss how to communicate one-on-one and how to conduct meetings.

You will also have plenty of chances to practice in a supportive, nonthreatening environment.

In other words, since this writer's goal is now to persuade as well as to inform, he has added information that will appeal to his readers and thereby motivate them to attend the session.

THE STRATEGIES OF PERSUASION

Any time you need to motivate readers in order to accomplish your goal, you are in a persuasive situation. But how do you persuade readers? Like the writer of the memo above, you use persuasive strategies; that is, you make the choices—of information, organization, style, and design—that will motivate them to identify with you and accept your point of view.

To figure out what persuasive strategies will motivate readers most effectively, you're going to have to decide how resistant they will be. If you think they won't resist very much, your job may be a simple one. For example, most people won't be too bothered if you have to switch the time of a meeting, even if the new time is a little inconvenient for them. In this case, just giving the reason for the change will probably be enough to motivate your readers to accept the new time and attend willingly. But when you think your readers will be more resistant—let's say you want an employee to accept a transfer to another division—you will have to be much more persuasive. You can picture the readers of your persuasive letters and memos on a kind of "resistance spectrum," ranging from those with little resistance to those with quite a lot.

Slightly Resistant	More Resistant	Very Resistant

In the following pages, we'll progress along this spectrum, discussing what strategies to use to persuade readers in these different categories.

Writing to Slightly Resistant Readers

When your readers are already prone to accept your ideas, your persuasive job will be an easy one. Perhaps your manager likes your suggestion to recondition some old machines rather than to buy new ones, and tells you, "Just write it up in a memo and I'll get it approved." Your memo can be relatively short, just long enough to state your proposal and support it with a comparison of reconditioning costs *versus* costs for new machines. But even in this situation, you should take the time to document the proposal with precise cost figures, just in case your manager has to have it approved by someone else who turns out to be more resistant.

Sometimes when managers write to subordinates, they assume that their readers will accept changes with little resistance. "After all," they think, "I'm the boss!" Thus, one supervisor wrote—

> Effective immediately, turn in all copies of load sheets going to the shipping dock after each shift.

But even in this kind of situation, a smart manager will motivate readers to accept the change willingly by adding a "please" and a brief explanation.

> Effective immediately, please turn in all copies of load sheets going to the shipping dock after each shift.
>
> This will enable us to see if we're meeting our Group Performance Bonus at the end of the month. Thanks in advance for your cooperation.

Writing to More Resistant Readers

Since many of the changes you propose on the job will involve someone's spending time or money, you'll often find that your readers will be more resistant than the ones we've been discussing. In these situations, you are going to have to win them through strategic information, organization, and stylistic choices. This section will show you how to make the most effective choices.

Choose information that will:

- *Explain your problem.* When writing a persuasive letter or memo to more resistant readers, choose information that will have the most appeal for them. Sometimes you can enlist their aid by *explaining your problem,* as this writer does in his second paragraph.

> Will you ask the Des Moines plant to inspect their stock for damage before it leaves their plant?
>
> Our Memphis Adhesive Bindery operation is still having high waste and too much time in rejogging because of the condition of stock received from Des Moines. The material is coming in full of dog ears, bent, torn, and creased so badly that it is almost impossible to run.

- *Describe your needs.* At other times, you might *describe needs* that your reader can help fulfill by approving of your proposal. Look at how one writer does this.

> The electronic technicians have been enrolled in a Heall Kit Micro Processor course for the past year. They have completed the course material and built the processor and trainer accessory.
>
> Now we need a video terminal such as the Heall Kit H-19 in order to successfully complete this course.

- *Stress the benefits to your reader.* A third strategy is to *stress the benefits* that your reader will receive by granting your request, as the customer service manager of a large motel does in the following paragraphs. He is responding to a customer's request about whether the motel has accommodations for a wedding.

We recommend you reserve our two best banquet rooms for this occasion. Our Queen Elizabeth room is an excellent choice for private dinner parties and rehearsal dinners. The Tudor room is our largest banquet room and is beautifully appointed for functions such as cocktail receptions. Two suites adjacent to the Tudor room are conveniently located for use by the bride and groom for changing before their honeymoon.

- *Appeal to your reader's emotions.* Until now, we have been talking about using information that will appeal primarily to your readers' intellect—describing your problem, stating your needs, or giving the benefits to be received by granting your request. But don't hesitate to use information that will make *emotional appeals* also. In fact, research shows that sometimes emotional appeals are more effective than logical ones. Note how the writer in the second paragraph of the following memo appeals subtly to a manager's pride in his subordinates' accomplishments by implying that naturally the manager will want to continue the success already attained (in underlined print). Then he buttresses this appeal in the numbered paragraphs by logically citing other advantages (as well as appealing again to the manager's pride in the department).

This is to request that we purchase two portable terminals to use for day and after-work hours. <u>These two terminals would enable people who have successfully completed APL computer school to help make our section even more efficient.</u>

The advantages of this purchase are the following:

1. It would allow three terminals to be on line during the day from this location. This would permit us to respond quicker to crisis requests and make the whole department look more effective and professional.

2. Data can be processed after working hours and weekends when computer time sharing is at a reduced rate. Based on last year's usage, we could save over $7,500 per year. This means we would return our investment the first year and make an additional $35,000 in savings during the next five years.

One particularly effective emotional appeal is to dramatize and personalize a problem so that the reader simply can't ignore it. For instance, a writer who wanted to persuade a company to install an automatic summer/winter changeover thermostat costing $925 began his letter this way:

Our major reason for recommending this installation is that in the last two months, your gas consumption has increased at the Elmont Street Plant by 800%. If this trend continues, your total cost for gas this year will be $1,235, which exceeds last year's cost by over $400.

Notice how figures (800%, over $400) dramatize the heightened gas consumption while the pronouns personalize it.

Organize information using either:

- *A priority pattern.* You may have noticed that six of the seven examples of persuasive requests we've talked about so far are organized according to the *priority pattern* discussed in the last chapter, with the recommendation for the change followed by its justification:

Recommendation (In one paragraph if possible)
Justification (Appealing to reason/emotions)

Use this pattern for most persuasive letters and memos, especially if you think there is any chance that your reader will be confused or misled if you don't.

- *A climactic pattern.* But there will be times when you may have to make your readers receptive to your request *before* making it. In these situations, you can use the more indirect, *climactic pattern*, leading with the justification and following with the actual recommendation.

Justification
Recommendation

By following this pattern, the writer of the following paragraphs from a letter to a client gets the reader to identify a need first and then to see how the product proposed can fill that need.

We recently became aware that some customers have to use an operator to manually feed materials into the machine in place of the infeed conveyor. This practice is potentially hazardous since the conveyor pulleys are exposed.

To help eliminate this problem, we have designed entry and exit belt guards, which can be easily installed on any equipment you have purchased. If you need an operator near exposed belt pulleys, we strongly recommend that you buy and install these belt guards for all machines sold since January 15, 19--.

Here is another writer who uses the same pattern, this time in order to demonstrate the potential benefits of a new product.

Presently Production Planning accesses the "UMSG" in the CICS network to send short messages to Capacity Planning in Des Moines.

Using the "UMSG" program saves numerous phone calls to Des Moines regarding job status, numbers, titles, dates, etc. However, using this program is costly and also inconvenient, since we can only use it on a part-time basis.

Therefore, I am requesting that a program similar to the "UMSG" program be purchased so that we can. . . .

The climactic pattern can work well when your document is short or when your reader is already familiar with your situation. It can also work when you can hold your readers' attention, perhaps by dramatizing the problem. But remember that you usually write persuasive letters and memos to busy managers who may not have the time to wade through your justification before getting to your recommendation. After wading through two pages of justification before finding a request for a new personnel position, one angry manager scrawled "Put your request first!" across the memo and shot it back to its writer.

Use a style that projects a positive personality to your readers:

Research has shown that readers are often as much convinced by their perception of the writer as they are by his or her arguments, whether logical or emotional. Therefore, you also need to present yourself as positively to your readers as possible, emphasizing—

- your *knowledge* of the subject ("In our 27 years in the industrial chemical business, we. . . .")
- your *honesty* ("While we try to do the best job possible, we cannot guarantee that all our graduates get a job immediately.")
- and your *goodwill* toward the reader ("Our customers have come to rely on our treatment of them because. . . .")

Your most powerful ally in creating such a convincing persona is your style.

To see how stylistic choices can create a persuasive personality, read the following paragraph from a letter written by a public utility to its stockholders. The goal of the letter is to counter adverse publicity the company has received because of setbacks suffered in constructing a nuclear power facility. The writer wants to persuade stockholders that the company is deeply concerned about its problems and will deal with them effectively. The first paragraph describes the problems—increased construction costs, negative reports from the Nuclear Regulatory Commission, and company bond ratings lowered. Here is the second paragraph.

In spite of these events, we've held steadfast to our plan to complete this project by late 1986, and we have not made excuses for the things that have gone wrong. We have strong reason to believe, for instance, that although the NRC reports may appear to give an indication that our project is in trouble, that's just not the case. We have met with the NRC, and we

```
understand their concerns. They have our full
attention, and we can accomplish what has to be done.
As a matter of fact, most of our corrective action
plans are already well underway. We want you to know
too that our follow-up work performed after the NRC
audit has demonstrated that our construction has
"built-in" quality. This was something we were unable
to prove at the time of the audit because of some
shortcomings in our inspection and documentation
programs. You may be assured that we've improved in
this regard and have found no need for major re-work
of the construction to date.
```

Notice how the pronouns "we" (used nine times) and "our" (used seven times) humanize the company and imply a personal relationship between it and the reader, a relationship that is reinforced by the use of the contraction "we've." And notice how carefully the writer chooses words and phrases to create a positive, confident tone—"that's just not the case"; "held steadfast"; "strong reason"; "full attention"; "well underway"; and "'built-in' quality."

Even the sentence structure contributes to the persuasive nature of the paragraph. For instance, the writer minimizes problems by couching them in short phrases ("In spite of these events") and subordinate clauses ("although the NRC reports may appear to give an indication that our project is in trouble"). But while using subordination to play down problems, the writer also uses coordinate clauses that create a sense of balance in dealing with these problems.

```
  We have met with the NRC, and we understand their
concerns. They have our full attention, and we can
accomplish what has to be done.
```

Taken together, these stylistic choices convey the image of a group of people who are as decent and human as the rest of us. "We may have suffered some momentary setbacks," the writer seems to be saying, "But we understand our problems, are willing to face them honestly, and are steadily and confidently moving to overcome them."

Writing to Highly Resistant Readers

If your readers are sharply opposed to your point of view, the best information you can give, even if well organized and presented in your most persuasive style, probably won't convince them. Such situations may not occur very often, but they will happen.

Acknowledge your reader's position, *then* seek to persuade.

Perhaps you need an expensive new system or want to hire new staff, but your manager doesn't think they are needed. In situations like these, your best strategy is to understand fully your reader's opposing position, acknowledge its validity in your letter or memo, but then persuade him or her that within this particular context, your argument is more compelling. Sometimes, you can do this simply by mentioning your reader's point of view briefly.

Would you help us solve the following problems we are having microfilming documents sent us by your department?

I can appreciate that some of these items may sound petty; however, they do reduce the time of our filming. . . .

At other times, you may need to deal with your reader's position in more detail. Imagine, for example, that you are a plant inspector who wants to persuade a plant manager to act on a quality control problem, even though the manager has previously refused to, arguing that no customers have complained. You might write—

In our spot inspections during the last week, we found several more samples of low quality sandwich wrap. Basically, the problem is the same as it was a month ago, when we caught that miscolored lot. The part that should have been blue was smeared and discolored.

True, we have not had any rejections for poor quality yet. But this is mainly because it is the store selling the food that sees the ink smears and discoloration, not the headquarters purchasing agent. Sooner or later, the problem will come to the attention of the purchasing agents, who may turn to another supplier.

I realize that our earlier attempts to control color quality on this product were expensive and time consuming. But I suggest we try again to solve this problem before we lose a customer.

Using the climactic pattern in your memo, you begin by describing the problem. Then you acknowledge that the manager is right when he says that you haven't lost any customers yet. But then you shift the context of the argument by making the point that the problem has not yet come to the attention of a headquarters purchasing agent. As soon as it does, you may lose customers. Therefore, the manager should solve the problem.

Deal with your reader's feelings carefully.

If you had written the memo above, you might have decided not to go to so much trouble to acknowledge and refute your reader's arguments, since you are the plant inspector and could therefore bring additional pressure to bear on the manager if you wanted to. But it is often wise to deal with your reader's feelings carefully and delicately, rather than coming down with a too-heavy hand. For instance, the writer of the following memo knows that the supplier must agree to this request for a change in procedure. But the writer also wants to maintain a cordial relationship, because there may come a time when some special help from the supplier will be needed. Therefore, the writer deals with the reader's arguments carefully, admitting that in the short run the new procedure will tend to increase costs and may cause flaws, but arguing that in the long run the new procedure will overcome these while increasing sales and profits.

From now on, would you supply us with film done in halftone gravure positives? As far as ad material is concerned, we can accept Group V ink halftone material to GTA standards.

We discussed this change in procedure at our meeting on October 15. At that time, you felt that this new procedure could increase your costs substantially as well as enhance flaws in artwork and supplied film. We agree that this procedure may increase your costs in the short run. But once you make the initial shift, you will begin to increase your profits because of faster turn-around time and increased sales as a result of the improved final product.

This new process, called Dynatone, will substantially improve the sharpness and detail of each page. Because of this, you may become aware of some flaws in artwork that were not visible before. But these will be easily corrected.

We feel that the sharper color and image enhancements will please your present customers and gain new ones.

We'd appreciate your help in making the shift to the new film by November 15. Thanks in advance for increasing the quality of our product.

MAJOR TYPES OF PERSUASIVE DOCUMENTS

In the last section, we focused on the readers of your persuasive letters and memos. You learned to choose the persuasive strategies that would most lower their resistance and thereby motivate them to your point of view. Now we are going to look at persuasive letters and memos from a different perspective, focusing this time on the major types you will write during your career. You will learn what each type is and the best persuasive strategies to use when writing each type.

Directives

A directive is an order that something be done. It is typically short, usually written within an organization (therefore in memo form), and comes down the chain of command—from someone who has the power to order that something be done to someone who must do it. Earlier, when talking about writing to slightly resistant readers, we used the example of this well-written directive, because it includes not only the specific directive, to "turn in all copies of *load sheets*," but the reason also.

> Effective immediately, please turn in all copies of load sheets going to the shipping dock after each shift.
>
> This will enable us to see if we're meeting our Group Performance Bonus at the end of the month. Thanks in advance for your cooperation.

You may have two questions when writing directives. The first will be how demanding a voice to use. On one occasion, you might decide to make your voice as mild as the following one:

```
Please modify ACF2 access rules to allow the
following production files to be created within the
General Ledger system. . . .
```

On another occasion, a stern voice like the one in this memo from a supervisor who is obviously angry at her production crew may be appropriate.

```
  Flammable materials must not be left in the work
area!
  Yesterday, the safety inspector found solvent in an
open glass jar on the table next to the heater. Had
that solvent been ignited, there could have been a
major accident.
  As you know, we don't just talk safety, we do it!
```

The voice you choose for a directive will depend on the situation and on your leadership style. But remember that words on paper carry a special sting, and once written, they cannot be retracted.

Another question you may have is how to organize directives. Generally, since the very position you hold as a manager will make strong resistance out of the question, you should lead with the directive and follow with necessary explanation. Some writers are tempted to build up to their main point even in a directive, but if you do this, you run the risk of confusing your readers about what you want them to do, as the writer of the following memo did:

```
  In order to enhance our credibility in the eyes of
the readers of our reports and to provide the readers
with management's intended course of action in the
comments addressed in our reports, we will include
management's response in future letters of
recommendation.
  The attached standard cover memo requesting
management's comments should accompany the final
draft given to management for discussion purposes.
Note that future report drafts should provide ample
space after each comment to permit management to write
in their proposed response. Issuance of the memo
requires auditor approval.
```

Since the specific directive is the most important part of this memo, the writer should have begun with it to emphasize its importance and then followed with his justification.

```
Please make the following two changes in our audit
reporting procedures:

   1. Enclose the attached cover memo, which requests
      that management respond to each of our
      recommendations.

   2. Leave sufficient space after each
      recommendation for management's responses.

This new procedure will enhance our credibility in
the eyes of our readers and provide them with
management's intended course of action.
```

Requests and Recommendations

Sometimes people at work make requests ("This is to *request* that our department buy two additional microcomputers.") or recommendations ("On the basis of our analysis of your needs, we *recommend* that your company purchase two additional microcomputers"). Although the meanings of these words may be different, the goal of both requests and recommendations is exactly the same—to persuade someone to take some action—and the document produced will be the same. Therefore, we'll consider them to be just different names for the same type of document. A request or recommendation might be as short as this one:

```
                    MEMORANDUM

TO: John Quinn
FROM: Ellis Stevens
SUBJECT: McCook Manuals
DATE: July 14, 19--

As we discussed on the phone, please assemble
300 training manuals and send them to me by
the 30th of January. Thanks in advance for
your help.
```

Or longer, like this one:

MEMORANDUM

TO: May Fontana
FROM: Larry Conroy
SUBJECT: Additional Computer Space
DATE: February 4, 19--

I am recommending that our department be given a private library to use to make several concurrent changes to the system.

First, we are working on one project that will require lengthening the master file; therefore, all update modules must be compiled.

Another project involves conversion to a 16-digit account number. This will, in turn, require changing every update module and most report modules, as well as some edit modules and many stand-alone programs.

In a third project, we are converting to a 23-digit microfilm reference number which, again, requires compiling all edit and update modules and all of BOSS II.

Earlier, in our discussion of writing to resistant readers, we covered the major persuasive strategies to use when writing requests/recommendations. When choosing information that will persuade a reader, one of these strategies may work:

Describe your problem;
State your needs; or
Give the benefits that your reader would get.

When organizing this information, use the priority pattern most of the time, putting your request/recommendation first so that busy readers will understand it quickly. However, when writing to readers who are highly resistant, you could use the climactic pattern, beginning by acknowledging the validity of their point of view before presenting your own. Be sure also to write in a style that creates a persuasive personality, emphasizing your dependability, honesty, and goodwill toward your reader.

Sales Letters

Even if you will never be in the position of writing unsolicited sales letters, you will probably have to respond to clients' requests for information about a product or service provided by your organization. Such requests are excellent opportunities to persuade your reader to buy the product or use the service. In effect, you will be writing a sales letter.

While writers follow different patterns in writing sales letters, one pattern that often works is the one that professionals are trained to follow when making a sale. To persuade someone to buy a product or service, they answer four questions a customer will have.

QUESTION	ANSWER
1. What is this?	1. Describe its *major features.*
2. How does this work?	2. Describe *advantages* of these features.
3. What does this mean to me?	3. Describe *benefits* of these advantages.
4. How do I buy this?	4. Describe *action* client needs to take.

To the right is the way a letter that follows this features/advantages/benefits/action pattern might look. This writer is responding to someone's request for information on a product.

You will have to adapt this pattern to your own needs. For instance, you might present features, advantages, and benefits in a different order, perhaps beginning a letter with the major benefits of a product or service in order to get your readers' attention. But no matter how you use it, you will find that this is an easy and effective pattern to follow in writing a sales letter, whether you are selling a product or service to clients or even yourself to a prospective employer. In fact, in Chapter 15, you will see how to use this pattern in job application letters.

Bad News Letters

Even though the last chapter was about writing informative letters and memos, we never really talked about how to write an unfavorable letter; that is, how to give bad news. This is because a bad news letter is not just informative; it is also persuasive. You are not just giving people bad news; you are trying to persuade them to accept it as well. This is sometimes a tricky task. Some writers approach the problem too mechanically, beginning with a buffer statement and then following with the bad news. This is a little bit like patting your readers on the back before you hit them on the head. The point is not to follow a formula, but to focus on your goal, which is to help somebody accept something he or she doesn't want to accept.

July 24, 19--

John Jacobs
Worcester Machine
Worcester, MA 03208

Dear Mr. Jacobs:

Thank you for your interest in our HXB Multiform Utility Bender.

Features The Bender has several important features. In the horizontal mode, you have the capability of doing pipe bending, tube bending, rebar work, flat work, "U" bolts, rod bending, etc. In the vertical mode, you have the capability of doing arbor press work for pressing out bushings or pressing in bushings or straightening, plus interchangeable tooling for doing press blade work, etc.

Advantages With these features, this new machine gives you a wide range of versatility. With it, you can form materials for onsite construction for general, electrical, or plumbing contractors.

Benefits With ever-increasing onsite costs, this versatility can result in significant savings on the job and yield increased profit for your organization.

Action We will be happy to place your order for the particular model that fits your needs. Send us prints of the parts you wish to form, the quantity needed, the type of material, and we will be happy to recommend a bender suitable for the job.

Our more than 80 years of experience is at your service.

The solution is not just to begin with a buffer; it's to choose the information, organizational pattern, and style that will accomplish your persuasive goal. Look at how the writer of the following difficult "no" letter, telling someone that he has been rejected for appointment to a medical post with an international relief organization, accomplishes the task:

October 18, 19--

Philip Roane
116 West Avenue
Wichita, KS 67203

Dear Mr. Roane:

Working with you during the past months as you moved through our appointment process has been a pleasure. And I want to assure you that our board carefully reviewed your own statement, your previous experience, your references, and the results of our own interviews.

But, as I told you by phone, the board's decision was finally a negative one. We based our decision on medical factors and on our feeling that the needs of your older children could best be met stateside.

In the near future I hope to visit with you in your home and go over in more detail the reasons for the position our board took.

Thank you for applying and for giving us so much of your time during the last few months.

This writer conveys the bad news to his reader, but because he understands his persuasive goal, he does it in a humane and considerate manner. First, he establishes rapport with his reader by a warm statement about their pleasant relationship and then assures him that a careful review process was followed. Only then does he break the bad news, after which he promises to discuss the reasons for refusal in more detail later in a personal meeting. Even his style conveys his warmth (" . . . has been a pleasure"); consideration for his reader ("And I want to assure you. . . ."); and regret at the bad news (" . . . the board's decision was *finally* a negative one").

As I've said, there's no easy formula you can follow in writing bad news letters. But you can remind yourself that your goal is not just to give the bad news; it's also to write in such a way that your reader will accept it.

Claims

One type of persuasive letter that illustrates the variety of persuasive strategies you may have to use is the claim. When you write a claim, you are asking someone to make an adjustment—to fix something that's broken, to replace faulty merchandise, or to pay money owed. A claim can be as simple as a direct request to repair something.

April 14, 19--

The Crystal Watch Company
1106 West Street
West Haversack, MA 90765

Gentlemen:

Can I still return my Crystal watch for repairs?

I bought this watch two years ago. Shortly before the end of a year, it began to lose time. I didn't think anything of it at first, but since then it has lost more and more time.

Since the problem began before the year's warranty period was up, I hope you will still repair the watch.

Thank you in advance for your consideration.

But claims also involve situations as challenging as requests for money. Here are some examples written by a woman in charge of a claims department in a large company. She has to claim payments from transportation companies when goods shipped by them are damaged. When she makes a first claim for payment, her job is a fairly easy one. In this situation, it is usually enough to make the request and substantiate it.

July 9, 19--

John Gallagher
Nelson Transportation Company
Loss and Damage Department
Birmingham, AL 76509

Dear Mr. Gallagher:

Would you please pay us the amount of $85.39 for two cases of containers lost recently by your company?

This shipment was covered by your freight bill #F-49861 dated July 2. We are attaching a copy of the bill, which was signed "two cases short" by your driver.

Thank you for your kind attention to this matter.

But her task gets trickier when the claims are overdue. Notice how her voice gets progressively tougher in each of the following requests for payment:

August 15, 19--

We request that you pay the above-referenced claim for $85.39 as soon as possible.

We wrote you on July 9 of this year about this claim. Perhaps you overlooked our letter—possibly you forgot.

At any rate, we have not yet received your check and are therefore requesting that you pay us as soon as possible.

September 15, 19--

The above-referenced claim, for the sum of $85.39, was first filed with your company July 9 of this year. It still remains unpaid. We now request that you pay it immediately.

This is the third request for payment of this claim. You have not even replied to our first two letters.

May we remind you that regulations of the Alabama Corporation Commission make it mandatory that all claims be handled thoroughly and promptly. Further delay exposes your company to criticism by the government.

Therefore, we urge you to send us a check for $85.39 immediately.

January 15, 19--

We cannot understand your not keeping your word. After we had written you three letters regarding the above-referenced claim for $85.39, you promised by phone on October 18 that you would pay it by return check. Sometimes mail is rather slow, but Mr. Gallagher, we cannot agree that mail is that slow.

You must pay this claim immediately so that we can draw this matter to an amicable conclusion as soon as possible. We are sincerely interested in keeping the goodwill of all our carriers; yet we cannot continue to build up a large collection expense.

As of this date, we are canceling all shipments with your company until this claim is paid. Furthermore, if it is not paid by January 30, we are turning the matter over to our attorneys.

What strategies did this writer use to put increasing pressure on the carrier for payment? First, she progressively toughened her voice, moving from a polite request, "Would you please pay us. . . ." (*1st letter*); to the slightly more distant, "We request that you pay . . . as soon as possible" (*2nd letter*); to the tougher, "We now request that you pay it immediately" (*3rd letter*); and finally to the sarcastic, "We cannot agree that the mails are that slow," and demanding, "You must pay this claim immediately. . . ."

But notice she brought another kind of pressure to bear also. First, she reminded her reader about the requirements of the Alabama Corporation Commission and implied that she might notify them. When that didn't work, she threatened to cancel shipments and to bring in her company attorneys. Probably the carrier finally paid the claim, but this company may have spent more money to collect the claim than it ever would have received in payment.

Writing claims letters is an art unto itself. People who do it regularly learn what strategies of voice and content (ways of bringing pressure) work best in particular situations. Because claims are usually handled by a special department within a company, you may never have to write a claims letter as such. But at some time you may have to remind a client to make a late payment. If you do, it's well to know that your main problem will be to apply pressure (perhaps just a little bit) without alienating your reader.

SUMMARY

Except perhaps for sales letters, there are no ready patterns or formulas to follow in persuasive situations. Rather, you will need to understand your goal in each situation and then decide how much your reader will resist this goal. The more resistance you encounter, the shrewder you will have to be about making the kinds of writing choices that will persuade a reader. But as we've said on the preceding pages, there are certain principles you can follow in persuasive situations.

1. Choose the information that will most predispose your readers to accept your goal.
2. Organize your ideas to motivate your readers. Usually it's best to follow the priority pattern; sometimes, though, you'll need to choose a climactic pattern.
3. Use a style that will create a convincing persona—knowledgeable, honest, and likeable.
4. As in informative situations, design your documents for ease and clarity of reading.

Let's apply these persuasive principles to the following writing situation.

A Writing Situation

Imagine that you interviewed for a job in the personnel department of a local bank. During the interview with your prospective manager, you mentioned casually that you took a course in business writing, thinking this might be one more thing in your favor. Now that you are hired, you realize that your manager must have taken your casual comment seriously, for your first assignment is to study form letters sent out by the personnel department to job applicants and revise them if necessary.

"I don't really like form letters," your manager says, "but with the volume of correspondence this department must answer, they are a necessary evil. Besides, our new word processing center system makes them easy to use. You just tell the transcriptionist which form to use, give a few facts, and he or she does the rest. But some of ours sound pretty bad to me. See if you can improve on them."

The first two letters you examine are letters sent to students graduating from college who are applying for positions in the bank's management training program. One of these letters is a good news letter that notifies an applicant that he or she has been hired, while the other conveys the bad news that the applicant has been rejected. The acceptance letter is on page 170.

As you read the letter, your throat constricts at its formality and coldness. In fact, you remember receiving exactly the same letter when you were hired. You were so put off you hardly even read it. "Mr. Sabriski was right! No question about it. This letter is terrible. Better see what I can do with it," you say to yourself.

You set to work, a little anxious since this is your first task for the bank. But you begin, first trying—

> This is in response to your recent application for employment. As a result of your interview, ________________ has authorized me to confirm an offer of employment to you.

But your version sounds just as cold and indirect as the first. Then you realize something: If you are giving your reader the important information that he has been hired, this ought to come first in the letter, following the priority pattern. So you try again.

> You have been hired. As a result of your interview, ________________ has authorized me to confirm an offer of a position in our management training program.

But this still sounds too cold and abrupt. And why do you need to mention the interview—isn't it obvious to the reader that the interview was a success? The more you think about the original letter, the more you realize that the whole thing is somehow wrong. And as you remember your own reaction on first reading it, you begin to realize its major problem. With its cold voice and forbidding information, this letter puts a reader off at the very moment when it should be convincing him that this bank will be a good place to work and that the training program will be exciting. In other words, the real goal of this letter should not just be to inform—it's to persuade the reader to take the job.

All of a sudden, you're flooded with ideas. For one thing, the voice needs to be changed. If your goal is to convince a reader to take the job, then the first thing you've got to do is set up a cordial relationship with him or her. This means that your voice has got to be more warm and personal. To personalize the letter even more, you decide to refer to some of the applicant's real strengths rather than just making that cold reference to "your interview." The more you think about the information in the original letter, the more you realize just how wrong most of it is. At the very time when you should be selling a prospective employee on the training program

Date

Name
Address
City, State, Zip

Dear __________________:

Thank you for your recent application for employment. As a result of your interview, __________________ has authorized me to confirm an offer of employment to you.

Therefore, we are confirming an offer for a position in our management training program at a starting salary of __________________. It is important that you report for work on _________, as that is the date on which this program begins. Please report directly to the Personnel Department on that date in order to complete all the necessary documents for our files.

It is our standard policy that the first three months of employment constitute a probationary period. We would like you to be aware that your employment with this bank is contingent, of course, on the receipt of satisfactory references from your teachers and former employers. At the end of _________ months, an evaluation of your performance will be made. If you have performed satisfactorily, an increase in salary may be recommended. Subsequent reviews will be on an annual basis.

We are happy that you considered employment with us, and hope that you will favorably consider the offer extended. If you accept the terms as set forth above, please sign and date the enclosed copy of this letter and return it to me in the envelope provided.

Sincerely,

____

Date

Name
Address
City, State, Zip

Dear ________________:

Congratulations. Your application to our management training program has been accepted. We welcome you to the bank.

You might be interested in knowing that ____, especially ______________________________, was particularly appealing to us. And your experience in/with ____________________________ indicates that you have had the opportunity to apply your education in practical situations.

The position of management trainee is a challenging one. You will take short courses in various aspects of management, including employee motivation, performance evaluation, and communication skills. In addition, you will get experience in a number of different capacities, ranging from operations, to personnel, to public relations.

Our company has an outstanding benefits program that includes medical and life insurance, as well as a strong retirement plan and an employee credit union.

In addition, since we are such a large and diversified company, opportunities for advancement are excellent.

Please contact ________________ as soon as possible if you have any questions and to arrange your starting date. We are looking forward to having you on our team.

Sincerely,

____

and on the bank, you're threatening him with a probationary period instead and "subsequent reviews" on top of that.

Your rewriting job is not an easy one. In fact, even after you've defined your real goal and seen some of the changes you will make, it still takes hours of painstaking work, consultations with your manager, and then more work, to come up with the draft on page 171, which you're both satisfied with.

At first you are a little worried about how a particular writer would fill in the blanks in the second paragraph, where you want to emphasize some of the new employee's individual strengths. But your manager reminds you that all these form letters are on a word processor anyway, so it will be no trouble for someone to tailor that paragraph to a reader's accomplishments. More importantly, your manager likes your letter, commenting that, "this is the way a letter ought to be written."

But your job is only half complete. Now you've got to revise that rejection letter. You pick it up and begin to read.

Date

Name
Address
City, State, Zip

Dear ____________________:

We write to inform you that your application to our management training program has been denied.

Your educational background and work experience are not appropriate for a position in this program at this time.

Sincerely,

____

"How would I feel if I got this letter?" you ask yourself. "Pretty terrible," you think. As you reflect on your own response to such a letter, you realize that the goal of this bad news letter is really just as persuasive as that of the acceptance letter. Only this time you're not trying to convince someone to take a job; you're trying to persuade him or her to accept some bad news.

Another way to describe your goal is that you're trying to convey some bad news but still leave the person with a sense of worth at the end of reading your letter. If that's the case, then this rejection letter doesn't work at all. Its voice ("We write to inform you") is too cold and its information too sketchy. You need to use a voice that will communicate concern for this person. And it'd be a good idea to let the person know that the bank doesn't just pass over applications lightly and then make a quick and arbitrary decision—that it really does consider applications carefully.

The more you think about it, the more you realize that this rejection has got to walk a fine line—on the one hand, you want to be as humane and considerate as possible; on the other, you want to be honest with your reader and clear that this is a rejection. After a number of drafts, you settle on the following version:

Date

Name
Address
City, State, Zip

Dear ________________:

Thank you for applying for a position in our management training program.

Your application has been given the most careful consideration by our staff. We studied your résumé, discussed various aspects of your interview, and ______________.

After careful deliberation, our staff determined that your ____________________ do not qualify you for this program. In particular, we are looking for people who ______________________________.

If we have another position for which you are qualified, we encourage you to apply.

Best wishes in your future career.

Sincerely,

____

One thing you've learned is that bad news letters are very difficult to write. Both you and your supervisor are a little worried that the paragraph in the letter about giving the application consideration may sound a little too positive. But after all, you tell yourselves, the personnel department does work hard to make sure that each applicant is given full and fair consideration. So the letter really does reflect what you do.

You won't have the opportunity to write good news letters every day, nor will you have the frequent burden of writing ones that give bad news. But when you do write them, remember that while your goal may look informational, it is often persuasive as well. In a good news letter, whether you are offering someone a job, congratulating someone on a promotion, or commending someone for a task well done, your goal is to convince that person to take the job, feel good about the promotion, or realize how much you appreciate extra effort. In the bad news letter, your goal is to persuade someone to accept the bad news without damage to his or her self-esteem.

APPLICATIONS

1. A student was ready to graduate when he discovered he was three hours short of the required credits. Even though the error was his advisor's, the catalog said he was responsible. To get the three hours, the student decided to petition the university academic status committee to allow him to count a project done previously for a professor as internship credit toward graduation. Read the letter on the right, paying particular attention to his voice and supporting arguments. Then revise the letter to make it more effective.

2. A problem exists on your job as a plant manager at a printing company. One person checks color quality as printed material comes off of one of your largest presses. This person must constantly run back and forth, making minor adjustments in ink concentrations, as well as keeping up with the visual checking. But one person is simply not enough to handle this important quality control job. You have seen some poor quality runs come off the press, despite this person's sincere efforts to keep up with the work. You would like to add a second person to assist in this task, but you know that your supervisor has argued in the past that the problem doesn't exist, and that if it did, your solution is too expensive. Write a memo persuading your supervisor to hire another person. Be prepared to explain why you organized the memo as you did.

Dr. George Rawlings, Chairman
Academic Status Committee
Indiana University
Ballantine Hall, Room 404
Bloomington, IN 47401

Dear Dr. Rawlings:

You may well imagine how embarrassed and upset I have been since I have learned that because of my advisor's error in calculating my credits, I am three hours short of graduation. This is especially upsetting since I have already been offered a full-time position contingent on my graduation. I wish to bring to the Academic Status Committee's attention that my three deficient credits are in the area of my electives, not my major.

This past summer, I assisted Dr. Sam Johnson in an intensive eight-week study of the off-campus housing for students. At the end of the study, I wrote a lengthy report. This project was more work and more informative than some of the classes I have taken. This is why I feel that assigning three credits to this work would not be inappropriate.

I would not ask the committee to consider this action if it were not for the unusual circumstances mentioned above. Up until two days ago, both my advisor and I believed that I had satisfied all the requirements for graduation.

3. The area where you live is zoned residential only. But a developer has petitioned your board of supervisors to be allowed an exception to the zoning regulation in order to build a shopping mall at the end of your street. You are opposed for many reasons—there will be increased traffic, many children live on your street, there is already a mall five miles away, and the aesthetic and property value of your home will be adversely affected. Write the board of supervisors, most of whom are realtors or developers themselves, requesting that they deny the developer's petition. Explain why you chose your voice, information, and organization.

4. Write a one-page description of the organization you work for or the school you attend to be used in recruiting efforts. Essentially, you will be writing a sales letter.

5. You have been asked to serve as one of the officers for a charitable organization. Though you are already an active member of the organization, the position of officer requires much more time and work than you feel you can give. You decide that you must refuse. Write the letter of refusal.

6. When you moved into your last apartment, you paid a damage deposit of $250. Now you are ready to move out and want your deposit refunded. Write the letter requesting the refund. Now suppose that you have waited a month, but have gotten no response to your letter. Write a second request for the refund.

7. Someone working under you has been violating established safety procedures by not wearing protective goggles while working around welding areas. Write a memo to that person directing that the problem be corrected.

PART

3

Long Documents

CHAPTER

8

Preparing to Write Long Documents

No matter what career you pursue, you're probably going to have to write long documents—reports, proposals, and perhaps even manuals. In addition, you may well have to make oral presentations to people within your organization and to people outside. The goal of the next six chapters is to prepare you for these kinds of writing situations.

This chapter will focus on how to prepare to write long documents. It will show you how to clarify goals, analyze readers, and identify the kind of information you need, as well as how to find, document, and organize this information. The next chapter will show you how to design long documents, especially how to prepare the graphics that often accompany them. In the three chapters after these, we'll discuss how to apply the principles we've derived to the writing of particular documents such as reports, manuals, and proposals. The final chapter in this section will show you how to prepare and present an oral presentation.

WHAT'S MY GOAL?

Your general goals for reports, proposals, or manuals will be the same as those for letters and memos. If you are writing a report or manual, your goal will be to inform your reader about something—in a report, perhaps to tell him about your progress on a project or what you recommend the organization do about a problem you have investigated; in a manual, perhaps how to use a word processing system or how to appraise an employee's performance. And if you are writing a proposal, your goal will be to convince someone to do something—maybe to switch to a new data processing system, to build a facility at a certain location, or to purchase a product or service from your company.

WHO ARE MY READERS?

But to know how to accomplish these goals, you're going to have to identify your prospective readers and analyze their needs and expectations. Sometimes this will be easy, especially if your reader is just one person whom you know well. If your manager asks you for a monthly status report, you know he or she wants a brief report on your activities for the month. And if a division head likes your idea for a new sales campaign and asks you for a proposal on it, you know what is wanted—probably a short proposal containing a minimum of supporting data. In both these cases, since you know your reader, you know his or her needs. And in situations like these, if you are not quite sure what your reader wants, you can always ask.

But since reports, proposals, and manuals are often written to a number of readers within (and sometimes outside of) an organization, your job of identifying readers and analyzing needs may not always be so easy. A manual you have developed to show someone how to use a computer program may go to many people, some of whom know the language of computers and some of whom don't. Or a report that you have written may be circulated to people with a variety of different backgrounds. A few, most likely those in your own department, will read it closely, but readers outside of your area will probably just skim it hurriedly for any impact it might have on them.

When writing long documents to multiple readers, you may have to understand a number of things about them. At times, you may have to ask yourself whether your readers are all within your organization or whether your document will be read by people on the outside as well. If your readers are outside the organization, you may well have a public relations job as well as a reporting job on your hands. There may be, for instance, certain problems that you just don't want to bring up with the readers of your company's annual report.

You may also have to consider the organizational hierarchy when preparing a long document. If you are writing a manual for readers mostly below you in the hierarchy, you may have to include detailed explanations of the processes you are describing. But readers above you in the hierarchy and not in your immediate field won't usually be interested in details. They will want to see the big picture—they'll want to know right away what you are recommending in a proposal or report and why you recommend it.

Distinguish Between *Primary* and *Secondary* Readers

How can you possibly visualize and understand the needs of so many different kinds of readers? It is often helpful to distinguish between your *primary* and *secondary* readers. Your primary readers are those who will take some action on the basis of your report, manual, or proposal. This action could be following instructions in your manual on how to process a claim, making a decision to adopt a new process or procedure that you have recommended in a proposal, or including information from your department's monthly progress report in their own division's progress report. Your secondary readers are all the others who will read your document, usually to keep up with what's going on in the organization. They might include managers in other divisions, people in your own division but in different departments, or even specialists in your own department.

When you have multiple readers for a report, manual, or proposal, begin by asking yourself, "Who are my primary readers and why do they need this document?" Your answer will guide you as you make information, organization, and stylistic choices. We'll discuss particular ways to adapt documents to primary and secondary readers. In the next chapters I'll show you, for instance, how to begin a report with information that is directed toward decision makers and end it with information for your colleagues.

WHAT DO MY READERS NEED TO KNOW?

Once you have identified your readers and analyzed their needs, you'll need to determine what kind of information will fulfill these needs. The easiest way to do this is simply to ask yourself, "In this document, what do my readers need to know?" Actually, there are only three types of information they could need—*facts, conclusions,* or *recommendations*. Usually, though, they will not want just one of these types—they will want them in some combination.

Facts

You may be surprised at how often your readers want to know the facts of a situation. "What happened?" or "What did you do?" they will ask. For instance, your manager might want to know what you did last month. The result would be facts like these that you would include in a progress report.

```
  Met with Guaranteed Foods in Newport News. This
account currently purchases $30,000 per week from
Johnson Foods. Mr. Kahn will make a decision on
switching suppliers in the next 30 days.
```

Or your manager may want to know what you observed in a test.

```
The test specimen consisted of a 6' x 3½' piece of
light gage corrugated sheet metal siding which was
painted a light gloss gray on the interior side and a
semi-gloss pale gray on the external side. Numerous
small specks and spots of rust were noted in several
areas on the exterior side of the sheet.
```

Or readers of a manual may want very concrete and factual instructions about how to do something.

TO ACCOMPLISH THIS:	DO THIS:
Add characters	Move cursor to spot, enter letters
Insert characters	Position cursor to left of where you want to begin inserting Press INSERT Insert text . . .

As you'll see in the next chapters, many short reports and most manuals are composed entirely of facts.

Conclusions

Employees often ask increduously, "Do you mean management really wants my opinion in this document?" Often the answer is "Yes." A simple recitation of the facts is just not enough. "What does all this mean? What do you think about this?" are the questions they will ask. Sometimes, readers want both a detailed description of the facts and your conclusions about them. This is frequently the case in test reports. For instance, the test report I quoted above goes on in the next paragraph like this.

```
                   Conclusions
 Based on the preceding examination, it is our
opinion that rust on the exterior of the panel is
occurring in areas where small bubbles, pin holes, and
voids in the paint are allowing moisture to come into
contact with the base metal. These voids probably
occurred at the time the paint was applied.
```

People on the job, especially those in management positions, often don't have the time to arrive at their own opinions. They don't have time to interview everyone who applies for a job or to evaluate the performance of all their employees. Instead they rely on the expertise of those reporting to them.

Of course, if you are reporting opinions, it is your responsibility to make sure that these opinions are soundly grounded in facts. Here are two short paragraphs of opinion that conclude a long factual report on a preliminary interview of applicants for a foreign assignment. The first paragraph summarizes the conclusions the writer has reached about the applicant and spouse. The second paragraph sets forth the writer's opinions about what should be investigated further. The manager who receives this report will no doubt rely heavily on these opinions when talking with the applicants and examining their application materials.

> The Thompsons are a likable, talented couple. They seem to relate happily to each other. Morris obviously is the more energetic of the two. He is a go-getter type and may be lacking in patience. Roberta is the more reserved type.
>
> My concerns, which I recommend be further investigated, are about the Thompsons' ability to relate well to foreign nationals and their capacity for coping with stress in another culture.

Recommendations

But often decision makers will want more than facts or even your opinion about the facts. In addition to such questions as "What happened?" or "What do you think about this?" they'll also ask, "What should we do about this?" Sometimes, you'll answer this question in some sort of action report. Here is the beginning of such a report written after an examination of the record-keeping procedures of a group of magistrates in a judicial system. It's obvious that the author studied the procedures (the facts) and reached some conclusions about them (that they needed to be improved). But probably because this is written to a reader who already knows enough about the problems, the writer gets right to recommendations about how to improve record-keeping procedures.

> Opportunities for improving uniformity and efficiency are as follows:
>
> 1. It is recommended that all magistrates record and code transactions on the magistrate log in accordance with the instructions and sample transactions provided by the Office of the Executive Secretary, thus insuring proper reporting of all transactions and insuring uniformity in the coding of each transaction.
> 2. It is recommended that the chief magistrate use the magistrate log each duty day to report all functions performed in the capacity of chief magistrate. Currently, the chief magistrate is

using the magistrate log only on those occasions when the chief magistrate is sitting as a relief magistrate.

3. It is recommended that Part I (the main body) of the log remain in the magistrate's office to be used by the magistrates to answer questions or inquiries.

Combinations of Facts, Conclusions, and Recommendations

Many of the documents you write will combine facts, conclusions, and recommendations. This can be true even in short documents, such as the following brief accident reports:

Accident Reports

Facts: While the tank of Flush Truck No. 1007 was being filled, smoke started coming from under the hood. When the hood was opened, fire broke out in the cab of the truck.

Conclusion: Fire apparently started from shorted wires.

Recommendation: That driver Samuel Kinney not be charged with the accident.

Facts: Truck No. 849 was hit on the right rear wheel by a car backing out of a private driveway. Driver of private vehicle stated he did not see city vehicle.

Conclusion: Driver of private car was at fault.

Recommendation: That driver Mary Booth not be charged with the accident.

The facts, conclusions, and recommendations in the accident reports above were identified for you. See if you can identify each kind of information in the following report on a training program, writing your answer in the margin beside the three paragraphs in each section.

Training Programs for
Electricians and Technicians

1. Electricians: The continuing education, self-instruction program has been used in the Electric Shop for the past three years. Sixteen electricians have completed the program, all with a grade of at least 80%.

   This has been a very successful program. It gives hands-on experience for better understanding of the subject and can be done on the job.

   We should continue with this program. Due to the increase in personnel in the shop, we will need eight additional texts.

2. Technicians: The technicians in the shop have now all completed both the A.C. and the D.C. Electronics programs, all passing with a grade of 80% or better.

   Therefore, they now all have a good basic background in electronics. More training is now needed in the areas of digital electronics, microprocessors, and specialized equipment.

   Each technician should be sent to school on microprocessor fundamentals and applications. We should continue on-the-job training using the microprocessor training course. All technicians should receive specialized training on new equipment such as the Field 160, scanners, and the etching machine.

In each of the two parts of the report, did you find that the first paragraph contained mostly facts, the second mostly conclusions about these facts, and the third recommendations that follow from these conclusions? As you will see in the next chapter on writing reports, most long reports and proposals are composed of a combination of facts, conclusions, and recommendations.

WHERE DO I GET THE INFORMATION MY READER NEEDS?

You may think you will have to do extensive formal research before you write a report, manual, or proposal. This is usually not true, for much of the information you will use in such documents will either come from your training and experience on the job or will be easily obtainable. The goal of this section is to survey the different resources you might use as you gather facts upon which to base your conclusions and recommendations.

Your Knowledge

Gained through training and experience, your own knowledge may well be your best source of information for many reports, manuals, and proposals. If you are in data processing and are reporting to someone on a problem that occurred and the solution you found, you don't need to investigate any further to write your report. If you are in engineering and want to propose that your organization buy new equipment that will process raw materials faster and more efficiently, your familiarity with the equipment and the manufacturing process may well give you the facts you need to support your argument. And if your manager asks you to write a short manual that explains to others how you are able to write monthly progress reports so clearly and concisely, you can rely on your own experience to do it.

Other People

Other people are sometimes an invaluable source of information. And finding out what they know may not be as difficult as you think. Sometimes just observing them is enough. Imagine that you are working on an operations manual for a new piece of computer hardware that your organization plans to use. One way you can develop the manual is to operate the system yourself and then record what you did. But you can also observe others as they operate the same system. And one excellent way to check the instructions in a manual you have developed is to observe others closely as they try to follow it in practice.

At work, you are surrounded by experts in different fields. Often, you can draw on this expertise just by picking up the phone and calling someone. If you are proposing a major public relations campaign for a new product, you can consult your own company engineers about how to describe the product and check with your people in marketing for suggestions about selling strategies. If you need some data for a report, you can likely find someone in the organization who knows where to find it quickly.

Interviews

An interview, in which you ask someone questions for an extended period of time, can be an excellent way of gathering information. But the key to a successful interview is to plan carefully ahead of time, knowing exactly what questions you want to ask. If you are more interested in getting facts, plan to ask lots of *factual* questions, questions that require specific answers. For example,

1. How much will it cost us to buy this new system?
2. What is your gross sales figure so far this month?

3. How many training programs have you conducted over the past year?
4. What do you do in order to delete material from your screen?

Opinion questions, on the other hand, require a more general answer, usually followed by an explanation. They work better when you are after a person's feelings or ideas on a subject. For example,

1. What are the major reasons we should buy this system?
2. How well are you progressing towards your sales goals for the year?
3. How successful do you feel last year's training programs were?
4. What do you think would be the best way to show the operator how to delete material?

When planning an interview, know in advance exactly what goal you want to accomplish. To make sure you have determined this goal, you might frame it as a question.

1. Should our organization purchase this new data processing system?
2. How should our sales goals be revised?
3. What training programs do we need to add, modify, or delete for next year?
4. What is the best way to perform these operations on this computer?

Once you know what you are after, you can then make a list of the questions you want to ask, making sure they are in the approximate order you want to follow in the interview. Even if you want to know someone's opinions about something, it's often best to begin an interview with factual questions, just to make sure the person you are interviewing has focused specifically on the subject. For example, in interviewing a participant of some in-house classes to measure the success of a training program, you might plan to open with a simple factual question such as "What training sessions did you attend last year?"

Begin your interview with a few pleasant comments to put the person you are interviewing at ease. After explaining the goal of your interview, begin asking questions, making sure you have phrased each question as precisely and clearly as possible. Listen closely to the person's answers, not interrupting even if you disagree. Most people don't mind having their answers tape recorded, if you can make the recorder unobtrusive. Even if you are tape recording, it's a good idea to take a few notes, both to make sure you have a written record and to let the person know you are listening closely.

During some interviews, you may find that you will have to alter the sequence in which you have planned to ask questions, because a particular answer may lead more naturally to a question you had planned to ask later or even to one that you had not planned to ask at all. Actually, you will get more information if you go with the flow of the interview, asking questions that fit best at a particular moment, rather than interrupting someone's train of thought with an irrelevant question. After the interview, be sure to follow up with a phone call or thank-you note.

Questionnaires

A questionnaire or survey is another excellent way of gathering information from others, primarily because it allows you to draw on the knowledge of many people efficiently. But the art of constructing a valid and reliable questionnaire is complex and specialized. We're just going to touch on the high points here, primarily for people who may need to use an informal questionnaire occasionally. If you plan to rely on many questionnaires, you should consult more detailed discussions.

Since respondents to a questionnaire can be influenced by their mood at a given moment or their perceptions of the reasons for the survey, most researchers know that they should take the results of a questionnaire with a grain of salt. They know that respondents tend to exaggerate some aspects of their lives, such as income, education, or social status, while minimizing ones that may seem less favorable.

Another problem that writers of questionnaires sometimes have is that either they don't get all the information they want or they get more information than they need. To avoid this, plan your questionnaire carefully. Since a questionnaire is really just an interview on paper, you can approach it in the same way. Make sure your questions are easy to understand, with no ambiguous or unclear wording. And make sure they are easy to answer, with responses that can be checked or numbers that can be chosen. If you want a written response, let respondents know it can be short. Otherwise, many people won't bother to answer. Arrange your questions for maximum ease and convenience, usually beginning with factual questions that can be answered quickly and progressing to more open questions that ask for opinion.

To make sure that people understand the purpose of your questionnaire, begin with an explanation of its purpose, either in a cover letter or preferably at the beginning of the questionnaire itself. And to insure the maximum number of returns, show how people will benefit, either in the short or long run, from answering your questions.

To illustrate these principles, here is a short questionnaire. Remember the flextime situation we discussed in Chapter 1. Imagine that you have been assigned the project of finding out whether such a system would work. To sample employee opinion, you might construct the questionnaire below. Notice how the questionnaire begins with a brief explanation of its goal and a description of how employees will benefit from answering it. Also note that most questions near the beginning are factual, to give the tabulators specific information, and that those toward the end deal more with opinion.

Introduction

We are trying to decide whether to adopt a flextime schedule as a way of improving morale and increasing efficiency. To help us, would you fill out the following questionnaire? Your answers will enable us to make the decision that will benefit the maximum number of employees.

Flextime is a system whereby different employees arrive and leave work at different times. Of course, schedules are staggered so that enough people are always available to do the job.

1. Your name:

2. The department in which you work:

3. Using the job descriptions published in the company's manual, describe your major responsibilities in about 25 words.

If the number of employees in your company were small, say 20 or fewer, you might want to send the questionnaire to everyone. But if the number were larger, you would probably want to save yourself tabulation time by selecting a sample that is representative of the whole. The size of your sample will depend primarily on how much you think the responses of people in the group will vary from each other. The more they will vary, the wider your sample has to be. Ordinarily, 25% of a group will give you a representative sample.

4. If the company were to adopt a flextime system, designate the hours you would prefer by numbering the following from 1 (most preferable) to 5 (least preferable).

   ________ 7:00 a.m. to 4:00 p.m.
   ________ 7:30 a.m. to 4:30 p.m.
   ________ 8:00 a.m. to 5:00 p.m.
   ________ 8:30 a.m. to 5:30 p.m.
   ________ 9:00 a.m. to 6:00 p.m.

5. Assuming that schedules are coordinated so that enough people are always available to meet responsibilities, would flextime increase or decrease efficiency in your department? Please check the correct answer and then give a brief explanation of choice.

   ________ Increase ________ Decrease

6. Would flextime help you coordinate your work and personal life better or not? Please give a short explanation.

7. Do you favor adopting a flextime schedule? Please check one:

   ________ Yes ________ No

8. What additional comments can you make to help us reach the best decision?

To make sure that your sample is truly representative of the whole group, you can use one of the following statistical methods:

1. *Random sampling.* If you are going to rely equally on the opinions of all employees, you can choose a *random sample* by putting all names in a container and choosing some, or by using a table of random numbers, which can be found in a college statistics text or in a reference book on basic research methods.
2. *Systematic sampling.* This method is much like random sampling. The only difference is that you choose your sample systematically, making a list of everyone you want to survey and then choosing every *n*th name on the list.
3. *Stratified random sampling.* If you plan to rely more heavily on the opinions of some rather than others in your group or if you want to see how different groups respond, then you will need to divide employees into appropriate subgroups and then sample each group either randomly or systematically. For example, you might divide your sample up into plant, clerical, and management personnel.

You can tell by now that the whole area of sampling is a very complex one. If you want to make sure that the data you collect from a questionnaire is as reliable as possible, consult a sampling statistician.

Printed Materials

Printed materials are another source of information. The major types you might consult are the following:

1. *Your organization's files and publications.* How much have our gross sales increased in the last five years? When did we first start offering that service and how has it changed? What was our marketing strategy when we first offered that product? When did we first introduce that policy and how did employees react then? Such historical questions can frequently be answered from your own organization's files—copies of surveys, reports, proposals, manuals, and company publications such as newsletters, bulletins, brochures, and pamphlets.
2. *General reference works.* For almost every area of research, a general guide has been published. If your question is a factual or statistical one (When were diamonds first mined in Africa? What is the population of the city of Chicago? What is the latest information on the conflict in . . . ?), you might consult the appropriate annual volume of the following compilations:

- *The World Almanac and Book of Facts*. New York: Newspaper Enterprise Assn.
- *Statistical Abstract of the United States*. Washington, D.C.: Government Printing Office.
- *Facts on File*. New York: Facts on File.

If your question is about business, you might check one of the following:

- *Where to Find Business Information: A Worldwide Guide for Everyone Who Needs the Answers to Business Questions*. New York: John Wiley, 1979.
- Paul Wasserman, ed., *Encyclopedia of Business Information Sources*, 3rd ed. Detroit: Gale Research, 1976.

Just about every field you can think of, from art to women's studies, has similar general reference works. They are frequently a good starting place for research.

3. *Periodical indexes*. If you think others might have published articles on your subject, you might check the appropriate annual volume of such periodical indexes as:
   - *Business Periodicals Index*. New York: H. W. Wilson.
   - *New York Times Index*. New York: New York Times.
   - *Readers' Guide to Periodical Literature*. New York: H. W. Wilson.
   - Eugene Garfield, ed., *Science Citation Index*. Philadelphia: Institute for Scientific Information, 1982.

4. *U.S. government publications*. The federal government has published guides, pamphlets, illustrations, and studies on an amazing number of subjects. To see whether they have published anything on your subject, consult:
   - *Guide to U.S. Government Publications*. McLean, Va.: Documents Index, 1973-Present.
   - Linden Pohle. *A Guide to Popular Government Publications*. Littleton, Colo.: Libraries Unlimited, 1972.

5. *Computerized data sources*. If you have a computer equipped with the appropriate software and a modem (to connect your computer by phone with others), you can gain access to an ever-increasing number of sources of information. There are now data bases that include specialized information on many subjects. The best-known one is KNOWLEDGE INDEX, a service of DIALOG information systems (a subsidiary of Lockheed Corporation). This data base contains a variety of kinds of information such as:
   - business information, including reports on earnings, latest mergers, management changes, as well as access to articles

in such journals as *Business Week*, *Forbes*, and *Harvard Business Review*;

- technical information on computers, electronics, physics, and engineering;
- medical and psychological information;
- current affairs, with indexes to *The New York Times* and *The Washington Post*, among other newspapers; and
- education information, including special education, computer assisted instruction, etc.

HOW DO I DOCUMENT THE INFORMATION I HAVE COLLECTED?

When you use someone else's words, facts, or ideas, you will have to document them by citing your sources. Through documentation, you acknowledge your indebtedness to someone else and tell your reader how to locate the information. Ordinarily, you should document information taken from interviews, surveys, and printed sources.

As you probably know, the subject of documentation is a complex one, primarily because there are so many different documentation styles. But unless you write complex technical or research reports, you can document your sources fairly easily. Just choose a method that best suits your purposes and then use it logically and consistently. I'm going to suggest that you adopt the following simple system[1], which can be used in business, economics, and other social sciences. It should suffice for most of the functional documents you write.

What to Tell Your Reader

In a citation, you are simply telling your reader how to find the same information you did. In general, give the following information: author, title, place, publisher, date, and page numbers. Here is the particular pattern to follow when writing citations for:

Books

Moore, Wilbert E., *The Conduct of a Corporation* (New York: Random House, 1962) 73.

Articles in Journals

Fielden, John, "What Do You Mean I Can't Write?" *Harvard Business Review* 42 (1964) 144–152.

[1]Adapted from Joseph Gibaldi and Walter S. Achtert, *MLA Handbook for Writers of Research Papers*, 2nd ed. (New York: Modern Language Association, 1984) 136–83.

Articles in Collections

Gieselman, Robert D., "Research in Business Communication: The State of the Art." *Teaching Business Writing*, ed. Jeanne W. Halpern (Urbana-Champaign, Ill: American Business Communication Association, 1983) 98–112.

Articles from Reference Works

"Advertising as a Career," *The Encyclopedia of Careers and Vocational Guidance*, ed. William E. Hopke (Chicago: J. G. Berguson, 1981) 48–64.

Unpublished Works

Donati, James, "The Office of the Future." Report to Personnel Department (New York: ABCA Corporation, April 19, 1986).

Interviews

Johnson, Robert, Operations Manager, Singer Corporation, personal interview, Clarkton, Ohio, January 12, 1986.

If you have to cite another kind of source, such as a video tape, computer disk, or speech, follow the basic pattern above of author, title, place, publisher, and date.

Where to Put Your Citation

If your document contains few references, you can make them immediately useful to readers by citing them as soon as they are used in your text rather than putting them in footnotes or endnotes at the end of the page or document. For example, in a proposal for a communications system, you might say, "Wilbert E. Moore feels that while the goal of communications is always shared values, it is not always shared information [*The Conduct of a Corporation* (New York: Random House, 1972) 73]."

But if you have a number of references in a document or if full reference information would interrupt the flow of your ideas too much, you can put a brief reference to your source in the text like this: after the information you have taken from a source, just enter the author's name and the page numbers, if they will not be in the list of references. Thus, if you were referring to the book listed above, you might say, "One authority on communication feels that while the goal of communications is always shared values, it is not always shared information (Moore 73)." Then list all your citations in an alphabetical list of references at the end of your document, so your readers can refer to it if they need more information.

You will find that various disciplines have slightly different ways of inserting citations in the text, some citing author and page while others number all references and cite this number within the text. If you need more help with documentation, you should check a guide to research and documentation in your field.

HOW DO I ORGANIZE MY INFORMATION?

Rarely can you present readers with raw information. In order to accomplish your goal, whether it's to inform in a report, persuade in a proposal, or instruct in a manual, you've got to find some way to organize information for your readers. If your document is fairly short, you may be able to use one of the organizing methods we discussed in Chapter 3—jot-listing, nutshelling, or reader questioning. For example, if you are writing a brief status report describing what you accomplished during the last month, simply jotting down your main points will be enough of an organizational plan. And an excellent way to organize a procedure for a manual is to ask yourself what questions your reader would have about the procedure.

But often your report, manual, or proposal will be such an extensive one that you will need to represent it to yourself in a more detailed plan. One way to do this is to use an outline. Outlining is simply a way of listing your points for a document and distinguishing major from minor ones with symbols.

The Number–Letter Outline

In school, you probably learned the *number–letter outline*, an outline that begins with a statement of your major goal and then uses Roman numerals for major points, capital letters for next most important, then Arabic numerals, lower case letters, and so on. You'll remember that this system looks like this:

```
Goal:
 I. First-degree head
    A. Second-degree head (less important)
       1. Third-degree head (less important yet)
II. First-degree head again, etc.
```

This system is especially helpful when you are outlining a particularly detailed document and need to distinguish among various levels of subordinate points. An outline of part of the first section of this book might look like this.

```
Goal: To teach people how to write effectively in
      on-the-job situations.
 I. The Writing Process
    A. The Writing Situation
       1. Group Report for Governor
       2. Group Revision of Memo
```

```
II. Analysis of Writing Situation
    A. Goals
        1. Three-Mile Island Memo
        2. Obstacles to Clarifying Goals
        3. How to Clarify Goals
    B. Readers . . .
```

The Number–Decimal Outline

Another kind of outline, called the *number–decimal outline*, is often used in documents written on the job, especially if they are written by technical writers such as engineers. This system follows the same logic as the number–letter outline, but uses numbers followed by decimals to distinguish among points.

```
Goal:
1.0 First-degree head
    1.1 Second-degree head
        1.1.1 Third-degree head
        1.1.2 Third-degree head
2.0 First-degree head, etc.
```

With this outline system, the outline of this book above would look like this.

```
Goal: To teach people how to write effectively in
      on-the-job situations.
1.0 The Writing Process
    1.1 The Writing Situation
        1.1.1 Group Report for Governor
        1.1.2 Group Revision of Memo
2.0 Analysis of Writing Situation
    2.1 Goals
        2.1.1 Three-Mile Island Memo
        2.1.2 Obstacles to Clarifying Goals
        2.1.3 How to Clarify Goals
2.2 Readers
```

A number–decimal outline is often incorporated into the final draft of a technical report, so its symbols serve as actual headings in the text.

Problems With These Outline Methods

Outline methods such as these can be helpful tools in organizing a long document. But they have their drawbacks. First, the methods are so intricate that they tempt some writers to try for too detailed an outline too early in their writing process. Later, sticking to this outline too closely may force them to filter out important ideas that occur as they write. It's best to begin with an informal outline as a guide to a project and then to use the detailed outline later on as a way of checking to make sure your document is logically organized.

The other problem with these methods, especially the number–decimal outline, is that some writers get so concerned about whether they are using the right symbols that they forget that the outline is just a tool to organize a document. I could produce the same outline of the first part of this book, for instance, by using another set of symbols.

```
Goal: To teach people how to write effectively in
      on-the-job situations.
The Writing Process
--The Writing Situation
   • Group Report for Governor
   • Group Revision of Memo
Analysis of Writing Situation
--Goals
   • Three-Mile Island Memo
   • Obstacles to Clarifying Goals
   • How to Clarify Goals
--Readers
```

It's not necessary to use any particular set of symbols in outlining a document. What's important is to find some way of distinguishing among major and minor points. Good writers use the symbols that work best for them. You'll learn to do the same.

Tree-Diagramming

Some writers prefer a more graphic way of outlining longer documents called tree-diagramming. A tree-diagram is an organizational chart of your document, in which you locate your most inclusive ideas at the top of your tree and then divide them at successively lower levels. A three-level tree diagram of the first section of this book would look like this.

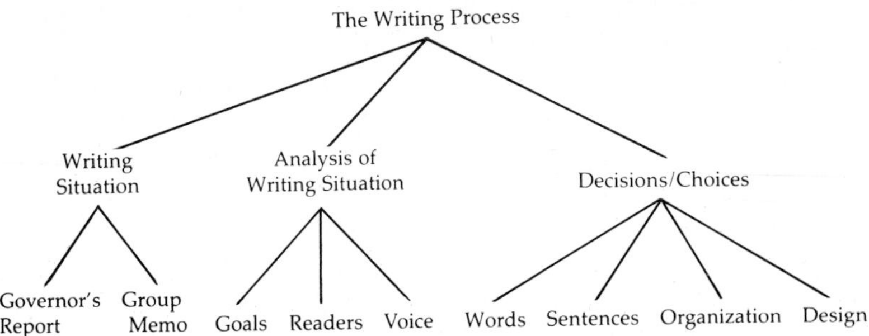

The advantage of a tree diagram over an outline is that it enables you to visualize relationships among ideas at a glance, since ideas of equal importance are on the same level.

As we talk about writing particular kinds of documents in the following chapters, you'll see how to use these methods of outlining. You'll realize that any method is just a tool to guide your thinking. In the earlier stages of developing a document, your best guide is a short outline that you can change as you develop your ideas and revise your document. After your document is written, a more detailed outline can help you visualize its structure to make sure that it is clear and logical.

SUMMARY

In this chapter, we've discussed how to prepare to write a long document such as a report, manual, or proposal. First identify your goal—to tell someone something you know in a report, to convince them to do something in a proposal, or to show them how to do something in a manual. Then identify your readers and analyze their needs, not an easy job when your document is going to a large number of people. After this, decide what kind of information your readers need, locate this information through research, document it, and begin to organize it with an outline.

APPLICATIONS

1. The following two paragraphs were taken from a report on a state welfare system. Determine whether the individual sentences in each are statements of facts, conclusions, or recommendations.

   To carry out these responsibilities, the bureau monitors local activities, holding ten administrative reviews per year and visiting each local office at least once. However, the department's view of local activities is fragmented. No central organizational unit coordinates findings to assess the overall performance of individual agencies or of the system. Moreover, the bureau does not exert sufficient influence to ensure that management problems are resolved, and little direction is provided to local agencies for the reduction of fraud and abuse. A central unit should be created as soon as possible to assess overall performance and make the changes needed.

The geographically dispersed nature of the welfare system requires clearly defined delegation of responsibility and an organizational structure that enhances system-wide communication and consistent administration. The bureau has created regional offices to increase frequency of contact with the 124 local welfare agencies and to improve response to local needs. Approximately half of the department's staff is located in these offices. In order to improve the efficiency and effectiveness of regional staff, the bureau must define the authority of regional directors and clarify the relationship between regional staff and the central office program divisions.

2. You have been asked to write a short report that briefs top management in your organization on one of the following topics. List eight to ten current sources of information you would use, including people you might interview and surveys you might do. When you list printed materials, use the documentation form suggested in this chapter.
   - stresses experienced by women in the workplace and ways to alleviate them
   - recent developments in technology to make offices more efficient
   - ways to train managers in effective oral communication
   - stock ownership plans for employees
   - performance appraisal systems

3. Your company, which relies heavily on oil for manufacturing purposes, is trying to decide whether to locate a plant in a Middle Eastern country to be closer to sources of oil. You are a member of a group of people assigned to do feasibility studies on a number of Middle Eastern countries. Choose a country that might be a possible site for your plant and draw up a research plan you would follow to write a feasibility report. List the topics you would cover in such a report and the sources, printed and otherwise, you might rely on in such a study. Then do a brief outline of the report.

4. A friend of yours has been approached about becoming the local dealer for a particular make of foreign car. He has asked you to find out whether he should do it or not. List five printed sources you would use in your research.

CHAPTER

9

Designing Long Documents

Document design is the art of formatting or laying out documents so readers can understand them easily. This chapter will show you how to design long documents effectively.

People will read the long documents you write in different ways. A few may pore over every word of a report, proposal, or manual, checking facts and evaluating conclusions. Others will read carefully but quickly, making sure they understand your recommendations and conclusions in a report, your request and the major reasons for it in a proposal, and the steps they should follow in a manual. Still others will read even more quickly, skimming for main ideas in summaries, lists, and lead sentences.

How can you help so many different kinds of readers understand your documents quickly and easily? The answer is to design them carefully, using the devices suggested at the end of Chapter 3. There, you remember, we talked about three groups of devices—*separators*, *enumerators*, and *illustrators*:

1. Separators
   a. Headings—center, side-bar, and run-in's
   b. Short paragraphs
   c. White space between paragraphs
   d. Parallels
   e. Different typefaces
2. Enumerators
   a. Numbers
   b. Letters
   c. Bullets

3. Illustrators
   a. Tables
   b. Charts
   c. Graphs

In this chapter, you'll learn how to use these devices to design long documents.

SEPARATORS

As the name suggests, separators are used to *separate* important pieces of information. Headings, which function to outline a document for your readers, are a good example. Use *center heads* to separate the major sections of a report, proposal, or manual. Then if you want to divide one of these sections further, you can use second degree headings, called *side-bar heads*. Finally, for your third category of information, use *run-in-heads*. Here, for instance, is the way you might separate the parts of a discussion in a proposal.

Discussion (center head)

Alternative 1: (side-bar head) This program provides for complete coverage of the following people:

Hospital patients not covered (run-in-head) by any other program, excluding Medicaid.

Hospital patients covered by Medicaid, if they receive less than. . . .

Convalescent-home patients who are. . . .

These three types of headings will cover the major divisions you have to make in a report.

The other ways to separate information—short paragraphs, white space, parallels, and different typefaces—are more familiar to you. See if you can identify how the writer of the following discussion of evaluation programs uses them all:

Evaluation Questions

Did the program accomplish its purpose?

Did the program operate as it was supposed to?

Were all outcomes observed attributable to the program?

ENUMERATORS

In addition to breaking up information the way separators do, enumerators often arrange it in a certain order. In a manual, for instance, you could enumerate steps to be followed by numbering them, as this writer does.

```
To convert a TR-80 system, do the following:
1. Pull old program out of . . . .
2. Be sure that old program is completely . . . .
3. Etc.
```

You could just as easily, of course, use letters to enumerate. And if you simply want to highlight information, without arranging it in a particular order, you can use bullets. For example, part of a document proposing the creation of a new department in a bank might look like this.

```
Our major objectives in this departmental shift will
be to—

• Appeal to the upper-income customer
• Offer new products
```

Look again at the excerpt we used before to illustrate separators, and you'll see how bullets can further separate and highlight particular items:

```
                Evaluation Questions

• Did the program accomplish its purpose?
• Did the program operate as it was supposed to?
• Were all outcomes observed attributable to the
  program?
```

ILLUSTRATORS

Illustrators, such as tables, charts, and graphs, enable you to present complicated facts simply and abstract ideas concretely. Since illustrators are commonly called "graphics" in discussions of document design, I am going to use this term throughout the rest of this chapter. In it, you will learn when to use graphics in long documents, which graphic will best suit your needs, and what principles to follow in using graphics.

There was a time when graphics were primarily the province of technical editors and designers. People in organizations wrote reports, proposals, and manuals, and then depended on editorial departments to add appropriate graphics. But with the proliferation of low-cost, easy-to-use graphics software for use on computers, any writer can produce professional-looking tables, charts, and graphs. But to use such software effectively, you will need to know what graphics are available and when to use a particular type. And even if you don't actually produce your own graphics, you will have to know enough about them to be able to work with the design people in your organization who do.

When Should I Use a Graphic?

Graphics make information, especially numerical information, easier for readers to understand and remember. Therefore, you should consider using a graphic any time you want to highlight some figures, present some complicated information compactly, or illustrate a difficult concept. For instance, the author of a newspaper article describing changes in the New York Stock Exchange for a particular day could have said that "while the stock of 444 companies increased in value, that of 429 remained unchanged, and that of 1,229 decreased in value." If the writer had done this, you would have understood the figures, although they wouldn't have had much impact. Instead, the writer chose to help you visualize the changes with the simple bar graph shown here.

MARKET PROFILE
New York Stock Exchange issues traded
Tuesday, April 1, 19--

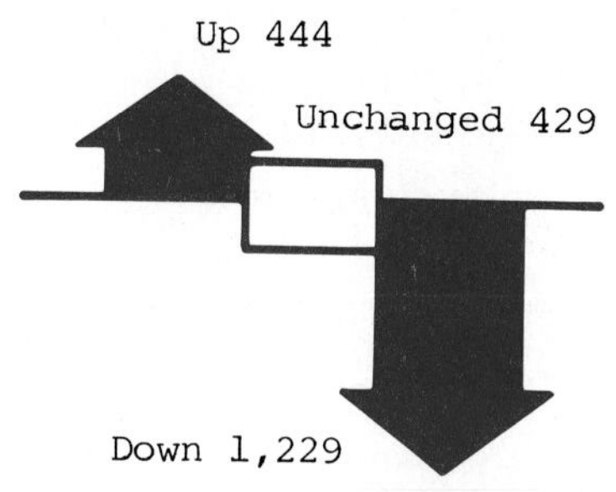

N.Y.S.E. Index	134.86	-1.85
S. & P. Comp.	235.14	-3.76
Dow Jones Ind.	1,790.11	-28.50

Volume	
N.Y.S.E.	167.4 million shares
N.Y.S.E. Comp.	200.6 million shares

Source: New York Stock Exchange.

By giving you a visual context for figures, this graphic helps you understand and remember them easily.

What Kind of Graphic Should I Use?

This will depend on the kind of data you are presenting and what you want to accomplish with it. To help you understand how to use various kinds of graphics, I'm going to ask you to imagine the following situation in which you have to write a long report. We'll then talk about how you could use different kinds of graphics at various places in the report.

A Writing Situation

Most state governments have special evaluation and review groups, whose job is to examine other state agencies to make sure they are operating efficiently. These groups are composed of people from a variety of backgrounds, including specialists in law, statistics, human relations, data processing, economics, and journalism, among others. Imagine that you are a member of such a group. Your group's current assignment is to evaluate the operations of the central motor pool for the state, the agency responsible for purchasing, maintaining, and assigning state-owned vehicles to government employees who need them for travel. You have been asked to write a report in which you describe the motor pool and its activities, analyze the problems you find, and recommend solutions.[1]

Your job is a big one, so it takes you several months just to study the agency and collect information. In your research, you conduct a written survey of both employees of the motor pool and users of the automobiles; you interview a selected number of employees and users; and you study stacks of records and reports. Finally, you are ready to write a draft of your report. On the next few pages are some of the graphics you might plan to use in this report. As you examine them, note two things. First, each graphic is specifically referred to in the report itself. Thus, it is integrated into the discussion, not just stuck in for ornamentation. Secondly, note that the source for the data in the graphic is given just below it.

Tables are used to present large quantities of information in compact form, especially when that information involves figures. As you describe the motor pool and its activities in the first chapter of your report, you might use a table to compare the use of motor pool vehicles with that of other kinds of vehicles. Your discussion and the accompanying table might look like this.

```
General purpose transportation cost $13.9 million in
fiscal 19--. Mileage and costs for each category of
vehicle use are shown in Table 1.
```

[1]Data and discussion in the following examples have been adapted from "Management and Use of State-Owned Motor Vehicles," a report written by the Joint Legislative Audit and Review Commission for The Virginia General Assembly, July 1979.

Table 1
PASSENGER VEHICLE TRAVEL
Fiscal Year 19--

Source	Mileage	Cost
Privately owned vehicles	52,853,865	$7,829,223
Motor pool vehicles	40,320,852	5,732,003
University owned vehicles	2,723,683	341,678
Other agencies	878,958	--
Total	96,777,358	$13,902,904

Source: Compiled from the records of the agencies cited.

A table is an explicit way to present facts and figures that your readers may have to look up or recall later. When you construct a table, there are a number of things you can do to help readers understand information quickly. First, arrange figures in columns for easy comparison and, if possible, construct your table so it can be scanned vertically rather than horizontally. In addition, round numbers off to not more than two digits after the decimal point. Most readers won't need and certainly won't be able to remember more precise figures. Also, provide column totals when you can.

Charts are not as explicit or precise as tables, but they do picture data in a more concrete way. Three commonly used types of charts are *flow, organizational,* and *pie charts.*

Flow charts are used to depict the steps or stages in a process. In your description of the activities of the motor pool in your first chapter, you might use the flow chart on the next page to explain the process by which a car is obtained from its central garage.

> The process by which users obtain cars from the motor pool is a straightforward one, as Figure 1 demonstrates.

Organizational charts are used to depict the structure of an organization. If you wanted to describe the way the motor pool is administered in your first chapter, you might use an organizational chart in your discussion.

> Since 19--, the motor pool has been administered under the direction of a motor pool committee appointed by the governor (Figure 2). The committee membership consists of the following people: the Commissioner of the Department of Highways and Transportation (Chairman); the Secretary of Administration and Finance; the Director of the Department of Planning and Budget; the Commissioner of the Division of Motor Vehicles; and the Commissioner of the State Health Department.

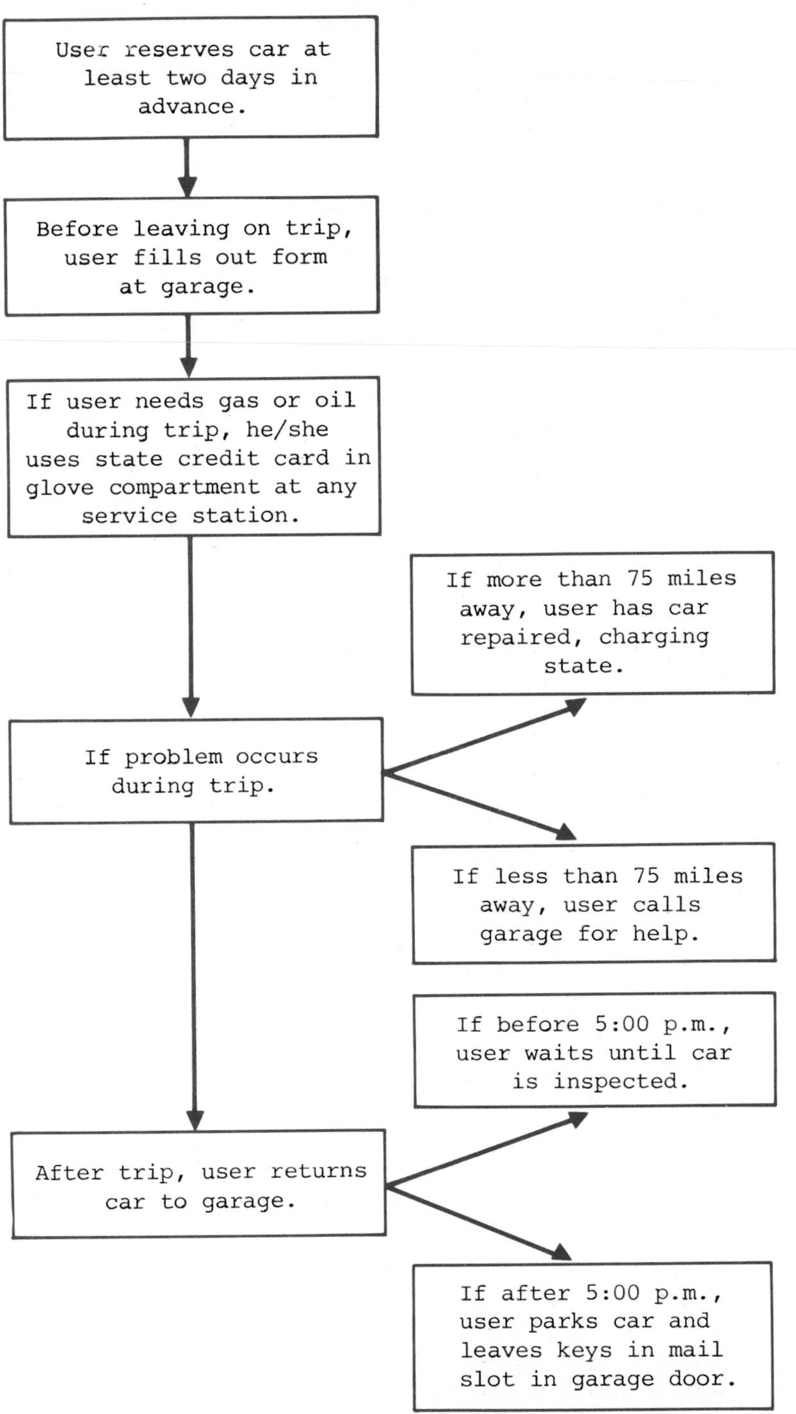
Figure 1
HOW TO OBTAIN, USE, AND RETURN MOTOR POOL VEHICLES
User reserves car at least two days in advance.
Before leaving on trip, user fills out form at garage.
If user needs gas or oil during trip, he/she uses state credit card in glove compartment at any service station.
If more than 75 miles away, user has car repaired, charging state.
If problem occurs during trip.
If less than 75 miles away, user calls garage for help.
If before 5:00 p.m., user waits until car is inspected.
After trip, user returns car to garage.
If after 5:00 p.m., user parks car and leaves keys in mail slot in garage door.

Figure 2

ORGANIZATION FOR STATE-OWNED VEHICLE MANAGEMENT

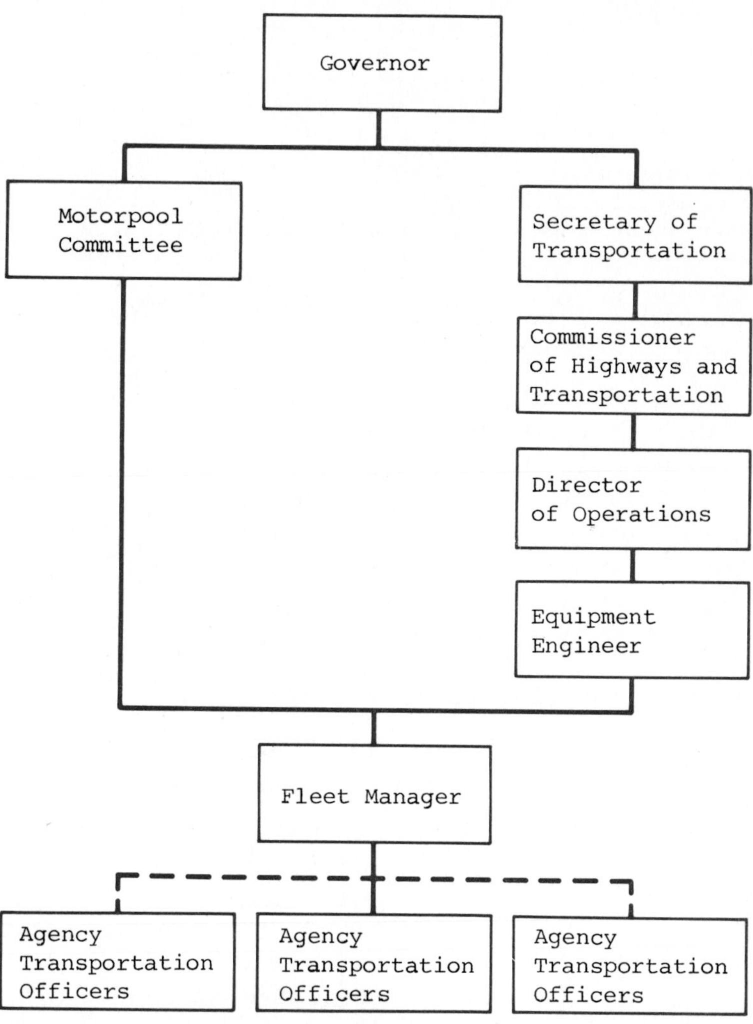

Source: Review investigation.

A full-time fleet manager coordinates fleet operations and reports to the Motor Pool Committee as well as to appropriate people in the Division of Transportation. The fleet manager reviews agency requests for vehicle assignments, makes recommendations to the Motor Pool Committee, and reviews fleet operating costs.

Each State agency has a transportation officer who is the liaison between the agency and the motor pool. In general, transportation officers approve vehicle requests, review agency travel needs, and monitor the use of assigned vehicles.

Pie charts, which are used to show relationships of parts, are especially useful for presenting numerical concepts simply and dramatically. In your report on the motor pool, you might use a simple pie chart to illustrate how economically vehicles had been used:

To measure how economically motor pool vehicles were used during the last year, we compared the costs of operating them with the costs of reimbursing employees if they had used their own cars. During this fiscal year, operating costs of 465 vehicles exceeded the reimbursement payments that would have been required if private vehicles had been used (Figure 3).

Figure 3

UTILIZATION OF MOTOR POOL VEHICLES
Fiscal Year 19--

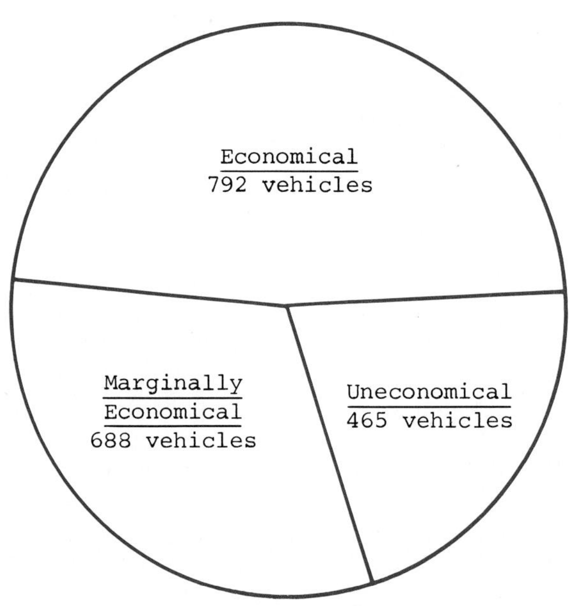

Source: Compiled from central garage records.

If you want to emphasize the separate parts depicted in a pie chart, you can leave space between the parts and draw them with a three-dimensional effect. You could also shade one part to make it stand out. If you did all these things, Figure 4 shows the way the chart on page 207 would now look.

Figure 4

UTILIZATION OF MOTOR POOL VEHICLES
Fiscal Year 19--

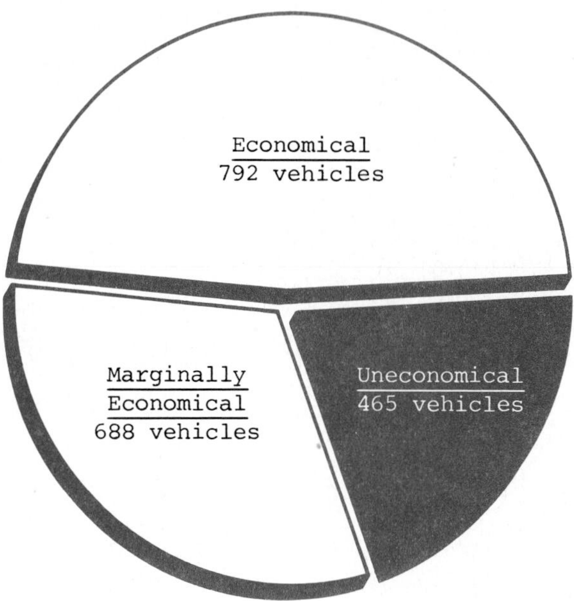

Source: Compiled from motor pool records.

The advantage of a pie chart is that it is so readily understood by your readers. But its disadvantage is that it cannot present very precise figures. If you want to do this, you will have to use a graph.

Graphs can be drawn with bars, lines, or pictures. *Bar graphs* can be used to present figures just as tables can, but their advantage over tables is that they are more concrete and graphic. Look at the following table, for example, which you might use in your report to show the percentage of mechanical problems that occurred to motor pool vehicles.

Respondents to our survey indicate that most Motor Pool vehicles provide dependable transportation. As the following table shows, engines and then air conditioning/heating systems were in most need of repair.

Table 2
MOTOR POOL VEHICLE PROBLEMS
(In Percentages)

Equipment	Never a Problem	Occasional Problem	Constant Problem
Lights	84%	15%	1%
Tires	59	37	4
Brakes	66	29	5
Steering	73	24	3
Engine	38	44	18
AC/Heating	41	39	20

Source: Motor pool records.

But because the table contains so many statistics, the data indicating that engines and AC/heating systems were most in need of repair don't stand out the way they would in a bar graph like Figure 5 on the next page.

Bar graphs are used to show size or magnitude of data at separate intervals. To show the number of miles traveled in motor pool vehicles at various times, for instance, you could use a bar graph. Note how the graph on the top of page 211 pictures the data at three different points in time.

In 19--, when the motor pool was first created, travel in its vehicles was low compared to that in privately owned vehicles (Figure 6). Five years later, in 19--, travel in both privately owned and motor pool vehicles had increased at about the same rate. But by 19--, travel in privately owned vehicles had decreased because of executive orders to reduce energy consumption by state agencies. This reduction was partially offset by increased travel in motor pool vehicles.

But to show a trend extending over a period of time rather than data at particular times, you would probably use a *line graph* rather than a bar graph. If, for instance, you wanted to depict the rising trend in travel in motor pool vehicles showed by the shaded parts of the vertical bars above, you would use a line graph like Figure 7 on the bottom of page 211.

Figure 5

INCIDENCE OF MAJOR REPAIR PROBLEMS

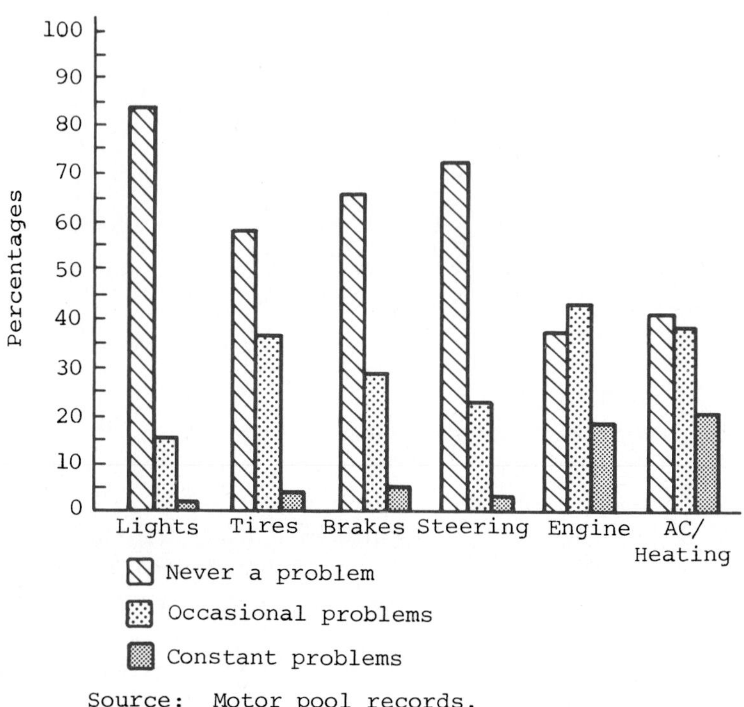

Source: Motor pool records.

Figure 7 indicates that travel in motor pool vehicles has increased steadily since 19--. In 19--, total mileage traveled was 20.2 million miles; by 19--, the total mileage had more than doubled, to 44.8 million miles.

You can even show more than one trend in the same line graph. On page 212, for example, are the trends in travel for privately owned versus motor pool vehicles, based on the data in the bar graph at the top of page 211. If there is any chance of confusion, you can use different kinds of lines (broken versus unbroken) or different kinds of shadings.

While travel in motor pool vehicles has more than doubled from 19-- to 19--, that in privately owned vehicles has fallen (see Figure 8).

When constructing line graphs, you need to be careful not to distort your data, either by starting your vertical axis at a number

Figure 6

TRAVEL IN MOTOR POOL AND PRIVATE VEHICLES
AT THREE DIFFERENT TIMES

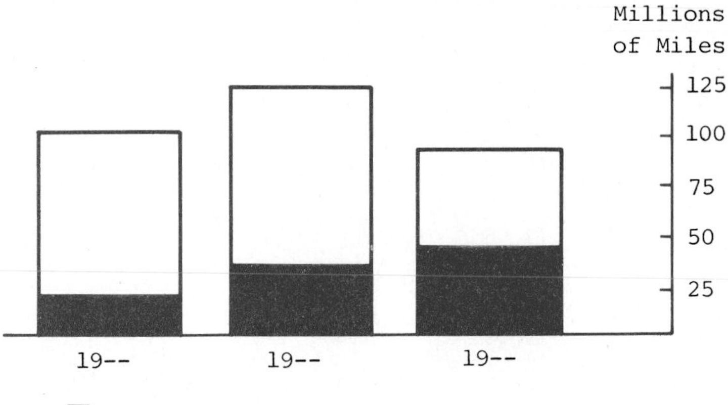

Source: Team investigations.

Figure

TRENDS IN TRAVEL IN STATE-OWNED VEHICLES
19-- to 19--

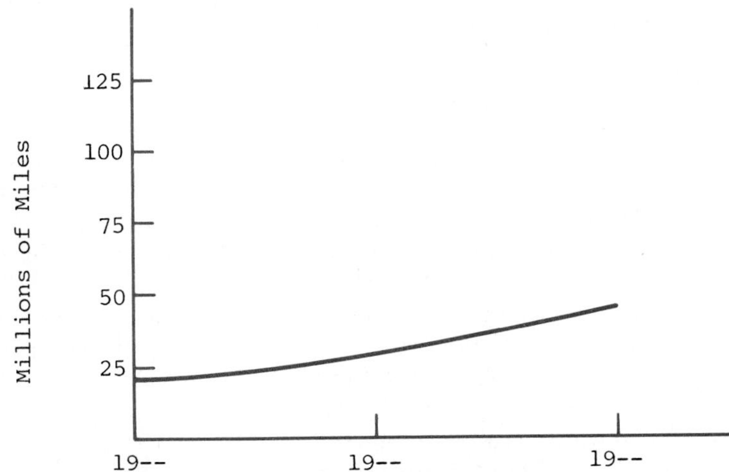

Source: Team investigations.

Figure 8

TRENDS IN TRAVEL OF STATE-OWNED AND PRIVATELY OWNED VEHICLES 19-- to 19--

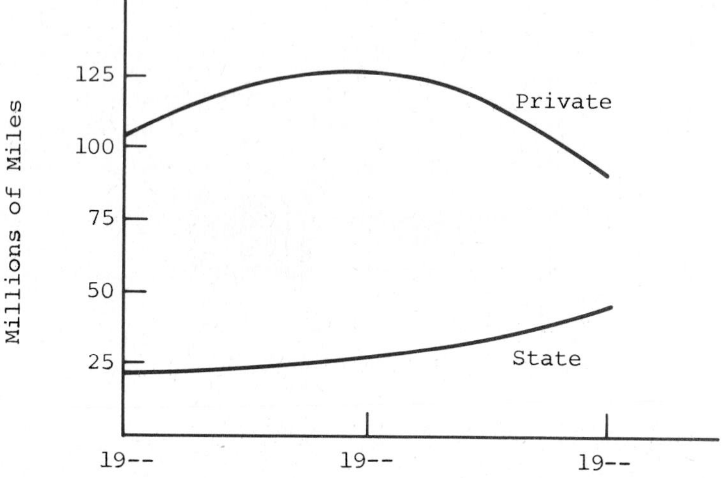

Source: Team investigations.

other than zero or by expanding or contracting the vertical or horizontal scale. Figure 9, for instance, is an original line graph showing how much average costs of maintaining motor pool vehicles increase with vehicle age. You can see that from the very first year of motor pool ownership, there is some cost for vehicle repair, but that this cost remains relatively low until the fifth year, when it rises sharply.

You could legitimately conclude from such data that vehicles don't need to be replaced for at least four years, but that sometime fairly soon after that it may be more economical to buy new vehicles than to repair old ones. But if you started the dollar amounts at $100 instead of zero to save space, as in Figure 9(a), you would make it appear that there were no vehicle repairs for the first two years, which is not true. This might not change your conclusion, but it would certainly mislead readers about total maintenance costs.

And if you were to contract the vertical or horizontal scale of the graph, you would make it appear that the repair rates rose either much less or much more dramatically than they really did. In Figure 9(b) (page 214), for example, note how much less dramatic the rise in costs looks if the vertical scale is contracted.

Figure 9

COSTS OF REPAIRING VEHICLES

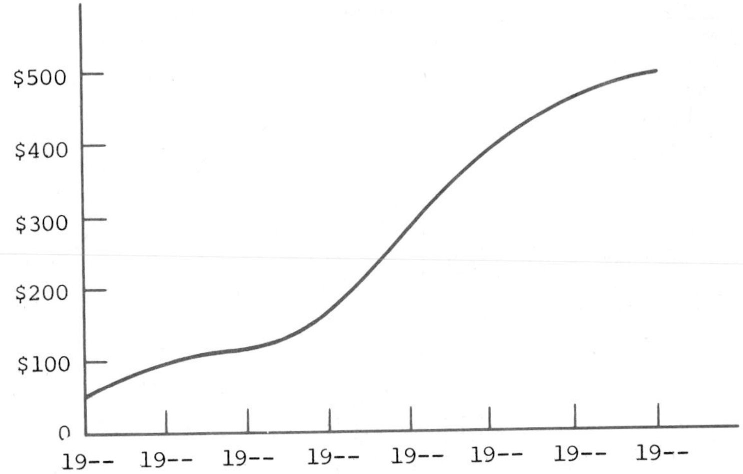

Source: Team investigations.

Figure 9(a)

COSTS OF REPAIRING VEHICLES

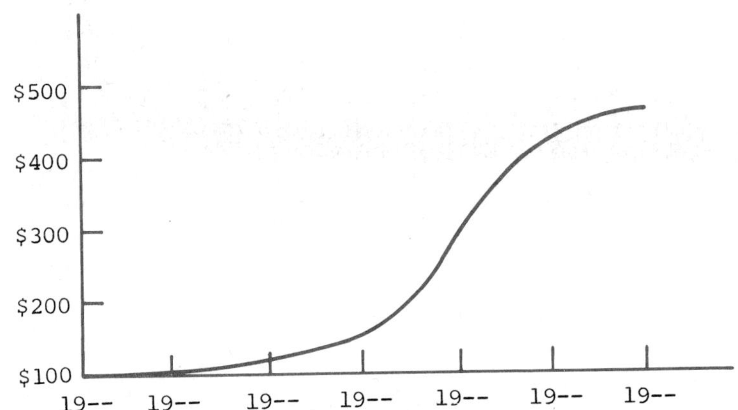

Source: Team investigations.

Figure 9(b)

COSTS OF REPAIRING VEHICLES

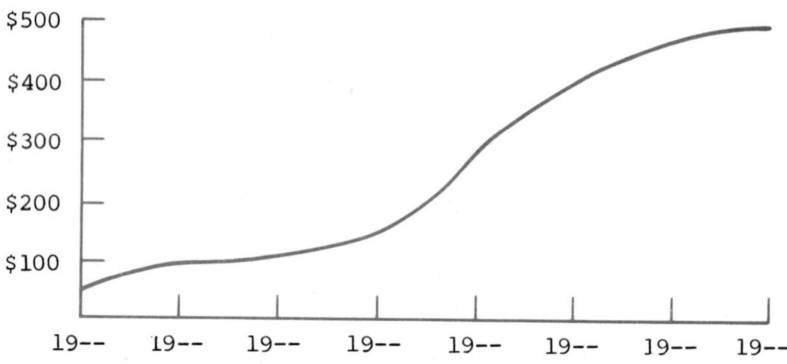

Source: Team investigations.

The graphs we've talked about so far are nonrepresentational; that is, they show statistical information about a particular subject very clearly, but the actual subject is usually read in a heading. A *pictorial graph* also gives statistical information, but it attempts to overcome the lack of appeal of line and bar graphs by representing the actual subject of the discussion. Here is an example of a pictorial graph.

Suppose you had discovered in your research that passenger cars from the motor pool were used much more heavily at certain times of the year than others. You could depict this in a bar graph, using bars to represent seasons or months. But since your finding could have important implications (for instance, that maintenance be scheduled during times of light use, or that idle cars could perhaps be rented to a municipality or county during periods of light use), you decide to depict it dramatically in a pictorial graph. Such a graph might look like the one on page 215.

Careful study of use records for the past five years has revealed that passenger vehicles are used much more heavily during the fall (September through November) and spring (March through April). Since use during the winter and summer is so light (Figure 10), we recommend that maintenance work be scheduled during this period. We also recommend that consideration be given to renting surplus vehicles during this period to a nearby municipality or county in order to use vehicles most economically.

Figure 10

SEASONAL UTILIZATION OF MOTOR POOL VEHICLES

Each car represents 1 million miles traveled.

Source: Vehicle use records from motor pool.

Because their symbols, called isotypes by their originator, Otto Neurath, are so representational, pictorial graphs can have strong visual impact. They are also readily understood by people irrespective of language or cultural barriers.

But when you use them, you'll need to be sure that the symbols are self-explanatory and have a strong association with what they represent. Also, avoid symbols that might go out of date. And when you depict differences in quantity, you must do it by adding more symbols (as I did above) rather than making the isotypes larger or smaller. Research has shown that readers quickly get confused by differences in size.

We've discussed the major graphics you'll probably use in the long documents you write. There are others, such as line drawings, maps, and even photographs. But since these graphics require specialized training to produce, you should consult a design specialist if you need to use them.

What Are Some of the Basic Design Principles I Should Follow When Using Graphics?

The basic principles to follow when constructing or approving graphics are simple and commonsensical. Most important, keep your graphics appropriate to your readers. There's no use constructing elaborate graphs for general readers who are not used to interpreting them. And by all means, keep graphics as simple as possible, even if you have to omit some less important data or give approximate figures. As one graphics specialist puts it, "To remember simplified pictures is better than to forget accurate figures."

Also, give each graphic an appropriate number (Figure 1 or Table 1) and title so your readers will understand its function. In addition, give the source of the data you are depicting. Remember also that a graphic is not an ornament for your document; rather, it is an integral element that should help to present information. Therefore, place your graphics as close to the information they depict as possible. (Don't put them all at the end of a document, so your readers constantly have to flip back and forth.) And integrate the graphic into your text by using it in some way—summarize its data if that is appropriate, refer to its most important figures, explain it, etc.

Finally, don't under- or overuse graphics. In the past, writers of long documents have sometimes not used enough graphics, because it took so much trouble to have them produced. With the advent of word processing programs that can produce professional-looking graphics at the press of a few keys, you may be tempted to go to the opposite extreme and use too many. The best way to avoid using too few or too many graphics is to think of them not as ornaments, but as simply another tool that you can use to present information clearly and effectively.

SUMMARY

In order to help people read your long documents with ease,

- use separators such as headings, short paragraphs, white space, parallels, and different typefaces
- enumerators such as numbers, letters, and bullets
- illustrators such as tables, charts, and graphs

APPLICATIONS

1. Your organization is in the process of providing life insurance for its management. To decide on an appropriate premium to charge, the life insurance company needs to know the age ranges of managers. The company doesn't need to know the exact ages of everyone, but would like the information in five-year increments, that is, how many people in a given category are 21–25, 26–30, 31–35, etc. You have been given the task of providing them with this information.

After checking personnel records, you find the following ages for people in different categories.

- Eight top-level managers, with ages of 48, 53, 64, 67, 49, 57, 53, and 61.
- Twelve mid-level managers, with ages of 52, 49, 36, 39, 42, 45, 58, 36, 44, 42, 38, 40.

- Eighteen lower-level managers, with ages of 28, 36, 42, 27, 26, 31, 33, 29, 28, 29, 38, 42, 34, 48, 41, 32, 26, 27.

Design a table that presents the above statistics to the insurance company as simply as possible.

2. Your organization gives employees the option of choosing one of three medical insurance plans. You have been asked to write a brief description of the three plans so that employees will understand the differences among them. Use a table to present the following data about the plans.

Plan A: This plan costs employees $250 per year. It will pay the reasonable charges of any licensed physician, excluding a dentist, who provides medical care, after the employee pays the first $150 of medical expenses every year. While it does not provide dental benefits, it will pay the usual fees for psychological counseling. For each family member to be covered by the plan, the employee must pay an additional $50 per year.

Plan B: This plan will also pay reasonable charges of all licensed physicians, including dentists but excluding counselors, and doesn't require the employee to pay any of the initial expenses. It is more expensive though, costing $325 per year. It will cover up to three members of the employee's family, with no additional charges.

Plan C: This plan is fairly inexpensive, only $125 per year, but its benefits are only paid to physicians, including counselors, who are members of the plan. It will cover up to $400 in dental charges per person per year, and will cover all members of an employee's family for $35 apiece. It also stipulates that an employee must pay the first 20% of any medical charge.

3. You are so good at writing research reports that your manager has asked you to design a flow chart that will show others the steps to follow in researching, planning, and writing reports. You will need to depict the major steps in the process and also show people what steps to follow if they get stumped anywhere along the way.

4. Construct an organizational chart that describes the structure of an organization you have been or are now a member of.

5. Prepare a pie chart and then a bar graph to depict the following sources of gross revenues for an appliance dealer. In what situation might you use one of these two graphics rather than another?

TVs	$158,865.23
Stereo equipment	$278,904.38
Kitchen appliances	$198,420.67
Video recorders/players	$147,320.29
Washers and dryers	$ 93,007.83

6. Six years ago, you set up a small consulting company, specializing in preparing self-study training materials for organizations. Over the years, you have bought necessary equipment such as a small computer, a copying machine, video recorder and player, etc. During the third year, you hired a part-time employee at $3,500 per year to help you prepare materials.

   You would now like to hire another part-time employee to help out. But you wonder whether you can afford one. As a matter of fact, you are worried about your profit margin. For the past two years, you have begun to notice a profit pinch. While your gross revenues don't seem to be rising that much, your costs do.

   After digging back through your records, you find the following cost and revenue figures:

Year:	1	2	3	4	5
Costs:	1,750	6,430	10,650	13,032	18,032
Revenues	11,730	15,749	28,750	34,540	36,940

   After preparing a multiple line graph comparing these figures, decide what your best course of action would be.

CHAPTER

10

Writing Reports

Reports help managers make decisions by answering questions like these: "What did you accomplish last month? What's the status of that project? What happened at that meeting you attended? How does that person perform her job? Do you think we should introduce that new product or service?" This chapter will show you how to write reports that answer such questions effectively.

Managers in organizations continually have to make these kinds of decisions—whether to offer a new product or service; whether to continue with a current project or program; whether to adopt a new policy or procedure; whether to hire new employees, and whether to retain or promote current employees. To make such decisions effectively, they need answers to questions.

- Should we develop this new product/offer this new service?
- How is this program or project progressing?
- Should we adopt this policy or procedure?
- Do we need new employees to do this job?
- Should we retain this person, give this one a raise, promote this one?

The basis for answering such questions is frequently a report that gives managers the facts, conclusions, and recommendations necessary to make the best decisions. In fact, the word "report" comes from a Latin word that means "to carry back." A report is simply the vehicle by which you carry back information to readers.

It's impossible in a book of this length to discuss all the particular kinds of reports you might write at work. Some reports are long, imposing volumes, containing hundreds of pages of charts, statistics, and analyses. But others may range from a paragraph to a few pages in length. And different organizations refer to reports in different ways. Sometimes, reports are referred to by the period of time they cover; for example, a daily activities report, a monthly status report, or an annual report. Sometimes they are referred to by their purposes; for example, an observation report, progress report, engineering report, or evaluation report. At other times, reports may be classified by their length and degree of formality; for example, a short, informal report versus a longer, more formal one.

Rather than try to cover this bewildering array, we're going to focus on the major principle behind all report writing—that no matter what kind of report you write, your goal is to answer the questions of your readers. Once you clarify your goal—that is, the questions you need to answer—you will know both the type of report to write and the information, organization, style, and design to choose. On the following pages, you'll see how to apply this principle of answering questions to the typical short and long reports you will write during your career.

SHORT REPORTS

No matter where you work, there are certain typical kinds of short reports that you will probably have to write. Many of these are so short, in fact, that we could just as easily have discussed them earlier, because they are often presented in the form of memos. But because people will often refer to these as reports, we're going to discuss them in this chapter. In particular, we're going to talk about the following types of short reports: *incident*, *status*, *contact*, and *performance* reports. The organization you work for may use other terms to refer to these types of reports. But no matter what they are called, they will always answer the same kinds of questions.

The type of report you write will depend on your goal, that is, the questions you want to answer. As you saw in the chapter on preparing to write long documents, you determine your goal by identifying your readers and deciding why they want your report. In each case, simply ask yourself: "Who is going to read this? What question(s) do they want answered?" Your answer will tell you what kind of report to write.

Incident Reports

Things happen in organizations—people have accidents, problems occur, incidents take place. And management needs to know about these events. Your report on such instances will be called different things in different organizations. It might be called an incident, occurrence, action, accident, inspection, or troubleshooting report. But no matter what your report is called, your reader's questions will be the same: "What happened?" and frequently, "What do you think about it?" Note how the writer of the following incident report answers these questions, first by describing the problem and then by giving his opinion about its effects:

```
Five problem areas in the PSD Payroll package,
Version 3.1, have been brought to my attention. They
are itemized below.

1. All check file records are being written out of
   programs with a record length of 3560 bytes instead
   of being variable length records. This is causing
   us problems with space allocation on direct
   storage devices for this file.
2. In the pay adjustment cycle, canceled checks are
   not sorting in front of manual checks. This is
   causing problems on deduction arrears when a
   manual and a canceled check for one employee are
   entered during the same adjustment run.
```

And even though the following inspection report looks totally factual on first glance, note how it combines facts *and* opinions. The reader will rely on these opinions to make sure that the proper quality of film is being maintained.

```
The following are the results of our final
inspections of corrected films:

   Date    Comments
   1/28    OK.
   2/3     Makeover. Magenta plus wanted color.
           Darken for reverse type.
   4/5     Magenta makeover--plus wanted color.
   4/6     OK.
   4/7     Rescanned because too flat. Midtone &
           3/4 tone plus.
```

You will quickly catch on to how to write the incident reports that your organization requires. You simply need to figure out what your reader wants to know, then organize your information (frequently you can just organize it chronologically—as it happened), and design your report for quick and easy reading, highlighting important points with short paragraphs, white space, and enumeration wherever possible.

Progress/Status Reports

"What did you do last month? How are things going on your projects?" managers frequently want to know. Your answer may be called a progress, status, or activity report, and you may have to write it on a weekly (Heaven forbid), monthly, quarterly, or yearly basis. Usually, readers just want to know the facts, presented so they can review them quickly and easily. Like incident reports, progress reports can often be arranged chronologically. The following short one, written by a sales representative for a food wholesaler, is an example:

ACTIVITY REPORT
February 26–March 25, 19--

- Met with Lancaster IGA ($30,000 per week) and presented our entire program. They will visit with Gray's in early April after which they will decide whether to sign or not.
- Met with Seashore in Newport. This account currently purchases $30,000 per week from Cordovan Foods. Mr. Kahn will make a decision on switching suppliers in the next 30 days.
- Continued to work with Ed Mahoney regarding the Jeff Mason Big Star.

Sometimes management may want to know more in status reports than just what you have done. In addition, they may want to know what you are currently doing and what you plan to do. The writer of the following report, for instance, had to cover all three categories:

Projects Completed

1. A new wiring machine has been installed and wired in the shipping area.
2. The new motors for the waste handling system have been wired and checked out.
3. The Elkgon units on press 309 have been modified to prevent fuse loss on start-up.

Current.Projects

1. We are installing five new rectifiers on the floor stands. This job should be completed by 6/4.
2. We are installing additional safety stops on the Comex conveyors on presses 503 and 502. This is being done as downtime permits.
3. Electrical work in the bromide area is on schedule. We are waiting for equipment at this time.

Upcoming.Projects

1. Press control room air purifying system.
2. Cylinder storage rack system.
3. Shuttle feeders in bindery.

When you plan progress reports, you're going to have to use your good judgment about what to include—and what to exclude. For example, if particular problems have arisen during the period, your manager may be as much interested in these (and how you solved them) as in an account of your major activities. And if you think that future problems may arise, you ought to mention these, especially if you think they may be serious. Good managers want to be informed, and they depend on their subordinates for this information.

But when talking about problems—whether past, present, or future—you're going to have to be careful about the details you include and the tone you use. On the one hand, you don't want to use such a negative tone that you arouse a manager's concerns unnecessarily; on the other, you don't want to conceal or misrepresent anything of possible importance. The best solution is simply to ask yourself, "What would I like to know about this situation/problem if I were the manager?" And then give your readers this information.

Contact Reports

People in organizations constantly work with others. They talk on the telephone, attend meetings, and make visits to other organizations. And because these contacts are often important to managers, they want to know: "What happened during that call, meeting, or visit?" To answer their question, you'll have to write what we're going to call a contact report. This category includes reports on telephone calls, interviews, meetings, and trips. A contact report could be as simple as the minutes of a meeting or a record of a telephone call. For instance, you may be required to keep a record of all important telephone calls.

David Laval called to discuss several matters pertaining to his and Anne's applications for the medical post abroad. He said that Anne is expecting July 17, 19--, and that they both are excited over knowing another baby is on the way. He indicated that Anne is having some morning sickness but is otherwise doing well.

David went on to state that in view of Anne's pregnancy, they have decided to plan for the summer departure date instead of spring, but wish to stay on the same schedule for conferences and meetings.

A report like this is easy to organize because the writer can just record the contact as it occurred. And note how the writer has underlined important points, so his manager can pick them up quickly. (Of course, you'll want to resist the temptation to underline too much in such reports. If everything is underlined, then nothing will seem important.)

But often, just presenting things the way they occurred in a phone call, meeting, or on a trip won't be the most helpful pattern for your reader. This person, usually your manager, just won't have the time to wade through details about everything that happened in order to get to the important parts. Therefore, you need to figure out what kind of information your reader needs in a given report and give it to him or her as quickly and easily as possible.

As an example, imagine for a moment that you are a company auditor whose job is to examine the accounts of different divisions. You have spent two days auditing a particular set of accounts looking for problems and making sure that procedures follow company policy. You could write a ten-page description of all the important transactions you checked and the people you talked with. Instead, you distill this discussion down to its major results and summarize these in a two-paragraph report.

EXAMINATION REPORT

Account: Greenland Products Division
Auditor: Greg Ackerman
Results: On this examination, I discovered that the manager had been adding credits on our Collateral Reports rather than subtracting them. I reversed

these transactions in the amount of $44,900.20 on Collateral Report #0075. This corrected the collateral overstatement.

I also found that none of the deposits had been applied to the loan. The new teller handling the transactions was advancing funds as requested on the Collateral Reports but not curtailing the loan as requested. Anne Cary and I reconciled the Grid Note to the loan outstanding on our Collateral Reports.

Your manager can now see immediately the results of your examination, for you have given your finding in the first sentence of each paragraph and your action in the next.

When people make frequent contact with clients to service accounts and solve problems, their companies often develop set formats for contact reports. One example for a large manufacturing company looks like this.

Account: National Balance Corp.
Region: Southeastern
Met.with: H. J. Rawlingson
Purpose: To analyze roll forming problems with alloy material. Approximately 10M pounds in house with total sales of 125M pounds for 19--.

Results: Adjustments made to the roll tools and the cut-to-length die, plus lubricating the input material to produce acceptable panels.

Discussion: This company started business in 19-- producing a product called . . . .

When you first write such reports, you may feel that a standard format such as this is just a bureaucratic constraint, which unnecessarily restricts your ability to communicate. You need to remember, though, that it enables a busy manager to skim your report quickly, understanding why you made the visit (purpose), what you found out (results), and the necessary background (discussion). Thus, your manager can read your report as quickly or as carefully as he needs to.

Performance Reports

If you are in a management position, one of your toughest tasks will be to evaluate the people who work under you. Since their pay increases, promotions, and even retention will depend on your assessment of the quality of their work, you will have to write performance appraisals or evaluations periodically. Sometimes your job will be made easier because your organization has a prepared form you can fill out, on which you can rate a person in certain categories before writing your evaluative comment. But since you will normally have to write some sort of evaluative comment even in these, you should learn how to do it.

The question your reader wants answered in a performance appraisal is "How well is this person performing his or her job?" Since your opinions will probably be relied on heavily, you will need to write a careful report, setting forth opinions that are derived from *facts*. Here is an example of a performance report on a U.S. Navy officer. Note how the first paragraph is primarily factual while the second is made up of opinions about the quality of the person's performance. The principal opinions are underlined:

PERFORMANCE REPORT

Description of Ratee's Duties and Responsibilities:

HM2 Smith is assigned as the corpsman for the unit. He assists the medical officer in conducting physical examinations, takes vital signs, and does sight testing, basic laboratory testing, and initial screening of medical problems. He has served as a member of the unit planning board for training. His mobilization assignment is in the medical section.

Evaluation of Ratee's Performance:

HM2 Smith is an <u>outstanding</u> petty officer in all respects. He has repeatedly demonstrated <u>superior proficiency and knowledge</u> of medical skills and information, both in a diagnostic capacity and in academic areas. His lectures on medical subjects to unit members <u>are thorough and extremely well delivered</u>.

Smith is <u>fully qualified</u> in his mobilization billet, and possesses an <u>excellent concept of</u> the unit's mission. He has participated in several METS and MOBEXs, providing <u>valuable assistance</u> to the command. Smith has <u>superior oral and written communication skills</u>.

Recommendation:

That HM2 Smith be advanced to the next pay grade.

Notice how much of the important material in this report consists of the writer's opinions about Smith's performance. To the reader, such opinions are the most valuable part of the report, for they will determine decisions about promotions and salary increases. If your reader's time is limited, you may have to restrict a performance report primarily to opinions. However, your opinions should always be grounded in the facts of the person's performance, and you should have documentation to support your opinions, even if you are not required to submit it.

There may be times, though, when your reader does want you to document (support) your opinions in a more detailed fashion than shown above. Such was the case with this yearly evaluation of a case worker in a social services division of a state government. Note how the writer documents this evaluation of the quantity and quality of the person's work with percentages and actual figures.

The _quantity_ of Ms. Smith's work last year was high. In fact, she exceeded her quantitative standard of 198 cases by 40%, processing a total of 277 cases.

The _quality_, though, needs to be improved because she made 21 errors in the 277 cases processed, for an error rate of 8%. This is 4% above the normal rate for this work. The more serious errors were 10 payment errors--in 6 of these, gross income was not counted; in 4 others, SSE income was counted inappropriately. The other errors were procedural ones, resulting from her missing or incomplete documentation.

Ms. Smith's error rate should be reduced during the next period because she now understands how to check all income calculations and how to insure that documentation is present in each file and complete.

Often, the best way to document your opinions about a person's performance is by measuring it against a previously established standard. The writer of the paragraph above does this, citing a quantitative standard in the first paragraph and a qualitative one in the second. Using such standards is an excellent way to make the basis of your evaluation clear, both to your manager and to the person being evaluated.

Frequently, the performance appraisal process begins with the employee evaluating his or her own performance and then submitting this report to a manager for further evaluation. If you have to write such a document, you will have to train yourself to be objective, being neither too kind nor too critical of yourself. Try pretending that you are a manager evaluating your performance. Of course, when you write the report, document your judgments with plenty of facts about your performance.

LONG REPORTS

People at work write long reports on every subject imaginable. In the stack on my desk right now are—

- technical reports on coagulation equipment for an aluminum company, on a missile launcher for the Navy, and on rust problems with sheet metal siding;
- annual reports issued by a state welfare department, a utility conservation program, and a nationally known publisher; and
- investigative reports about the implementation of a Medicaid policy, the administration of a state highway department, and the allocation of a company budget.

There is no one set of procedures that will enable you to write all these kinds of reports. Technical test reports require one kind of research and reporting format, annual reports another, and investigative reports another. But the principle behind writing long reports is the same as that for writing short ones. Decide on your goal—that is, the questions you want to answer in your report—and then choose the information, organization, style, and design that will enable you to answer these questions best.

Your Information

The source, type, and amount of information you include in a long report will depend on the question(s) you want to answer. If the question is a technical one—how do tests indicate this product or process will work?—your information will probably be drawn from experimental observation. If it is more of an explanatory question—how does this procedure work, or how does this department or division operate?—your information will come from your own knowledge, study of records, and interviews with others. The same sources might also serve to answer more evaluative questions—how is this project or program working and how can we improve it?

The tendency of too many report writers is to spend too much time getting information before they begin to write their actual report. The result is that they often end up collecting information they don't need or neglecting to get information they do need. To avoid this problem, begin drafting your report early in your research. While you are still making observations, reading documents, or interviewing others, begin to outline your report and even to write sections of it. In this way, you'll be able to devote your research to getting just the information you need.

Your Organization

One of your major problems in writing a long report will be organizing it to answer your readers' questions most efficiently. But the solution is not as difficult as you might think. Even though there are lots of ways to organize reports, there is a way to think about organizational methods that will make the task easy for you. No matter what kind of report you are writing, you can either organize your information into parts or groups. The difference simply lies in whether the subject you are writing about is singular or plural. Let me explain.

Analysis If you are reporting on one entity—whether it is an event that took place, an organization that you are examining, or the impact of a new policy—you will break your information down into parts. That is, you will *analyze* your subject in some way. The parts you focus on might consist of the causes of an event, the effects of a proposed change on your organization, or the components of a program.

One analyst, for example, was told by a state budget office to evaluate the activities of a new division of the state welfare bureau. This division had been set up four years ago to involve welfare participants in decisions about their welfare benefits. The analyst was told that on the basis of the study, the budget office would decide whether to continue to fund the division or not. But the analyst was not asked to make a recommendation, only to present the evaluation on which the recommendation would be made.

If you had been given this assignment, what components of the division and its activities would you focus on? Basically, your reader's question is as follows: "How well is this division accomplishing its goal?" So you'd probably begin with a description of its major goal. Then follow perhaps with a brief description of the division itself—its structure, number of employees, etc. Finally, you would probably need to discuss its major accomplishments and costs. Here is the rough outline the analyst developed to guide the research and writing.

```
1. Introduction—state purpose of the report
2. Purpose of division
3. Organizational structure
   a. Number of employees
   b. Functions
```

```
    c. Positions
4. Major costs
    a. Personnel
    b. Operational
5. Impact on clients
    a. Positive
    b. Negative
```

On the basis of these parts of the report, the budget office should be able to decide whether or not to continue the division. Of course, if the report were very long, the writer might well include a summary at the beginning that would state the purpose of the report and quickly enumerate major benefits, drawbacks, and costs. Why? So readers who need a quick capsule of the report can get it from the summary alone.

You will use analysis in any number of report situations during your career. The short performance report we discussed earlier in this chapter was based on analysis. First, the writer set forth the duties of the person and then described how well the duties had been performed. If you are asked to study a situation, say a conflict between an employee and supervisor, you will analyze it, probably breaking your final report down into discussions of the problem, its causes, and your recommended solution. And you will find that an annual report describing how well a department or division has performed will be based on an analysis of its functions and a description of how well it has fulfilled them.

Classification When you classify, you simply sort things into groups. You already know how to classify since you use this method all the time to understand experience. For example, if you were to mention to someone that you want to replace your subcompact car with a compact model, you are basing your statement on a classification—of automobiles by size. And as soon as you begin to talk to someone about the types of music you enjoy or the kinds of TV programs you can't stand, you are classifying.

Many of the reports you write during your career will be based on classification. Look back, for example, at the incident or progress reports that we discussed at the beginning of this chapter, and you'll see that both are based on classification. In each case, the writer pigeonholed facts into categories—problems in one case and activities in another. Here is a budget request that its writer organized into categories, describing various programs and their needs:

```
  The Human Resources Subcommittee is reporting to you
today on its recommendations for budget allocations.
We recommend that the following amounts be allocated
to the following programs:
```

Developmental Disabilities Program. This program has been underfunded for the past four years. It should receive $450,000 to study the availability of jobs for the disabled and $500,000 for individual grants.

Medicaid. The subcommittee concurs with the governor's overall proposed funding for this program. We recommend the following amounts be allocated: . . .

Community Mental Retardation Program. We recommend that. . . .

A Classic Pattern Often reports are organized by a combination of analysis and classification. This is frequently the case with long reports that are written to answer questions about a study or investigation. In fact, such reports are so common within organizations that a basic pattern has evolved to organize them. It is now widely accepted and used. This pattern was developed to answer the five basic questions readers of investigative reports usually have:

- "What is in this report?" will be their first question, which is answered in the *summary* section of the report.
- "Why did you do this report?" will be your readers' next logical question. This question is answered in the *introduction/purpose* section of the report.
- "What action do you recommend we take on the basis of your conclusions?" This most important question will be answered in the *Recommendations* section.
- "What did you find out?" will be the question you will answer in the *Conclusion* section, which will give your readers the basis for your recommendations.
- "How did you perform this study?" they will also ask, a question you will answer in the *Discussion* section, which will set forth the basic facts of the study.

This classic pattern is almost always followed in technical reports, such as those written by engineers or research scientists. But it is also a useful pattern for any type of investigative report. I've seen it used to analyze the cash flow problems of a large department store, the pros and cons of a merger between two companies, and even the problem that someone from a company encountered on a trouble-shooting trip. This pattern works especially well when you are writing a report for readers with different needs, for you can address different components of the report to these different groups of readers. Here is what should go into each section.

Summary. Your summary is addressed to everyone who might read your report. By presenting the report in miniature—its purpose, as well as major recommendations and conclusions—it enables busy readers to understand your project quickly and decide whether to read further. Long, technical reports often include an *abstract* along with the summary. The abstract condenses the report's contents in 150 to 200 words and is often circulated separately from the report or published in an index or information retrieval system.

Introduction. An introduction, sometimes called *foreword* or *purpose*, prepares readers for the rest of your report. Different organizations have different requirements for what the introduction should contain, but it always tells readers the subject of your study and the purpose of your report. In more elaborate reports, the introduction can also contain a description of the scope of your study, a discussion of the background or context of your study, or a description of the problem you wish to solve.

Recommendations. The most important question for the decision makers who read your report will be what you recommend they *do* on the basis of your study. If your report recommends that a program be eliminated, a project be started, or a product or service be offered by the organization, busy executives will want to know this right away. In fact, many executives turn to this section of a report immediately, and only after finding out what the report recommends will they read the rest of it.

Conclusions. Your recommendations will be based on what you have found out in the course of your study; that is, the conclusions you have arrived at. The same people who read your recommendations may well glance at your conclusions as well to find out whether they provide a sound basis for your recommendations.

Discussion. This is the most factual part of your study, for it is here that you explain the methods—observations, surveys, interviews, researching records—by which you arrived at your conclusions. Decision makers may just skim this section of your report, but other people on your level may read and analyze it closely. For this reason, your discussion must describe with precision and in detail exactly how you arrived at your conclusions.

At first glance, this pattern may seem complicated and unfamiliar to you. Actually, it follows the same priority sequence we followed when organizing informative letters and memos—leading with parts important to all readers and then following with parts of decreasing importance. Newspaper reporters also use it to organize most news articles, calling it the inverted pyramid, because important ideas are placed at the top and less important ones near the bottom. You can think of this pattern as having three major parts, each addressed to a different group of readers—

For all readers	"What is in this report?"	*Summary*
For decision makers	"Why did you do this?"	*Introduction*
	"What should we do?"	*Recommendations*
	"What did you find out?"	*Conclusions*
For technical people	"How did you perform this study?"	*Discussion*

YOUR STYLE

Let's talk about report writing style. First, there isn't any such thing, although the writer of the following introduction to a report on corrosion must have thought so when he wrote:

This organization is experiencing the loss of substantial sums of money each and every year because of unchecked corrosion. The occurrence of this corrosion comes about as a direct or indirect result of improper preparation for the handling, the shipping, and the storage of in-process and finished products. While the company is cognizant of the fact that the accumulated loss is extremely expensive, it is very unlikely that any individual can confirm exactly how costly the total loss is or what it accumulates to in terms of delayed or unacceptable deliveries and the loss of quality customers who will not bother to investigate the company's record at a future date so never come back.

Imagine yourself as a busy executive sitting down to read a 20-page report beginning with that paragraph. How far will you read before you simply give up in disgust? Look at some of the stylistic features that make this paragraph so unwieldy. The words are abstract ("experiencing," "substantial sums"), too Latinate ("cognizant," "accumulated," "investigate"), and impersonal ("This organization," "The company"). More important, there are too many smothered verbs ("organization," "occurrence," "preparation"). These features, coupled with the long sentences (while the first sentence is only 19 words long, the second is 29 words, and the third is 66 words long), make the paragraph unnecessarily difficult to read.

Does this style occur often in reports? Too often, unfortunately. Why? Probably because people think of report writing as a situation in which they must project a formal personality by writing in an abstract, complex style. What's the solution? To remind yourself that even in a long, technical report you are talking to your readers on paper, attempting to answer their questions in a down-to-earth, human manner. Since your information will usually be complicated to begin with, you will be wise to aim for the simplest, most personal voice possible. How do you accomplish this? Remember the stylistic choices we discussed in Chapter 4. Here are the word choices.

INFORMAL STYLE	FORMAL STYLE
Simple	Complex
Concrete	Abstract
Personal	Impersonal
Active	Passive
Verbs	Nouns
Nontechnical	Technical

Whenever you can, try to choose more informal words. These will create a simple, direct voice. And even if you can't use personal pronouns, you can still use words that are simple, concrete, and nontechnical. Remember also the sentence variables of length and variety that we discussed in Chapter 4. Since the subject you are talking about in a report will probably be difficult enough for your readers, try to keep your sentences fairly short and as varied as possible.

YOUR DESIGN

In the last chapter, we talked about how to design a long document for efficient reading by using separators, enumerators, and illustrators. All reports, whether short or long, use these design devices to make information available to readers quickly and easily. To see how they can be used, take a moment to skim back through the excerpts from short reports in the first part of this chapter. You should find separators such as white space, short paragraphs, headings, underlinings, and different typefaces, as well as enumerators such as numbers and bullets. And in the report sample that follows, you will see how a graphic such as a table can be used to illustrate complicated cost information for readers.

A Writing Situation

You work in the human relations department of a large organization employing thousands of people. Among other things, your department is responsible for conducting all training throughout the organization. This includes conducting orientation courses that explain policies to new employees, locating people who can conduct training seminars in technical and management skills, and developing instructional materials for self-study courses.

One day your manager calls you in and says, "I just received this memo from John Briggs [a senior vice-president]. He's concerned about the level of writing skills in our organization. Just last week, someone on his staff complained about a mistake in a letter he had received from our accounting department. And John says that his people periodically complain that employees can't write a concise memo or a clear report. He wants to know whether we think we should begin a training program in effective written communication.

"Would you do a little study to find out whether we need such a program? You might check with managers in the organization, look at some possible outside sources of training, that sort of thing. Give me about a six- to eight-page report in a week or so. If you think we need such a program, recommend the best type, and I'll pass your report right up the ladder."

To begin planning your study, you decide to get some background information by doing a little reading about the general quality of writing on the job. Using the *Business Periodicals Index* and the *Readers' Guide to Periodical Literature*, you find plenty of information; in fact, too much to digest. You see that *Time Magazine*, *Newsweek*, and *Harper's Magazine* all published articles on the "writing crisis" back in 1975, complaining that students and professionals could not write.

You find more recent articles in *Business Week*, the *Harvard Business Review*, the *S.A.M. Advanced Management Journal*, and even *Chemical Engineering*, all lamenting the inability of employees to write and suggesting solutions. You even find a series on effective letter writing published by the Royal Bank of Canada and another series on effective reading and writing published by the International Paper Company.

As you read and think about your assignment, you realize that your manager wants you to answer two questions in your report.

1. Do we have enough of a writing problem in this organization to require a training program in effective writing?
2. If so, what would be the best type of program to recommend?

In order to answer the first question, you interview some key managers to find out about the quantity and quality of writing done in their departments and divisions. You discover that employees write more memos, letters, reports, and proposals than you thought. In fact, some managers spend as much as half their time

SURVEY

1. What department do you work in and what is your position?

2. What type of writing do you typically do? Is it mostly letters, memos, reports, or other types? Write the number of each you write per week below.
   ________ Letters
   ________ Memos
   ________ Reports
   ________ Other Types

3. How many hours per week do you spend writing? (Count your planning time as well as actual writing.)
   ________ Hours

4. Do you feel that you write effectively? Why? Do you feel that your fellow workers write effectively? Why?

5. Do you think that people in the organization write poorly? If so, what do you think is the cause?

6. Do you think the organization should institute a training program in effective written communication?

7. Would you be interested in participating in such a program?
   Yes ________ No ________

working on writing, either writing themselves or critiquing the writing of others. And most managers agree that the quality is not very high, although they don't all agree on the cause. Supervisors of lower level employees feel that the problem is caused by poor grammar and spelling. But those who supervise people in management feel that the cause is more that people just can't communicate their thoughts clearly. The comment of one manager sums up the general feeling, "Listen, if we're above the level of manual labor, communication skill is not *one* of the reasons we're hired; it is *the* reason. No matter what the cause of poor writing, we've got to correct it!"

To get opinions about writing skills from a wider group of people throughout the organization, you decide to do a quick survey. After enlisting the help of a statistician in your data processing department to select a representative sample, you construct a questionnaire. You decide not to ask respondents to identify themselves, because some may be embarrassed about their writing. Your questionnaire, which is attached to a brief memo explaining that you want to find out whether or not the organization needs a training program to improve writing skills, is on the left.

Some results are what you expected. Throughout the organization, people write a wide range of documents, including letters, memos, and reports, but also sales proposals, brochures, even newsletters and legal briefs. Many people don't think they or their colleagues write very well. Your respondents seem to agree with the managers who said that people at lower levels have more trouble with grammar, while people at the upper levels have the most trouble with clarity and conciseness.

But two results are surprising. Your management people spend lots of time on writing, with people at higher levels averaging from one to two days per week. And over 60% of your respondents would participate in a training program.

Your answer to the first question is now obvious. People in your organization think that the quality of writing is low, and many are willing to do something about it. So you start to answer the second one—what type of program to recommend—by investigating alternative methods of training. You examine textbooks on business writing, courses commercially developed for self-study, and even popular books on clear writing. You call several consulting companies that offer courses in effective writing. They will conduct in-house training seminars, usually one or two days long, but most are expensive, ranging from $500 to $1,500 per day. You also call several local colleges, both to find out what writing courses they offer and to interview several professors about the best methods for improving writing skills.

During this period in your research, you begin to jot down some notes for a preliminary outline of the report. They look like this.

```
    Problem:   Many in organization can't write--
               documented from interviews,
               surveys, reading.

      Cause:   Don't really know--some say poor grammar,
               some say lack of clarity/conciseness.

  Solutions:   Self-study--motivation levels?
               In-house training--expensive?
               High school/college courses--effective?
```

After thinking for a few days, you decide that the problem is serious enough to warrant a new training program, but that since there is probably more than one cause, you will need to attack it in different ways. Therefore, your goal for the final report will be to recommend a program composed of several alternative training methods. At this stage, you do a tree diagram of the report that looks like this:

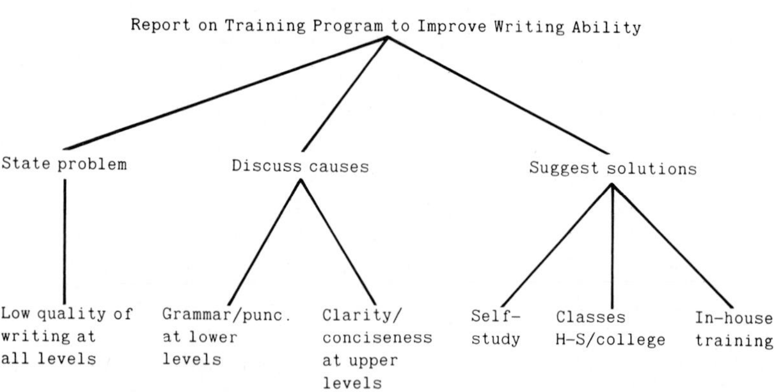

Following this diagram, you start to write a draft of your report. You begin with an introduction that describes the goal of your report—to analyze the writing problem in your organization and recommend a solution. In your first section, you describe the problem, on a national and local level, citing facts from your reading as well as from your interviews and surveys. Your next section is a discussion of the causes, admitting that no one fully understands

Rem. 407

ADMIT SLIP

DATE JAN 22 1990

PLEASE ADMIT Pizzoferrato, Emilio

TO Eng 210 ITEM NUMBER 593

Class Name

Susan B. Salowitz

Susan B. Salowitz
Assistant Director
of Admissions and Records

them, but that they seem to be either lack of knowledge of basic rules of grammar (at the lower levels) or inability to explain a subject clearly and concisely (at the upper levels). Your last section recommends a three-part training program: self-study courses for people weak in grammar; organization-supported high school and college courses for those willing; and in-house training, beginning with upper management and working down through lower levels.

To get some feedback on your first draft, you pass it around to colleagues in your department and also ask your manager to look at it. Most of your colleagues like it, suggesting a few changes in style and catching a few errors in grammar. But your manager suggests a major change. "Look," he says, "I really like this study. You've done your homework, your analysis is good, and your recommendations are practical. In fact, I'm going to distribute it to all third-level managers and division heads. I think we'll get some action on this.

"But," he continues, "this means you've got to change the organization of this report. Most of your readers will just want the high points, so put them first, then follow with your discussion. You've just about got to flip your whole report over, leading with your solutions and then discussing the problem and its causes to support the solutions.

"And there is nothing in this report so far about the costs of the program you recommend. I suggest you end with a section setting forth the major costs of the program, in an easy-to-read table if you can. And try to make your style a little less formal. The people who will decide about this program like to read reports that are written simply and directly."

After two more drafts and more feedback, you finally have the whole report reorganized, this time following the classic report pattern your manager recommended. You begin with a summary of important points for all readers; then follow with your purpose, recommendations, and conclusions for those who will make the final decision about the program; and conclude with a more detailed discussion of the problem and its causes for those who want the fine points. After a good deal of editing, your final report looks like the one on pages 240–42.

At first glance, this kind of report may seem very different from the reports you have written in the past. Actually, it is based on the same thinking processes as the long papers you have written before. For most of these papers, didn't you first investigate a subject through research in the library, interviews, or perhaps an experiment, and then draw some conclusions from your research? This classic report pattern highlights this thinking process, often called *induction*, because your reader can quickly see that your conclusions are based on the *facts* you uncovered in your investigation. The major difference between it and other papers you have written is that you include recommendations with your facts and conclusions, since your reader will usually want to take some action as a result of

REPORT ON TRAINING PROGRAM TO
IMPROVE WRITING ABILITY

Summary
As a result of interviews with key managers, surveys of company personnel, and background reading, this study concludes that written communication is important to this organization, and that its quality needs to be improved. Therefore, the human relations department recommends a program consisting of self-study courses, high school and college classes, and in-house training. The annual budget for such a program would be in the range of $30,000.

Purpose
The purpose of this study was to determine whether a problem of poor writing existed and to recommend possible solutions.

Recommendations
That we institute a training program with three major components.

1. Self-study courses in the rules and use of correct grammar for employees in operational and clerical positions. Approximate costs for development would be $4,500 for original materials.
2. Organization-funded high school and college classes in effective writing for employees wishing this training. Based on surveys of people interested in this option, costs for a year would be approximately $5,000.
3. Intensive in-house seminars in effective writing for mid- and upper-level management. The cost for a two-day seminar, including materials and trainer, would be about $1,500.

Conclusions

These recommendations are based on three conclusions.

1. That writing good memos, letters, reports, etc., is important in this organization, occupying considerable amounts of time and costing large amounts of money.
2. That division heads, managers, and many employees agree that writing skills are presently low and need to be improved.
3. That the best way to improve writing skills is to implement a flexible program, with various components adapted to people with different needs.

Discussion

1. Quantity of writing. To determine quantity and quality of writing within this organization, six key managers were interviewed and a survey was distributed to a sample of 100 employees. The results of the interviews and the survey (70 returned) indicate that managers average two days per week at a variety of writing tasks, including memos, letters, reports, as well as proposals, brochures, newsletters, etc. Results also indicate that nonmanagers may write less, but their reports, memos, and letters are important in their work. (Returned survey forms are attached as the appendix of this report.)
2. Quality of writing. Seventy-two percent of the people who returned surveys (see appendix) feel that people in this organization do not write effectively. Four of the six managers interviewed feel strongly that many employees cannot write well enough to be effective on the job. One manager who was interviewed said, "No matter what the cause [of poor writing], we've got to correct it."
3. Causes of the problem. It is difficult to assign one cause. Both interviews and surveys indicate that on the lower levels, the cause of poor writing is primarily poor grammar and punctuation. At upper levels, it is usually a lack of clarity and conciseness.

4. Solutions. To determine the best type of training program, I examined books on business writing, wrote several consulting companies, and called local colleges. This research indicates that the best solution will be to create a program to meet different needs: self-study courses in grammar and punctuation for some; high school and college courses for others; and in-house training for management.

Program Costs

The following table presents the costs for the first year of the program. These are approximate, based on estimates of personnel time, materials costs, and consultant fees.

YEARLY COSTS

Type.of.Program	Individual Costs	Totals
Self-study	10 modules @ $450 per module	$ 4,500.00
Academic courses	25 people @ $200 per course	5,000.00
In-house seminars	10 seminars @ $1,500 per session	15,000.00
Personnel	Time allocated from H.R. Dept. to manage program	5,500.00
Total costs		$30,000.00

the report. And you lead with your recommendations and conclu sions, since these are what your busy readers are most interested in.

Some people are at first dismayed at the amount of repetition when they first write a report following the classic pattern. "After all," they say, "why give the purpose in the summary paragraph when you are giving it later? Also, it looks like the recommendations are implied by the conclusions. Why spell them out? And, for that matter, the discussion repeats part of the conclusions section."

If you think for a minute about the way different readers will read your report, you'll understand why some repetition is necessary. First, many readers will just read your summary; therefore, you'll need to give them a thumbnail sketch of your report in it. Secondly, even readers who go beyond your summary may well just skim certain sections. They will probably read just your recommendations and your conclusions. Only a few will want to know your methodology in detail. So think of this kind of report pattern as responding to readers with very different needs and expectations.

Of course, not all the long reports you write will follow this classic pattern. Often, especially when you are describing or evaluating a program, project, or process as opposed to investigating something, you will use other organizational methods based on analysis or classification. To decide on the most appropriate organizational pattern in a particular instance, focus on the questions you want to answer in the report and then choose the pattern that will best enable you to answer these questions.

SUMMARY

In this chapter, we've discussed the following points:

1. You will write various kinds of short reports during your career, including incident, progress, contact, and performance reports. But whatever you call a short report, your task is always the same—to answer your reader's questions in the best way possible.
2. Many of the investigative reports you write can follow the classic pattern of *recommendations, conclusions,* and *discussion.* You will frequently have to include *summaries* and *introductions* or purpose statements with these reports also.
3. Don't get trapped into thinking that there is a style for all reports. Even though reports may be longer and more formal than memos and letters, you should still make your style as readable as possible.
4. Help readers understand your main ideas and data quickly by using such design devices as separators, enumerators, and illustrators.

APPLICATIONS

1. *Incident report.* Recently, you witnessed a heated argument between an employee and a supervisor where you work. Insults and even a few blows were exchanged. A plant committee is about to hold a hearing to determine who was at fault in the dispute and what action should be taken. They have asked you for a brief report describing the incident and pointing out the person at fault. Write the report, imagining any details about the argument that you need to.

2. *Progress/status report.* Your manager has asked you for a one-page progress report describing your activities for the past month. Although the report should be brief, your manager does want to know what you have accomplished as well as what you are currently working on. The highlights of your report will be included in your manager's own monthly progress report to management. If you are not currently working, focus the report on your academic activities.

3. *Performance report.* Your manager has asked you for a two-page self-evaluation of your performance for the past six months to be used in her periodic performance evaluation of your work. Be as objective as possible, neither overplaying nor underplaying your accomplishments. Remember to document what you say. Again, if you are not currently working, focus on your academic accomplishments.

4. You work for a large organization that has many employees. Each day, hundreds of employees drive their cars to work. Your organization has decided to investigate ways to cut individual transportation costs and conserve energy. Your manager has given you the job, asking you for a report that can be passed up the line to top management.

   You investigated two alternatives, vanpooling and carpooling, by attending a meeting at which both were discussed. When you returned from the meeting, you wrote the following report. Two days later, your manager returned it to you, complaining that it was unnecessarily complicated and therefore not yet ready to be submitted to busy managers. After reading the report, revise it according to the principles of this chapter. Pay particular attention to the amount of information you include, to the way you organize that information, and to the way you design the final report.

REPORT

On Tuesday, July 24, I attended a workshop sponsored by the Greater Little Rock Chamber of Commerce and the State Energy Offices. Governor Bill Clinton, the Federal and State Energy Offices, and local business and industry representatives discussed the pros and cons of mass transportation. Enclosed is a copy of the program and a packet of material they gave us.

The purpose of the meeting was to encourage employers to implement a vanpool or carpool program for their employees. Governor Clinton is asking our state to be a leader in energy conservation.

ConVoco Oil has around 160 vans across the country transporting their employees to and from work. They are very high on vanpooling. The vans cost between $9,000 and $11,500 and seat 8–12 people. They enlist an employee to drive and be responsible for upkeep and collection of fares from riders. In turn, that employee gets the use of the van on weekends and free fare during the week. They also reimburse the employee for upkeep expenses.

ConVoco receives reduced parking facility costs, improved employee relations, wider labor market, and improved community relations through reduced congestion, pollution, and energy consumption. On the other hand, they have a full-time employee and several part-time helpers that do the necessary paperwork. There is purchasing, insurance, fares received, and various forms for driver and riders to complete. Also, workmen's compensation and all that it entails is involved. ConVoco is mainly office/salaried personnel who do not punch time clocks.

I do not believe we should attempt vanpooling. We have predominantly hourly employees who work shift work and use time clocks. The administrative costs and workmen's compensation exposure would be a detriment in my opinion.

Carpooling seems to be the best approach for us. Several businesses and industries in our area have already started this, and they shared ideas with us. Mostly, the company posts a map of the area with sections or zone numbers. Employees are encouraged to sign the list for their area/zone; then those on the different lists are asked to get together and arrange their own plans for carpooling. The employer is not directly involved in who or how after promoting and encouraging the employees. This saves on administration costs and workmen's compensation is not affected, but everyone does his or her part to help conserve energy. Some good employee and community relations can be derived from it, too. It was suggested that incentives be offered to carpoolers. For instance: special parking spaces, flexibility in time to start work or get off work, or monthly or yearly parties for participants. We might arrange for parking spaces, but I do not believe we should get too involved for reasons already mentioned.

I definitely believe we all should, individually as well as collectively, conserve energy. Carpooling is a good idea for us, and I would like to see us promote it.

5. You are a member of a team that has been asked to evaluate the class you are taking on business writing, using the book *Writing: A Guide for Business Professionals.* You are to recommend the continuation, modification, or elimination of the class. After doing the appropriate research through interviews, surveys (if necessary), and printed sources, write your report. You might consider using the classic report format discussed in this chapter, although you could also develop your own format.

CHAPTER

11

Proposals: Persuading People

There will be times during your career when you will want to persuade people in an organization to buy a product, change a procedure, or institute a new program. To accomplish this, you may have to write a proposal. This chapter will show you how to write a successful one.

The car you drive, the TV set you own, the medicines your doctor prescribes, even this book, all began as proposals on someone's desk. If you want to build a new machine, develop a cure for a disease, implement a new program, sell a large order to a customer, or just make a little change in the way things are done in your office, you'll probably write a proposal. Engineers write technical proposals to recommend new products or systems, scientists write research proposals to get funds to support their research projects, and sales representatives write product proposals to sell products, programs, or services.

But even if you're not an engineer, scientist, or sales rep, you are going to have to write proposals some time during your career. The situation may be a pretty simple, everyday one. You may notice how something in your organization can be done better—perhaps you realize that production in your office can be scheduled and controlled more efficiently by a new data processing system than by the old handwritten forms. You approach your manager with the idea. "Might work," he says, "Why don't you give me a two-page proposal on it first of the week." Or you're a manager who's tired of the lousy performance appraisals submitted to you by people in your department. "These people need some training in how to write a good appraisal," you say to yourself. So you write a three-part proposal: the first section describing the problem, the second recommending a one-day effective writing workshop to solve it, and the third outlining the program and setting forth costs.

Or take a more complicated situation. You are the new member of your local city council. For months, council has been talking about the deterioration of the downtown area. Stores, restaurants, and even theaters are closing because of new shopping malls in the suburbs. The prevailing sentiment is that council has got to take some action before your inner city becomes as blighted as downtown areas elsewhere. But what action?

"Why don't we hire someone to study the problem and recommend a solution," suggests one member of council. "That's fine," pipes up another, "but where are we going to get the money?" You remember reading an article about grants of money offered by the federal government to enable cities with problems such as yours to hire consultants to analyze the problem. You suggest this, and before you know it, you are appointed to investigate further and write the proposal requesting the money.

Proposals come in different shapes and sizes. Here are some of the major types you may run across during your career.

- ***Research proposals.*** Research proposals may also be called *grant proposals*. If you work for a large organization that is involved in research of any kind—say a drug company, a large manufacturing company, or a university or research center—you may have to write a proposal to a federal agency or charitable foundation in order to get funds to do needed research. Most modern scientific research is funded by such proposals. These proposals are submitted to government agencies like the National Science Foundation or the National Institutes of Health, or private foundations like the Kellogg or Mellon Foundation. They are frequently long, running to hundreds of pages, and quite elaborate, with their formats spelled out in detail by the funding agency.
- ***Research and development proposals.*** These proposals, often called R & Ds, are the basis of much work done for the government, ranging from studies of the environment to large-scale weapons systems. Often they are responses to RFPs (requests for proposals), which are circulated by government agencies asking for proposals to develop particular projects. Like research proposals, they are usually long and detailed, with formats dictated strictly by the funding agency. Successful proposals of this type can often be worth millions and even billions of dollars and involve cooperation and coordination among large numbers of people, departments, and even different companies.

  The development of the B-1 bomber is a good example. In 1969, the Pentagon asked three aircraft companies—General

Dynamics of Fort Worth, Boeing of Seattle, and North American Rockwell of Los Angeles—to submit proposals to develop the B-1 bomber, a plane with a speed of 2,000 mph and the ability to carry missiles plus nuclear bombs. In addition, two companies—Pratt & Whitney of Hartford and General Electric of Evendale, Ohio—were asked to submit proposals to develop the engines for the plane. Each of these prime contractors in turn asked subcontractors to submit proposals to them to build different parts of the plane. These were then assembled into overall proposals that were submitted to the Pentagon. The B-1 contract, worth "a minimum of 5 billion dollars, involving thousands of workers from laborers to engineers and management personnel," was won by North American Rockwell and General Electric.[1]

- ***Sales, program, and consulting proposals.*** If you are a sales or marketing representative for your firm, you may have to write *sales proposals* to clients. Sometimes these are done on standard proposal forms that provide sections to fill in price, delivery schedule, etc., but sometimes you will have to invent your own format. Most large sales of manufactured goods begin with such proposals. If you work in human relations or personnel and want to implement a new training program, you will probably have to write a *program proposal* recommending it. And if you work for a government agency or a large corporation, you may well have to request and then evaluate *consulting proposals* requesting outside consultants to help on various projects.

It's impossible to learn the names and formats of all the different types of proposals you may have to write during your career. But luckily, the basic principle for writing successful proposals is always the same. Whether you write in-house proposals for changes within your own organization, research proposals to government agencies or charitable foundations, or proposals selling products or services, your choices of information, organization, design, and style will be determined by your readers' attitudes toward your subject. If your readers are favorable toward your idea, your job will be a relatively easy one—you may have to explain the details of your proposal, but you probably won't have to spend much time arguing for its acceptance. But if your readers are less favorable or even hostile to your idea, you're going to have to choose the information, organization, and style that will convince them.

In the following pages, you will learn how to write proposals that will *persuade different types of readers*—favorable, relatively neutral, and finally hostile readers. You need to understand that these are

[1]Steven Pauley, *Technical Report Writing Today* (New York: Houghton Mifflin, 1973) 163–64.

just three points along a reader resistance spectrum. You will have to locate the readers for each of your proposals somewhere along this spectrum.

Favorable — Neutral — Hostile

We'll refer at times to another reader variable—how much your readers know about the subject of your proposal. The less they know about the subject, the more you're going to have to explain. You also have to understand that what we are discussing are not formulas for proposals but principles to guide you. You'll have to adapt these principles to suit the particular proposal situation you are in.

WHEN YOUR READERS ARE FAVORABLE TO YOUR IDEA

This is the easiest kind of proposal-writing situation to be in, because your readers are already favorably inclined toward your idea. This is sometimes the case with in-house proposals, especially in those situations where a manager likes your idea and simply wants you to write it up so it can be presented to another supervisor. Since your reader already understands what you are proposing and the reason for it, you only need to give a minimum of information.

Basically, the questions most favorable readers want answered are—

- What exactly are you recommending?
- Why are you recommending it?
- And how will your recommendation be implemented?

And since your readers are already pretty well convinced, you won't have to write a long, detailed proposal. You should know, though, that sometimes the person you are writing to may submit your proposal to a higher ranking manager for approval. Since that person may not be so favorably disposed toward your project, be sure to provide enough evidence to convince him or her also.

After you collect your information, organize it as directly as possible. Most of the time you can just begin with a description of what you are proposing, followed by your justification of it. Since your readers are already favorably inclined, you don't need to convince them before presenting your proposal. Sometimes, in fact, you will have to resist the temptation to begin with the reasons justifying your proposal. Usually, it's best to follow the priority pattern of organization we discussed earlier in this book.

PROPOSAL

We propose that the billing department be allowed to create two new personnel positions . . . .

JUSTIFICATION

Our justification for this request is that during the past six months our workload has increased to more than. . . .

IMPLEMENTATION (if needed)

People hired in these two positions can immediately be assigned to preparing bills more than 60 days old and to. . . .

A Writing Situation

To understand how to develop and write a proposal for a favorable reader, imagine the following situation. You have been asked by the vice-president for development at your university (he's the person in charge of getting funds for the university) to meet with a small group of students and faculty to discuss a project he has in mind. At your first meeting, he announces to your group that a major fund drive is about to begin at the university. The funds your state-supported school currently receives from taxes have been adequate to build necessary buildings and hire sufficient faculty, but they haven't allowed the school to buy those "extras" that are necessary for it to do a first-class job—video equipment for large classrooms, computers for student use, sophisticated lab equipment, scholarly leaves for faculty, and the like. Now the university has decided to appeal to alumni, large corporations, and charitable foundations for the money to buy these things. The goal of the drive is one million dollars.

At the end of his description of the drive, the development VP says, "The reason why I've called this group together is to see what you think of using some of the money collected from this drive to establish a student scholarship program. Because both federal and state funding sources are starting to dry up, we have many students in need of financial aid. A scholarship fund would help us support these students."

Your group, composed of students and faculty known around campus for being especially interested in student welfare, thinks that this is a fine idea. After all, says one student member, "If students can't afford to attend this school, what's the use of buying TV's, computers, and lab equipment?"

"Okay," responds the VP, "what I need from you is a proposal that some of the money we receive from our campaign be set aside in such a fund. I'll then present it for approval to the university committee in charge of the campaign. If they like it, they'll submit it in turn to the Board of Visitors, who must give the final approval for all campaign fund allocations."

Your group begins to draft the proposal. After a good deal of discussion (and some pretty petty haggling, you think) over how much money you should request and how it should be allocated, the group settles on a percentage of the total funds collected, 25%, to be awarded partly on the basis of achievement and partly on the basis of need. When you have written and revised it, your proposal is ready to be sent to the VP.

```
Proposed: That 25% of all funds collected in the
university fund drive be allocated to a student
scholarship fund. One-half of these funds will be
awarded on the basis of achievement in classes (as
measured primarily by GPA) and one-half on the basis
of need, as determined by the student's income from
parents and other sources measured against the
student's expenses.
```

"Hey, wait a minute," says someone in the group. "Before we send this thing, don't we need to provide some justification to prove why we should receive the funds?"

"Why?" asks another. "After all, we know the VP's in favor of this. He's the one who suggested it to us."

"Sure," says another, "but he's got to present it to the university campaign committee and the Board of Visitors. And he'll need some proof for them."

So you agree to include in your proposal a justification section, giving the reasons why the scholarship fund should be created. In order to collect information, your group decides to interview ten students from the various schools at the university to find out whether students would need such a scholarship. You discover that seven out of ten say that their parents' income is not enough to support their education fully. All these students work in the summer and seven work part-time during the school year to contribute to their expenses. But all students tell you that jobs are getting harder and harder to find.

You also call the financial aid office to find out what funds are available to students needing them. You discover that the level of aid has fallen sharply in the last year. The director in charge of financial aid says, "Last year, the federal government stipulated that no student could receive more than $1,500 from tuition assistance. Until then, that was the principal source of financial aid." She also tells you that the state has recently raised the minimum family income required to qualify for loans. In order for a student to qualify for a loan, his or her family must make below $35,000 per year.

Armed with these facts, your group redrafts the proposal. After some discussion and a good deal of rewriting, it looks like this:

Proposal

That 25% of all funds collected in the university fund drive be allocated to a student scholarship fund. One-half of these funds will be awarded on the basis of achievement in classes (as measured primarily by GPA) and one-half on the basis of need, as determined by the student's income from parents and other sources measured against the student's expenses.

Justification

In our opinion, many students at this university need the additional financial support that a scholarship fund would provide. Last week, this committee interviewed ten students from the colleges of business, arts and sciences, education, and fine arts. Almost without exception, these students said that they would need more than their parents' income could provide in order to complete their educations. Of course, many of our students already work, part-time during the school year and full-time during the summer, but our understanding is that such jobs are getting harder and harder to find.

And as jobs are getting harder to find, financial aid funds also seem to be diminishing, both on the federal and state level. Last year, for instance, the federal government stipulated that no student could receive more than $1,500 from federal assistance funds. And just recently, the state has raised minimum family income requirements for its loans: now if a student's family income is above $35,000, that student does not qualify for a loan.

Implementation

Because we will not know how much money will be in the Scholarship Fund until the current fund drive is completed, we cannot describe all the details of the implementation of this proposal. We suggest that a committee composed of students, faculty, and administrators be formed to set up a detailed system.

We do recommend the following:

That 25% of all funds collected in the university fund drive be allocated to a student scholarship fund. One-half of these funds will be awarded on the basis of scholastic achievement (as measured primarily by GPA) and one-half on the basis of need, as determined by the student's income from parents and other sources measured against the student's expenses.

```
                    Conclusion
  We hope that these reasons are sufficient to justify
the scholarship fund we have proposed. Some students
have proven that they deserve such support; many
others need it. We hope that the university will set
up the fund to help both groups.
```

In about a week, the VP for development asks to address the group again. "I liked your proposal, mainly because it was so short and to the point. So I presented it to the campaign committee yesterday, but I didn't get quite the response I'd hoped for. As some of you know, that committee is composed of a few students, but most are faculty and administrators. While all the student members agreed with the proposal right away, a number of the faculty and administrators were more skeptical. In a nutshell, they told me that it's not that they really disagree with the proposal. It's just that they were not as convinced by it as they were by the proposals for more equipment, additional classroom space, and scholarly leaves. Through facts and statistics, these proposals really made their case. Frankly, they weren't convinced that the ten students you interviewed really represent the circumstances of the 6,000 students on this campus. And even though some financial aid programs have been cut, they think there are still others. The funds we collect will only go so far. In essence, they're just not convinced that a scholarship fund is the best way to spend our limited funds."

Even before the VP is finished, you notice how people are reacting. Most are looking disgusted. A few are muttering under their breath. One student, whose face had been getting redder by the minute, says, "Wouldn't you know those people are more interested in their TV's, computers, and scholarly leaves than they are in students. That washes it, I guess."

"Not necessarily," responds the VP. "I think a number of people on the committee are on your side. The students already agree with you. And some of the faculty and administrators are not against you; they're just neutral. You've got to remember that there are lots of different groups competing for this money. Naturally, the committee is going to award the money to the groups that are the most persuasive. I suggest you rewrite the proposal and see if you can't make it more convincing. If it is, you may get the funds yet."

In the discussion that follows, your group decides to revise the proposal and resubmit it to the campaign committee. Most people agree that your proposal was weak because it didn't give enough specific justification. So you resolve to get more hard facts for your revision. But you also realize that you are in a very different situation, this time for you're writing to an audience that is not so familiar with your ideas, nor is it entirely sympathetic to them.

Before going any further with our imaginary situation, let's discuss what principles to follow when your audience is neutral toward your idea and therefore needs to be persuaded. Then we'll apply these principles to your revision of the proposal.

WHEN YOUR READERS ARE NEUTRAL TO YOUR IDEA

Since proposals almost always request that money be spent in order to make changes, your readers will usually fall more in the middle of the spectrum on page 251; that is, they will need convincing. This is often the case with in-house proposals, and frequently the case with research and sales proposals. If your readers are neutral, they will usually have the following general questions:

- What exactly are you proposing?
- Why are you proposing this?
- What benefits will this proposal have?
- How much will it cost?
- How will it be implemented?
- How will we monitor its success?

The information you include in your proposal will answer these questions. Sometimes, and this is especially true for proposals to a state or the federal government, you will have to adapt your answers to a specified format. At first glance, for instance, the format for proposals for the National Science Foundation looks very different from the questions above, for it requires four major sections.

- narrative
- abstract
- budget
- cover sheet

But as you write various parts of the narrative section, you will end up answering five of the six questions I've listed above, and you'll answer the remaining question about cost in the budget section. If a company or government agency wants you to write a proposal in a particular way, this will be specified, usually in a request for a proposal. And sometimes, both government agencies and companies hold pre-proposal conferences, at which questions about the information required can be asked. But no matter how different proposal formats may look, readers usually want you to answer the questions I've listed above.

The specific information you use to answer these questions will be determined by what you think will best persuade your readers. Smart proposal writers try to press their readers' "hot buttons," by giving the kind of information that will particularly appeal to them. Often, it's important to show exactly how much money your proposal will save, perhaps by reducing personnel or by making production more efficient. In other cases, readers may be convinced by a fast delivery schedule or a guarantee of high quality. Sometimes, you will have to touch a number of bases, as the proposer of a new data processing system did when he described how his system would save a company money by allowing more efficient administration, shorter training periods, lower initial equipment costs, and cheaper repair bills. Whatever information you choose to include, the general rule is the more specific, the better.

How do you organize this information? Most writers begin their proposals by answering the second question above, "Why are you proposing this?" Their answer usually is that there is a need to be met or a problem to be solved. Naturally, their proposal, which they usually describe in the second section of the document, is the solution to the problem. Then they follow these sections with discussions of benefits, implementation procedures, and costs. In other words, most of these kinds of proposals generally follow the priority pattern—putting important information (the problem and your solution) at the beginning.

A Writing Situation (continued)

Now let's return to the campaign fund situation and see how these principles of choosing convincing information and organizing it in the priority pattern might be applied. Remember that the Campaign Fund Committee wasn't convinced before because your proposal lacked enough facts to justify it. Well, this time your group resolves to do a thorough job of research.

To make sure your interviews are representative, you interview ten students, selected randomly, for each college in the university. And you send a written survey about family income, financial aid, and part-time work to a much larger sample of students. But you don't stop there. You also get figures about average family income from the dean of students, an estimate from your accounting office of the costs of attending four years of college for a typical student at your university, and information from your financial aid office on exactly what has happened to federal and state funds during the past five years. By the time you have finished, you have assembled an impressive list of facts and figures to support your position.

1. Average income for families with students attending your university is $45,000 per year.
2. Twenty-six percent of the families you surveyed will have two or more children in college at the same time.
3. Financial aid has fallen from an average award of $2,400 to $950 in the last five years. The two federal loan programs that your students relied on most heavily have been cut substantially in the past two years.

a. The Guaranteed Student Loan Program has been restricted to families earning less than $35,000 per year, not taking into account how many children of a particular family are in college.
b. The National Defense Student Loan fund has been cut more than 40% in the last two years.

4. Sixty-four percent of your students work during the summer to earn college funds—the average amount earned is $1,400.
5. Forty percent of the full-time students at your university work at least 20 hours per week during the school year.
6. Costs of attending your university have risen 80% in the last five years. Now the total cost, including tuition, room, and board, is $7,500 per year.

You decide to organize your proposal by beginning with a statement of the need for the fund, then describing what you are proposing, then its benefits, and finally how it can be implemented. After a great deal of discussion and rewriting, the final draft of your proposal looks like the one on pages 259–61.

You can imagine what happens this time. Almost to a person, the members of the Campaign Fund Committee are persuaded by your proposal, especially by its careful use of facts and figures. Some members are shocked by how much costs of attending the university have risen. Others comment that they certainly didn't know of the financial problems faced by many of their students. After some discussion, the committee votes to allocate 20% of the funds collected to the Scholarship Fund. Considering how much other proposals received, this is more than generous.

But don't count your chickens yet. You still have one more hurdle—final approval by the Board of Visitors. The Campaign Fund Committee submits its overall proposal to the board, recommending that the funds be allocated to a number of projects, including the 20% to yours. But by the time the board has finished its considerations, your proposed scholarship fund ranks near the bottom of approved projects, to be funded if most of the others are first—an unlikely prospect.

You are told that a few members of the board supported your proposal, but that most were either neutral or opposed. Two of the most powerful members were sharply opposed, one commenting that students should work during the summers and part-time during the year and not spend so much time partying and on vacations. The other kept insisting that there must be other funding sources available. Luckily, the board plans an open hearing for all proposals, at which you will have a chance to present your full proposal. Even though your group is disheartened and discouraged by this time, you are encouraged by the VP to rewrite the proposal, making the board understand just how pressing student financial problems are at your university.

PROPOSAL FOR A SCHOLARSHIP FUND
AT CITY UNIVERSITY

The Need

Many students attending City University are facing a financial crisis: many simply do not have the money to continue attending school. According to facts supplied by the university accounting office, the costs of attending this school have risen approximately 80% over the past five years, from $4,200 in 19-- to a present cost for tuition, room, and board of $7,500 per year (see Figure 1).

Yet, as Figure 1 also shows, the amount of money available to support students during college has decreased by more than 60% during the same period, from an average award of $2,400 in 19-- to $950 in 19--. The major reason for this dramatic reduction is that two major federal loan programs, the Guaranteed Student Loan Program and the National Defense Student Loan Program, have been cut drastically during the last five years.

Figure 1

COLLEGE COSTS VS. FINANCIAL AID

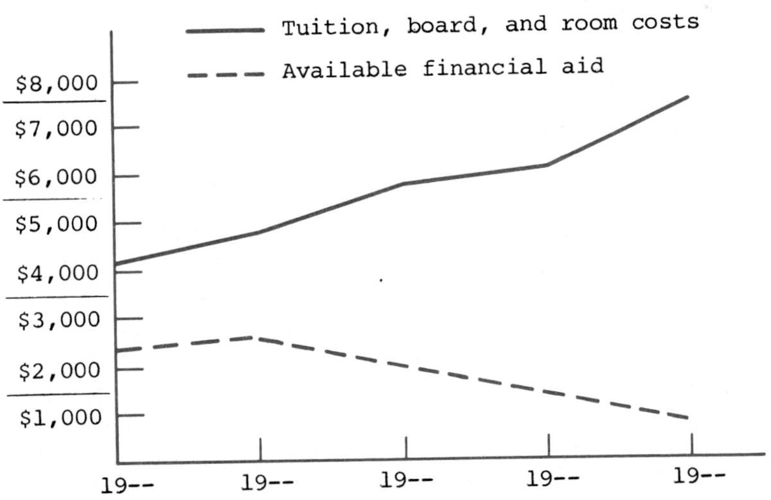

These conditions put many of our students in a financial bind. Their families (with an average income of $45,000 per year) cannot supply any more money. A further problem is that 26% of our students' families must support at least two children in college at the same time.

Many of our students work to help defray the costs of their education. But the amount they can work is limited by the number of jobs available and the hours they can work. Many of our students simply cannot earn enough to make up the difference between what parents can pay and what our university charges. Therefore, we recommend the following solution.

The Solution

That 25% of all funds collected in the university fund drive be allocated to a student scholarship fund. One-half of these funds will be awarded on the basis of scholastic achievement (as measured primarily by GPA) and one-half on the basis of need, as determined by the student's income from parents and other sources measured against the student's expenses.

Benefits

This fund would have two major benefits:

1. It would help provide funds to replace the money that our students have lost in financial aid during the last five years. A survey of students attending all colleges in the university indicates that 35% would benefit from additional support.
2. It would be a tangible way of rewarding students who have done exceptionally well in their academic work. Records at the registrar's office indicate that over 250 of our students presently have a GPA of 3.7 or higher. Even a small scholarship would provide these students with additional incentive and support to pursue their studies.

Implementation

Because we will not know how much money will be in the scholarship fund until the current fund drive is completed, we cannot describe all the details of the implementation of this proposal. We suggest that a committee composed of students, faculty, and administrators be formed to set up a detailed system.

We do recommend the following:

1. That funds for academic achievement be awarded on the basis of GPA combined with recommendations from appropriate faculty members.
2. That the present system used by the financial aid office to determine financial need be applied to the need for scholarship funds also.

Conclusion

We request that the Campaign Fund Committee give our proposal the most careful consideration. Through our research, we have discovered that many students at our university are in serious need of financial help. The scholarship fund we recommend can provide that help.

Now you are in a third kind of proposal situation, writing to an audience that is unsympathetic and even hostile to your point of view.

WHEN YOUR READERS ARE HOSTILE TO YOUR IDEA

You won't often face this situation, but you should know what methods to use when you do. Basically, you will have to adapt the methods we discussed with the more neutral readers to this situation. The information you use to justify your proposal will have to be very "hard"; that is, you will need to be specific, give figures if appropriate, and cite authorities that your readers trust for your evidence. Organizing your proposal may present a problem, because you will have to decide whether to use a direct or more indirect method. If you choose the direct pattern, you would put your actual proposal near the beginning of the document, as the writers of the second version of the scholarship fund proposal did. If you choose a more indirect pattern, you will lead with a justification for your proposal, in order to prepare hostile readers for the proposal itself.

There is no easy choice here. If you opt for the direct method, you may raise the hackles of your hostile audience even more. But if you use the indirect method to prepare them, you may lose their interest before you get to your proposal. If your audience is not familiar with your proposal, it's probably best to be fairly direct, stating the problem or need and then your solution. If they are familiar with it but still oppose it, you can be more indirect.

Your major concern when writing to a hostile audience will be to try to deal persuasively with their thoughts and feelings. This may mean offering more evidence than you ordinarily would, building up to your actual proposal indirectly with a discussion of the problem or need, or even acknowledging and dealing with arguments that they have previously made. In these situations, it will help you to remember that the root of the word persuade (suade) means "sweet," and the old saying that "You catch more flies with honey than with vinegar."[2]

A Writing Situation (continued)

Your group decides to revise the proposal one more time, taking the board's opposition and objections into consideration. Luckily, you can use a large part of the original proposal, since the board has never seen it. But you decide to add information and change your organization. This time, you will lead with a more detailed discussion of the financial problems currently faced by students. Then, to

[2]James Kinney, David E. Jones, and John Scally. *Understanding Writing* (New York: Random House, 1983) 149.

counter the arguments that there are other solutions, you will show why alternative solutions won't work. Finally, you will recommend your scholarship fund as the solution. You hope that this detailed discussion presented in an indirect organizational pattern will convince the board that a problem exists and prepare them for your solution. Specifically, you decide to organize your proposal like this.

---

1. A description of the problem, this time including details about how most students do work during the summers and part-time during the year in order to counter the argument that students waste time rather than contributing to their education.
2. To drive home the impact of the problem on students, you decide to describe some specific students with financial problems.
3. To take into account the argument that there are other solutions, you decide to discuss and dismiss alternative solutions.
4. You will describe your solution, the Scholarship Fund.
5. You will describe its benefits.
6. You will describe the way you will implement the new system.

Since you are spending so much time making your case at the beginning before giving the actual proposal, the group decides to begin the document with a quick summary of the proposal and its benefits. Some members argue that this may have the effect of turning the board off before you convince them that a problem exists, but most finally agree that if you don't let them know at the beginning what you are proposing, they will have no reason to read your long first sections on the problems, its effects, etc. And in addition to the line graph you included last time, you decide to include a pie chart to dramatize how many students are affected.

The revised proposal is on pages 264–68, with changed or added sections bracketed. Note that the first sentence has been changed slightly to present the need more dramatically. The fourth paragraph has been made more specific, primarily to counter the board member's comment about students taking vacations instead of working. And new sections on effects and alternative solutions have been added.

PROPOSAL FOR A SCHOLARSHIP FUND
AT CITY UNIVERSITY

The Need

Students attending City University are facing a financial crisis: they simply do not have the money to continue attending school. According to facts supplied by the university accounting office, the costs of attending this school have risen approximately 80% over the past five years, from $4,200 in 19-- to a present cost for tuition, room, and board of $7,500 per year (see Figure 1).

Yet, as Figure 1 also shows, the amount of money available to support students during college has decreased by more than 60% during the same period, from an average award of $2,400 in 19-- to $950 in 19--. The major reason for this dramatic reduction is that two major federal loan programs, the Guaranteed Student Loan Program and the National Defense Student Loan Program, have been cut drastically during the last five years.

These conditions put many of our students in a financial bind. Their families (with an average income of $45,000 per year) cannot supply any more money. A further problem is that

Figure 1

COLLEGE COSTS VS. FINANCIAL AID

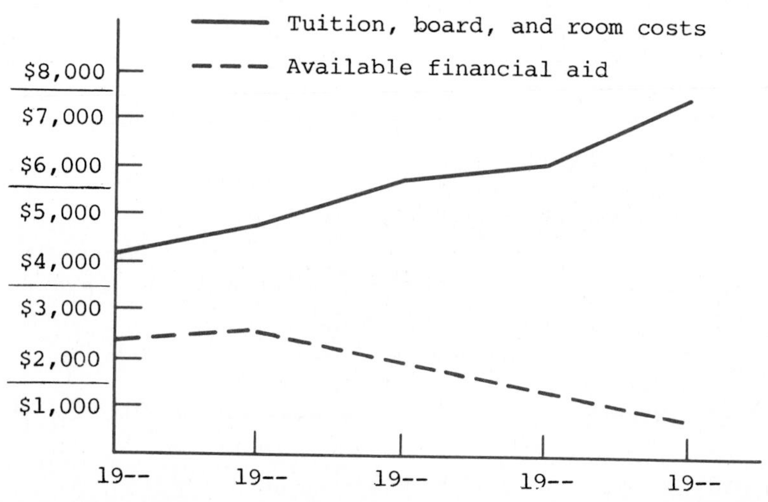

26% of our students' families must support at least two children in college at the same time.

Even though 64% of our students work during the summer to earn college funds, the average amount they earn is only $1,400, much of which must be paid toward their summer support. Thus, summer earnings provide only a fraction of the money needed for college fees. Forty percent of our students also work part-time during the year to help defray costs, but their hours and thus their earnings are limited by academic responsibilities.

Effects of this Problem

As the following chart shows, a survey sample of over 400 students reveals that at least 70% of our students are being hurt by their lack of financial resources. Students are affected in various ways. Some have to drop out of school for a year to earn enough money to return. Many of the ones who hold part-time jobs find that they must cut the number of courses they take per semester. Others receive lower grades.

Figure 2

EFFECTS OF LACK OF FINANCIAL RESOURCES

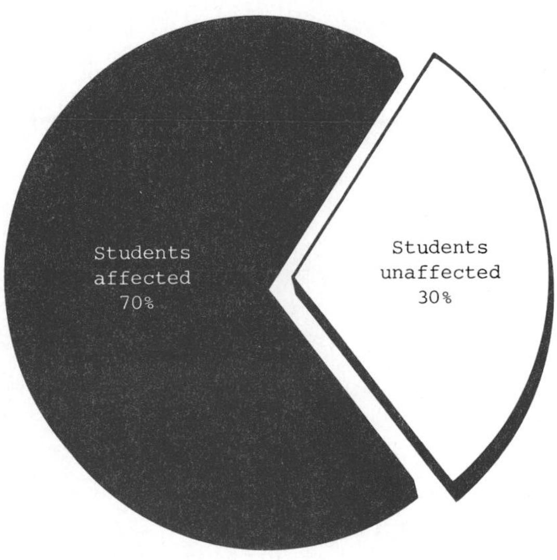

Source: Responses to survey.

The following three students are typical examples of the kinds of problems students now face.

Student No. 1. Mary Ann is a junior in the School of Business Administration, with a GPA of 3.84. Until last summer, she worked as a waitress, earning more than $2,000 per summer. From this sum, she was able to contribute $1,500 toward her college expenses. But last summer, because of a decrease in jobs in her hometown, she had to take a lower-paying job. As a result, she is working part-time this year to pay her fees. Because of this, she says, her GPA last semester fell to 2.9.

Student No. 2. John is a sophomore in the School of Fine Arts. His parents are both public school teachers and receive a combined income of only $36,000 per year, hardly enough to support him and his brother in college. As a result, John has to work 30 hours per week. Therefore, he cannot take certain studio courses he needs in his program. John says that he will probably have to drop out of school for a year to earn his fees.

Student No. 3. Vanessa is a senior in the College of Arts and Sciences. She is majoring in biology and wants to do graduate work. She is a good student, but because she has had to work for 22 hours per week for the last three years, her GPA is 3.3. Compared to that of most students, this GPA is impressive, but it is not high enough to get her into the first-class graduate school that she chose. Therefore, she will have to attend a lesser-known one.

These are only three examples among many others. But they are typical of the financial dilemmas our students face.

Alternative Solutions

1. This university could create a scholarship fund to help support such students. Half this fund would be awarded on the basis of academic merit, the other half on the basis of need. While the school doesn't presently have the funds to do this, a portion of the funds received during the fund drive could be allocated to this.

   Money from this fund would go to Mary Ann and Vanessa on the basis of merit and to John on the basis of need.
2. Other sources of funding, either governmental or private, could be sought. We talked with the development offices of a university in Minneapolis and one in Illinois because both had tried to do this. They have had very limited success after extended efforts.
3. Students could work more to contribute to their educational costs. As we have shown above, however, limited summer salaries do not provide enough funds in many cases. Many of the students we interviewed tell us that available local, part-time jobs are very limited. Some students, especially those in fine arts and the sciences, cannot work part-time and keep up with work in school.

Solution

We recommend that 20% of all funds collected in the university fund drive be allocated to a student scholarship fund. One-half of these funds will be awarded on the basis of scholastic achievement (as measured primarily by GPA) and one-half on the basis of need, as determined by the student's income from parents and other sources measured against the student's expenses.

Benefits

This fund would have two major benefits:

1. It would help provide funds to replace the money that our students have lost on financial aid during the last five years. A survey of students attending all colleges in the university indicates that over 35% would benefit from additional support.
2. It would be a tangible way of rewarding students who have done exceptionally well in their academic work. Records at the registrar's office indicate that over 250 of our students presently have a GPA of 3.7 or higher. Even a small scholarship would provide these students with additional incentive and support to pursue their studies.

Implementation

Because we will not know how much money will be in the scholarship fund until the current fund drive is completed, we cannot describe all the details of the implementation of this proposal. We suggest that a committee composed of students, faculty, and administrators be formed to set up a detailed system.

We do recommend the following:

1. That funds for academic achievement be awarded on the basis of GPA combined with recommendations from appropriate faculty members.
2. That the present system used by the financial aid office to determine financial need be applied to the need for scholarship funds also.

Conclusion

We hope the Board of Visitors will give our proposal the most careful consideration. Through our research, we have discovered that many students at our university are in serious need of financial help. The scholarship fund we recommend can provide that help.

PROPOSAL DESIGN AND STYLE

The design and style of your proposal can also be important. Especially when your proposal is fairly long, you will need to use headings to separate sections and enumeration to highlight points. It's even more important to choose a style that will project a credible and confident persona. People give money to those they trust to get the job done; therefore, successful proposal writers use a positive and upbeat voice. If you skim back through the last version of the scholarship proposal, you will hear this voice. There, it comes through primarily in statements made without qualification ("Students attending City University are facing a financial crisis . . . ,"), and in the use of specific evidence, particularly in the descriptions of the three individual students.

But this voice can be created through other techniques as well. In scientific proposals, it may be created by careful qualification of statements to convince a reader that you are not overstating or oversimplifying your argument. It can even be expressed in the use of positive adjectives, as in this example from the summary of a proposal to recruit and educate minority students (adjectives are underlined).

> To complement its academic program, the VST Program will develop support services in a <u>strong</u> counseling component. . . .
>
> The University's philosophy and the Program's philosophy are <u>compatible</u>. The University is <u>unique</u> in that it is. . . .
>
> The Project design is of <u>high quality</u>. The VST Program objectives <u>clearly show</u> how goals will be met. The management is <u>designed to support</u> each activity.

Take the opportunity to use a positive voice anywhere you can in a proposal. If you are writing a technical proposal, the only chance you get may be in the cover letter, as in the following letter accompanying a proposal to install a new office communications system. Notice how the writer chooses words with positive connotations like *benefits*, *increase*, and *smooth implementation*.

> We have proposed a system which we feel will provide two key benefits to . . . . First, we believe that this system will increase the productivity of both management and staff, as well as the secretaries that support them. Second, the early installation of this system will enable D/MIS to gain the expertise so necessary to the smooth implementation of Office Automation in the user department.

SUMMARY

A proposal is essentially an attempt to persuade someone to make a change, whether that change is buying a new product or service, adopting a new procedure or system, or awarding someone money to pursue research. To write a convincing proposal, you're going to have to figure out where your readers stand—whether they are generally favorable, neutral, or even hostile to your idea. Once you decide this, you can choose the information, organization, style, and design that will best convince them.

The three scholarship proposal situations you read about in this chapter are very like the situations you'll face when you write proposals.

- First, some of your proposals will be written with a group, just as these were, because you'll need the expertise of people with different kinds of training in order to write successfully.
- Second, you'll frequently have to do research to write a proposal, but you may not use the traditional "library" techniques you learned in school. Like the writers above, you may have to telephone to find out information, to interview numbers of people, and even do surveys. If you are competing with other proposal writers for a particular grant or sale, you may want to do some research to find what they are offering to do—if you can.
- Third, if you write very many proposals, you will find yourself using parts of older proposals in your new ones, just as the writers in this chapter did. In fact, organizations that write lots of proposals keep materials like the résumés of people who will be involved in a project, specifications of products, and descriptions of methods on file so they can use these again and again. These materials, often called "boilerplate," are sometimes used as they are and sometimes revised to fit a different proposal.

APPENDIX: PROPOSAL RESOURCES

There are literally thousands of private foundations and government agencies that are possible sources for grant funds. Here is a list of some resources you can check for possible support of a project.

Annual Register of Grant Support: A Directory of Funding Sources. Wilmette, Ill.: National Register Publishing.

Published annually, this register includes details of grant support programs of government agencies, public and private foundations, corporations, etc. It covers a broad spectrum of interests such as academic and scientific research, project development, travel and exchange programs, publication and support equipment, construction grants, in-service training, and competitive awards and prizes in a variety of fields. Each program description contains details of the type, purpose, and duration of the grant, amount of funding available, eligibility requirements, and so forth.

Catalog of Federal Domestic Assistance. Washington, D.C.: Government Printing Office.

A government-wide compendium of federal programs, projects, services, and activities that provide assistance and benefits to the American public. Published annually, it includes procedures to be followed in proposals and requirements of various programs.

Corporate Foundation Profiles. New York: The Foundation Center.

This source analyzes over 200 of the largest corporate-sponsored foundations and provides brief profiles on some 300 other corporate foundations.

Federal Assistance Programs Retrieval System.

This is a computer-based information program of sources of federal funds. Access is available through regional offices of federal agencies, some libraries and universities, and some state and county government offices.

National Data Book. 9th ed. New York: The Foundation Center, 1985.

Designed primarily for preliminary research on funding sources, it is particularly helpful in identifying the many small foundations that are often important sources of local funding. These foundations give hundreds of thousands of small grants ranging in size from as little as one dollar to several thousand dollars. Provides information needed to further research the foundations' application procedures and primary giving interests.

The Corporate Fund Raising Directory. 1985–86 ed. Hartsdale, NY: Public Service Materials Center, 1984.

A directory of over 600 corporations that provide grant support for various projects. For each corporation, the telephone number, contact person, application information, geographic preference, primary giving interests, and guidelines on grant programs are given.

Loren Renz, ed. *The Foundation Directory*. 10th ed. New York: The Foundation Center, 1985.

An index to 4,402 foundations that account for $63.1 billion in assets and $4.1 billion in annual grant giving, including independent, company-sponsored, operating, and community foundations. For each foundation, the directory gives donor, financial data, purpose and activities, type of support awarded, limitations, etc.

Elan Garonzik, ed. *The Foundation Grants Index: A Cumulative List of Foundation Grants Compiled by the Foundation Center*. 14th ed. New York: The Foundation Center, 1985.

An index covering 34,040 grants of $5,000 or more awarded by 460 foundations.

APPLICATIONS

1. The organization you work for has decided to diversify into new areas. You have been asked to propose a suitable product (for example, an automobile safety device, a line of clothing, a new high tech device) or service (for example, nursing care for the elderly, counseling of some kind, home improvement). After deciding on a product or service and investigating it, write a short proposal recommending that the organization adopt it.

2. You are a member of a neighborhood community association that has decided to establish a recreational facility for the area with provisions for both children and adults. After careful planning, the group projects the following initial expenses:

$3,200	Purchase of four acres of land
$ 700	Purchase of two used modular homes as clubhouse
$1,200	Cost of moving homes to site and assembly of homes
$ 900	Construction of three rooms inside the clubhouse—open room for large group activities; smaller room for social events; room for association office
$21,000	Construction of a 25-meter pool
$ 2,300	Design and paving of two tennis courts
$ 4,500	Miscellaneous expenses—lights, landscaping, fences, etc.

Your county board of supervisors has funds to provide up to one-half of the support for such projects, provided applicants demonstrate that they can provide the rest. Even though the association can collect only about $10,000, you can make up the rest of your half in the services of members who have volunteered to donate their time.

Write a proposal for the funds. The board of supervisors has no particular format you have to follow, but they do request that you keep the proposal to no more than five typewritten pages.

3. Your local chamber of commerce wants to create a program to teach underprivileged adults the functional skills of reading, writing, and computation. You have been asked to plan a suitable program and write a proposal to an appropriate foundation for funds to implement it.

You decide to begin by proposing a small program built around self-instructional materials, teachers, and aides. The first year's costs look like this.

$70,000	Three teachers—science, math, English
$15,000	Three part-time aides
$ 7,500	Self-instructional materials and equipment, including texts, programmed materials, and tape players

Classes will meet in a local school during afternoon and evening hours. The lab containing the self-instructional materials will be open during these hours also.

Using the references at the end of this chapter, locate some foundations that might fund such an undertaking. Write a persuasive proposal to one of these organizations, organizing it as you think best.

4. You feel that an expensive piece of equipment (you decide what it should be) is needed for your organization. You suggested it to your manager, who didn't seem very enthusiastic. In fact, your manager explained that the organization just couldn't afford the necessary expense right now. But you are convinced that the equipment is necessary. Your manager has agreed to consider a proposal if you keep it to one page. When writing the proposal, use the techniques suggested at the end of this chapter for dealing with hostile readers.

CHAPTER

12

Manuals: Explaining Things

Manuals are the road maps of organizations, explaining how to use equipment, operate systems, and implement policies. This chapter will show you how to write manuals that guide rather than confuse readers.

You already know what a manual is, although you may not be aware that you do. Certainly you have used manuals in the past. If you ever had a flat tire, you probably pulled your automobile manual out of the glove compartment to see how to change it. When you prepared for your driver's license test, you studied a manual published by your state division of motor vehicles. And no doubt you have used other kinds of manuals. You have probably used a college catalog or bulletin, which is essentially a manual describing how to be successful in college. And if you know how to use a computer, you probably learned from a manual. You may have used manuals telling you how to lift weights, play tennis well, or put something together.

Everywhere you turn on the job, you'll find a manual. Large corporations and government agencies have policy manuals that explain the general principles they follow in purchasing materials, producing and marketing goods, hiring new employees, and promoting old ones. They also have procedures manuals that show employees how to operate plant equipment, how to make purchases or sales, how to request reimbursement for travel, how to apply for insurance benefits, and how to do myriad other tasks. And there are thousands of additional manuals and guides published every year for the public, explaining how to use computers, repair cars, use a bank card, buy the best auto insurance, or pay your taxes. All these manuals have the same function—their purpose is to explain policies and procedures so people will be able to follow them.

But often, people don't consult manuals when they need them. They'd rather take the additional time to ask a manager about a new policy, consult fellow workers about how to operate machinery, call the insurance department with complicated questions, or just muddle through something as best they can. Why? Because many manuals are so badly written that people simply cannot use them. These manuals tell too much of what readers don't want to know or too little of what they need to know. They are often so poorly organized and designed that readers can't find the information they need, and they are written in an almost impenetrable style.

GOOD VERSUS BAD MANUALS

Here are excerpts from two manuals. Read them to see which is better and why. The first is from a welfare agency manual, whose purpose is to explain to workers how to help people in need of welfare services. This particular section explains how they can help protect adults who are aged, ill, or disabled. As you read it, imagine that you are a new employee in a local welfare agency and have just completed your first interview with an older lady who is living with her daughter's family. She claims she is being neglected and abused. She says she is only getting one full meal a day, is frequently locked in her room when the family goes out, and is sometimes even bruised by the oldest child who plays too roughly with her. You consult the appropriate section of your manual to find out what to do and read the following:

LEGAL BASE

The law of this State authorizes each local department to provide protective services to adults who are sixty years of age and older or eighteen years of age and older who are incapacitated. This authority to provide such services shall not limit the right of any individual to refuse to accept any of the services so offered, except as provided in Section 80.2–33.6 (State Code). If an adult lacks the capacity to consent to receive protective services, the services may be ordered by a court on an involuntary basis through an emergency order or through the appointment of a guardian (State Code, Section 80.2–33.8).

1. OBJECTIVES
   a. To reestablish and/or maintain a stable level of functioning within the maximum potential of the adult.

b. To assure that the adult, who wishes them, receives services which will afford proper care, necessary supervision and protection from himself and/or negative environmental surroundings harmful to his well-being.

c. To assure that the adult, who lacks the capacity to consent, receives services that may be ordered by the court on an involuntary basis.

d. To assist the adult, who is at risk, to remain in the community.

e. To assist the adult in obtaining appropriate institutional care if the intensity of the situation requires it.

2. DEFINITION

Protective Services to Aged, Infirm, or Disabled Adults is defined as provision of services on behalf of aged, disabled (including blind), and infirm adults who are unable to protect themselves without help from neglect, abuse, or exploitation and which assist in assuring security, refuge and safety. Definitions of terms used in this chapter are as follows:

a. <u>Abuse</u>--Willful infliction of physical pain, injury or mental anguish or unreasonable confinement.

b. <u>Adult</u>--Any person eighteen years of age and older who is incapacitated and any person sixty years of age and older, both of whom reside in the Commonwealth; are in need of temporary or emergency adult protective services.

c. <u>Neglect</u>--An adult is living under such circumstances that he is not able to provide for himself or he is not being provided such services as are necessary to maintain his physical and mental health and that the failure to receive such necessary services impairs or threatens to impair his well-being.

d. Exploitation--Illegal use of an incapacitated adult or his resources for another's profit or advantage.

e. Incapacitated adult--Any adult who is impaired by reason of mental illness, mental retardation, physical illness or disability, advanced age or other causes to the extent that he lacks sufficient understanding or capacity to make, communicate or carry out responsible decisions concerning his or her well-being.

f. Emergency--An adult is living in conditions which present a clear and substantial risk of death or immediate and serious physical harm to himself or others.

g. Protective Services--Services provided by the local department of public welfare/ social services which are necessary to prevent abuse, neglect or exploitation of an adult. . . .

3. BASIC DEFINED ELEMENTS OF PROTECTIVE SERVICES

a. Establishing Need for Protective Services
The basic defined elements of Protective Services are:

(1) response to request, complaint, or report
(2) investigation and determination of validity
(3) assessment of service needs
(4) provision of services

b. Delivery of Protective Services
The delivery of protective services consists of counseling to the individual, his family and other responsible persons and arrangement without cost to the agency, for alternative living arrangements, legal representation, health care and assistance in guardianship/commitment if needed.

4. ELIGIBLE PERSONS
Any adult who is sixty years of age and older who resides in the State or eighteen years of age and older who is incapacitated is eligible, without regard to income, for the basic defined elements of protective services and optional components. However, non-residents of the state in both of the above groups may also be served when they are in need of temporary or emergency adult protective services.

Here is the other manual excerpt. This time imagine an entirely different situation—you own a year-old Honda Accord and want to adjust the brakes. You are by no means a mechanical genius, but want to experiment with a few repairs to see whether you can save yourself some money. So you buy a repair manual called *How to Keep Your Honda Alive*. Its table of contents sends you to the chapter on brakes and you begin to read.[1]

Chapter Nine: Brakes

How are you able to slow and stop your one-ton Honda with just your right foot? It's done through the magic of hydraulics—you're forcing hydraulic brake fluid through small-bore pipes and hoses to each of the four brakes. When you push down on the brake pedal it moves a piston in the ***master cylinder*** which pushes hydraulic fluid through those tubes and hoses (the ***brake lines***), creating pressure in the cylinders at the wheels which activates the brakes.

Hondas have ***disc brakes*** on the front wheels, and ***drum brakes*** at the rear. At each front brake there is a ***disc*** (sometimes spelled *disk* and also called a *rotor*) that turns as the wheel turns. The hydraulic pressure causes a ***caliper*** with some friction ***pads*** to squeeze the disc and,

[1]Fred Cisin and Jack Parvin, *How to Keep Your Honda Alive: A Manual of Step by Step Procedures for the Compleat Idiot* (Santa Fe, NM: John Muir Publications, 1983) 113–116.

through friction, to slow it down. It thus slows and stops the wheel to which it is attached. The caliper and disc work very much like a bicycle's hand brake. When you let go of the pedal, the caliper stops squeezing the disc and lets it turn freely again. The pads normally ride against the disc, but without the pressure provided when you step on the brake pedal. . . .

The front brakes self-adjust. This means that as the brake pads wear and become thinner, the ***brake piston***—the device that controls the positions of the pads—moves in on the disc to keep the thinning pads near the disc. This is why you can't just slap thick new brake pads into the same spots where the old thin ones had been. You have to pry the brake piston away from the brake disc to allow room for the thicker new pads.

Each brake pad has two sides, a metal side and a side that's a mixture of asbestos, brass, glue, and miscellaneous other substances. The asbestos side pushes in on the disc to resist its turning, and gradually the asbestos wears down. If the pad is allowed to wear down too far, it'll lose its asbestos right down to the metal, and the metal backing will start to rub against the disc. The brakes might still work, but you'll hear hostile growling sounds as the disc gets gouged up. The disc very quickly ends up looking like a very groovy worn out record, and must be replaced or reground. . . .

Since most of a Honda's weight is carried by the front wheels, the rear brakes are under little load. (The main task for the rear wheels on a front-drive car is to keep the tailpipe from scraping the ground.) The front wheels take all of the engine's power and do most of the braking. The rear (drum) brakes are somewhat like an inside out version of the front (disc) brakes. Here the pad-like ***brake shoes*** are on the *inside* of a hollow turning piece called the ***brake drum***, which resembles a cake pan. The brake shoes slow and stop a rear wheel by expanding outward against the inside of the brake drum. The drums rotate as the wheels rotate. Stop the drums and you stop the wheels.

Inside each rear brake drum is a hydraulic cylinder called the ***rear wheel brake cylinder***. Brake fluid comes through the brake line to the cylinder and forces a little piston to push the asbestos linings of the shoes out against the drum.

Unfortunately, the cylinders sometimes leak. Brake fluid is corrosive enough to dissolve both the brake shoe linings and the glue that holds the linings on. When a cylinder leaks, the brake pedal feels "soft," and the brakes don't work very well. A leak from a cylinder is usually not bad enough to slosh brake fluid onto the brake shoes, but if there is a hefty leak, and fluid does contact the linings, they will be ruined and will need to be replaced along with the cylinder.

PROCEDURE 1: REAR BRAKE ADJUSTMENT FOR 1973-79 CIVIC AND 1976-78 ACCORD

Conditions: Maintenance every 5,000 miles. Or any time the brake pedal feels too low, or the handbrake handle comes up too high. This procedure is for *all* models that do not have self-adjusting brakes. The brake shoes should be as close as possible to the brake drum without crowding it; the shoes should not have to move far before contacting

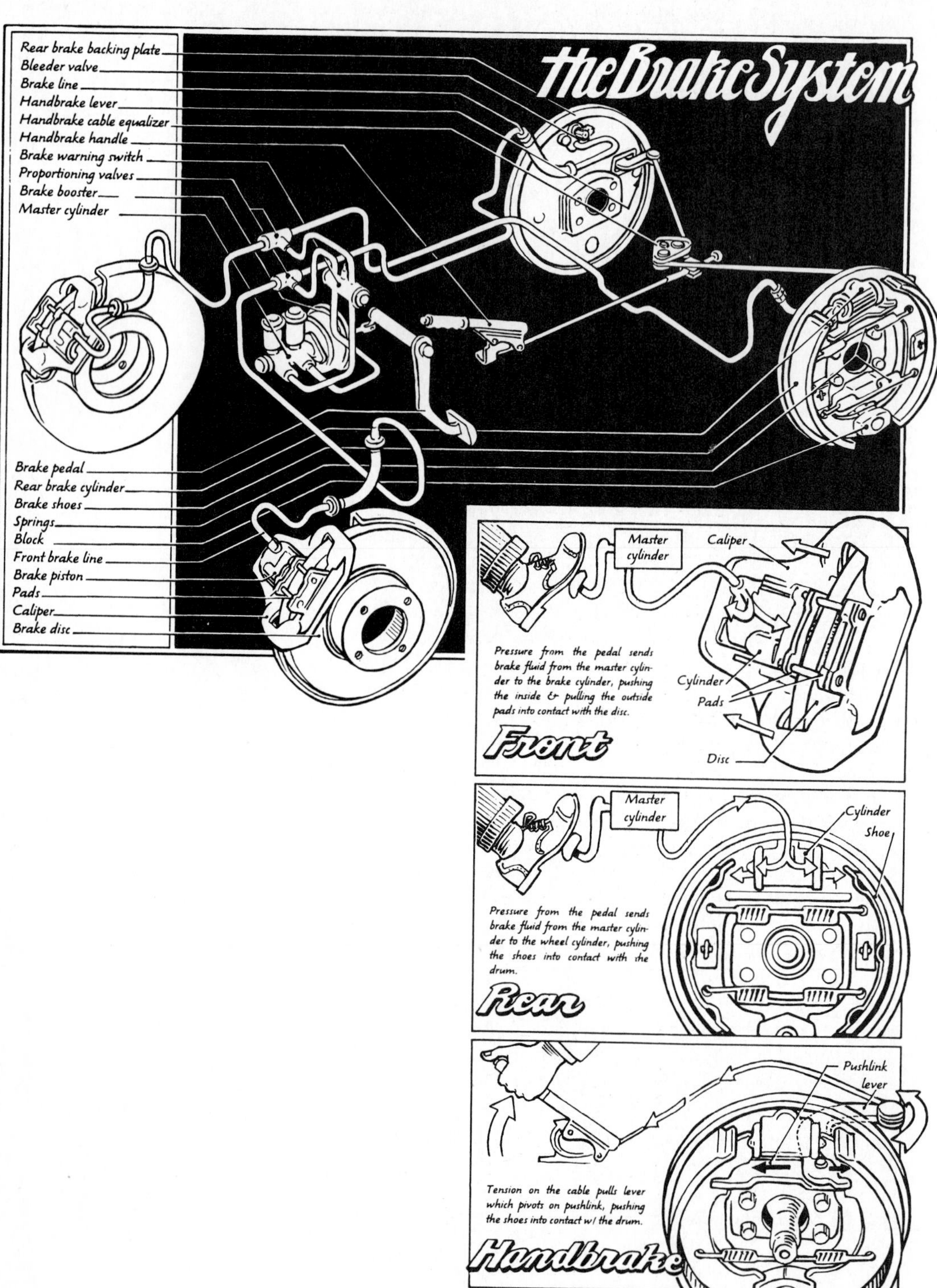
the Brake System
Rear brake backing plate
Bleeder valve
Brake line
Handbrake lever
Handbrake cable equalizer
Handbrake handle
Brake warning switch
Proportioning valves
Brake booster
Master cylinder
Brake pedal
Rear brake cylinder
Brake shoes
Springs
Block
Front brake line
Brake piston
Pads
Caliper
Brake disc
Master cylinder
Caliper
Pressure from the pedal sends brake fluid from the master cylinder to the brake cylinder, pushing the inside & pulling the outside pads into contact with the disc.
Cylinder
Pads
Disc
Front
Master cylinder
Cylinder
Shoe
Pressure from the pedal sends brake fluid from the master cylinder to the wheel cylinder, pushing the shoes into contact with the drum.
Rear
Pushlink lever
Tension on the cable pulls lever which pivots on pushlink, pushing the shoes into contact w/ the drum.
Handbrake

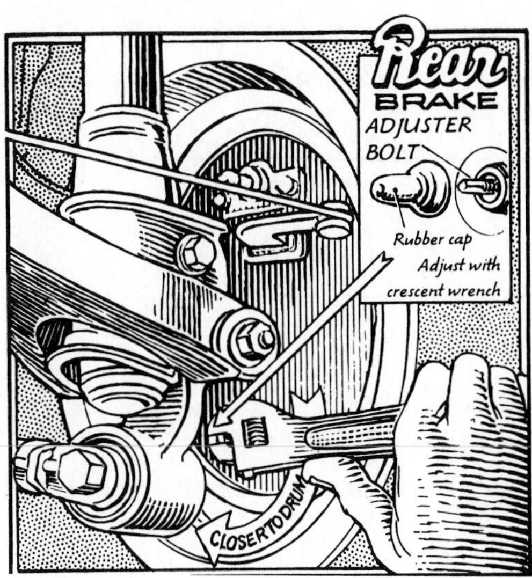

with force against the drum, so the brakes will engage as soon as possible after your foot hits the brake pedal.
Tools and Materials: Jacking equipment. *Maintenance tools:* Honda brake adjusting tool or 4- to 6-inch crescent wrench, 14mm wrench.

Step 1. **Jack 'er Up.** Put the car in gear, block the front wheels, and jack one rear wheel off the ground (see Jacking Up Your Honda in Chapter 1). The wheel being adjusted must be off the ground enough so that it can turn freely. IMPORTANT: Make sure the parking brake is *off*.

Step 2. **Remove the Rubber Cap on the Brake Adjuster.** Sometimes it can be a little stubborn. Put your adjusting wrench on the adjuster.

Step 3. **Tighten the Adjuster Bolt.** Turn it clockwise, feeling it advance one notch at a time until you can't turn the wheel *at all*. Don't worry, we're not going to leave it that way. If the adjuster won't turn, try some penetrating oil on it; forcing things might mangle the shaft.

Step 4. **Loosen the Adjuster into Position.** Back off the adjuster one or two clicks counterclockwise until the wheel turns "easily"—not as easily as a bike wheel spins, but easily enough so there's no heavy drag on it from inside the brake drum. If you can turn the wheel with one finger, then it is loose enough. You might hear a slight scraping sound as you turn the wheel (*whish, whish*)—it's OK. If the wheel being adjusted won't turn easily, loosen the adjuster bolt one more click by turning counterclockwise. Make sure you're exactly at the click point by wriggling the wrench to see that the adjuster bolt is firmly in place, not between notches. This brake is now adjusted.

Step 5. **Put the Rubber Cap Back on the Adjuster.** If the old cap's lost buy a new one. When dirt gets into the adjuster, it gets hard to turn. It's easy to damage the adjuster by turning it too hard. . . .

If you had decided to adjust the rear brakes on your Honda, what questions would you have? They would probably be *What*, *When*, and *How*. In other words,

- *What* is this brake system like, anyway? Give me a quick overview.
- *When* should I adjust these brakes?
- *What* tools do I need to do this?
- *How* do I do it?

Notice how quickly and easily the Honda manual answers your questions, describing the brake system, explaining when you should adjust the brakes, and then telling you how to do it. And this information is organized in just the way you need it. Furthermore, the whole thing is designed for a quick reading, with technical terms highlighted, illustrations, headings, and enumerations. And its style is so down-to-earth, with its contractions, questions, and fragments, that it sounds as if someone is actually talking to you.

Now imagine what questions you'd have if you were the welfare worker trying to help the lady. They'd probably be—

- Does this agency have a way to help this lady?
- If so, what is it?
- Is this lady eligible for this program?
- What should I do to help her?

Does the welfare manual answer these questions? Probably, if you are willing to wade through lots of extra information and read between the lines. But it's obviously ready for the intensive care of a thorough revision. After a good deal of work, a writer might come up with the following improved version, which focuses squarely on the questions a reader would have:

Protective Services to Aged,
Infirm, or Disabled Adults

1. What is this program? This program is authorized by law to provide protective services to adults who are unable to protect themselves from neglect, abuse or exploitation because they are aged, infirm, or

disabled. (All underlined terms are defined in Section 4 of this section.)

2. Who is eligible? Adults who are either
   (1) aged--sixty years of age or older; or
   (2) incapacitated--so sick or disabled that they cannot take care of themselves.

   If the person lacks the capacity to consent to these services, a court may order that they be provided. However, the person may refuse to accept these services.

3. What services are provided? The local welfare agency can help in the following ways:
   a. Investigate all reports of abuse, neglect, and exploitation to determine their validity.
   b. Report such acts to the proper local authorities, if this is felt to be necessary and appropriate.
   c. Remove the adult who needs help from the harmful situation, if this is thought appropriate. (To do this, see Section VI, Homes for Adults.)
   d. Provide counseling for people involved in the harmful situation, either by the local welfare worker or by professional counselors approved by the agency. (See Appendix III for the approved list.)

4. What do the following terms mean?

   - Abuse--Willfully inflicting physical pain, injury, or mental anguish or unreasonable confinement.
   - Adult--Any person eighteen years of age and older who resides in this state.
   - Exploitation--Illegally using an incapacitated adult or his resources for another's profit or advantage.
   - Incapacitated--Whenever an adult cannot provide for his own welfare because of conditions such as mental illness, retardation, physical illness, disability, or advanced age.
   - Neglect--Whenever an adult does not receive the necessary services to provide for his or her well-being.

With a manual such as this, you can find the answers to your questions quickly, learning what the program does, whether the lady is eligible for help, and what help can be provided. Notice that now the manual gives only the information you need, omitting unnecessary information about the legal base for the policy and the objectives, information that may make it look important but that you don't need. Furthermore, the excerpt is organized in the same order that you will need the information, with definitions relegated to the list at the end, where they can be consulted if needed. The design is now clear, with underlining used to highlight important points and terms. And the style is simplified. It is not as chatty and conversational as that of the repair manual, because this would not seem appropriate in a welfare manual, but the bureaucratic voice is gone.

Manuals are written to explain programs, policies, and procedures to people. But they often confuse rather than explain because of the "absent reader" problem we discussed in Chapter 2. Because readers are not present to tell them what they need, too many writers of manuals get totally wrapped up in their own concerns—including information that their readers don't need, organizing that information so that it makes sense to them but not to their readers, casting that information in a too-complicated format, and writing in a stilted, "official" style. The rest of this chapter will show you how to avoid these pitfalls and write manuals that will explain subjects clearly and concisely.

In the next few pages, you're going to be in a situation in which you have to write a manual, beginning by identifying what information your readers need, then researching to find that information, and finally outlining and writing a first draft. From this practice, you will derive a set of principles for writing good manuals—a kind of manual on manuals. Along the way, I'll help you avoid some of the major pitfalls that lie in wait for all manual writers.

A Writing Situation

You are an employee of your state employment commission. Your manager has assigned you, along with three other employees, to a special task. She wants your group to write a job search manual for people who will use the commission's out-placement center. The manual will describe procedures they should follow in choosing a new career field, finding a job, and applying for it. She explains that intake counselors are so busy they don't have enough time to explain these detailed procedures to every client. She thinks that if unemployed people had access to such a manual, they would understand general job search procedures and could spend their time with a counselor more profitably, focusing on particular questions and individual problems.

You and the other manual writers meet with the manager, who outlines the project. "I want a clearly written, complete manual of about 25 pages that will guide clients in their job search," she says. She explains that the placement center presents the job search to clients as a six-step process. She wants you to cover each of these steps in the manual.

1. How to assess interests, abilities, values, and past experiences in order to locate some career fields that fit these.
2. How to use research techniques to find out about these careers.
3. How to target particular locations, companies, and jobs within these careers.
4. How to prepare a résumé.
5. How to prepare a cover letter.
6. How to interview for a job successfully.

She suggests that your group divide up the work, each person taking a section or two. She also wants the group to follow a standard format. She suggests that you use traditional outline symbols—Roman numerals, capital letters, Arabic numerals, lower case letters, and then numbers and letters in parentheses—to outline each section.

You volunteer for the last section on job interviewing, offering to try to keep your draft to about five pages. To begin your research, you go to the library to find out what experts say about successful job interviewing, wondering whether you'll find enough information to write your section. You look in the card catalog under such topics as "Interviews," "Job Interviews," "Applying for Jobs," "The Job Search," etc. You find two books on job interviews, one by Anthony Medley called *Sweaty Palms: The Neglected Art of Being Interviewed* (Berkeley, CA: Ten Speed Press, 1978), and the other by Phyllis Martin called *The Job Interview: The Job-Hunt Success Kit* (Cincinnati, OH: Center for Career Development, 1981). You also find chapters on interviews in six other books about finding jobs. In addition, when you consult *The Reader's Guide to Periodical Literature* (for articles on interviewing in general-interest magazines) and *The Business Periodicals Index* (for those in business, industrial, and trade magazines), you find over 25 articles written just in the last five years.

Later, as you sit at your library desk surrounded by piles of books and stacks of articles on job interviewing, you wonder, "Where do I start?" You decide to plunge in, reading and taking notes as you go. Four or five hours later, you still haven't been through half your materials and already have 15 pages of notes for your five pages of the manual. "Something's wrong," you tell yourself, "I can't possibly use all this information."

Finally, you realize the problem. You don't know what you're looking for. Because you haven't yet found out what your readers need to know about interviewing, you have no way of knowing what information will be important to them. "But how do I figure out what readers of this manual will need?" you ask yourself. Then it hits you—you are surrounded by potential readers of your manual. "Every day, there are clients who are getting ready for job interviews. I'll ask them what they'd like to know. And there are others who have already interviewed. I'll ask them what they wish they had known before they interviewed."

You begin by talking with some clients who will be interviewing for jobs shortly. In each case, you ask them, "What would you like to know about job interviewing?" Some shrug their shoulders, seeming confused about the whole process. Others give you a variety of answers—they wonder how they should dress for an interview (whether to wear a shirt and tie, for instance); they wish they could prepare themselves for the questions they might get, but don't know how; they hope their answers to questions will be long enough; and they worry about what to do if they get nervous during the interview.

You also talk with some clients who have already been through the interview process, asking them, "What do you wish you had known about job interviewing?" Lots of their concerns are about how to prepare for the interview—some still don't know whether they were dressed properly or not. Others wish they had known some of the questions they were asked so they could have practiced answers beforehand. One person says that her interviewer surprised her by saying that she was expected to ask questions about the company as well as answer them. Another mentions that he had read a really good article on relaxation techniques to use if you got nervous before the interview. Another is sorry because she didn't learn that a particular company was holding interviews for a job opening until it was too late to sign up.

Gradually, your readers' needs are coming into focus. You realize that there are at least three major areas of concern.

1. How to find out about job openings and get an interview.
2. How to prepare for job interviews.
3. How to conduct one's self during the actual interview.

But you still need more information. Then an idea strikes you—"Why not talk with some people who actually do the interviewing for local companies and ask them what they look for in an interview?" So you call the personnel officers of two local businesses and set up appointments with them. Much of what they say you already know. They really are concerned about how people dress for an interview, expecting professional looking attire. And they are impressed when people ask questions about their company and the job, especially questions revealing that they have done some research on the company. You are a little surprised to discover that both interviewers ask pretty much the same questions, although they phrase them differently. But what really surprises you is the discovery that interviewers are interested in more than how a person dresses, or asks and answers questions. Even more than *what* the person does, they are interested in *how* he or she does it. They are looking for a certain style—a way of looking and acting that will convince them that this is the person for the job.

Finally you decide to consult one more person in your research—your manager, the person who gave you the assignment in the first place. "Surely she will have lots of ideas about interview techniques," you say to yourself. Sure enough, she does, mentioning many of the things you have already learned from other interviews, but adding some things also. She notes, for instance, that lots of people who are unemployed just don't seem to know how to use outplacement resources to find out where the jobs are in the first place. And she says that it's important for applicants to follow up on each interview, with a thank you letter and a phone call, if appropriate.

She also says that people should know that most of their initial interviews will be "screening interviews," where the primary purpose is to weed out unqualified applicants. If the applicant successfully passes this hurdle, he or she then has a "selection interview," where the purpose is actually to choose someone for the job. Applicants, she says, should prepare for the two types of interviews in different ways. Finally, she gives you materials her office has already collected on job interviews—excerpts from *The Honda How to Get a Job Guide*, written by the staff of *Business Week* and published by McGraw Hill, 1985; articles from other periodicals; a bibliography that includes some references to interviewing; and a handout on "How to Interview," prepared by the training department a few years ago.

As you go over all your interview notes, your project begins to take shape. You realize that all your sources are saying the same thing—that there are five basic questions readers of your manual will have.

1. How do I find out about job openings and then get an interview?
2. What am I trying to do in an interview anyway?
3. How do I prepare myself for an interview?
4. What should I do during the interview?
5. How should I follow up after the interview?

Now you return to your reading and notetaking with a focus, trying to find information that will answer these questions. Your research goes faster now. You discover that Medley's *Sweaty Palms: The Neglected Art of Being Interviewed* gives you lots of information in these areas, as do chapters from three other books. And not surprisingly, you find that the best articles you have are those given you by your manager. In addition, her interviewing handout gives you information in a more succinct form than any book or article you have. But your best sources turn out to be the first-hand experiences of the applicants and company representatives you interviewed. Soon you feel that you have collected plenty of information for the manual. And since it's all focused on your five reader questions, it's already organized into the five major areas you'll have to cover.

Now you start to write a draft of the manual. It will begin with an introduction that explains what an interview is and defines the two types, screening and selection interviews. Then it will continue with a section answering each of the five questions you had planned.

After you have written two rough drafts, the first part of your manual looks like this.

Job Interviews

I. Introduction. A job interview is a situation in which a representative of a particular organization meets with a candidate for a job to assess that candidate's qualifications.

II. Types of interviews: There are two types of job interviews:

   A. The screening interview: The purpose of this type of interview is to screen out applicants who are not qualified for the job. It is usually conducted in the personnel department.

   B. The selection interview: The purpose of this type of interview is to select a person for the position in question. It is usually conducted by the manager who will hire you at the organization's location.

III. Interview modes: Interviews can be conducted in different modes:

   A. Formal interviews: These interviews are very structured, with the interviewer asking a set of questions that have been planned in advance.

   B. Informal interviews: These interviews are less structured, with the interviewer letting the direction of the interview determine the questions.

C. Combination interview: An interview that is a combination of A and B above.

IV. Interview preparation: The person desiring an interview should take careful steps to prepare for it.

A. He or she should begin to prepare by finding out what organizations have job openings and will be interviewing. This can be done by checking the bulletin board periodically in Room 131 of the Outplacement Center.

B. When the person has identified organizations he/she is interested in, he/she should notify the secretary of the Placement Office, that an interview with that organization is desired.

C. The secretary will then have the person fill out Form 18, which is Appendix I of this manual, giving name, address, phone number, job desired, education, and prior work history (if any).

D. An interviewee should dress properly for an interview, making sure to wear proper business attire.

1. Men should wear conservative clothing—a suit and tie, if appropriate. Hair and nails should be trimmed properly.

2. Women should wear a conservative suit or dress. Their hair should be done neatly and make-up applied sparingly.

E. Interviewees should prepare themselves for interviewing with a particular organization by researching that organization carefully in the library. Some research resources are listed in Appendix II.

F. Interviewees should also prepare themselves by practicing answers to questions that might be asked. Some of these questions are the following:

1. Why do you think you might like to work for our organization?
2. In what type of position are you most interested?
3. What is your education? How has this education prepared you for the career you are interested in?
4. What community activities have you participated in? Why?
5. What parts of your previous job did you like best? Least? Why?
6. Why did you leave your last job?
7. What qualifications do you have that would make you successful in this field?

At this point you realize something: "I'm not even through my interview preparation yet, and I've used up two of my allotted five pages. I've still got to list 20 other questions that are frequently asked. How can I do that and still cover what happens during and after the interview in three more pages?" And you realize too that you have wandered away from your original plan a little with that Section III on interview modes. "Do applicants really need that information there?" you wonder. You show the draft to your manager, thinking she'll be able to solve your problems. Instead, she suggests you see how some applicants react to the manual. After all, they will be your readers.

You ask applicants to read the draft, some who are preparing for interviews and others who have already been through the process. A few think it looks okay, but to your disappointment, most are critical of what you have done. One complains that your format is so complicated that it confused her. "I just gave up reading," she says. Another says, "I kept waiting for you to get to the important things about how to get ready for an interview and how to act, but I had to wade through a lot of useless stuff at the beginning. And," she continues, "I forgot all the steps you gave. Could you summarize them in some way?" Another wonders whether you could make it sound less formal. "I guess manuals should sound pretty formal," she says, "but I found it pretty boring."

After you ponder these and other comments awhile, you realize that there are three major problems with your draft—readers are confused by your format, don't feel that all the information you have included is needed, and don't especially like your formal voice.

And the more you reread what you have written, the more you agree. But you do see ways to improve it. To revise, you could just begin with a short introduction giving the purpose of your section, and then immediately get to the major questions you want to answer. You could include whatever you needed to say about types and modes of interviews under preparation. To get rid of unnecessary information, you could cut much of that information about how to sign up and also cut the list of specific questions, putting them in an appendix. Also, to help people remember the steps they should follow, you could draw a simple flow chart at the end, summarizing them all. Finally, you realize you can make your voice more personal if you just relax and pretend you are talking to your readers. You even decide to use a simpler format, getting rid of the Roman numerals and A's and B's.

By the time you are finished with all your revisions, the first part of your manual now looks like this.

Job Interviews

<u>The purpose of a job interview</u>. In an interview, someone tries to find out your qualifications for a job with their organization. The purpose of most interviews conducted in a personnel office is to <u>screen out</u> unqualified candidates; those conducted by a manager are usually to <u>select</u> someone for the job.

<u>Your objective in an interview</u>. You are trying to let the interviewer know by the way you act, dress, and ask and answer questions that you are the person most qualified for the job.

<u>Preparation for an interview</u>. Follow these steps:

1. Contact the Outplacement Center to find out what jobs are available and when to make appointments for interviews.
2. Prepare to dress appropriately for an interview, wearing formal and fairly conservative business clothing.

3. Find out all you can about the organization you are interviewing with. Research resources are listed in Appendix 1.
4. Plan the interview by anticipating questions and practicing how you will answer them. See Appendix 2 for particular questions interviewers may ask. Most will come from the following areas:

   - Your background--family, education, work experience.
   - Your personal qualities--strong and weak points, likes and dislikes, leisure-time activities.
   - Your goals--personal and professional, salary expected, types of people with whom you want to work, preferred location.
   - Your knowledge of the position--what their organization does, what the position entails.

5. Be prepared either for a formal interview, where the questions follow a structured pattern, or a more informal one, where the answer to one question might suggest another; or for a combination of the two.

The following chart summarizes the important steps to follow:

Figure 1
Follow These Steps for a Successful Interview

Schedule Interviews
↓
Prepare Yourself
↓
Research the Organization
↓
Anticipate Questions

You feel a lot better about your draft now, although it's still a long way from being finished. You need to complete it by telling people how to conduct themselves during the interview and how to follow up afterwards. Then you will need to meet again with your manual group to see whether your piece fits in with theirs. (You already know, for instance, that you have chosen a different format. You will have to see how they react to this.) And finally, the whole manual will have to be critiqued by people who have actually tried to use it during the interviewing process. Then it will have to be revised again.

SUMMARY

The major pitfalls lying in wait for all manual writers are apparent from the writing situation we just discussed. Because you get so caught up in your own concerns that you forget your reader's, you may—

- include information your reader doesn't need,
- omit important information that your reader does need,
- organize the manual from your own point of view rather than your reader's,
- use a format that is too complicated to follow,
- and write in a bureaucratic, "official voice."

You can usually avoid these pitfalls by following the principles listed below. But you have seen that writing a manual is too complex a process to apply any procedure literally and simple-mindedly. Therefore, you will have to adapt the following principles to suit each new situation.

1. Begin a manual with your reader's needs, not yours. Ask yourself, "What does my reader need to know about this subject?" The best way to do this is to find out what questions readers will have as they use your manual.
2. Then do research to answer these questions. Frequently, the most effective research method for a manual will be interviewing two groups of people: those who know the policy or procedure already and those who will have to use your manual in order to follow it.
3. Whenever you have questions about the manual, consult people who will read it. They are the experts on how you should do it.
4. Be sure to get all the information your readers will need, but be sure to restrict yourself to just what your readers need to know.
5. Organize the information in the sequence your readers will naturally follow as they consult the manual.

6. Design the manual so your readers can find what they need to know quickly and easily—make ingenious use of headings, indentations, boldface, enumerations, illustrations, etc. See the appendix at the end of this chapter for ways to design and punctuate lists in a manual.
7. Imagine that you are talking to your readers and use as natural and conversational a voice as possible.

APPENDIX

Whenever you can in a manual, use a list to simplify an explanation. Here is one method for creating and punctuating lists, adapted from *How to Write a Computer Manual: A Handbook of Software Documentation* (Menlo Park, CA: Benjamin/Cummings Publishing, 1984) 255–56, written by Jonathan Price and the staff of the User Education Group in the Apple II Division of Apple Computer, Inc.

Enumerated lists. Use enumerated (numbered or alphabetized) lists for sequential steps or to show a hierarchical relationship. Introduce a numbered list with a main clause followed by a colon. The first word of each item should be capitalized, and each item should end with a punctuation mark.

Example: The steps to follow in preparing for an interview are the following:

1. Identify organizations that have job openings;
2. Schedule interviews with appropriate organizations;
3. Research the organizations;
4. Prepare for the interview by practicing answers to questions that might be asked.

Bulleted lists. Use bulleted lists when items can occur in any order. Punctuate bulleted lists as follows:

---

1. When a sentence is broken into a list to emphasize the parts of a series, don't capitalize or use a colon, but do end with a punctuation mark.

Example: The three parts are

- a central power unit
- one or more disk drives
- a video display.

2. When a complete sentence is followed by a series, use a colon but no capitals or end punctuation.

   Example: The three parts that you will encounter most often are already familiar to you:

   - a central power unit
   - one or more disk drives
   - a video display

3. When a complete sentence is followed by a series that is itself made up of complete sentences, capitalize the first word of each item in the series and end each item with an appropriate end mark.

   Example: You will have the following three questions about this system:

   - Will it provide the power needed?
   - Will it be easy to use?
   - Will it be flexible enough?

APPLICATIONS

1. An excerpt from a performance appraisal manual is shown on the next page. Its purpose is to guide managers in their yearly appraisals of subordinates. Under this system, managers first fill out an appraisal form on each person working under them. Then they submit this form to their supervisors for approval. If their supervisors approve their appraisal, the managers discuss it in an interview with the person being appraised. After reading the excerpt, revise it so it can be understood quickly and easily by someone who must use it.

Prior to the interview, two appraisal forms should be filled out. One should be marked "original" and the other "copy." Pages 1 and 2 should be completed in their entirety. When the appraisal form has been completed, it should be put away for several days. Then, it should be reevaluated to reduce the influences of personal feelings in your evaluation. After this process, the original form should be given to your immediate supervisor who will review, approve, and/or comment and send it up for further review and approvals. After the final approval is given, the appraisal form will be returned to you.

When the appraisal form is returned, you will then see in Section 4, "Overall Rating," whether or not your rating has been changed and at what level of supervisor the change occurred. At this point, before the appraisal interview with the employee, you will have an opportunity to appeal the final decision, if it has not already been discussed with you. If you think an employee has been unjustly ranked, contact your supervisor and the overall ranking can be reconsidered.

Once these decisions are definitely finalized, hold an appraisal interview with the employee. The appraisal should be given to the employee for review and discussion during the appraisal interview.

2. The beginning of a section of a manual used in a department of welfare appears on pages 297–98. Its purpose is to guide welfare counselors in advising clients about correct nutritional practices. Like the poorly done manual we discussed in this chapter, this excerpt gives readers information they don't need and organizes it badly. After reading the section, revise it so it can be used in the day-to-day work of welfare counselors. Imagine that counselors are already familiar with good nutritional practices and have

PURPOSE

The purpose of nutrition services is to improve a person's eating habits, nutritional intake, and knowledge of nutrition for increased physical and mental functioning, thereby providing a means of maintaining independence to the fullest extent possible; to remove or reduce neglect of individuals caused by a lack of adequate quantity and quality of food intake; to improve an individual's capacity to continue living in his/her own home or the home of others to avoid institutional placements; and to provide a means for aged and/or disabled adults to maintain or regain their living situations in the community.

1. NUTRITION COUNSELING AND EDUCATION SERVICES
   a. <u>Definition</u>
      Nutrition counseling is defined as the provision of information, advice, and counseling about nutritional needs, meal preparation, and how to purchase wisely to meet daily nutritional needs. The service includes instruction and education. Educational fees are a component of the service for classes or courses related to nutrition.

[continued]

references available to consult for additional information. In other words, they know what to say to clients about good nutrition, they just need to understand how to go about saying it.

3. Choose some procedure that you know well and write a manual showing others how to do it. You might write about something you do at work, such as solving a particular kind of problem or

```
b. Eligible.persons
   Individuals are eligible for
   nutrition services based on income
   maintenance or income level status
   when the service and the population
   to be served are in the geographic
   area served by the department.
c. Methods of service delivery
   (1) Direct service provision:
       Direct services such as
       information, advice, or
       counseling can be provided by the
       local welfare department.
   (2) Purchase of service:
       Under certain conditions,
       counselors may purchase
       nutrition-related education.
       These conditions and appropriate
       methods of education are listed
       below. . . .
```

operating a system; something you do at home, such as balancing your checkbook or repairing your car; or something you do in connection with school, such as studying a chapter in a textbook or solving a math problem.

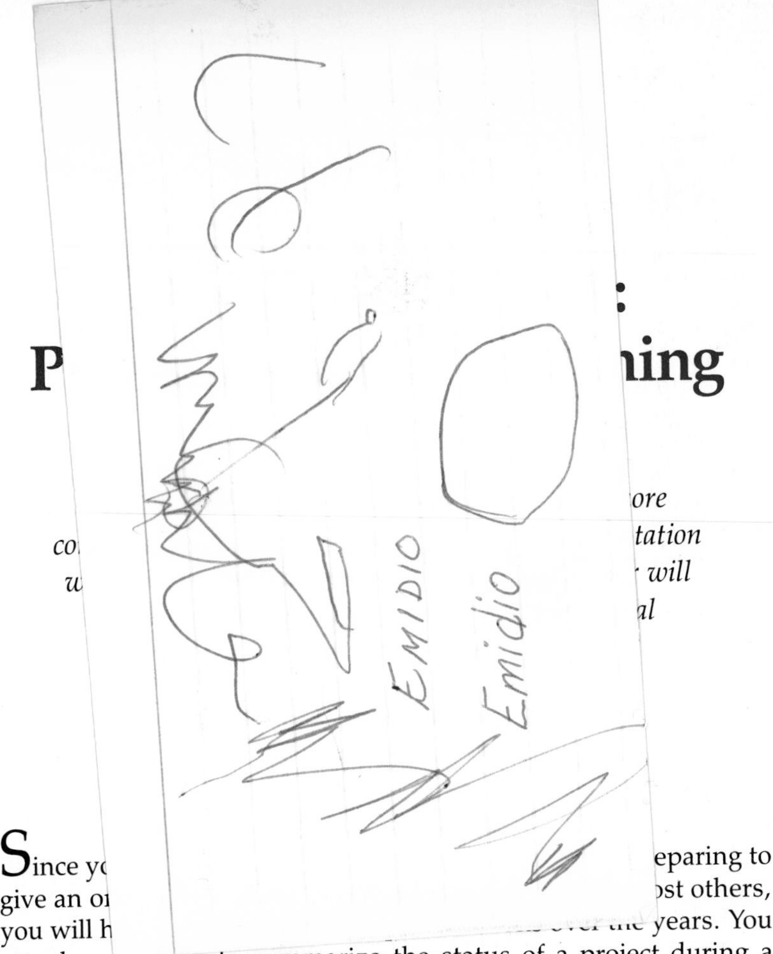

:
P ning

ore
co tation
w will
al

Since yo eparing to give an o ost others, you will h years. You may be called on to summarize the status of a project during a meeting, make a proposal before a group of managers or customers, or even give a speech to a community group. The goal of this chapter is to prepare you to make such presentations effectively.

TYPES OF PRESENTATIONS

No matter what kind of oral presentation you make, it will fall into one of three groups.

Brief Talks

The type of presentation you'll have to make most frequently is just an ordinary, garden-variety talk that you might make at a meeting on almost any subject, either to subordinates or peers. You might describe a new policy,

```
Look, because of this new policy, we're going to have
to change the way we handle annual leave. From now
on . . . ;
```

explain a new procedure,

> In the future, we're going to have to run all the previous day's entries before we close. This means that we'll have to . . . ;

or summarize progress on a project,

> We're moving forward quickly on the McHanna project. In fact, I'd say that by Wednesday the 22nd we'll be far enough along to. . . .

As you rise through the managerial ranks, you'll have to make these kinds of short, informal presentations more frequently. But with practice will come proficiency. You'll learn to plan them quickly, setting your goals and jotting some notes. Since you'll almost always know your listeners well, you won't be very nervous. And because you'll rarely use any visual aid beyond a simple flip chart or a handout, these presentations won't be difficult to prepare for.

Formal, In-House Presentations

If they are given to a group of your superiors, in-house presentations will be longer and more formal than brief talks. Your goal in one of these presentations might be to describe a major problem that has developed and propose a solution. For example:

> Our failure to meet environmental standards at the Red River plant has troubled many of us during the last six months. But now we think we've found the answer. Today, I'd like to describe our problem to you and then propose a way of solving it.
>
> The problem, as we see it, is that. . . .

Or you might recommend that your organization institute a major policy change, implement a new data processing system, or develop a new product.

> Interest rates on commercial loans are at their lowest point in the last six years. And the latest figures show that demand for office space in the area exceeds supply by 35%.
>
> Therefore, we think it's time for the company to develop the Laras tract as an office park. If we can complete the project in eight months, we stand to gain over. . . .

Since this type of presentation will be made to a group of busy decision-makers, you will need to prepare carefully, organizing ideas so they are crystal clear, finding convincing evidence to persuade your audience, and using professional-looking audiovisual materials to clarify and support your points.

Formal, Outside Presentations

This third type of presentation is more like the kinds of formal speeches you may have learned to make in a college speech class. Generally, it is made to people outside your organization. It might be a major sales presentation to a client, an oral proposal to a foundation or government organization, an annual report at a stockholders' meeting, or even a speech to a local community group.

No matter what type of oral presentation you are giving, all have two things in common—preparation and performance. That is, even though you may be speaking to your staff at one time and to top managers at another, even though you may talk for three minutes explaining a new procedure and for thirty minutes when giving a major proposal, and even though you may give a brief handout at an informal meeting and use elaborate charts, graphs, and transparencies in a more formal situation, you will always have to do two things—prepare for a presentation carefully and then perform it effectively.

PREPARATION

Experts on oral presentations all stress one theme: "Preparation is the key to a good presentation!" If you want your presentation to be clear, you've got to *prepare* by organizing your ideas carefully. If you want to persuade people to accept a new idea, you've got to *prepare* by marshaling your evidence carefully. If you want to be able to answer people's questions effectively, you've got to *prepare* by knowing them in advance. The more time you spend in preparation, the better your presentation will be.

As you prepare to give a presentation, three issues will arise:

- whether to give an oral presentation at all
- how to analyze the speaking situation
- how to plan the actual presentation

Let's discuss each one.

Should I Give an Oral Presentation?

Sometimes, the answer is no. It all depends on what you have to say. If what you have to communicate is fairly routine, for example, the announcement of the place and time for the company picnic; if what you have to communicate needs to go to many people at different locations, for example, news of a new plant opening; most important, if you need to describe something in detail, to say something precisely, or to give people something to refer to later, for example, the description of a division reorganization, an explanation of an agreement between disputing parties, or a notice of a change of health insurance benefits; then you'd better write it out.

But there will be many times when you will want to take advantage of the more personal quality of an oral presentation. If your audience will be resistant—perhaps to a new overtime policy, an increased production quota, or a new quality control procedure—you may want to present it to them face-to-face, so you can use your voice and gestures, as well as your words, to convince them. And if you want to encourage people to ask questions and express their own feelings about a subject—perhaps to ask how a policy should be applied, how a procedure should be carried out, or why something can't be done a different way—you should make an oral presentation.

One way to gain the advantages of both speaking and writing is to supplement your oral presentation with a handout that summarizes what you say. This way, you can present your ideas orally and respond to questions, but the handout will describe the system in more detail and give people something to refer to later. If you do use such a summary handout, be sure to distribute it *after* rather than *before* your presentation. If you give it out before or during your talk, your listeners will be tempted to read the handout rather than listen to what you are saying.

How Do I Analyze My Speaking Situation?

To plan your presentation, analyze your speaking situation just as you would a writing situation—clarify your goals, understand your audience, and decide on your voice. If you need to, review Chapter 2 for a detailed discussion of how to do this. Here, we'll review the main points of that discussion.

1. ***Clarify your goals***. If anything, effective goal setting is even more crucial for an oral presentation than it is for a written one, since you get only one chance at your audience. If they don't understand what you're trying to say because you yourself aren't clear about it, you've failed.

Whether you are just explaining a new policy to a group of subordinates in a 15-minute meeting or making a major sales presentation about a highly sophisticated computer for a prospective client, you've got to know exactly what you want to accomplish. One way to do this is to use the "so that" technique described in Chapter 2. Say to yourself: "I'm making this presentation *so that* my audience will follow this new safety policy or sign the contract to buy our X-1310 computer. And keep saying it until you can picture your audience doing what you want them to do. You may have to work and work to get your goal precisely stated, but if you haven't done this at some stage in your planning, you could waste your listeners' time and not get anything accomplished besides. Let's see how you might go about clarifying your goal for a particular presentation.

An Oral Situation

Imagine that you work in the personnel department of a large organization. About a month ago, the vice president of the sales division requested that someone in personnel recommend a new performance appraisal system for the division. The VP said, "All we have now is a yearly appraisal form that is filled out by a manager on each sales rep. It just isn't working. My managers fill out the form as fast as they can and then write a two- or three-sentence summary. How can they recommend a salary increase or promotion on the basis of that? And for that matter, how can the sales reps tell whether they've done a good or bad job for the year?"

Even though you had been in the personnel department only a little over two years, you got the assignment of developing the new system. You did a careful job of research, examining a number of performance appraisal systems. The system you finally recommended contained these steps:

1. At the beginning of the year, sales reps meet with their manager to agree on objectives for the coming year.
2. At the end of the year, the sales reps write out their own appraisal of how well they have achieved their objectives. Then they meet with their manager to discuss this appraisal.
3. On the basis of this discussion, the manager then fills out his or her own appraisal, evaluating the rep's performance and recommending appropriate salary and promotion actions.

The VP of sales liked your new system, especially because it included sales reps as well as their managers in the appraisal process. In fact, it was adopted for the division, and you were asked to present it at a meeting of the sales managers. In your presentation, much like the "brief talk" presentation described earlier, you were able not only to explain the system clearly, but also to show how similar systems had increased sales for other companies. Your presentation was a success and now your task is complete.

But not quite. That afternoon the VP calls and says, "Congratulations, you did a super job this morning! You explained the system well, and you convinced even my most skeptical managers that this system will get results.

"Would you be willing to present this same idea to the company executive committee? It's made up of all the vice presidents. Some of them have been as dissatisfied as I am with the old rating system, and I'll bet they'll go for your ideas. Who knows, maybe the whole company will adopt it eventually.

"Anyway, I think I can get you put on the agenda of the next meeting for 20 minutes or so. That'll give you the time to outline the system and its benefits. This is a high-level group, so better make your presentation a little more formal than the one for my managers. Maybe you could spruce it up with some visuals. And you'd better be prepared for some tough questions. Some of those old-timers are going to be suspicious of anything that doesn't seem to turn a buck right away. But you'll do fine. Your system's a good one and you'll present it well."

"Sure," you respond, full of confidence born of your successful presentation to the sales managers. "There's no reason why this system won't work well anywhere in the company." Only later do you realize what you've done—committed yourself to giving a major presentation to the top management of your company. "It's one thing to explain a system to a few managers of one division, especially when their boss has already decided that they have to use it," you think to yourself. "It's going to be a lot harder to convince people to accept it in the first place. And top-level people at that."

But second thoughts or not, you have no choice. So you begin to set your goal for the presentation. At first, you think this will be a snap. "After all," you think to yourself, "the VP said I was to present my ideas about performance appraisal to the committee. So, I guess that's my goal. But is it, really? Don't I have a deeper goal? Doesn't the VP really want me to persuade the committee to adopt my system? I guess that's my goal, then.

"But that's not very specific. And it's not realistic either. I'm not going to persuade every person in that group to adopt this new system. I've got to limit myself. Let's see. There are twelve members of that committee, so suppose I say my goal is to persuade at least seven of them to adopt this new system. That's specific, but not too realistic. I can't expect even seven of them to shift from the present system to my system overnight. But I might be able to persuade them to try it on a limited basis, maybe for one year with a limited number of people.

"Okay, so now my goal is to convince at least seven members of that committee to try the new performance appraisal system on at least a pilot basis—with a limited number of people for a limited period of time. Good. I ought to be able to accomplish that. But how?"

2. ***Understand your audience***. The answer is, of course, to understand your audience—its knowledge, values, and possible responses—the same issues we discussed in Chapter 2. The best way to understand your audience is to picture them listening to your presentation as you ask yourself the following questions.

- *What does my audience already know about this subject and therefore what will they need to know?* Beginning speakers often make the mistake of telling their audience too much about what they already know (explaining concepts or defining terms unnecessarily) and not enough about what they do need to know (omitting important explanations or details). To avoid this mistake, keep your goal in mind and give only the information needed to accomplish this goal.

To convince the VP's to adopt the performance appraisal system, for instance, you won't need to explain what a performance appraisal is or how it is used, since they will already be familiar with the answers to these questions. But you *will* need to describe in detail how the system you are proposing works, since there are so many different systems in use.

- *What values are at stake here? In other words, what is particularly important to my audience about this subject?* Most successful speakers seem to know instinctively what is most important to the listeners of a particular oral presentation. They know that if they are describing a new safety policy, their listeners want to know how it will protect them. If they are trying to sell a new computer, they understand that their listeners want to know how it will save them time and effort. They understand, in short, that what is most important to people on the job is what will benefit them and their organization.

  For example, you can assume that people on the executive committee to whom you will be presenting the performance appraisal system will have pretty much the same bottom line question: "How will the system you are proposing bring in more revenue to the company?" In addition, of course, they'll want a system that will be easy to implement. To respond to these concerns, you might decide to collect all the materials you can find to prove that effective performance evaluation does increase production and therefore brings in more revenue. In addition, you might resolve to demonstrate to people on the committee that your system will be an easy one to implement.

- *How will my audience respond to my presentation?* Since an oral presentation is a face-to-face, immediate situation, this is a crucial question to be answered in your preparation. People can have all kinds of reactions to oral presentations, ranging from apathy to anger. In fact, one way to anticipate how a particular audience might respond is to locate your listeners on a kind of reaction spectrum.

Apathetic Know-It-All Accepting Critical Angry

You will find that some audiences will fall at the left side of the spectrum, reacting with little interest to your presentation. Workers in a plant, for instance, might be ready to react to a pep talk about increasing production with little enthusiasm, feeling they've heard it all before. And data systems operators might respond to the explanation of a new procedure in the same way, unless you are able to get their interest.

Some audiences will fall more in the middle of the spectrum, being willing to accept your ideas, especially if you can show how they will benefit from them. If you can manage to strike the right chord, plant workers might be receptive to your explanation of a new safety policy, even if following it might take a little extra effort. And managers will certainly welcome any proposal that will save their division money or increase its productivity. Of course, your audience could also react more critically or even hostilely to a presentation. For instance, if you have to ask your staff to readjust their vacation schedules, you might get some angry responses.

Let's return to the performance appraisal presentation we talked about earlier and see how you might go about understanding your audience in this situation.

An Oral Situation (continued)

As you begin to focus on your audience, you recall that even your earlier successful performance appraisal presentation to the sales managers did evoke a few negative reactions. A couple of the old-timers sort of sat back with a smirk that said, "Hey, I'll bet I've heard all this before." Others seemed more interested, especially as you began to explain how your system might raise morale in their division. But there's no doubt about it—you did get a few hostile questions, mostly from people who felt that your system would take a lot of extra time and not accomplish anything new.

To prepare yourself fully for the reactions of members of the executive committee, you decide to do a little research to find out in advance how they feel about performance appraisal and therefore how they might respond to your ideas. At first, you are going to call several for appointments and interview them. But on reflection, it doesn't strike you as a particularly good idea to bother busy VP's with questions about a 20-minute presentation that is three weeks away. Instead, you call a few friends in different divisions to find out what they might know, but you get almost nowhere. Your friends are just too far down the hierarchy to know how their VP's might respond to a particular issue.

Then it hits you: "Why not consult the VP of sales, who asked me to do the presentation in the first place? After all, since the VP's meet every month, who else would know better how they will react?"

At first, thinking you just need a little assurance, the VP dismisses your questions with a wave and a quick, "Oh, come on now, don't worry. People on the committee are really going to go for your ideas." But you say that you really do want to know how they might respond to your ideas, so the VP begins to think about it.

"Well, let's see. I think John Allen over in the finance division will really be enthusiastic. He's the kind of guy who really wants managers to stay in touch with their people. He'll especially like your suggestion of an appraisal conference with each employee. He's always saying that we spend too much time with figures and not enough with people.

"And Clark Martin, your own chief over in personnel, has already told you how much he likes it. He's the one on that committee who's been complaining for years that we base salary and promotion decisions on almost no real information.

"Some of the other people I'm less sure about. Joan Hollander in marketing may resist a little at first, but I'm betting she'll come around pretty easily. She's always wondering how she can keep better tabs on what some of her creative types in advertising are doing.

"But you may have a little trouble with Jane Stennis, the chief of production. She's pretty new on the job, and still trying to prove herself by keeping production figures up. Unless she sees a direct connection between your system and increased production, she may be pretty skeptical. Why don't you expand on those figures you gave to us on increased production. That may help.

"Frankly, I just don't know how some of the others will react. A couple of those people are so close to retirement that they probably won't care one way or another. And Helen Armrein over in legal will probably be pretty skeptical. I suspect that she'd dread trying to appraise the performance of those six lawyers she's got working under her.

"Joe Capristo, the senior VP in charge of the committee, is the one you're going to have to target. If he goes for this idea, then some of the skeptics will tag along."

The VP of sales has been very helpful. You realize now that you've got to be prepared to prove to some members of the committee that your system can really increase production. So you resolve to emphasize this in the presentation, documenting your point with examples and figures taken from your research on other companies that have tried it. You may even be able to find an example of someone who has used the system successfully with high-level personnel like attorneys. At the very least, you can be ready for some of the hostile questions you might get.

3. ***Decide on your voice.*** In Chapter 2, you learned that the words you choose and the sentences you put them in create a "voice," a projection of yourself on paper. You also found that you have to adapt your voice to particular writing situations. Exactly the same principle holds in speaking, although you will find that the self you project in a given situation (often called your *persona*) is created by the way you act and dress as well as by the way you actually speak.

The persona you assume for a given oral presentation can be the most persuasive tool you have. Often, your most appropriate persona on the job is one that communicates both a commitment to your own ideas *and* an openness to the ideas of others. For example, a note of quiet intensity in your voice or an appropriate gesture at just the right moment can convince an otherwise apathetic audience to listen closely to your description of an important new policy or procedure. At the same time, an interested look or occasional nod of the head as someone else is talking may motivate them to listen a little more closely to what you have to say.

By the time you have thought about a particular oral situation enough to clarify your goals and understand your audience, you will probably have decided, perhaps without quite realizing it, on the most effective persona to adopt. For the presentation on the performance appraisal system for the VP's, for example, you would probably want to communicate an air of quiet confidence. On the one hand, you would certainly not want to presume that your superiors in the organization would accept your proposal without question. But neither would you want to be apologetic or overly modest about your ideas. After all, you will have researched carefully the system you finally recommend.

How Do I Plan the Actual Presentation?

To plan an actual presentation, you'll need to decide how you want to organize your ideas and what visual aids to use.

1. ***Organize your ideas***. Given the one-shot nature of an oral presentation, if it's not organized so its main ideas are crystal clear to the audience the first time, it's not going to be successful. But there's not always an easy way to organize an oral presentation, especially if it's a major one about a complicated topic. Old sayings like, "Tell 'em what you're going to say, say it, and then tell 'em you've said it," aren't often very helpful. But this old chestnut of a saying does make an important point: every oral presentation must have three parts—a beginning, middle, and end.

- ***The Beginning***. An effective introduction should accomplish three goals: (1) get your audience's attention and interest; (2) create a favorable image of yourself with the audience; and (3) state your major goal, purpose, or thesis.

  Of course, there is no end of specific ways to begin a talk. You can get attention by beginning—
  - with a baffling question
  - with a description of an unusual event
  - with a startling statistic, statement, or a story
  - with a quotation that establishes the context
  - with a reference to individuals in the group
  - with a statement about the importance of your subject
  - with a reference or analogy that connects what the audience already knows with your subject.

And you can establish your own credibility with an audience by—

- greeting them straightforwardly and sincerely
- linking yourself with them and their concerns
- modestly referring to your own experience or expertise with the subject.

Because these lists of introductory techniques are not tied to particular situations, they may not be much help to you. It may make more sense to think of adapting introductory strategies to the way you think different audiences will respond to your presentation.[1]

RESPONSE	STRATEGY
Apathetic	Get attention—through a startling statement, a story, a quote, humor, a demonstration
Bored/Blasé	Create new perspective through reference to someone who has respect, through startling statement or statistic, through "insider" statement (e.g., "As we all know . . . .")
Accepting	Reinforce this with appealing human interest story, appeal to authority, telling details, great ideas, or goals
Critical	Admit the validity of this attitude by stating your basic goals, assumptions, and viewpoints, describing your procedures, admitting the points where your argument is weakest
Hostile	Eliminate or diminish opposition through appeal to common values or beliefs, using respected sources or people, commending audience for previous achievements, placing disagreement in broader context, offering to compromise

Tying your introduction to your audience's possible response should help you remember what any good introduction should do: Enable you to make your audience—whether apathetic, accepting, or hostile—as open to your ideas as possible. In one case you might accomplish this with a humorous story or a startling statistic; in another, with a description of a problem or a statement that appeals to your audience's sympathies; in some cases, even with a statement that is slightly self-critical or apologetic.

- ***The middle***. You organize ideas for the body of an oral presentation in the same way you might organize them for a long

[1]The following strategies are adapted from George T. Vardaman, *Making Successful Presentations* (New York: AMACOM, A Division of American Management Associations, 1981) 102–132.

memo, letter, report, or proposal. Some topics—an explanation of a new procedure, for instance—would best be organized chronologically. Others—a description of a new machine or plant site—would best be organized spatially. Still others might be organized by topics, by problem and then solution, by causes and effects, from most important to least important, etc. No matter how you decide to organize your presentation, just remember its one-shot nature and be sure your organization is simple and crystal clear.

- ***The ending.*** If you are like most of us, you have probably always had trouble ending presentations. Most of the ways you may already be familiar with—ending with a summary, appropriate quotation, story, plan of action, challenge to the audience, inspirational words—may seem removed from any actual presentation. After all, an ending shouldn't be mechanically tacked onto a presentation; it should seem to grow naturally out of what you've said and how you've said it. Rather than trying to remember a bunch of ways to end presentations, it may be more helpful just to remember the function of any effective ending—it should help your audience remember your main points and understand their significance. Any ending that accomplishes these goals will be a good one.

To see how you might organize a particular presentation, let's return again to the performance appraisal situation.

An Oral Situation (continued)

You begin by thinking to yourself that organizing the presentation will be pretty easy. "I'll just pick techniques that will work for me, taking the best beginning technique and combining it with the best way of organizing the middle, and then finding a good method for ending."

So you begin to set up your presentation. First, you try to begin by getting a quotation about performance appraisal that will get people's attention. But you just can't find one you like. You're no more successful in finding a good story that would illustrate the need for an appraisal system. And when you check the list of introductory strategies for different kinds of audiences, you realize you're not sure whether to characterize your audience as apathetic, critical, or accepting. Some members seem to fall into each category. At last, you decide in desperation to begin with a question like, "Why should we appraise people's performance, anyway?"

You're not much more successful when it comes to organizing the middle of your presentation. At first, the chronological method seems best. You could begin by describing how the employee would appraise his or her own performance, then explain how the supervisor would fill in the form, and finally show how the appraisal interview would work. Then you remember that your goal is not so much to explain your system as it is to get committee members to try it. So you consider organizing the presentation around causes and effects, beginning by explaining the reason why the company needs a new system, then describing the one you are proposing, etc. But both these methods seem so dull.

"There's something wrong," you say to yourself. "I'm getting nowhere doing this. Maybe I'd just better take a break for a little while." Two coffee breaks and one trip to the water fountain later, you're still trying to think of a way to organize your presentation. The longer you sit, the more you worry and the less you get done. Finally, you decide to talk with your own boss, the chief of personnel, about the problem. After all, he has a reputation in the company for being a good speaker.

"You know," he says, after you summarize some of the techniques you've tried in organizing your presentation, "good speakers do use all those techniques at one time or another, but they don't approach the job as mechanically as you are. You're trying to put a presentation together the way you would a puzzle, and it's just not going to work.

"What the good speakers do is to look for an 'angle' on their subject, some way of approaching it that will allow them to accomplish their goal."

"I'm not sure what you mean by 'angle,'" you say.

"Well, newspaper reporters use the technique. After they research a story, they try to find some way of setting it up so it will make the most sense and have the widest appeal. Essentially, they begin by thinking about their goal and then come up with the approach that will help them accomplish it best. Good speakers do the same thing. I've heard supervisors explain a new procedure by contrasting it with the old one, managers describe a policy change by explaining why it's necessary and what it will accomplish, and engineers convince people to buy a new system by explaining what's wrong with the old one. Why don't you approach your speech in this way? Just look for the right angle on the subject."

Even though this seems like a helpful way to think about organizing your presentation, coming up with your own angle is not easy. But after skimming through your notes on performance appraisal and taking a few more coffee breaks, an angle does occur to you.

"One way to convince that committee to try my system is to show them what's wrong with the old one. So why not begin by showing the problems the old system creates and then showing how my system will solve them. Better yet, why not think of it as a kind of three-part presentation?"

1. Begin by showing the problems with the old system.
2. Then explain my system, showing how it will solve these problems.
3. Finally, show that my system will raise morale and thereby increase productivity.

The more you think about this approach, the more you like it. You even hit on a way of introducing the presentation—by actually quoting what some of the supervisors you spoke to said about the problems with the old system. And you could conclude with some statistics that prove that systems like yours have increased production at other companies.

Because you have to go back to your research notes and dig up these statistics, it takes you most of another week to get a draft written. But by Friday, you do have a first draft of about eight pages. And you know it's just about the right length, because you read it aloud once, timing yourself.

"Whew!" you say to yourself. "Glad that job's done. I'm ready to give the presentation."

Then you remember the VP of sales' advice to use some audio-visual aids. So, it's back to the drawing board once more.

2. ***Use Audiovisuals***. Well-designed audiovisuals can help you *show* your audience what you could otherwise only *tell* them. A color transparency can summarize the important points of a presentation; a video vignette can dramatize an important concept about human behavior; and a chart or graph can demonstrate an important change or contrast. Studies have shown that when information is just presented orally, immediate audience recall is 70% and three days later only 10%. But if the oral presentation is accompanied by visuals, immediate recall increases to 85% and three days later is still at 65%.[2]

Here are the most widely used visual aids, with a short discussion of when they work best and how they should be used.

- ***Handouts***. A simple handout that outlines or summarizes your presentation can be a most effective aid. Handouts are usually easy to prepare and can be done at the last minute if you are in a hurry. If you intend to refer to the handout during your presentation, make it simple to read by not cluttering it up with details and by highlighting the points you want people to notice. And give your audience a few minutes to glance over it before you begin; otherwise, they'll be reading while you're talking.

  People who have attended a presentation welcome a summary handout afterward because they have something to refer to later or to share with colleagues. Summary handouts

[2] Cited in W. Linkugel and D. Berg, *A Time to Speak* (Belmont, CA: Wadsworth, 1970), p. 69.

can be quite detailed, elaborating on the points you made during your presentation. But don't hand them out before you've finished. If you do, you know what's going to happen.

- ***Blackboard***. Blackboards are particularly flexible media because you can find them at so many presentation sites and use them in so many ways—outlining the important points of a presentation before or as you give it, putting up an illustration of an idea and then erasing it, or recording points made by people in your audience. But you need to be careful using them—they can be messy, look too informal, and make your audience feel that they are getting more of a "school" than a professional presentation. If you do use a blackboard, stand to one side so your audience can see what you've written, and keep what you write simple and orderly so your audience can pick it up at a glance.
- ***E-Z rite boards***. These boards have a baked-on white surface that allows you to write with felt-tip pens containing water soluble ink in various colors. They are becoming more and more popular in presentation areas because they have the flexibility of the older blackboard but look more professional. You can use them just as you would a blackboard—for outlining, illustrating, and noting. But be careful of the writing instruments you use—if you don't use water soluble ink, you can't erase your marks. And the same advice holds true for these boards as for blackboards—keep what you write simple and orderly and stand off to one side so your audience can easily read what you've written.
- ***Flip charts***. A flip chart is simply a pad of paper mounted on some sort of stand, usually called an easel. Some flip charts are small, but the most visible ones are large, with pads measuring 24 by 48 inches. Flip charts are probably the most popular visual aid for oral presentations—and for good reason. You can use them just as you would a blackboard, but you can also move them from place to place in the room. In addition, you can tear off important pages and hang them in the room for later reference.

  Most people feel that a flip chart makes a presentation look more professional than a blackboard does. Sometimes, it's best to prepare important pages in advance, even getting someone with professional training in graphics to design charts or graphs. (Most large organizations have someone who can do this for you.) If you do use a flip chart during a presentation, follow these guidelines.

  —Print neatly.
  —Limit each page to a few key points or to a particular theme.
  —Stay to one side so your audience can see the chart.

- ***Transparencies.*** These are specially prepared acetate sheets (sometimes called "slides"), which you lay over a projector table to produce an image on a screen. Well-designed transparencies can create sharp and colorful images, which give your presentation a professional polish that nothing else can. You can use a transparency just as you would a chart or blackboard—to highlight the main points of a presentation (perhaps in different colors for emphasis) or to demonstrate an important concept with a chart, graph, or picture.

  Transparencies are relatively easy to prepare, but you're probably better off getting a trained professional to prepare yours. Such an individual will know how to make them particularly effective through the use of color, numbers, etc. One advantage of a transparency is that you can keep it handy, referring to it over and over as you progress through a presentation. But practice with them a little before your presentation, so you learn how not to project your fingers or shadow onto the wall. A finger enlarged ten times will look pretty funny to your audience. Also, since a transparency projector uses a little fan to keep the high intensity bulb cool, you're better off cutting the projector off when you're not going to use it for awhile, so the motor noise doesn't interfere with what you are saying.

  The most effective way to use transparencies is the following one:

  —Turn on projector when you are ready to use your first transparency.
  —Place transparency on glass table.
  —Now turn screen light on to reveal the transparency.
  —To control the amount of information you reveal, put a piece of paper under the transparency and gradually slide it out to reveal one point at a time.
  —Read information directly from the transparency, not from the screen behind you.
  —Use a pen, pencil, or small pointer to point out particular items on the transparency.
  —Turn screen light off between transparencies because the white glare on the screen is distracting.

There are other types of audiovisual equipment (opaque projectors, slide projectors, video tapes, films, audio tapes), but the ones we've discussed are most frequently used in ordinary presentations. The keys to using any visual aid are—

- to design it very simply, so it can be read and interpreted quickly and easily;
- to be careful not to interfere with its impact by getting between your audience and the aid; and

- to use it to supplement, not replace, your presentation.

Also, a few simple aids used gracefully are much more effective than scads of professionally produced ones used amateurishly. Remember that you're making a short oral presentation, not producing a major motion picture. Now let's return to the performance appraisal system presentation.

An Oral Situation (continued)

For your presentation on performance appraisal, you decide to prepare a handout that summarizes the main features of the system you recommend. In addition, you order a flip chart that you will write on to illustrate important points. Finally, you order five transparencies made by your organization's publications division. You will use one to give an overview of your presentation, and others to illustrate the main features of your system, its benefits, etc.

Here is how your first transparency will look.

PERFORMANCE APPRAISAL: AN OVERVIEW

PROBLEMS: PRESENT SYSTEM

1. EXCLUDES EMPLOYEES FROM PROCESS
2. DOES NOT PROVIDE SUFFICIENT INFORMATION

SOLUTION: A NEW SYSTEM

1. EMPLOYEES SET YEARLY OBJECTIVES
2. EMPLOYEES
   - APPRAISE OWN PERFORMANCE
   - DISCUSS APPRAISAL WITH MANAGERS
3. MANAGER APPRAISES EMPLOYEES' PERFORMANCE

BENEFITS: RAISE MORALE/INCREASE PRODUCTIVITY THROUGH

- PARTICIPATION
- STANDARDIZATION
- EFFICIENCY

In addition to preparing your visuals, you also make a list of possible questions you could get after your presentation, questions about how a particular aspect of the performance appraisal procedure will work, about how long appraisal interviews will take, about how to deal with difficult employees, etc. Then you rehearse your answers. After all, you don't want to damage your credibility and undercut your presentation just by failing to give a satisfactory answer to a question or two.

PERFORMANCE

To make an oral presentation is to give a performance. Like an actor, you've got to play a role by projecting a certain kind of image. You've got to consider your audience, making sure that you speak and gesture so they can understand and get the meaning you want, and you've got to plan your entrance and exit carefully, for maximum effect. And like most good actors, you're probably going to experience stage fright, what most people call plain nervousness.

Nervousness: What Is It, Why Do I Get It, and How Do I Overcome It?

You might as well face the fact that you're going to be nervous before at least some oral presentations. Your hands may get moist, your heart may pound, your stomach may feel full of butterflies, and your breath may come rapidly.

How do you get over nervousness? Well, you don't want to, at least not entirely. In fact, a friend of mine says, "If it's a major presentation and you're not nervous, you got troubles!" A certain amount of nervousness is just the sign that your body is marshaling its resources to help you give the best oral presentation you can. Adrenalin is charging your muscles, sugar and insulin are preparing your body, and additional blood is providing oxygen to alert your mind.[3] Thus, your task is not to eliminate nervousness; it's to control it, so you can use it effectively.

Researchers don't know exactly why people get nervous, especially why some get more nervous than others. Some researchers think you get more nervous if you have a particular kind of personality, others that it comes from lack of self-confidence, and others that it comes from an unrealistic desire to achieve. Two writers say that nervousness comes from two sources:

- A constant stream of internal negative comments—"I'll never be able to do this successfully. They are not going to like this."
- Hyperresponsibility; that is, assuming that you are totally

[3]"Symptoms and signs of nervousness" taken from Michael E. Adelstein and W. Keats Sparrow, *Business Communication* (New York: Harcourt Brace Jovanovich, 1983) 35.

responsible for making your presentation a success for everyone present.[4]

There are almost as many remedies to control nervousness as there are suggested causes for it. But what most have in common is careful preparation of yourself beforehand. Here are some remedies that have worked for others.

1. Prepare yourself physically by eating protein about two hours before the presentation to control blood sugar. Avoid greasy foods and other things that are hard to digest to control gastrointestinal symptoms. Stay away from alcohol and too much caffeine. And don't take any drugs except those prescribed for you regularly.
2. Prepare mentally by talking positively rather than negatively to yourself. Say,

   - "It's OK to be nervous. Everyone gets that way."
   - "I know this subject better than anyone else. Even if I make a mistake, who's going to notice it?"
   - "Most of the people here want me to succeed."
   - "I'm going to think about my audience, not myself. What I care about is not how I feel, but what they'll get out of this."

3. Prepare for the actual presentation by practicing it just as you would deliver it. Picture the room you'll be in, see the people who will be in front of you, and listen as you make the presentation. Each time you do this, you'll prepare yourself a little more for the actual event.
4. Make sure that everything is prepared in advance: Lay out the clothes you'll wear the night before; get to the site a half-hour before you're scheduled to begin; make sure that everything in the room is the way you want it.
5. Finally, plan not to take all the responsibility for success yourself. Remember that members of your audience will have helpful ideas too. If you get a question you can't answer, ask people in the audience if they have the answer.

Delivery

When it comes to actually delivering an oral presentation, you've got three choices: you can memorize it, read it, or talk from an outline or notes. *Do not*, I repeat, do not try to memorize your presentation. At first thought, memorizing may appear to be the

[4]Marya W. Holcombe and Judith K. Stein, *Presentations for Decision Makers: Strategies for Structuring and Delivering Your Ideas* (Belmont, CA: Lifetime Learning Publications, Wadsworth Inc., 1983) 133.

solution to nervousness. After all, how can you be nervous if you know your speech cold? But what happens if you forget a point, or for that matter, just one line? You'll falter, lose your place and composure, and all will be lost.

Reading is not much better. Scholars do read papers to each other at professional meetings, but since the material they are talking about is often complicated, reading is expected. On the job, you'll find that most oral presentations are not read. For one thing, people quickly get bored when they are being read to. Also, reading a presentation can create an atmosphere of stiff formality, just what you want to avoid in most presentations.

Most good speakers try not to think of themselves as giving a formal "presentation." Rather, they try to create the illusion that they are simply talking with people in the room about a subject that they care about. To accomplish this, they usually make up a brief list of talking points, detailed enough to remind them of their important ideas, but not so detailed that they can't pick up ideas in a quick glance. Then they just present their ideas in as relaxed and as comfortable a fashion as possible. Here is how a list of talking points might look for your presentation on performance appraisal.

Here are some other things you can do to communicate clearly and comfortably with your audience.

1. *Talk* naturally and clearly to people, just as you would in conversation. As in conversation, when you want to emphasize something, raise or lower your voice. And consciously try to vary your pace and pitch a little. Most important, to make sure everyone can hear you, talk to a few people at the very back of the room. This will force you to project your voice so it can be heard by everyone.
2. *Move* around a little as you talk. For example, go to one side of the room and then the other, or move toward your audience and then away from them. And gesture a little, just as you would in conversation. Use your hands to emphasize an important point or a smile to indicate enthusiasm for an idea.
3. *Look* directly at people and talk to them. Pick out one person and talk to him for a moment or two. Then, pick out another and talk to her. And so on. Say this to one person, that to another, and still something else to another. And it helps to aim important points at people in the room who will make decisions. But resist the temptation to keep glancing at your boss. Remember, you're talking to everyone in the room.
4. The key to effective delivery is to *practice* as much as you can. If possible, practice in the actual place where you'll be giving your presentation. Getting the feel of a room often helps reduce nervousness. If you have access to videotaping equipment, have yourself videotaped during a practice ses-

PERFORMANCE APPRAISAL: TALKING POINTS

INTRO: Show problems with the old system

- Excludes employees from process
- Does not provide sufficient information--quote from VP of Sales

BODY: Explain new system

Step 1: First of year--sales reps meet with managers to set objectives

Step 2: End of year

- Sales reps write out their own appraisal of how well they have achieved their objectives
- Meet with managers to discuss appraisals

Step 3: Manager fills out appraisal form

- Evaluating rep's performance
- Recommending appropriate salary and promotion actions

ENDING: Show how system will raise morale/ increase productivity

<u>Participation</u>--People set own objectives for year and participate in evaluation at end of year

<u>Standardization</u>--Each division evaluates in same way, making training easy and results understandable

<u>Efficiency</u>--Trial runs show this system takes 2 hours per person vs. 3.5 hours with old system

sion. Then critique the tape carefully, making sure you talk naturally, move around the room, and look at different places. Or find a friend to listen to your presentation and critique you. Check especially for little nervous habits like shuffling your feet or saying "Ah" at every pause.

The more you practice, the easier it will become to be natural. After a while, you won't even notice that you really are raising and lowering your voice and even varying your pitch and pace a little. And you'll gradually use body language more effectively—moving from side to side a little and actually using your hands and facial expressions. In short, as you gain competence and confidence, you'll become more relaxed and natural.

You may not believe it while preparing for your first major oral presentation, but speaking to a group can be very satisfying, even fun. Any teacher or trainer will tell you that there's nothing quite like the feeling you get at the end of a presentation when smiles, compliments, or even informed questions indicate that you've been a success.

SUMMARY

As you prepare to give presentations over the next few years, practice these techniques.

1. Know what type of presentation you have to make, so you'll know how elaborate your preparations need to be.
2. Decide whether you even need to do an oral presentation. Sometimes it's easier just to put something in writing.
3. Set a limited and realistic goal for yourself, one you can make clear to your audience and accomplish with them.
4. Analyze your audience carefully, asking—
   - What do they need to know?
   - What values are at stake?
   - What will be their probable reaction?
5. Find an angle on your presentation that will enable you to organize it with an effective beginning, middle, and end.
6. Make use of appropriate audiovisuals, but be sure to use them well and don't overdo them.
7. Deal with nervousness by preparing yourself in every way—physically, mentally, and with plenty of practice.
8. Practice your delivery as often as you can, giving your presentation to people who can critique you.

APPLICATIONS

1. Reports are frequently given as oral presentations before they are written. Look back over the types of reports described in Chapter 10 and give a short oral report on—
   - A meeting you attended recently. Your audience will be the other members of the class and your goal will be to summarize the important points covered in the meeting.
   - The progress of a project you are working on. You could report on your progress investigating a possible career for yourself, giving your methods of research and findings to date.
   - The high points of the van-carpooling report you revised as Application 4 or the evaluation report you did in Application 5.

2. Proposals are given as oral presentations even more frequently than reports. Look back over the proposals you wrote for the applications at the end of Chapter 11 and make a short proposal presentation to the class.

3. Reread the situation in Chapter 12 involving the group that had to write a manual for job seekers. Imagine you are the group coordinator and give a short introductory presentation to the group describing the project and explaining how it can be done most efficiently. Be ready to answer any questions members of the group might have.

4. Give a short presentation in which you explain a procedure you have learned this semester such as how to write an effective report, proposal, or manual, how to write a persuasive letter or memo, or how to write a letter or memo that informs.

PART

4

Your Job Campaign

CHAPTER

14

Choosing a Career and Finding Jobs

The goal of the next two chapters is to help you apply the principles you have learned to a real situation—deciding on a career and writing the documents that will help you get a job. Even if you are in a career that you plan to continue or if you have already found a job for when you graduate, read them carefully. Not only will you learn how to apply principles of effective researching and writing to a real situation, but you may well be able to use this information later to plan and implement a career or job change.

Not long ago, the daughter of a friend of mine graduated from college with a double major in English and psychology, ready to enter the world of work. A year later, she had an excellent job in the public relations department of a local hospital, earning a good starting salary for writing brochures, interviewing hospital personnel for articles she contributed to the weekly newsletter, and coordinating a variety of public service activities. Her education had prepared her for just this kind of job and she loves it.

But what happened to Sarah in that year between graduation and employment is a horror story, one I'm going to tell you in the hope that you won't repeat her mistakes. She arrived home after graduation, determined to relax for two weeks before beginning her search for a job. After two weeks of soaps, Pepsi, and potato chips, she launched her campaign. First, she browsed through about one-hundred pages of Richard Bolles' excellent book, *What Color is Your Parachute*. Then she borrowed a friend's résumé and typed her own, devoting about a line to each of the jobs she had held during the summers. Finally, she had 500 copies made.

Next, she began to wonder where to apply. Since she wanted to settle in a large city, friends of her family offered to let her stay with the family in Philadelphia while she looked. After wandering around the city for a week, and either being brushed off by secretaries or filling out complicated application forms for faceless personnel departments, she was thoroughly discouraged, so much so that she returned home.

My friend's most vivid memories of his daughter during the next few months are of her sitting on the sofa, alternately crying, stuffing herself with junk food, and watching lousy TV. Occasionally, she'd gather herself together, read the want ads in our local newspaper or in the *Washington Post*, and drop her résumé in the mail accompanied by a cover letter, the kind that begins—

> Dear Sir or Madame:
>
> I recently graduated from college with majors in English and psychology and would now like to apply for a ________________ position.

Most of the time, she never heard anything from the prospective employer. Occasionally, she was asked in for an interview, from which she usually returned home only to cry some more.

But something else happened during that unhappy year. Between the TV, tears, and terrible interviews, Sarah learned how to go about applying for a job. First, through self-examination, she learned a lot about herself—about her interests and abilities. She reread journals she had kept in college, talked about herself with friends and relatives, and even went for counseling at a local university career planning and placement center. Through this process, she finally arrived at the decision to pursue a career in public relations. Next, she approached a friend of her family who supervised a public relations department in a large hospital and asked if she could intern (without pay) so she could learn something about the field. At the same time, she took a course in public relations at a local college.

As time went on, she began to apply for public relations jobs, some she read about in newspapers and others she heard about from people with whom she worked. Gradually too, she improved her résumé, focusing it on the writing skills she had developed in college and during her internship, and on the administrative and people skills she had learned in the jobs she had held during the summers. And each time she applied for a particular position, she rewrote her cover letter, emphasizing the skills and experiences that seemed most appropriate for that position. All the while, she was learning about public relations first-hand, meeting people in the field, and building a portfolio of her own work that she could show to prospective employers.

One day her break came. The supervisor of her department took her to a banquet given by the local public relations society. Sarah found herself seated beside a very friendly woman who asked a number of questions about what she was learning in her internship. At the end of their pleasant conversation, the woman identified herself as the supervisor of another hospital public relations department in the area. Moreover, she said that she would shortly be advertising an entry-level position in her department. You've probably guessed the rest by now. Sure enough, Sarah applied for and got the job.

Was that meeting an accident? Perhaps. On the other hand, it never would have occurred if Sarah hadn't made a decision about her career and taken that internship. Was it an accident that she landed the job? In no way. Through self-analysis, preparing a résumé and cover letters, interviewing for jobs, and working in her internship, she had spent a year preparing to get that job.

By now, of course, you know the moral of the story: you can find a job, a job leading to a rewarding career. But to find a good job and to avoid the kinds of frustrations Sarah experienced, you've got to pursue your job search in an organized fashion. In fact, you'll need to organize yourself as if you were conducting a military campaign, marshaling all your interests, talents, and efforts until you succeed. This chapter and the next one are about how to do this.

You will learn six steps to follow as you pursue your job campaign. This chapter will describe the first three, which focus on *assessing* your skills, interests, and values; *identifying* a career (or careers) that matches these; and *locating* some actual jobs within that career. The next chapter will show you how to prepare a convincing résumé, write an effective cover letter to accompany that résumé, and prepare for your job interview. Here are all six steps.

1. *Know thyself.* Inventory your interests, abilities, values, and experiences so you can locate a career that will fit these.
2. *Identify and research some careers.* On the basis of your inventory, choose some possible career areas. Using the research tools I will describe, find out all you can about these careers—what qualifications you would need, what kind of work you would do, what the salary and benefits would be, what future you would have, etc.
3. *Target particular locations, organizations, and jobs.* Using the research materials I will describe, pick out the locations and organizations you want to target.
4. *Prepare your résumé.* On the basis of your self-inventory and career research, prepare a résumé that will highlight your preparation for a career.
5. *Write your cover letter.* For each organization you have chosen, prepare a cover or application letter that is targeted directly to that organization and the position you are applying for.

6. *Interview successfully.* Obtain interviews from appropriate people at your target organizations and prepare yourself to interview successfully.

If you have not done much thinking about a career choice up to now, you may want to use all six steps. On the other hand, you may be fairly certain of your career. If so, you may want to skip Steps 1 and 2 and go on to Step 3, locating jobs within your career. But even if you are fairly sure of a career, you may want to use Steps 1 and 2 to check the suitability of your choice and prepare yourself to write a solid résumé. You should also know that this is certainly not the last time you will examine your career choice. If you are like most of us, you will go through these steps several times during your lifetime, reassessing your career and current job.

STEP 1: KNOW THYSELF

The key to choosing a rewarding career is to match your own interests and talents with occupations that will enable you to use these. Therefore, the first step in your job campaign is to study yourself, to find out what kind of person you have become. The best way to do this is to consult a counselor in the career planning and placement center found at most universities. Such a person can lead you through a systematic process that will enable you to assess yourself and then locate a suitable career. Many career centers offer workshops and classes on choosing a career, some even with class credit. These can be helpful too.

Another thing you can do is to browse through the self-assessment sections in the following books. You will find most of them in your career counseling center or library.

- Robert S. Barkhaus and Charles W. Bolyard, *Threads: A Tapestry of Self and Career Exploration* (Dubuque, Ia.: Kendall/Hunt, 1977).
  A detailed manual on career planning.
- Richard Nelson Bolles, *What Color is Your Parachute*? (Berkeley, Calif.: Ten Speed Press, 1983).
  "The Quick Job-Hunting Map" on pages 206–241 gives a detailed method for self-assessment.
- Howard Figler, *The Complete Job-Search Handbook* (New York: Holt, Rinehart, 1979).
  Contains a detailed discussion of self-assessment skills in Chapter 1.
- H. B. Gelatt, et al., *Decisions and Outcomes* (New York: Educational Testing Service, 1973).
  A step-by-step manual on how to go about making career decisions.

Autobiography[1]

The purpose of this 10- to 15-page essay is to enable you to analyze yourself, trying to find out what kind of person you have become, and to discover some of the factors in your life that have created this person. Be sure to address yourself to all the questions in the following areas that pertain to you. You may organize the essay chronologically or topically.

1. Home life: Where were you born and reared? Where have you lived? What are your parents like and how have they influenced you over the years? Any other family members who influenced you as you grew up?
2. School: Where have you gone to school? Have you been happy and successful in school, or otherwise? What courses/programs have you particularly liked over the years? Which have you adamantly disliked? What scholarships or awards have you won? Why did you choose your present major? Looking back now, was it a wise choice?
3. Jobs: What kind of jobs have you held over the years, both paying and volunteer? What were your actual duties? What qualities/

On the next few pages are three activities that you can use to study yourself. Even though they are not meant to substitute for career counseling, they will give you an introduction to self-assessment methods and a basis for career research. If at all possible, supplement these with help from a career counselor.

Your Life Story

Whether you are aware of it or not, you have spent your life preparing for a career. Your experiences—with family, friends, and in school—have led you to develop certain values, interests, and abilities. One way to discover what these are is to write a detailed autobiography of yourself, a sketch of the kind of person you have

[1]This exercise has been adapted from one developed by Professor Janet Kotler, School of Business, University of Richmond, Richmond, VA.

abilities did these jobs demand of you (tact, brute strength, ability to use computer, etc.)? How successful and happy were you in these jobs? Were you hired again? Promoted? Fired? What did you learn on these jobs?

4. Personal interests: What are you like: When you're not working or studying, do you tend to spend time by yourself? Doing what? With a few close friends? Doing what? With one other person? Do you feel you should have more friends? Get rid of some? Do you play any sports? Which? Any good at them? Do you read? What? Know any languages besides English? How well? Traveled? US? Abroad?
5. Personality: How do you feel about yourself? What are you proud of having accomplished? What past performance gives you the creeps just to think about? Does living come easy or hard for you? Do you take the initiative in most situations? Are you a good follower? What do you do best? What do you not do so well? Are you pretty intelligent? In what way? Personable? In what way? Responsible? About what? Do you wish you were physically stronger or more attractive?

become over the years. Write the 10- to 15-page autobiography according to the following instructions. You might do it just for yourself, or get someone else to read and comment on it.

Your Career Profile

Imagine that you have been asked to write a profile of yourself for a prospective employer, focusing on your skills, interests, and personal attributes. Prepare to write your profile by doing the following. (Suggestion—consult others who know you well as you do these):

1. *List ten achievements during your life that you are proud of.* These might include doing a job particularly well, winning an athletic event, doing well in a difficult course, playing in a recital, winning a scholastic honor, accomplishing a difficult

task, or sticking to something that you didn't like. Now choose three of these and describe in detail how you accomplished them.

2. *List all the jobs you have held up to now.* Include not only major jobs such as camp counselor or store clerk, but also others such as babysitting or carrying newspapers.
3. *Now look over your list of achievements and jobs and list the important skills you needed to accomplish these.* Some of the basic skills you might include are the following:
   a. *Mental skills*—reading, writing, working with numbers, solving problems, using computers.
   b. *People skills*—getting along with, helping or caring for, supervising, persuading, motivating people.
   c. *Artistic skills*—playing music, dancing, acting, writing, designing clothing or stage sets, painting, drawing.
   d. *Mechanical skills*—operating or repairing complex machines or electronic equipment.
   e. *Athletic skills*—swimming, running, jumping, playing ball.
   f. *Self-management skills*—dependability, integrity, efficiency, drive.
4. *List ten activities that you currently enjoy.* You might include reading, sailing, engaging in athletics, listening to music, being by yourself, or being with friends.
5. *Fantasize for a moment and list ten activities that you would enjoy doing if you had the chance.* You might include traveling to Europe, racing sports cars, dancing, or fishing.
6. *Fantasize again and choose ten perfect careers for yourself.* Think about what you would like to do, where you would like to live, how much money you want to make, etc.
7. *List the ten courses you have most enjoyed taking in high school and college.*
8. *Now look over your last three lists and make a list of your principal interests.* Include such things as working with machinery, helping people, playing tennis, building things, listening to music, taking care of animals, or working with computers.
9. *Make a list of your principal personal attributes.* Here is a list of personal attributes to help you think of some:

precise	energetic	hard-working	dedicated
assertive	sensitive	helpful	easygoing
perceptive	imaginative	diligent	intelligent
responsible	persistent	friendly	humorous
analytic	persuasive	organized	flexible

A Personality Assessment

In his *Making Vocational Choices: A Theory of Careers* (Englewood Cliffs, N.J.: Prentice-Hall, 1973), the psychologist John Holland says that the key to an effective career choice is to understand your personality and then choose a career that suits this personality. All of us, says Holland, have a personality pattern, formed primarily by heredity and early experiences in schools, with friends, and so on. This personality pattern determines how we will conceive of ourselves and our environment, what our values will be, how we will react to rewards and stress, how we cope with problems, etc.

Holland has developed six basic personality types. An individual's personality pattern is a combination of three types, with one usually predominating. One of the surveys designed to help someone determine his or her personality pattern is given below. Take the survey and then compare your results with the descriptions of Holland's personality types listed after it.

WORK VALUES SURVEY[2]

To determine your basic personality pattern, rank each of the following as—

1—not important to you
2—important to you
3—very important to you

1. ______ *Improve society*. Do work that will make the world a better place. (S)
2. ______ *Be part of a group*. Work as a team member of an organization. (C)
3. ______ *Exercise artistic creativity*. Do creative work in any of several art forms. (A)
4. ______ *Compete with others*. Do work that matches my abilities against others with clear win-or-lose outcomes. (E)
5. ______ *Have social contact*. Do work that requires frequent contact with people. (S)
6. ______ *Work alone*. Do projects by myself, without any significant contact with others. (R)
7. ______ *Be philosophically curious*. Work to try to understand the laws of nature, add to cultural heritage, make scientific discoveries, or question society's beliefs. (I & A)
8. ______ *Have power and authority*. Control the work activities or work development of others. (E)
9. ______ *Possess security*. Be assured of keeping my job and a reasonable financial reward. (C)

[2]This instrument is adapted from one used by the Career Planning and Placement Office at the University of Richmond, Richmond, VA.

10. ______ *Be generally creative.* Create new ideas, programs, or organizational structures by not following a format previously set by others. (A)
11. ______ *Acquire knowledge.* Study books, people, activities, etc., in the pursuit of knowledge or truth. (I)
12. ______ *Work with others.* Work with a team toward common goal. (S)
13. ______ *Experience physical challenges.* Have a job that makes physical demands that I find rewarding. (R)
14. ______ *Appreciate beauty.* Work to study the beauty of things, ideas, etc. (A)
15. ______ *Influence people.* Work to persuade others to change their beliefs or actions. (E)
16. ______ *Have friendships.* Have a job that results in the development of close personal relationships. (S)
17. ______ *Have intellectual status.* Be regarded at work as highly intelligent and/or an "expert." (I)
18. ______ *Work predictably.* Work in an environment that is routine and has a minimum of unexpected changes in schedule or job duties. (C)
19. ______ *Live adventurously.* Have work duties that involve frequent risk-taking. (R)
20. ______ *Earn profits or gain.* Have a strong likelihood of accumulating large amounts of money or other material gain. (E & R)
21. ______ *Do precision work.* Work in situations where there is very little tolerance for error. (I)
22. ______ *Be organized.* Work in a methodical way, keep things organized, and help facilitate the work of others. (C)
23. ______ *Experience moral fulfillment.* Feel that my work is contributing significantly to a set of moral standards that are very important. (S)
24. ______ *Attain recognition.* Be recognized for the quality of my work in some visible or public way. (E)
25. ______ *Gain independence.* Be able to determine the nature of my work without significant direction from others; not have to do what others tell me to do. (A & I)
26. ______ *Perform specific tasks.* Work in a job in which I know what is expected, work on well-defined problems or tasks, and am able to check work in detail. (C & R)

At the end of each item there are one or two letters that fit that item into a personality category. Total the items in each category. If an item is in two categories, count it twice. Your three highest numbers will give your basic personality pattern.

______ Realistic
______ Investigative
______ Artistic
______ Social
______ Enterprising
______ Conventional

To identify your pattern, compare your results with the descriptions of the patterns listed below (adapted from Holland; pp. 14–18). You may find, for example, that you are a social type first, then enterprising, then another type. Remember that these types are extremes; you probably won't fit exactly into any. But if you combine three, you should have a pretty good idea of your general pattern.

1. *Realistic.* People who have athletic or mechanical ability, prefer to work with plants, animals, objects, machines, tools, or to be outdoors. They may perceive themselves to lack human relations abilities. Concrete things and tangible qualities such as money, power, and status are important to them.
2. *Investigative.* People who like to observe, learn, investigate, analyze, evaluate, or solve problems. They usually perceive themselves as scholarly, intellectually self-confident, but perhaps lacking in leadership ability. They enjoy research and scientific activities.
3. *Artistic.* People who have artistic, innovative, or intuitional abilities and like to work in unstructured situations using their imagination or creativity. They may perceive themselves as expressive, original, nonconforming, introspective, and disorderly. They value aesthetic qualities.
4. *Social.* People who like to work with other people to inform, enlighten, help, train, develop, or cure them. They perceive themselves as liking to help others, understanding others, or having teaching ability, but lacking in mechanical and scientific ability. They value social and ethical activities and problems.
5. *Enterprising.* People who like to work with people, influencing, persuading, or managing for organizational goals or economic gain. They perceive themselves as aggressive, popular, self-confident, social, possessing leadership and speaking ability, but lacking scientific ability.
6. *Conventional.* People who like to work with data or have numerical ability, carrying out things in detail or following through on instructions. They perceive themselves as conforming and orderly, and they value business and economic achievement.

Besides the survey above, there are other ways to determine your basic personality pattern. Try the two below and see whether your results approximate the results you obtained from the survey.[3]

[3]Adapted from Richard Nelson Bolles, *What Color is Your Parachute?* (Berkeley, Calif.: Ten Speed Press, 1983), pp. 209–210.

1. Reread the descriptions of the six personality types above. Then imagine you are attending a party in a room full of these people. In one corner are a group of realistic types, in another a group of investigative types, in another corner another group, etc. Rank the three groups you would be most drawn to during the evening, scoring the group you most prefer with a 3, the next most preferred group with a 2, etc.
2. Using the same scoring method, imagine that you are choosing types of people with whom you would prefer to work.

Now compare the personality codes you derived from all these activities. They should not be very much different from each other. You will use these codes to find appropriate careers in the next section.

Of course, no one ever understands him- or herself completely, but if you have used the Life Story, Career Profile, and Personality Assessment, you should understand many of your dominant values, interests, skills, and personal traits. If you want to pursue your research further, you might take a career interest assessment such as John Holland's, *The Self-Directed Search* (Odessa, Fla.: Psychological Assessment Resources, 1985), or the *Strong-Campbell Interest Inventory* by Strong, Hansen, and Campbell, revised in 1985 and published by Consulting Psychologists, Palo Alto, Calif. Both of these instruments are based on the Holland codes and most career counseling centers have them.

STEP 2: IDENTIFY AND RESEARCH SOME CAREERS

Now that you have completed your self-assessment, you should have a pretty good profile of yourself. You may have found that you are more of a "numbers" person, someone who might be happy teaching math, working with computers, or holding a job in the financial world. On the other hand, you may now see yourself as more of a verbal person, interested perhaps in personnel work, mass communications, public relations, etc. You will, of course, have discovered many other things about yourself—whether you prefer to be outside or inside most of the time, to work with others or by yourself, to rely heavily on your intuition or reasoning ability, to take the lead in a situation or follow, and so on.

Keep your self-profile in mind as you begin now to locate some careers that match it. Since there is no easy way to research careers, you will have to be ingenious and persistent. But the results will be rewarding. Also, remember that, at this stage, the object of your research will be to locate a career field, but not yet a particular job within that field. Identifying these will come later.

What's the difference between a career and a job? A career is an occupation, such as public relations, accounting, equipment sales, teaching, or data processing, that you can pursue for a long period of time (perhaps a lifetime) in a variety of organizations and jobs. A job is a particular position, such as records administrator in a hospital, auditor for a bank, director of sales for a heavy industry, that you hold with one organization, probably for a limited period of time.

As with any research project, you should know the kind of information you are looking for before you begin. The best way to decide this is to list the general questions you will have about a career. You might divide them up into areas like the following:

1. *Description*. What would I actually *do* if I worked in this career? That is, what kind of product or service would I produce? Would I work mostly with data, things, or people? Would I spend lots of time in meetings, writing reports, or talking on the telephone?
2. *Working conditions*. Would most of the work be done inside or outside the office? In what part of the country would I be located? What would the working hours be like? Would they be flexible? How much room would there be for innovation or self-expression? What kinds of people would I be working with? Would this career prescribe a particular lifestyle for me?
3. *Preparation*. How have I prepared for this career? Specifically, how have my courses, major, and job experiences prepared me?
4. *Benefits*. What benefits would I receive? What are the tangible benefits such as salaries (starting and continuing) and fringe benefits (health insurance, life insurance, etc.)? And what are the more intangible job satisfactions?
5. *Future*. Specifically, what are the possibilities for advancement within this career? And more generally, what does the future for this career look like? Will it expand, remain about the same size, or shrink during the next 10 to 20 years? Will there be particular jobs that will grow more than others in this field?

As a first step in researching careers, try to set up an interview with a counselor at a university career planning and placement center. If you don't have access to a center, try your state employment agency. Since you will have completed your self-assessment and will have a list of general research questions, you will be well prepared to talk with the counselor about research possibilities. He or she might suggest that you consult people in career areas that are of interest to you. If so, consult the discussion of information interviews in the last part of this chapter to learn how to go about this process. In addition, your counselor might suggest that you consult the various career guides and materials the center has and that you browse through materials on some particular careers. Some career centers have computer programs that you can use to locate careers within your state or region.

As you begin your research, you will find some reference works particularly useful. Two are particularly well-known within the field of career counseling and will certainly be in a career center and probably in the public library. Here is a brief description of each.

- *The Occupational Outlook Handbook* (Washington, D.C.: U.S. Department of Labor, Bureau of Labor Statistics, U.S. Government Printing Office, latest edition).

This easy-to-use reference work, which is published every two years, provides employment trends and projections, showing employment shifts as well as projecting the number of people needed in particular occupational categories in the future. From these projections, you can get some idea of the types of occupations that will employ the most people in the future.

It also describes over 300 particular occupations in a nontechnical, narrative form, giving the nature of the work, places of employment, training required, other qualifications, opportunities for advancement, the employment outlook, earnings and working conditions, and sources of additional information. Finally, for readers interested more generally in whole industries, it discusses 35 major industries, giving for each such information as its nature, purpose, employment outlook, earnings and working conditions, particular occupations associated with it, qualifications for workers, and methods of entry.

- *The Dictionary of Occupational Titles* (Washington, D.C.: U.S. Department of Labor, 4th ed., 1977).

First published in 1939, this book is now in its fourth edition. Based on 75,000 on-site analyses of jobs in various industries, it lists and describes all major occupations in this country. Because it is such a comprehensive and detailed reference work, you will have to spend a little time getting used to it. But it is a very useful tool, for it will give you information such as the tasks and skills used in a particular occupation; the tools or work aids used; the services, products, materials, and academic subjects included; the industries where the occupation is found; what workers are required to do; and so forth.

Each occupation in the *DOT* is classified by a nine-digit code that places it within an occupational category, indicates whether people in this occupation work mostly with data, things, or other people, and distinguishes it from other similar occupations. At this stage in your research, you will find a supplement to the *DOT* called *Selected Characteristics of Occupations Defined in the Dictionary of Occupational*

Titles (Washington, D.C.: U.S. Department of Labor, Employment Service, U.S. Government Printing Office, 1981) to be most helpful. It classifies jobs into work groups that accord with particular interest areas and then describes each work group in a nontechnical narrative form, giving particular occupations within each work group.

You will find a number of other reference works to be useful.

- Thomas F. Harrington and Arthur J. O'Shea, *Guide for Occupational Exploration* (Circle Pines, Minn.: American Guidance Service, 1984).

  This guide helps you match information about yourself—your work values, leisure activities, school subjects, and desired work settings—with particular careers.
- William E. Hopke, ed., *The Encyclopedia of Careers and Vocational Guidance*. 2 vols. (Chicago: J. G. Berguson, 1981).

  Volume I gives guidelines for planning a career, discusses what the future world of work will be like, and shows you how to use test results in matching yourself to a career. Then it gives a series of articles that describe various career fields such as advertising, data-processing, electronics, management, publishing, and radio and TV. Volume II describes particular careers by giving a history of the career, the nature of the work, requirements to enter the career, opportunities, etc.

If you did the self-assessment activities based on the Holland personality patterns, a book that should be especially useful to you is—

- Gary D. Gottfredson, John L. Holland, Deborah Kimiko Ogawa, *Dictionary of Holland Occupational Codes: A Comprehensive Cross-Index of Holland's RIASEC codes with 12,000 DOT Occupations* (Palo Alto, CA: Consulting Psychologists Press, 1982).

  Here, you can look up your personality pattern code and find occupations that match it. Each entry gives the title of the occupation, such as "Lighting-Equipment Operator," the level of education required by the job, the training time required, and a nine-digit code referring to the *Dictionary of Occupational Titles.*

A book that may help you match your college major with various careers is—

- Lawrence R. Malnig, with Anita Malnig, *What Can I Do with a Major In . . . ? How to Choose and Use Your College Major* (Ridgefield, N.J.: Abbott Press, 1984).

Based on studies to find out what careers students in different majors choose, it describes various majors, gives job titles, DOT and

Holland codes, institutions that would hire for these jobs, and specific jobs entered by the graduates of St. Peter's College in Jersey City, New Jersey.

You may be surprised to learn that the authors of this book have found that the occupations college graduates choose are not necessarily determined by their major. They say:

> The most surprising thing about our findings was the fact—which surfaced so consistently we couldn't help but be impressed by it—that regardless of their major, *college graduates enter a wide range of occupations, many of them seemingly unrelated to undergraduate studies.* These findings have forced us to conclude that any major, apparently, equips students with knowledge and skills that they can apply to a wide range of jobs in many diverse fields.

If your career placement center has it, a very helpful system to use in matching yourself to a career is the Career Information System. It divides possible careers up into 12 areas—such as artistic, scientific, nature—and then subdivides each area into a number of job groups. The most helpful part of the system is—

- David W. Winefordner, *Worker Trait Group Guide* (Bloomington, Ill.: McKnight Publ., 1978).

  For each of the twelve career areas, this book gives a general description of the group, describes the kind of work performed, sets forth the kinds of skills, abilities, and interests workers in the group have, and gives clues for deciding whether you have them. It also tells you how to prepare for and enter that field and what else you should know about the jobs.

Finally, three helpful series contain books that discuss particular careers in detail, giving the kinds of jobs to be had in each field, ways to prepare for the career, typical salaries and working conditions, etc. Three of them are—

- *Opportunities in . . .*, VGM Career Horizons Series (Skokie, Ill.: National Textbook, 1981).
- *Exploring Careers in . . .* (New York: Richards Rosen Press, various dates).
- *Your Future in . . .* (New York: Richards Rosen Press, 1980).

You have seen by now that identifying and researching a career you want to enter will not be an easy job, especially if you have not done much thinking about a career choice before. But with the help of your placement center, using some of the reference works I have just described, and trying out your ideas on your friends and/or spouse, you will, in time, be able to identify a rewarding career for yourself.

STEP 3: TARGET PARTICULAR LOCATIONS, ORGANIZATIONS, AND JOBS

Once you have identified and researched a career, you are ready to locate some jobs that will allow you to pursue it. If you are successful in this step, you will find some jobs for which you wish to apply and identify the people to whom you will apply. Your research task may be a relatively easy one, because in the process of assessing yourself and identifying and researching a career, you have probably learned a lot about the kinds of jobs available within that career. You may even have learned the names of some companies you could contact.

On the other hand, if you have not yet located many jobs and organizations with these jobs, your research task will be more complex. For one thing, there is no one reference work that will enable you to match your career interests with particular jobs. Why? Because there are just too many organizations with jobs in a particular career field. The task would be monumental, if not impossible. But there is a kind of narrowing-down process you can follow that will lead you to particular jobs within your chosen career. The next few pages will show you this process.

Let's begin with your broadest concerns—where you wish to live and the kinds of organizations you might like to work for. In your career research, you will almost certainly have learned that there are a number of locations and organizations where you can do what you want to do. If you have chosen retail sales, for instance, you can locate almost anywhere in the country with a number of different kinds of companies. And if your interest is accounting, you know that there are positions in various sections of the country with accounting firms, as well as with banks, businesses, and government organizations. The same is true for most other career fields. If you are entering public relations, for instance, you are by no means limited just to public relations agencies. You should consider public relations jobs in government and large private industries, as well as in hospitals and trade organizations. So, you probably do have some job choices—both as to where you want to live and as to the kinds of companies to which you will apply.

Targeting Particular Locations

First, let's consider geographical location. If you are like many people, you will already have chosen where you wish to work. You may wish to live in the area where you grew up, or you may wish to locate a position closer to where you received your college education. But perhaps you shouldn't dismiss the issue of location without considering it just a little. After all, locating a job or shifting from one job to another provides an ideal time to move.

Of course, for some career fields, one location may be preferable to another. If you want to enter public relations with a trade organization, for instance, Washington, D.C., with its many trade organizations, might be an ideal place to locate. The same might be true if you are considering a job with the federal government. And during your career research, you will have learned that there are certain places in the country where occupations such as investment banking, data processing, or TV production seem to cluster.

But if you can locate in different sections of the country, you might consider those places that will grow the most during the next few years. John Naisbitt, the author of *Megatrends: Ten New Directions Transforming Our Lives* (New York: Warner Books, 1984), says that population (and therefore job opportunity) is shifting from the North and East to the South and West. During the 1970s, for instance, the states that grew the most in population were Florida and Texas in the South-Southwest and Alaska, Arizona, Colorado, Idaho, New Mexico, Nevada, and Utah in the West. He feels that California, Florida, and Texas will grow the most economically during the rest of this century. And the cities that will provide the greatest opportunity, says Naisbitt, are all located in the Sun Belt—Albuquerque, Austin, Denver, Phoenix, Salt Lake City, San Antonio, San Diego, San Jose, Tampa, and Tucson.

Richard Bolles, author of *What Color is Your Parachute*, generally agrees. His ten fastest growing cities are (in order) Fort Lauderdale, Tucson, Houston, Phoenix, Austin, San Diego, Oxnard (California), Columbia (South Carolina), Tampa, and Albuquerque. You will probably know of other fast-growing places where you can pursue your career.

Of course, other factors besides rate of growth are important as you consider location. Two references that describe some of these factors in connection with particular locations are the following:

- Richard Boyer and David Savageau. *Places Rated Almanac: Your Guide to Finding the Best Places to Live in America* (Chicago, Ill.: Rand McNally, latest ed.).

  This guide describes 329 metropolitan areas, discussing such topics as climate, terrain, environment, housing, health care, transportation, education, arts, recreation, taxes, and even crime rates.

- Thomas F. Bowman, George A. Giuliani, and M. Ronald Minge. *Finding Your Best Place to Live in America* (New York: Red Lion Books, 1981).

  This guide describes the overall quality of life in 50 to 100 cities, discussing topics such as cost of living, weather conditions, air pollutants, crime rates, concentrations of religious groups, health hazards, etc.

But don't let location be the only determining factor in locating jobs. Remember that the more flexible you are about location, the better chance you have to get particular jobs. And you may well move around the first few years anyway, especially if you go with a large organization.

Since you will probably have a choice of industries (or government organizations) to apply to for jobs, you should be aware of which ones will probably grow the most during your working life, for you may well be able to locate your career within one of these. Various authorities say slightly different things, but most agree on areas of real growth. In *Megatrends*, for example, John Naisbitt says that we are shifting from an industrial to an information society; from the heavy technology of mining and manufacturing to the high technology of electronics and computers; and from a national economy to being a part of an interdependent global economy. (Of course, this does not mean that you should eliminate heavy industry or restrict yourself just to electronics and high tech. We will still need automobiles and buildings in the future.) In addition to the areas Naisbitt mentions, areas such as office management, bioengineering, health care, and other human services will continue to grow.

Targeting Particular Organizations and Jobs

Let's assume now that you have at least tentatively decided on some sections of the country where you'd like to locate and perhaps even some possible industries. Your next step will be to identify particular organizations and jobs for which you wish to apply. There are several different ways to do this.

One effective way to match your chosen career with particular jobs is to consult a placement or employment service. Here again, as with choosing a career, a university career planning and placement center is probably your best bet. It will have particular books and possibly audiovisual materials on jobs available in different career fields. Such centers even arrange "interview days," during which particular organizations come to campus and hold interviews.

If your local university doesn't have a career placement center, you can try the public employment service in the area in which you choose to locate. Finally you might contact a commercial employment agency. But be careful—remember that commercial agencies are in business to make money, usually a percentage of your salary after you are hired. Too often, their counselors are just salespersons, who are more interested in producing a job for you rather than really helping match your career interests with jobs.

Another way is to look at the jobs available section in newspapers within your geographical area. Large Sunday editions of newspapers, especially the *New York Times*, will give you some especially good ideas about what companies are hiring people with career interests like yours. And you can also consult national newspapers such as *The Wall Street Journal*, which advertises jobs in the entire country and abroad. *The Wall Street Journal* also publishes the *National Business Employment Weekly* each Sunday, which describes jobs available in organizations throughout the nation. In addition, you might consult some professional journals within your field, which sometimes advertise available jobs. You should not rely too heavily on newspapers for actual job leads, because many positions never appear in the paper at all.

Besides newspapers, there are some general reference works that you can consult.

- Heinz Ulrich and J. Robert Connor. *The National Job Finding Guide* (Garden City, N.Y.: Doubleday, 1981).
  Gives job prospects for the 1980s, with the percentage of increase or decrease of clerical workers, sales people, professional and technical people, etc. It also contains a list of employment agencies across the nation classified by job, as well as discussions of special opportunities for women, minorities, and the handicapped.

Three other guides that may be helpful are

- *The Occupational Outlook Handbook* (Washington, D.C.: U.S. Department of Labor, Bureau of Labor Statistics, U.S. Government Printing Office, latest ed.).
- *Occupational Outlook for College Graduates* (Washington, D.C.: U.S. Department of Labor, Bureau of Labor Statistics, U.S. Government Printing Office, latest ed.).
- *College Placement Annual* (Bethlehem, Penn.: College Placement Council, 1985–86).

If you want to focus more on particular companies, some standard corporation reference guides are

- Dun and Bradstreet's *Million Dollar Directory* (Parsippany, N.J.: Dun and Bradstreet, 1986).
- Standard and Poor's *Register of Corporations, Directors, and Executives*, 3 vols (New York: Standard and Poor's, 1986).
- *The 100 Best Companies to Work for in America*, by Robert Levering, Milton Moskowitz, and Michael Katz (Reading, Mass.: Addison-Wesley Publ., 1983).
  This last guide gives not only facts about these companies, but also their characteristic atmospheres.

In addition to these general reference works, two other helpful guides to particular companies are—

- *The Career Guide: Dun's Employment Opportunities Directory* (Parsippany, N.J.: Dun and Bradstreet, annual).

This guide gives an overview of particular companies, as well as employment opportunities, benefits, and the names of people to contact about job applications.

- J. Michael Fiedler, *National Job Bank: A Comprehensive Guide to Major Employers in the United States* (Boston, Mass.: Bob Adams Inc., 2nd edn., 1985).

  Organized by state, this guide describes the functions of particular companies and their facilities, as well as identifying whom to contact for job information.

Professional associations are another excellent source of information about jobs in particular fields. To see whether there is a professional association for your career, consult the guide to *National Trade and Professional Associations of the U.S.*, John J. Russel and Patricia Becker Lee, eds. (Washington, D.C.: Columbia Books, 1986).

Information Interviews

The best way to research geographical areas, companies, and particular jobs is to use all the means I have described so far—placement agencies, newspapers, and reference works. But these are not enough. In fact, I have yet to mention the most effective way of researching and, ultimately, of finding a job. In 1970, the U.S. Department of Labor reported on a study in which thousands of job holders were asked how they found their employment. Seventy-two percent reported that they got their jobs through people, either through direct contact with employers or through friends or relatives. So your most helpful resource will be other people. But besides relatives or friends, how do you make contacts?

The answer is that you conduct "information interviews" with people working in your career field. Your interviews will have three goals. First, to find out as much as you can about your chosen career, including what jobs are available and how you might apply for these jobs. Second, to find out how you can match your skills and interests with particular jobs. And third, to establish a network of people who can help you locate jobs that match your interests, skills, and values.

How do you go about conducting information interviews? First, you use the research tools described previously to identify some companies you are interested in. Then, identify the people within these companies whom you wish to interview. If possible, steer clear of personnel departments; rather, make appointments with people in the field itself. You can get their names from your placement counselor as well as from teachers, parents, and friends. In addition, you can also consult your university or local library for a directory that gives information on all companies within your area. Such a directory, sometimes published by a local chamber of commerce, describes companies and gives the names of people in major positions. You can then contact these people for the names of people whom you might interview. Emphasize the fact that you are not interviewing for a job; you are simply interested in their career and want to find out more about it. They will usually find someone with the time to grant you an interview.

Your first goal in an information interview is to find out as much as you can about your chosen career field. To do this, you will need to prepare your questions well. In general, you want to know what the career is like, how to prepare for it, what the tangible and intangible benefits are, what working conditions are like, and what the future of the career looks like. Make yourself a list of 15 to 20 questions to ask. Your list might look like the following:

<u>Description</u>

1. What do you do during a typical day/week?
2. How much of your time do you spend on various activities such as writing, talking with people on the phone, meeting with groups, traveling?

<u>Working Conditions</u>

3. Where is most of your work done, inside the office or outside?
4. What are your usual working hours?
5. What kinds of people do you work with?
6. How much room do you find for self-expression and innovation?

<u>Preparation</u>

7. How did you prepare yourself for this career?
8. What courses have been most helpful to you?
9. What sort of job experiences will best prepare me for this career?
10. How do I go about getting an interview and eventual job in this field?

<u>Benefits</u>

11. What are typical starting salaries in this field? What are mid-career salaries like? What are the top salaries?
12. What are the normal fringe benefits?

13. What are the intangible job satisfactions you have experienced?

Future

14. What are the possibilities for advancement in this field?
15. What does the future of the whole field look like? Will it expand, contract, remain the same?
16. What particular jobs do you think will grow the most?

General

17. What do you enjoy most/least about this field?
18. If you had it to do again, would you enter this field? Why?

Besides finding out all you can about a particular career, your information interviewing has two other goals. First, you want to find out how you can match your skills and interests with particular jobs. The best way to do this is to find out what problems are faced by people working in your career and by the organizations with which you interview. You can be assured that if you look hard enough, you will uncover problems, even though the people you talk with may prefer to call them challenges. Whatever they are called, companies are always looking for people who can solve their problems. They might have sales problems—how to market a particular product or reach a certain area; management problems—how to handle employee grievances, organize an office more effectively, or produce a certain product more efficiently; or training problems—how to better motivate employees, or improve their safety record. Once you have discovered these problem areas, you will be ready to demonstrate in your résumé, cover letter, and job interview how your skills can help solve them.[4]

You also want to create a network of people who can help you locate jobs. To do this, just keep asking for names. During your interview with one person, ask for the names of some other people with whom you could talk. (But word your question so the person has an "out" if he or she doesn't want to provide you with other names.) By the time you have interviewed 10 or 15 people, you will know the names of many individuals and companies to which you can return when you are ready to apply for jobs.

[4]See Bolles, Chapter 6, pp. 132–168, for more on information interviews and discovering problems in organizations.

SUMMARY

This chapter has given you a three-step process for identifying your career and locating jobs:

Step 1: Begin by examining yourself, identifying your major skills, interests, and values.

Step 2: Then look for careers that match these, using all the resources at your command, including a career placement center, some of the reference works I described, and parents, friends, and teachers.

Step 3: Finally, try to locate some suitable jobs within these careers, through research in newspapers and reference works, but most of all, through information interviewing.

If you have tried to follow this procedure, you know by now that choosing a career and finding a job is not as easy as it looks. The process of self-examination can be difficult, even agonizing. And the idea of making a long-term career choice from so many possible careers may overwhelm you. But if you do use the materials and methods I've suggested, somewhere along the way—in an interview with a career counselor or employer, in a want ad or reference work, or perhaps just in a chat with a friend—you should discover a career that will challenge and reward you.

APPLICATIONS

1. Self-Assessment: If you have not already done so, try some of the self-assessment activities suggested in this chapter. Do at least a rough draft of the autobiography suggested on pages 328–29, write the notes for the career profile suggested on pages 329–30, or do the personality assessment on pages 331–33. After you have tried some of these assessment activities, summarize what you have learned by writing a paragraph or two describing yourself—your interests, values, abilities, and personal traits.

2. Using some of the resources suggested in the second section of this chapter, research a possible career for yourself and then write a report describing this career for others in your class. You might organize your report around the categories suggested on page 335:

    - description of the career
    - working conditions

- benefits, both short and long term
- future possibilities

If you want to investigate more than one career, you could contrast several careers in this report, perhaps using the topics suggested above.

3. Using materials on targeting locations described in the third section of this chapter, research locations (cities as well as sections of the country) that look particularly appealing. Consider such factors as growth potential, climate, natural and industrial environment, crime rates, recreation, and availability of educational, health, and transportation services. Give an oral (and/or written) report on your research to others in your class. Your goal will be to recommend suitable locations for people in your audience.

4. Consulting directories that describe particular companies (see pages 342–43), your career planning and placement center, and employees whom you might know, research two organizations in your area that might have jobs that appeal to you. Give the results of your research in an oral or written report to the rest of the class.

5. Arrange, prepare for, and conduct three information interviews with people working in a career or careers that you are interested in. You might work with a group of people in preparation for your interview, reviewing the material about information interviews on pages 343–45.

CHAPTER

15

Résumés, Cover Letters, and Interviews

Let's assume that you have assessed your skills, interests, and values; that based on this assessment you have identified a career field you are interested in; and finally that you have located some possible jobs within that field. Now you need to prepare the persuasive package that will convince an employer to hire you. This package consists of a convincing résumé, an effective cover letter, and a "you" ready for a successful interview.

STEP 4: PREPARE YOUR RÉSUMÉ

You already know what a résumé is. Or do you? If you think that it's the story of your life, you're wrong. A résumé is not a biography. Rather, it is an easy-to-read, factual presentation of your qualifications, whose purpose is to convince an employer to interview and then hire you. In *What Color is Your Parachute?*, Richard Bolles calls it an *extended calling-card*. It can also serve as an agenda for an interview and as a memory-jogger for an employer after the interview.

Who Are Your Readers?

An effective résumé is based on the same kinds of decisions and choices we have been discussing throughout this book. Let's begin with your reader. Exactly who will read your résumé? If you send it to an organization, it may go first to the personnel department to be read very fast by a person facing a stack of résumés from applicants for a particular job. This person's task may be to cut a pile of 200 résumés down to 25 for someone else to examine more closely. If your résumé survives this first cut, it will be sent to the department that will actually hire you. Here it may be read by an individual or a group of people assigned by the department supervisor to find the five most outstanding applicants. Finally, it will be read by the department supervisor just before his or her interview with you. Of course, it could be read by other people in other situations. For instance, it could be read by a representative of an organization interviewing on a college campus. And it could also be read after an interview, to remind someone of your qualifications.

You can assume two things about the readers in these situations. First, that your readers will be busy and will therefore read fast, often just skimming for main points. To accommodate them, you need to keep your résumé as short as possible, setting forth only the highlights of your career. The general rule is to keep a résumé to one page in length.

Second, you can assume that different readers will be looking for different things. The reader in the personnel department facing a stack of 200 résumés will probably be looking for negatives—for some reason to eliminate you. But those readers who will play a greater role in hiring you will be looking more closely for the skills needed to do a particular job.

What Is the Goal of Your Résumé?

The goal of your résumé may vary slightly, depending on what kind of reader you have in mind. For instance, for the reader in the personnel department, you will be trying not to say anything that can be taken negatively and thereby exclude you from the stack. But generally, your goal will be the same—to convince *all* your readers that you possess the skills they are looking for and are therefore the person for the job.

What Voice Should You Use?

Since all readers will be reading fast, they will probably most appreciate a concise, professional-sounding voice. Think of yourself as answering a series of questions about your education, experience, etc., in an efficient, business-like way.

What Information, Organization, Design, and Style Should You Use?

The kinds of information you include, the way you organize that information, and the way you design and style the whole résumé will grow out of the decisions about reader, goal, and voice that we've just discussed. Keeping these major choices in mind, let's build some model résumés step by step.

SOME MODEL RÉSUMÉS

Imagine that you are applying for a job in public relations. What kind of information do you include and how do you organize that information? Just think of yourself as answering series of questions about yourself for a prospective employer. The questions will be pretty standard ones, about your career objective, education, work experience, personal interests, and references. But remember, the goal of your résumé is *not* to tell your life's story—it's to persuade someone to hire you. This means that any information you do include should show your reader that you are qualified for that job. Let's discuss the questions and your answers in light of this principle.

What Is Your Name and Address?

Begin your résumé not with the word résumé (since any reader will know this), but with your name, current and/or permanent address, and phone number. This information will enable a prospective employer to get in touch with you easily. And highlight this information by putting it in the center at the top. Thus,

```
                Sarah Gilvari
            141 Aldersmead Road
             Richmond, VA 23230
               (804) 272-9452
```

What Is Your Career Objective?

If your answer to this question is too specific, it can eliminate you from possible jobs; on the other hand, if it is too general, it can confuse your reader. So should you even try to answer this question? Yes, if your answer will help convince an employer to interview and hire you. A convincing objective lets an employer know (1) what you will perform—the level and scope of your job; and (2) how you will perform it—the particular ways you can benefit the organization, perhaps by increasing production, quality, sales, or morale. The following example, for instance, doesn't accomplish either one of these aims. It is too general in scope and focuses too much on what the organization should do for the applicant rather than on what she can do for it.

```
Objective:  Position in marketing with an
            organization that rewards communication
            and human relations skills.
```

But this objective can be rewritten to give prospective employers the specific job desired and the ways the applicant can benefit the organization:

```
Objective:  Position in public relations that
            utilizes clear writing skills, desire to
            work with a variety of people, and ability
            to manage time well.
```

If you cannot write an objective statement that is convincing—one that really identifies the kind of position you want and emphasizes the skills you bring to the organization—this may mean that you haven't really assessed yourself fully yet. You may need to do more work in this area.

Notice also that we have designed and styled the objective statement to be read as quickly as possible. We have used the side-bar heading, "Objective," to identify that block of information for the reader. And we have written it in a terse style, actually a sentence fragment, so we don't waste the reader's time with unnecessary words. We will continue both these practices throughout the rest of the résumé.

What Is Your Educational Background?

The more recent your education is, the more important it will be to your reader. Therefore, if you are a college student about to graduate, you should put your education after your job objective. (This is true unless you think your work experience supports your objective better. If this is true, put this information first.) If you will be a college graduate, it is not necessary to include your high school education. Put your degree, major, date of graduation, college, and location. If you have not received the degree yet, simply put the word "expected" after the date. Also include any accomplishments in this category that might qualify you for a job, such as GPA (if high), grades in major subjects (if good), and other honors. If you have done an internship or taken courses that will particularly qualify you, you might list them. But don't overdo it. Here is the way our public relations applicant might describe her education.

```
Education:  B.A., English and Psychology, 19--,
            Susquehanna University, Slinsgrove, PA.
            GPA in English, 3.6. Elective courses in
            marketing, public relations, and writing
            for the mass media. Reporter and then
            editor for college newspaper.
```

What Kind of Work Experience Have You Had?

Since your work experience is their basis for predicting your future performance, prospective employers will read this section of your résumé more carefully than any of the rest of it. Include any job that has prepared you for your career, including internships and volunteer work. And remember that employers not only want to know when and where you worked, they also want to know what skills you learned.

You can either present this information *chronologically*, emphasizing where and when you worked, or you can present it *functionally*, emphasizing the skills you developed. A chronological presentation is most convincing when you have held a number of jobs that have prepared you for your desired career. Here is the way our applicant for the public relations position would write a chronological description.

Experience: <u>Public Relations Staff Writer</u>
St. Mary's Hospital, Richmond, VA, Public Relations Department, Summer Intern, 19--. Wrote press releases, interviewed and wrote stories for employee newsletter, wrote announcements of key events for employees.

<u>Ride Foreman</u>
King's Dominion Amusement Park, Richmond, VA, Summers, 19---19--. Supervised, trained, and evaluated five employees on children's rides. Ensured customer safety, scheduled employees, checked time cards, wrote reports.

<u>Sales Clerk</u>
Thalhimer's Department Store, Cloverleaf Mall, Richmond, VA, Summer, 19--. Waited on customers in various departments and took inventory.

<u>Counselor</u>
YMCA, Summer Camp, Richmond, VA, 19--. Supervised and coordinated activities of ten children, ranging from 5-7 years old.

Now let's imagine the same applicant has had only two jobs, the internship at the hospital and the job at the amusement park. Note this time how she organizes the information functionally to emphasize the skills she learned rather than calling attention to the fact that she has had only two jobs.

Skills:

<u>Writing</u>
Wrote press releases, articles for employee newsletter, and announcements of key events.

<u>People</u>
Worked for four summers with people from different racial and educational backgrounds in large amusement park.

<u>Management</u>
As public relations intern at hospital, coordinated two public information programs. As amusement park ride supervisor, coordinated employee work schedules, trained employees in operations and safety procedures, and checked employee time cards.

Experience: <u>Public Relations Staff Writer</u>
St. Mary's Hospital, Richmond, VA, Summer, 19--.

<u>Ride Foreman</u>
King's Dominion Amusement Park, Richmond, VA, Summers, 19---19--.

Even though the entries are organized differently, notice that the style of both is the same concise style we have been using. The writer notes her skills not with complete sentences but with phrases beginning with active verbs.

What Were Your Activities in School or College?

A short time ago, a prospective employer of one of my students called me for a reference. His major question was, "Can this person get along with others?" The activities you have participated in during school or college provide one way to demonstrate to an employer that you can. List whatever you have done while in school, whether it's serving on the school newspaper, holding a position in student government, or even participating in discussion series or leisure activities. If you don't have any activities to list, try to get involved in some right away.

```
Activities:  Student Judiciary Board, Academic
             Honesty Board, Student Government,
             Orientation Committee, Student Advisor
             for Freshmen, Woodrow Wilson Visiting
             Fellows Committee.
```

What Can You Tell Me About Yourself?

"Should I even try to answer this question?" you may ask yourself. "After all, I may include information that will eliminate me from consideration." The answer is "yes," if the information you include will convince an employer to interview and hire you, but "no" if it won't. Thus, if you are single and have five children to care for, you need not mention this. But if you think such information as your family, travel, or hobbies might help qualify you, by all means include them. Here is an example of personal information that might help our applicant by convincing her readers that she is an active, social person.

```
Personal        Enjoy playing the piano and listening
Information:    to music. Active sports fan and tennis
                player.
```

What Are Your References?

When choosing references, avoid people who have a vested interest in seeing you do well, such as doctors, ministers, or family members. Prospective employers won't trust them. Rather, choose people like college professors and people who supervised you on the job, those who can testify to your knowledge, ability to get along with others, and ability to do a job conscientiously.

It's accepted practice to ask prospective references whether they can give you a strong recommendation or not. If they cannot, find someone else. Also, make sure that the people who will write your references have enough information about you. If you are applying for a particular job, tell them that. Give them a copy of your résumé and catch them up on anything you have been doing since you knew them. To protect your references from being unnecessarily bothered, don't list their names on your résumé. Instead, just put the following:

```
References:  Available on request.
```

Now let's see how each complete résumé will look, looking first at the chronological (p. 355) and then at the functional skills (pp. 356–57) one.

Sarah Gilvari
141 Aldersmead Road
Richmond, VA 23230
(804) 272-9452

Objective: Position in public relations that utilizes clear writing skills, desire to work with a variety of people, and ability to manage time well.

Education: B.A., English and Psychology, 19--, Susquehanna University, Slinsgrove, PA. GPA in English, 3.6. Elective courses in marketing, public relations, and writing for the mass media. Reporter and then editor for college newspaper.

Experience: Public Relations Staff Writer
St. Mary's Hospital, Richmond, VA, Public Relations Department, Summer Intern, 19--. Wrote press releases, interviewed and wrote stories for employee newsletter, wrote announcements of key events for employees.

Ride Foreman
King's Dominion Amusement Park, Richmond, VA, Summers, 19---19--. Supervised, trained, and evaluated five employees on children's rides. Ensured customer safety, scheduled employees, checked time cards, wrote reports.

Sales Clerk
Thalhimer's Department Store, Cloverleaf Mall, Richmond, VA, Summer, 19--. Waited on customers in various departments and took inventory.

Counselor
YMCA, Summer Camp, Richmond, VA, 19--. Supervised and coordinated activities of ten children, ranging from 5-7 years old.

Activities: Student Judiciary Board, Academic Honesty Board, Student Government, Orientation Committee, Student Advisor for Freshmen, Woodrow Wilson Visiting Fellows Committee.

Personal Information: Enjoy playing the piano and listening to music. Active sports fan and tennis player.

References: Available on request.

Sarah Gilvari
141 Aldersmead Road
Richmond, VA 23230
(804) 272-9452

Objective: Position in public relations that utilizes clear writing skills, desire to work with a variety of people, and ability to manage time well.

Education: B.A., English and Psychology, 19--, Susquehanna University, Slinsgrove, PA. GPA in English, 3.6. Elective courses in marketing, public relations, and writing for the mass media. Reporter and then editor for college newspaper.

Skills: Writing
Wrote press releases, articles for employee newsletter, and announcements of key events.

People
Worked for four summers with people from different racial and educational backgrounds in large amusement park.

Besides the chronological and functional skills résumés, there is a third type called a *targeted résumé*. You would use this format if you wanted to apply for a particular kind of job or with a particular kind of organization.

Let's imagine, for instance, that our public relations applicant decided in her sophomore year of college that she wanted to work in public relations, particularly in health care settings. To prepare herself for this work, she interned for a semester at a large metropol-

	<u>Management</u> As public relations summer intern at hospital, coordinated two public information programs. As amusement park ride supervisor, coordinated employee work schedules, trained employees in operations and safety procedures, and checked employee time cards.
Experience:	<u>Public Relations Staff Writer</u> St. Mary's Hospital, Richmond, VA, Summer, 19--. <u>Ride Foreman</u> King's Dominion Amusement Park, Richmond, VA, Summers, 19---19--.
Activities:	Student Judiciary Board, Academic Honesty Board, Student Government, Orientation Committee, Student Advisor for Freshmen, Woodrow Wilson Visiting Fellows Committee.
Personal Information:	Enjoy playing the piano and listening to music. Active sports fan and tennis player.
References:	Available on request.

itan hospital, working in various jobs—admissions, patient counseling, and public relations. And in addition to her public relations courses, she also took three courses in health care—medical terminology, medical records science, and medical economics.

On the next two pages is what her targeted résumé might look like. Note in particular how her job objective is now aimed specifically at health care work, how she includes courses in health care, and how she emphasizes her skills that relate specifically to a hospi-

Sarah Gilvari
141 Aldersmead Road
Richmond, VA 23230
(804) 272-9452

Objective: Public relations position in a health care facility that utilizes clear writing skills, desire to work with a variety of medical personnel as well as the public, and ability to manage time well.

Education: B.A., English and Psychology, 19--, Susquehanna University, Slinsgrove, PA. GPA in English, 3.6.

Public relations courses: marketing, public relations, and writing for the mass media.

Health care courses: medical terminology, medical records science, and medical economics.

Skills: <u>Writing</u>
Researched, wrote, and laid out stories for hospital newsletter.

<u>People</u>
Worked with hospital personnel, ranging from maintenance staff to physicians.

Worked for four summers with people from different racial and educational backgrounds in large amusement park.

tal setting. Notice also that she has had to shorten descriptions of her experience as a ride supervisor and her school activities as well as completely delete personal information in order to keep the résumé brief. This was probably the right decision to make. Quite possibly, she could mention other activities in her cover letter.

On the next several pages are three other model résumés. Look them over carefully to see different ways to organize and design an effective résumé. The first was done by James Cahill, a student with a degree in liberal larts. Notice that he has used the functional skills

	<u>Management</u> As intern in large metropolitan hospital, assisted in public relations department and in patient admissions. As public relations summer intern at hospital, coordinated two public information programs. As amusement park ride supervisor, trained employees and coordinated schedules.
Experience:	<u>Public Relations Staff Writer</u> St. Mary's Hospital, Richmond, VA, Summer, 19--. <u>Patient Representative Intern</u> University of Maryland Hospital, Baltimore, MD, 19--. <u>Ride Foreman</u> King's Dominion Amusement Park, Richmond, VA, Summers 19---19--.
Activities:	Student Judiciary Board, Academic Honesty Board, Student Government, as well as other committees.
References:	Available on request.

format in order to emphasize the skills he has learned during college and on the job rather than his particular work experiences.

Imad Falah, the student who did the next résumé on pages 362–63, chose to emphasize his work experience by using the chronological format.

Finally, on pages 364–65 is a résumé by Evelyn Richardson targeted at the metallurgical industry by someone who wants to advance to a higher-level position after seven years of experience. Note how she put her experience before her education and then highlighted all the

James Cahill
1535 West Avenue
Phoenix, AZ 85026
(602) 358-8547

Job Target: Human resources position in which I can use my abilities to relate well to people, to identify and solve problems, and to communicate effectively.

Education: B.A., English and Philosophy, Spring, 19--, University of Arizona, Tucson, AZ.

Skills:

Reasoning

- Ability to think logically and critically
- Ability to analyze complex problems
- Ability to synthesize information

Communication

- Ability to write clearly, persuasively, and analytically
- Ability to write for different audiences
- Ability to communicate orally in public with confidence
- Ability to read with understanding and attention to detail

positions she had held, even though they were with the same company.

STEP 5: WRITE YOUR COVER LETTER

If you have written a chronological or functional skills résumé, you can use it to apply for a variety of jobs in your field. But now you need something to bridge the gap between the facts on your résumé and the particular job for which you are applying. This is the

Human Relations

- Ability to recognize and understand the different needs of various kinds of people
- Ability to establish warm, friendly, and mutually respectful relationships
- Ability to maintain control when dealing with people under stressful conditions and to ease and alleviate those conditions
- Ability to show enthusiasm and good humor in relating to people

Experience:	President, UA Philosophy Club, 19---19--. Planned budget and lecture series, spoke in public.
	Student Manager for UA Housing Department, 19---19--. Managed dorm, acted as public information representative, liaison between students and university police.
	Retail Sales and Stock for Pep Boys, Phoenix, AZ, 19---19--. Managed stock and worked with public.
	Customer Service Representative, Delta Airlines, Phoenix, AZ, 19---19--. Assisted passengers with problems, made airport announcements, handled stressful situations.
References:	Available on request.

function of your cover letter. It interprets the skills on your résumé to demonstrate that they match the particular job you are applying for.

Because each cover letter applies to a particular job, it must be individually typed and addressed. Sometimes, of course, you can use the same cover letter to apply for the same kinds of jobs. For instance, if you are applying for an auditing job with large banks, you can use the same cover letter for all banks. But if you are also applying for auditing jobs with private firms and the federal govern-

Imad Falah
2316 Hampstead Avenue, Apartment 3
Carlsbad, CA 92008
(619) 288-4741 (Home)
(619) 270-8268 (Work)

Objective: A position in computer programming, utilizing technical proficiency, understanding of large organizations, and ability to relate to people in the United States and abroad.

Education: B.S., Information Systems, Spring 19--, San Diego State University, CA.

Career Oriented Courses:

- Advanced Programming (Cobol and JCL)
- Advanced Program Design Techniques (BASIC)
- Data Base
- System Analysis
- System Design

Employment: <u>Proof Operator</u>, San Diego Bankshares, San Diego, CA, 19---Present

- Settle various transactions involving commercial as well as personal accounts
- Use automated check clearing system

ment, you will need to rewrite the letter. In any case, make sure each letter is individually typed and addressed to *the person who will hire you*. Both of these practices send a message to your reader that this job is personally important to you.

You may be able to find the name of the person you should write to by consulting the guides described on pages 342–43 of the last chapter. If you cannot, seek help from friends, parents, and teachers. Another method is to get the names of appropriate people

Grocery Clerk, Giant Food, San Diego, CA, 19---19--

- Served customers and managed delicatessen department
- Maintained and organized dairy products inventory

Bank Teller, The Bank of Kuwait and the Middle East, Kuwait, 19---19--

- Initiated commercial and personal accounts
- Conducted training programs for new employees
- Worked in foreign exchange department and prepared wire transfers

University Activities: Vice-President of SDU International Students Union

- Prepared 19-- budget proposal
- Developed expanded recreation program

References: Available on request

to contact during your information interviews. Probably the least satisfactory way to get names is to call organizations; too often, you will simply be referred to a personnel department.

What Does Your Reader Want to Know?

To write a good cover letter, decide what your reader wants to know. As he or she reads through letters and résumés, your reader's basic question will be, "Can this person do this job better than

Evelyn G. Richardson
2964 Woodbridge Crossing Drive
Seattle, WA 98109
(206) 744-3542

Objective: Position as Technical Director with a major metallurgical industry, which would allow me to use my technical background, supervisory skills, and ability to interact with employees and customers

Experience: Foil Process Metallurgist, Flexible Packaging Div., Reynolds Metals, Seattle, WA, 19---Present

- Responsible for alloy development, customer service, and product development
- Required to interact with all types of people and perform in unstructured environment

Quality Assurance Manager, Flexible Packaging Div., Reynolds Metals, Hot Springs, AR, 19---19--

- Responsible for monthly production of 30 million pounds of aluminum, management of nine quality assurance technicians
- Required to solve quality problems, handle customer complaints, train plant employees, and write quality control manual

anyone else?" Of course, this question will mean different things, depending on the particular job. If you are applying to be an auditor in a large bank, your reader may want to know how careful you will be in examining accounts, how clear and succinct your reports will be, how well you can get along with other auditors on your team, and how willing you are to travel and work hard.

If you are applying for a job in employee training, the questions will be different. In this case, your reader may want to know how carefully you plan programs, how stimulating a trainer you will be,

	Start-Up Metallurgist, Flexible Packaging Div., Reynolds Metals, Paris, FR, 19--
	• Responsible for setting up a lab in new plant design, lay out, order new equipment • Conducted training program for all technicians
	Metallurgical Engineering Trainee, Mill Products Div., Reynolds Metals, Grand Rapids, MI, 19---19--
	• Exposed to D.C. casting, extrusion presses, heat treating, forming lines, aging ovens, and anodizing • Involved with trouble-shooting customer problems
Education:	B.S., 19--, Materials Engineering, Michigan State University, East Lansing, MI.
Activities:	Junior Chamber of Commerce and Rotary Club
References:	Available on request

and whether your training programs really will have practical impact on participants. And if you are applying for a job in public relations in a large organization, your reader may want to know how well you can interview busy professionals, how clearly and interestingly you can write stories for the newsletter, and how quickly you can learn other facets of your job. To write a convincing cover letter then, you need to figure out what kinds of skills your reader is looking for and then highlight the skills from your résumé that match these.

What Format Should You Use?

Every textbook you read will have a slightly different way to write cover letters. My suggestion is that you write a fairly short (three to four paragraphs and certainly no longer than a page) letter with a beginning, middle, and end. Why short? Because most of your readers will simply not take the time to read a long letter; rather, they will skim it, looking for the highlights. Since this is true, you might as well just present the highlights.

While there is no set formula for cover letters, you might adapt the pattern suggested for effective sales letters at the end of Chapter 7. After all, your cover letter will probably be the most important sales letter of your career. To follow this pattern, answer three questions your reader will have about any product or service.

Question	*Answer*
1. What is this?	1. Describe *major features.*
2. How does this work?	2. Describe *advantages.*
3. What does this mean to me?	3. Describe *benefits.*

In this case, of course, you are selling yourself, so you will need to describe the major features about you that will appeal to an employer, explain the specific advantages of these features, and finally show how the features will benefit your prospective employer. You need not follow this pattern rigidly; rather, adapt it to suit your abilities and the position you are applying for. Here is how you might apply it in writing a three-part cover letter.

1. ***Begin with a strong opening*.**

   Begin with a strong opening that identifies the job you are applying for and describes the *features* that set you apart from all other applicants. Here are three openings that do this. The first is by the woman who wants a job in public relations in a hospital (her targeted résumé is on pages 358–59). Note that the features she emphasizes are her specific educational preparation and her internship experience.

After our interesting phone conversation yesterday about the public relations assistant position open in your hospital, I am convinced that I am suited for the job. Not only have I prepared myself for such a position with course work in both public relations and health care, I have also had internship experience in two hospitals.

Here is the beginning paragraph of a cover letter written by the liberal arts graduate applying for a job as a college recruiter (résumé on pages 360–61). He emphasizes his educational background and the experience he acquired as student manager.

Your advertisement for someone to work as a college recruiter in your personnel department caught my attention. My strong liberal arts background coupled with my experience as manager of a college dorm has prepared me for this position.

Now here is the applicant for the computer programming job (résumé on pages 362–63). He focuses on his technical preparation, job experience, and international background.

Is there a need in your organization for a computer programmer with a strong technical education, practical experience in large organizations, and an international background?

---

2. ***Continue with a specific middle.***

Continue with a specific middle that explains how the *features* you identified in your first paragraph will serve as advantages to your prospective employer. This is also a good place to reveal something you have learned about the organization through your research.

Here is the middle section of the letter written by the applicant for the job of public relations in a hospital. She now points out specific courses that have prepared her for the position and describes her experience as an intern. She emphasizes that her experience has been at large, metropolitan hospitals, since she is applying to such a hospital.

Three years ago, I decided to pursue a public relations position in a health care setting. The courses I elected to take in public relations, marketing, and writing for the mass media, coupled with courses in medical terminology, health management, and medical economics, have prepared me well for such a position.

But my strong suit is my practical experience with two large metropolitan hospitals. I interned for a semester at Baltimore General Hospital in Maryland, working in both public relations and admissions. Last summer, I interned in the public relations department of St. Mary's Hospital in Richmond, Virginia, gaining experience in writing articles and coordinating activities for the public.

Now here is the applicant for the college recruiter job. He shows how his educational background has prepared him to work for a diversified company and given him skills that will enable him to communicate with students and judge their value to the company.

A college recruiter for a company as diversified as yours must be familiar with a variety of educational backgrounds. My liberal arts degree, which has trained me in the humanities, the social sciences, and the natural sciences, assures that I have this background.

In addition, my double major in philosophy and English has given me important reasoning and communication tools. With this preparation, I can communicate effectively with students and make clear judgments about their possible value to your company.

Finally, here is the computer programmer who says that his education has trained him in recent developments, notes his experience in two large banking systems, and emphasizes the advantages of his Middle Eastern background.

You will note from my résumé that my degree in information systems has given me particularly strong preparation in system analysis and design as well as in the most recent programming languages. But I also combine this education with five years of practical experience in two large banking systems.

Since your company has a subsidiary in the Middle East and does a high volume of business there, you should be especially interested in my Middle Eastern background. My ability to speak Lebanese and my understanding of Middle Eastern customs and traditions, coupled with my training in data processing, should serve your company well, both here and abroad.

---

3. *Close with a strong ending.*

Close with a strong ending that will make you stand out in the mind of the employer because of the way the features you have described will directly *benefit* the organization. If possible, also refer to your résumé and request an interview. In the following cover letter, note how the applicant for the public relations job shows how the training she has already received will benefit the hospital she is applying to. The implication is, of course, that the hospital won't have to spend as much time and money training her as they would someone else.

All the evidence I am familiar with shows that the need for health care services will increase dramatically in the next 20 years. Therefore, the industry will need people trained to bring these services to the public. My résumé shows that I have already acquired much of the training necessary to help your hospital accomplish this goal. I shall call you soon to arrange an interview.

The applicant for the college recruiter position stresses the skills he has that will make him an effective recruiter.

> As my résumé indicates, my two years' experience as student manager in a college dorm has taught me how to communicate with and evaluate the personalities of college students. I would now like to put these skills to use as your recruiter. In a few days, I shall call for an interview.

The applicant for computer programmer emphasizes the fact that his background and training will enable him to work effectively with both American and Middle Eastern members of the company.

> I am sure that your company has employees who understand either American or Middle Eastern language and culture. My résumé indicates that my background and training have prepared me to understand both. I will contact you soon to set up an interview.

While these three letters follow the features-advantages-benefits pattern we described, it is not necessary that your cover letter follow this pattern rigidly. More important than following any particular pattern is simply remembering that an effective cover letter demonstrates to your readers that you possess the skills required to do the job. If you can convince them of this, they will read your résumé more closely and call you for an interview.

STEP 6: INTERVIEW SUCCESSFULLY

The key to a successful job interview is to prepare yourself in advance. How do you do this? First, by understanding what your interview will be like, and second, by practicing answers to questions that you may be asked. In an interview, a representative of an organization you are interested in will meet with you to assess your qualifications for a job. The interview might be on campus, conducted by someone from an organization who travels around to different colleges. Or it might take place in the personnel department of an organization, conducted by someone who will decide whether or not to send you on to a second interview with the person actually doing the hiring.

What Will Your Interview Be Like?

There are two basic types of interviews—the screening interview and the selection interview. Screening interviews are usually conducted by people in personnel departments or by visitors to a college campus. Their purpose is to screen out applicants who are not qualified for a particular job so they can send on to the next interview just those people who are qualified. Since screening interviewers are interested primarily in your qualifications for a particular job, their questions will be mostly factual ones about your background, education, and work experience.

If you pass the screening interview successfully, you will then go on to a selection interview. This is usually conducted by someone, a supervisor for instance, who can actually hire you. This person will be less interested in facts about you and more interested in assessing you as a person. He or she will be trying to find out about the inner you—how you think, how you express yourself, how well you would get along with others, and whether you would tackle a job with enthusiasm. Some screening interviewers, especially those who interview at college campuses, will be interested in these things also. The bottom line for this person is whether he or she develops a good feeling about you. If so, you will probably be hired.

Interviews can be conducted in different ways. Usually, you will be interviewed by one person, but you could be interviewed as part of a group of applicants, or by a panel of people from a company. And even individual interviews can be different from each other. Some are very formal and structured, with the interviewer asking a set of questions that have been planned and even written down in advance. An interviewer might begin a structured interview by asking you about your education.

1. What is your major?
2. Why did you choose this particular major?
3. What are the courses you enjoyed the most?
4. What are the courses you didn't like?
5. What is your current GPA?

Or you might be asked about the job you are applying for and your knowledge of the company itself.

1. What type of position are you most interested in?
2. Why do you think you would like this particular kind of job?

3. What do you know about our organization?
4. Why do you think you might like to work for our organization?

On the other hand, the interview could be more informal and unstructured. For example, the interviewer might begin by asking some of the questions above, but then take cues from your answers for the next questions. For instance, if you were to say that you especially liked certain courses in school, you might be asked why, how you plan to use what you have learned from these courses on the job, or even the major things you learned from these courses. Screening interviews will usually be more structured, while selection interviews may be less so. Some interviews will be both structured and unstructured, possibly with the interviewer beginning in a more structured manner and becoming less structured as the interview moves on.

How Can You Prepare for Your Interview?

1. **Practice answering questions**. Your best preparation for a successful interview is to practice answering questions ahead of time. The appendix at the end of this chapter contains interview questions reported by companies surveyed by *The Northwestern Endicott Report*, published by the Placement Center, Northwestern University, Evanston, Ill. As you look over this appendix, notice that some questions are very specific; for example, "What percentage of your college expenses did you earn?" "What extracurricular offices have you held?" "How much money do you hope to earn at age ____?" These are factual questions and require very specific answers. But many of the questions are opinion questions, which require more general answers as well as explanation. Some examples from the list are "What are your future vocational plans?" "Why did you choose your particular field of work?" You should prepare for both kinds of questions.

   In addition, prepare yourself for what Anthony Medley in *Sweaty Palms: The Neglected Art of Being Interviewed* (Berkeley, CA: Ten Speed Press, 1984), calls "blockbusters—statements like "Tell me about yourself." At first glance, this looks easy, because you could have so much to say. But how do you decide what to talk about? And your ability to reach a decision is probably just what the interviewer is trying to test. Probably the best way to handle vague questions is to remind yourself that the interviewer wants you to talk about yourself in relation to the particular job.
2. **Remember the goal of the interview**. Review in your own mind exactly why you will be at the interview. As Richard

Lathrop puts it in *Who's Hiring Who*, you are at the interview for three reasons:

- to convey information regarding your accomplishments, abilities, and personality that will convince the employer that *you* are the one to hire;
- to uncover as much information as possible about the opening and the person you would be working for so you can determine whether this is the right job for you supervised by the kind of person you can work with happily and productively;
- to provide a resounding answer to the one question dominating the employer's view of the discussion—however foggily formulated it may be. That is, "How will hiring this applicant best serve *my* interests?"[1]

3. **Research the company and the job**. Use some of the resources I suggested on pages 342–43 to find out as much as you can about the company. Also, try to find out all you can about the job you are applying for. Then prepare yourself to answer the questions in the appendix.
4. **Plan to ask some questions yourself**. Make plans to ask some questions yourself. This is an important step, because you will almost always have the chance to ask such questions—about the job itself, about where the job fits into the whole company, about your future with the company, or about the work situation. Ask also about challenges facing the company or about plans for future directions. Your questions will show the interviewer that you are definitely interested in the company and may give you a chance to show how you can fit into the company's future.
5. **What about nervousness?** What do you do if you get nervous before or during the interview? First of all, realize that you're not alone—practically everyone gets nervous before an interview. Second, a little nervousness is not such a bad thing—it will put a sharp edge on you. But if you tend to get too nervous, there are some things you can do to overcome it.

   - Practice answering questions at home—actually simulate the interview situation with the help of a friend or family member. The more times you put yourself through a simulated interview, the more relaxed you will be during the real thing. (Even if you think you won't get nervous, it's a good idea to practice before the interview.)
   - During the interview, don't think about yourself, but about the interviewer and the questions being asked.

[1]Taken from Richard Lathrop's *Who's Hiring Who* (Berkeley, CA: Ten Speed Press, 1977) 178–79.

- If you get a momentary case of the shakes, take a deep breath or two.

6. **Create a good impression**. Your goal in the interview is to get the interviewer to like you so much that he or she will be convinced that you are the best person for the job. You do this by creating as good an impression of yourself as possible—be on time for the interview; dress well, as you imagine your prospective boss would dress; sit up straight; try to maintain good eye contact; and speak clearly. And above all, be so well prepared that you can turn what might be a scary question and answer session into a real conversation, with you asking and answering questions knowledgeably and enthusiastically.
7. **Follow up with a thank-you note**. Finally, be sure to follow up your interview with a thank-you note. Not only is the note important just to be polite, it can also provide you with the opportunity to address something you neglected to say during the interview or something you thought of since.

SUMMARY

This chapter has completed the process begun in the last chapter by discussing the last three steps in your job pursuit campaign. To obtain a challenging and rewarding position, prepare the following persuasive package:

Step 4: Prepare a succinct résumé that convincingly presents your qualifications.
Step 5: Prepare a cover letter that shows an organization how the qualifications on your résumé will benefit it.
Step 6: Prepare yourself for the give and take of a successful interview.

APPENDIX

Questions Typically Asked During Interviews

Family Background

1. What was your father's occupation?
2. What was your home life like when you were growing up?
3. Do you live with your parents? Which of your parents has had the most profound influence on you?
4. When did you first contribute to your family income?

[2]Adapted from *The Northwestern Endicott Report* (Evanston, IL: Northwestern University).

Educational Background

1. How did you rank in your graduating class in high school? College? Graduate school?
2. Why did you go to college? Why did you decide to go to the college you attended?
3. When and how did you choose your college major?
4. Have you ever changed your major field of interest? Why?
5. What courses did you like best? Least? Why?
6. What school activities did you participate in? Why? Which did you enjoy most?
7. Do you think that your extracurricular activities were worth the time you devoted to them? Why?
8. What extracurricular offices have you held?
9. If you were starting school all over again, what courses would you take?
10. What percentage of your college expenses did you earn? How?
11. How did your college grades after military service compare with those previously earned?
12. Which of your school/college years was the most difficult?
13. Did you enjoy school? College?
14. Do you feel you have received a good general training?
15. Have you ever tutored another student?
16. Do you have any plans for future education?

Work Experience

1. What jobs have you held? How were they obtained, and why did you leave?
2. How did previous employers treat you?
3. What have you learned from some of the jobs you have held?
4. Can you get me recommendations from previous employers?
5. What was your record in military service?
6. Do you feel you have done the best work of which you are capable?
7. What jobs have you enjoyed the most? The least? Why?

Knowledge of the Organization/Career Field/Job

1. What do you know about our organization?
2. What job in our company would you choose if you were entirely free to do so?
3. What job in our company do you want to work toward?
4. What is your idea of how our industry operates today?

5. What do you know about opportunities in the field in which you are trained?
6. Why do you think you would like this type of job?

Personal and Professional Goals

1. What are your future vocational plans?
2. What type of position are you most interested in?
3. Are you primarily interested in making money, or do you feel that service to your fellow men is a satisfactory accomplishment?
4. Would you prefer a large or a small company? Why?
5. Are you interested in research?
6. Why did you choose your particular field of work?
7. Are you looking for a permanent or temporary job?
8. How long do you expect to work?

Personal Qualities

1. What personal characteristics are necessary for success in your chosen field?
2. What qualifications do you have that make you feel that you will be successful in your field?
3. How did you spend your vacation while in school?
4. What have you done that shows initiative and willingness to work?
5. What are your own special abilities?
6. What are the disadvantages of your chosen field?
7. Do you think that grades should be considered by employers? Why or why not?
8. What do you think determines a person's progress in a good company?
9. Is it an effort for you to be tolerant of persons with backgrounds and interests different from your own?
10. Can you take instructions without being upset?
11. How would you define cooperation?
12. Will you fight to get ahead?
13. Do you have an analytical mind?
14. Are you eager to please?
15. Do you demand attention?
16. Do you like routine work? Do you like regular work?
17. What is your major weakness?
18. How do you keep in good physical condition?
19. How old were you when you became self-supporting?
20. What types of books have you read?
21. Would you tell me a story?

Preferences as to Location and Types of Colleagues

1. Do you prefer any particular geographic location? Why?
2. What kind of boss do you prefer?
3. Do you prefer working with others or by yourself?
4. What types of people seem to rub you the wrong way?
5. What size city do you prefer?
6. Are you willing to go where the company sends you?

Likes and Dislikes

1. Why do you think you might like to work for our organization?
2. What kind of work interests you?
3. Do you like to travel?
4. Who are your best friends?
5. How interested are you in sports?
6. Do you enjoy sports as a participant? An observer?

Leisure Time Activities

1. What do you do in your spare time? What are your hobbies?

Salary Expectations

1. What are your ideas on salary?
2. How much money do you hope to earn at age ____?

APPLICATIONS

1. After studying the first section of this chapter carefully, prepare drafts of three résumés, following the chronological, functional skills, and targeted patterns. Which pattern seems best for you to follow for your final draft résumé? Why?

2. Following the pattern that seems best for you, prepare a draft of your résumé for critique by others in your class or by colleagues or friends. Using the feedback you receive from this critique, prepare the final draft of your résumé, making sure that it is succinct and convincing.

3. Write a letter to a former teacher or employer requesting a letter of reference either for a particular position or for your file in a career planning and placement center. Be sure to give the person enough information (especially about your activities since you knew the person) so he or she can write the most effective letter.

4. Choose two or three organizations where you would like to apply for jobs. Now write a specific cover letter to each one, showing how the qualifications on your résumé will benefit that organization.

5. Write the appropriate letters for the following situations:
   a. An organization that you are not particularly interested in offers you a job. Write a letter refusing the offer.
   b. An organization that you are very much interested in has interviewed you twice. But now they write to tell you that they want to interview some other applicants before making an offer. Write a reply that convinces them you are the right person for the job. You'll need to be persuasive, but avoid overselling yourself. That could turn them off.
   c. A month ago, you interviewed for a job but have heard nothing from the organization since. Write to find out what the situation is. You might use the opportunity to sell yourself once more.

PART

5

Editing Your Writing

CHAPTER

16

Some Conventions of Writing: A Guide

The goal of this chapter is to help you write and edit correctly. You can work through it section by section or use the following guide to turn to particular sections for help.

CHAPTER GUIDE

Donald G. Hill
Personel Department
Johnson Controls
San Diego, CA 92101

Dear Mr. Hill:

After the converation we had a few days ago, about the office manager's position, I am convinced, I am qualified for the position. My strong asset is the experience I have recieved in training, and interacting with people on a consistent basis. Also, my experience in having to think through problems to reach a decision.

All the satistics I have read in weekly magazines and newspapers, indicate that companies are earning profits, but at the same time losing valuable employees. For the simple reason, they do not know how to work with their people.

I am convinced that I have the qualifications to do the job. To do the kind of job, not only to help Johnson controls make a profit, but help them to operate more eficiently.

I hope you contact me soon for an interview.

Sincerely Yours,

Lawrence Jacobs

How do you think the personnel manager of a company would react if the following letter were received from a job applicant?

This letter is a minefield of mistakes, a disaster about to happen.[1] The hesitant first sentence, with its flow interrupted by too many commas, would lead the manager to suspect that the applicant lacked the necessary confidence for the job. But there are other

[1]"No college student could write this badly," you may say. You'd be right, but the letter does contain the typical errors some writers make when they are working fast and not editing.

errors. Maybe the manager would miss the misspelled "Personel" and "converation," but not miss "recieved," "satistics," and "eficiently." These, coupled with the sentence fragments at the end of each paragraph, would convince the manager that the author of the letter was a careless writer and an inadequate thinker, incapable of holding any job with the company.

This manager's reaction would be a typical one. In fact, a recent study concluded that most readers on the job react strongly to serious mistakes in writing. Some errors—for example, "Calhoun has went," or "When Mitchell moved, he brung his secretary with him"—will so outrage them that they'll probably assume the writer to be illiterate. Other mistakes—for example, run-on sentences and lack of subject-verb agreement—seem very serious lapses, while still others seem less serious.[2] In a textbook she wrote after the study, the author concluded that "the middle-aged, educated, and successful men and women who occupy positions of responsibility in the business and professional world . . . seem to believe that writers should observe the conventions of standard English usage."

What exactly are "conventions of standard English usage"? They are the patterns your readers expect you to follow as you write. You know most of them already. In a letter or memo, you just wouldn't say, "The supervisor has went over there," "When we was in that department yesterday," or "He don't think that's acceptable," because you know these unconventional ways of saying something will violate your readers' expectations and cause them to focus on you and the way you write rather than on your message.

But there are probably some conventions of writing that you are less sure of, usually because you don't always observe them in speech. In talking to someone, even if you are trying to be careful, you might say "different from" when you should have said "different than," or "less people than I thought" when you meant "fewer people than I thought." And since speaking uses a different punctuation system from writing, relying on pause and pitch rather than commas and semicolons, you don't get very much practice at using the conventions of paragraphing or written punctuation correctly.

The purpose of this handbook is to help you observe the conventions of writing so the documents you write on the job will be clear and acceptable to your readers. But wait a minute before you roll your eyes and close this book in fear of another dull and confusing compendium of grammar and punctuation rules. This handbook will contain a few such rules, but only the ones you'll need to know in order to correct the major mistakes you'll be likely to make. To write clean copy, most writers on the job just need a review of some of the more tricky conventions of writing. These are the ones we'll

[2]Maxine Hairston, "Not all Errors are Created Equal: Nonacademic Readers in the Professions Respond to Lapses in Usage, *College English*, 43 (December 1981) 794–806.

focus on in the following sections, which will discuss paragraphing, sentence structure, punctuation, agreement, and spelling. You may want to work your way through the chapter section by section, studying the principles and practicing them in the applications. On the other hand, if you have a reader who will point out your problems—a friend, spouse, or teacher—you may want to focus just on the sections that discuss these.

PARAGRAPHS

For a complete discussion of the principles of good paragraphing, you may want to consult a good handbook on writing and editing, such as the *Harbrace College Handbook*, by Hodges, Whitten, and Webb (San Diego: Harcourt Brace Jovanovich 1986). But you probably don't need the full treatment at this stage in your writing career. Why? Because by now you can probably fulfill most of your reader's expectations more by intuition than by rules or principles. And most of the time your intuitions will be sound. You will know as you write or revise whether you need to add more information to a paragraph to make your point, to drop a sentence that doesn't have anything to do with the rest of the paragraph, or to move a sentence from one place to another.

But as you write on the job, you may have certain questions. Your major ones will probably be these two: "When should I break for a new paragraph?" and "How can I make my ideas in a paragraph seem to flow naturally from one to the other?" There are no hard and fast answers to these questions. In the same situation, two equally good writers might write paragraphs of different lengths or tie ideas together in different ways. But the following discussion will give you some ways to think about the problems.

When do I break for a new paragraph?

In school, you were taught not to break for a new paragraph until you had developed your topic or point completely, because your academic readers were trying to teach you to sustain a thought. The result was a paper made up of relatively long paragraphs, pretty uniform in length.

But busy readers on the job will often expect you to break up your information into fairly short paragraphs. You will usually break a paragraph for one of the following reasons:

1. ***To emphasize a point***. The person who wrote the following memo announcing and describing a new employee wellness program should have emphasized his two lead sentences by breaking for a new paragraph after them. Compare these two versions and see whether you don't agree.

(1)

YES--The rumors you have heard are true. Beginning May 1, 1985, there will be a new employee wellness program that will have something for everyone. There will be an Olympic-sized pool, a weight room, an indoor track, and locker room facilities. In addition, the company will provide, at no charge, classes in aerobic dancing, diet control, and classic dance. In the area of mental health, there will be private counseling on smoking, depression, and alcohol.

(2)

YES--The rumors you have heard are true. Beginning May 1, 1985, there will be a new employee wellness program that will have something for everyone.

There will be an Olympic-sized pool, a weight room, an indoor track, and locker room facilities. In addition, the company will provide, at no charge, classes in aerobic dancing, diet control, and classic dance. In the area of mental health, there will be private counseling on smoking, depression, and alcohol.

In a similar way, you can use short, even one-sentence paragraphs, to emphasize a request at the beginning of a letter or highlight an important point at the end.

2. ***To present information in a simple and readable form.*** Often you can make information easily available to busy readers by listing it in separate paragraphs rather than including it in one long paragraph. Remind yourself to write so that a busy reader can just skim a paragraph quickly to pick up its main point. For instance, don't you agree that the second version of the following paragraph is easier to read than the first?

(1)

The solution to our slow turnaround time in the lab is to buy a new computer. Although its initial cost will be high, it will be justified for the following reasons: First, it will cost $60,000 to develop software for the present office computer to accomplish the needed efficiency in reporting laboratory results. The cost of the new computer, in contrast, is $23,000. Second, the computer program will generate lab reports that will allow sequential results in one letter-size copy instead of several reports to be lost, placed out of sequence, or rendered unreadable by repeated use. Third, the lab reports can be placed in front of the patient's chart for quick access.

---

(2)

The solution to our slow turnaround time in the lab is to buy a new computer. Although its initial cost will be high, it will be justified for the following reasons:

1. It will cost $60,000 to develop software for the present office computer to accomplish the needed efficiency in reporting laboratory results. The cost of the new computer, in contrast, is $23,000.
2. The computer program will generate lab reports that will allow sequential results in one letter-size copy instead of several reports to be lost, placed out of sequence, or rendered unreadable by repeated use.
3. The lab reports can be placed in front of the patient's chart for quick access.

---

3. ***To provide readers with either visual or psychological relief.*** Readers, especially those who might have some difficulty following all your intricate points, may need a new para-

graph just for a moment's relief. Sometimes, therefore, you may have to break a long unit into two short ones, even if strictly logical considerations would have you include them in one paragraph. Thus, the following paragraph, taken from a bank examiner's report, should probably be broken at the phrase "This situation" (underlined below), since the report is meant to be understood (at least in its general outlines) by people on the board of directors as well as by officers of the bank. Since readers on the board may have trouble with the technical language and intricate details, they will need periodic breaks just to catch their mental breath.

The tremendous change in the liquidity position since the last examination is a result of the bank's use of seasonal demand deposits. The bank is recognized as having a seasonal trend in that large real estate escrow funds are deposited from April through August. From September through December, these funds leave the bank. The problem the bank is experiencing is a result of its use of these "volatile funds." Instead of investing them in temporary investments (as it was doing at the last examination), the bank is funding loans. As seasonal deposits run off, the bank is left in a deficit funding position. <u>This situation</u> is what led to the purchase of approximately $3,000,000 in brokered deposits in September 1984. This trend is clearly indicated in the changes in the "Sources and Use of Funds Analysis" on page 16. In 1983, however, $5,500,000 in loan growth has been funded primarily by brokered deposits. In addition, the bank purchased federal funds 181 times in 1984, ranging in amounts from $100,000 to $4,275,000. It is particularly distressing to note that even since the purchase of the brokered deposits, the bank has purchased federal funds 55 times.

I suspect that even another examiner reading this paragraph would appreciate the relief of two short ones.

But keeping your paragraphs short enough to be readable does not mean you should write skimpy, insubstantial paragraphs. Often, you will have to give your reader a number of facts to support a general statement. You may have to give examples to back up a judgment about an employee in a performance appraisal or a number of details to prove that your department deserves a new computer or personnel position. In fact, your challenge will be to give your reader enough information but to present it in paragraphs that are short enough to be quickly and easily understood.

How Can I Make my Ideas in a Paragraph "Flow" Better?

People who attend on-the-job writing seminars ask this question more than any other. What they mean is that they want ideas to move in an easy progression, where one seems to grow naturally into another. Linguists call this sense of flow *coherence* or *cohesion*, and they are just beginning to understand some of the techniques writers use to achieve it.

Luckily, most of your paragraphs will seem to flow automatically, because either in writing or revising you will find a logical, orderly way to say what you want to say. Occasionally, though, you may write a paragraph like the following one:

In most firms, an individual will not start fresh as an Operations Manager. An individual needs years of experience before he or she can qualify for the job. The person who will be considered for the job needs to have an understanding of the various tasks that are performed in the sub-departments. In most cases, the individual selected for the job was a department head in one of the sub-departments. The Operations Manager must fully understand all aspects of the manufacturing process. The person therefore must have experience in all aspects of the manufacturing process. An individual also needs experience in communication skills. The manager will be communicating with many different types of people. He or she will communicate with factory personnel as well as with professionals.

As you read this paragraph, don't you find yourself saying: "This thing just doesn't seem to go anywhere. Every time I read a sentence, I have the feeling that I'm starting over again."

How would you fix this paragraph? Probably the best place to begin is with the idea that readers expect a paragraph to move—to take them from one point to another. But on first glance, this paragraph just doesn't seem to go anywhere. Rather, each sentence seems to start over again by referring to the same person—"an individual," "The person," "the individual," "The Operations Manager," etc. But after studying it for a while, you will probably see that the paragraph really does move through a set of topics. It's just that the movement isn't apparent on the surface. The sequence of topics seems to be this.

> An individual–Operations Manager–Experience–Department Head–Manufacturing Process–Communication–Factory Personnel/Professionals

Once you have identified the sequence, you could try rewriting it, using what students of writing call the "old-new" principle. According to this principle, to make a paragraph understandable to your reader, begin a sentence with something your reader is already familiar with (the old topic) and then introduce the new topic. This practice gives your reader the feeling of moving in an orderly way through your topics. If you were to apply this principle to the paragraph above, you might write it as follows.

> An individual cannot start fresh as an Operations Manager. To be an Operations Manager, an individual needs years of experience. Experience can be gained by being a department head. Department heads learn to understand the manufacturing process. Department heads learn to communicate with all types of people. These people are factory personnel and professionals.

Because the topic at the beginning of the sentences repeats the topic of the last sentence, the progression of topics is now clear.

"Sure," you might respond, "now I can see the movement from topic to topic, but the thing is so repetitious that it's boring!"

You're right. So let's eliminate some of the repetition by substituting a few pronouns and using two introductory phrases to link topics (these are underlined).

> An individual cannot start fresh as an Operations Manager. <u>To qualify for such a job, he or she</u> needs

```
years of experience. This can best be gained by being
a department head. In this position, the person
learns to understand the manufacturing process.
He or she learns to communicate with all types of
people, from factory personnel to professionals.
```

In addition, to make sure that readers understand exactly where we're going at every stage, let's put in a couple of transitional words (underlined), to signal them that we're moving from one point to a different one.

```
  An individual cannot start fresh as an Operations
Manager. Rather, to qualify for such a job, he or she
needs years of experience. In most cases, this can
best be gained by being a department head. In this
position, the person learns to understand the
manufacturing process. In addition, he or she learns
to communicate with all types of people, ranging from
factory personnel to professionals.
```

Actually, we may have overdone it a little, so we might decide to eliminate the transitional word, "Rather," since the reader already knows that a contrast is coming from the word "cannot."

Most of the time when writing or revising paragraphs, you'll use these coherence techniques automatically. Certainly you will if you know where you want the paragraph to go and are clear about the relationships of ideas. But if you do have to revise a paragraph so it will flow better, remember that your reader expects two things—*movement* and *continuity*. To provide movement, make sure you move through a sequence of topics, as we did above. To provide the continuity, try the linking and transitional techniques we used.

1. ***Use the old-new principle***. Try to structure individual sentences so the first part refers to old information while the second part introduces the new information.
2. ***Use linking words and phrases***. Link sentences by using personal (you, she, he, they, etc.) or demonstrative pronouns (this, that, these, those) or by repeating key words.
3. ***Use transitional words***. Here are some you will use most often. Good handbooks contain more complete lists.

TO INDICATE:	USE:
Addition:	and, moreover, further, furthermore, besides, also, too, in addition, next, first, second, in the first place, finally, last
Comparison:	similarly, likewise
Contrast:	but, yet, however, still, nevertheless, on the other hand, on the contrary, in contrast
Place:	here, beyond, on the other side
Purpose:	for this purpose, to this end
Cause, Result:	so, hence, therefore, consequently, thus, as a result, then
Summary or example:	to sum up, in brief, in short, in other words, for example, for instance, in fact
Time:	meanwhile, at length, soon, afterward, later, now, then

Academic Status Committee
Medical College of Virginia
Richmond, VA 23298-0001

Ladies and Gentlemen:

In order to fulfill my graduation requirements, I am writing to request that the Academic Status Committee grant me academic credit for internship hours served last summer. Recently, my academic advisor and I discovered that I am three credits below the minimum graduation requirements for the BS Pharmacy degree. Although we are not sure exactly how or when this miscalculation occurred, we have a proposal that we believe will rectify this unfortunate situation. In July 1985, I assisted Dr. Thomas Reimer on a project entitled "Analysis of a Drug Monograph Subscription Service," which was funded by a Special Interest Group on Drug/Poison Information, American Society of Hospital Pharmacists (ASHP). Dr. Reimer selected me from several applicants, citing my past performance in two prerequisite classes, PHA 357 (Research Design) and PHA 501 (Drug Literature Evaluation), my previous experience with Drug Information Services, and a personal recommendation from the Chairman of the Pharmacy Administration Department, Dr. C. D. Goldberg. During the

APPLICATIONS: PARAGRAPHS

1. Following the principles discussed in this section, break the following letter into paragraphs of appropriate length. Be prepared to defend your choices if asked.
2. Write a paragraph of five to six sentences explaining to a high school student how to apply to a college. Make your ideas flow smoothly by using the "old-new principle," linking words, and transitional expressions. Underline each device you use and be prepared to discuss your strategy.
3. Revise the following paragraph so its ideas flow smoothly:

   Dr. Blick was a biologist in industry before she began teaching. Dr. Blick is able to make lectures on her subject more "real." Dr. Blick has a good speaking voice and chooses interesting parts

month I worked with Dr. Reimer, I had the opportunity to directly apply principles learned in PHA 357 and 501 to a practical problem—the initiation of a contract drug monograph subscription service. I have enclosed a copy of my project proposal so you may get a better idea of the scope of the project and how it related so uniquely to my previous undergraduate coursework. The time I spent with Dr. Reimer was insightful and challenging. I spent over 40 hours per week here at the school, collecting and analyzing data. Much of my work was completed independently. Since Dr. Reimer had deadlines imposed on him from ASHP, he and I met twice weekly to monitor my progress. In five weeks, we completed the project and have submitted it for publication to the American Journal of Hospital Pharmacy. I was never formally examined during the project, but it was expected that my understanding of statistical analysis and research design methods was sophisticated enough to handle this project with depth and clarity. I believe that the experience I gained while involved in this project was equivalent to, if not superior to, the educational experience gained in a classroom. Therefore, I ask you to approve my request for academic credit to be applied to the internship hours served this past summer. Thank you for your consideration.

of the subject for her lectures. Dr. Blick sometimes rambles in her lectures and does not always finish on time. The students become anxious and angry. Dr. Blick should organize her time better. Dr. Blick has experience. Dr. Blick has the ability to make her subject interesting.

SENTENCES

When people learn a language, they are programmed to expect that words will occur in certain patterns and not in others. That's why, if you were to ask any native speaker of English to rearrange the words

French the young girls four,

he or she would say, "the four young French girls." And while "Grennick is a furient drack with many neebs" may sound like nonsense, the words are arranged in the normal pattern for English—subject (Grennick), verb (is), complement (drack)—so it sounds like English, and not German or Chinese, nonsense. In the next few paragraphs, we'll discuss the major problems that may occur as you try to write sentences that will fulfill your readers' expectations.

Sentence Fragments

The dominant *sense* pattern in language seems to be, as its root indicates, the sentence. Listeners and readers simply expect that words will occur in sentence patterns, built around subjects, verbs, and often complements. This is not to say that we don't often talk in what seem to be fragments, such as "Go, now!" "Can't help it if you don't!" But understood in the first sentence is the subject, "You," and in the second, "I." Occasionally, you can even use what looks like a fragment in writing. When writing instructional materials and manuals, you could say, "Do this!" "Don't do that!"

But if someone expects you to write in complete sentences, either because the situation is a formal one or because you have created this expectation by writing in a formal voice, then you've got to oblige your reader. Otherwise, your reader is going to get the impression that you're an unclear thinker or careless writer, as the personnel manager did at the beginning of this chapter.

A sentence fragment may occur because you are writing and editing so hastily that you have omitted a word.

```
My practical experience with South Animal Hospital,
where I learned both animal care and laboratory
techniques.
```

Or you have punctuated a phrase or clause as a sentence.

```
You learn self-defense by practicing certain
movements with your hands and feet. Specifically,
blocking, punching, and kicking.

If we bought three instead of six RLM-300s, this
would cost us $34,750 instead of $104,250. Saving the
company $60,500 and cutting our training almost in
half.

When reviewing the answers received, we found that
writers are more careful about tone in letters than
in memos. Although in general no one was aware of
projecting a personality.
```

The reason why you may not catch these fragments in writing or editing is that you are thinking in complete sentences. In your mind, you have included the omitted words or are attaching the fragments to a sentence, usually the one before. Therefore, unless you edit carefully, you will tend to see the complete sentence you meant rather than the incomplete one you wrote.

The key to editing for fragments is to locate them. Once you find them, you will immediately know what you meant to say and can revise accordingly. But finding them can be difficult. The only way I know to do it is just to have the self-discipline to take your time in editing. If you are prone to fragments, read each sentence in isolation from every other, making sure it makes sense and is complete by itself. Motivate yourself to do this by reminding yourself that any fragment could mean a lost job or promotion.

Introductory Modifiers

Read the following sentence:

```
In discussing this project with the logistic officer,
this equipment has not been assigned to any company.
```

Don't you have the nagging feeling that there's something wrong with it? This is because a reader automatically expects that an introductory phrase will usually modify (tell him or her something about) the subject of the sentence. In the sentence above, the reader would expect that the phrase "In discussing this project with the logistic officer" will modify the subject "this equipment." But if this is true, then the sentence seems to imply that the equipment discussed the project with the logistic officer. Of course, the reader knows what the writer really means is probably—

```
In discussing this project with the logistic officer,
[I discovered] that this equipment has not been
assigned to any company.
```

But it takes the reader a moment to figure this out. A good writer tries to avoid costing the reader that moment's confusion.

To do this, make sure that an introductory modifier containing an -ing or -ed word really does have a logical subject to modify. Apply this principle to the following sentences, mentally editing as you read:

```
When talking about the R.A.I.N. program with several other volunteers and professional care-providers, three points of improvement were discovered.

After researching three other programs and conducting interviews with a number of employees, the results indicate that the company should adopt the program recommended below.

After having talked with my adviser this morning, however, my joy began to subside.
```

You should have corrected the three sentences so that the introductory modifiers, "talking," "researching," and "having talked," don't illogically modify "three points," "the results," and "my joy." One way to do this is as follows:

When talking about the R.A.I.N. program with several other volunteers and professional care-providers, <u>we discovered</u> three points of improvement.

After researching three other programs and conducting interviews with a number of employees, <u>he realized</u> that the company should adopt the program recommended below.

After having talked with my adviser this morning, however, <u>I became</u> a lot less happy.

Parallelism

Sometimes, writers create expectations in the minds of their readers just by using a particular pattern of words. Then if they don't stick to this pattern, their sentence will sound a little peculiar, the way a song does when a musician hits a wrong note. See if you can find the wrong note in the following sentence:

```
Readers of grant proposals expect writers to project a certain personality, which is usually authoritative, knowledgeable, and sensitivity.
```

As soon as the writer uses the adjective "authoritative," the expectation is created in the reader that the following words will also be adjectives. When one is not—the noun "sensitivity"—the reader will notice it.

There will be times when you will need to parallel words, phrases, or even whole sentences. It just depends on what expectation you create in the reader's mind. Most often, problems in parallelism occur in series or lists. Find the parallelism problems in the following sentences and correct them:

> Other problems of single, working college students are lack of sleep, overlapping school and job responsibilities, not being able to socialize, and lack of study time.
>
> Dr. Jameson has been active in various aspects of university life, including teaching, research, and students.
>
> The five steps in solving a problem in public relations are as follows:
>
> 1. Analyze the need
> 2. Establishing objectives
> 3. Developing the plan
> 4. Implementing the plan
> 5. Evaluating results

You should have seen that the following elements are not parallel in these sentences: "lack of study time" in the first, "students" in the second, and "Analyze the need" in the third. You might correct the problems as follows:

> Other problems of single, working college students are lack of sleep, overlapping school and job responsibilities, <u>inability to socialize</u>, and lack of study time.
>
> Dr. Jameson has been active in various aspects of university life, including teaching, research, and <u>advising</u> students.
>
> The eight steps in solving a problem in public relations are as follows:
> 1. <u>Analyzing</u> the need
> 2. Establishing objectives
> 3. Developing the plan
> 4. Implementing the plan
> 5. Evaluating results

Here is a sentence that is an absolute disaster because of its faulty parallelism. See if you can meet the challenge of unraveling it.

> All nine of the unskilled writers worry about relatively simple matters: forgetting to cite a source, how their reader will respond to their paper, they worry about whether they covered the topic, grammatical and typographical errors, and whether they will finish a paper on time.

This sentence is tricky, isn't it? You might have decided to split it into two separate sentences to correct it. Another way is to turn the phrases in the series into questions like these.

> All nine of the unskilled writers worry about relatively simple matters:
>
> - Did I forget to cite a source?
> - How will my reader respond to this paper?
> - Did I cover the topic?
> - Did I make any grammatical and typographical errors?
> - Will I finish this paper on time?

Some of these examples may seem outrageous to you. "Surely no one could write that badly," you might say. But people actually made these mistakes in letters, memos, and reports written for courses in business writing. As soon as they learned to listen to the sound of their sentences as they edited, they corrected the problems. If you tend to make mistakes in parallelism, you can do the same thing. Just edit slowly and listen to the patterns you have created in a sentence. If you hear a discordant note, revise the sentence.

Awkward Phrasing

There is a whole grab bag of other sentence structure problems that you could have. You could insert a long modifier that makes the sentence sound clumsy.

> For you, <u>the new owner of this blood pressure self-monitoring kit</u>, we hope that this unit will give you many years of high quality service.

You could misuse a word.

> Many students prefer to <u>living</u> in apartments located near campus.

You could write a phrase that just doesn't quite fit the rest of the sentence.

```
Because of the increase in the cost of housing and
because your commission is a percentage of the
selling price, has caused an increase in yearly
income for realtors.
```

Or you could omit an important word.

```
Or if you want to specialize in a particular area,
such as urban real estate, [this] will require a
bachelor's degree.
```

But these problems will occur very seldom, especially if you are writing in a voice you are comfortable with. To catch the few that might occur, train yourself to edit carefully, listening to the sound of your sentences and attending to their meaning.

APPLICATIONS: SENTENCES

1. To practice some of the sentence principles discussed above, revise the following sentences as needed:
   a. By reducing fatigue, the firefighter will be able to operate more safely.
   b. While he possesses good qualities as well as bad. It is my opinion that his bad qualities outweigh the good.
   c. We formulated an equation that will give the time of expected high sales, productivity, and when the cash flow would be the greatest.
   d. After interviewing the users and the training coordinator, the best answer to the problem seemed to be to eliminate the program entirely.
   e. As information is gathered, notes are made. Even thoughts are jotted down for later use.
   f. Because of an error, my academic advisor and I have discovered that I am three credits short of fulfilling the requirements needed for graduation.
   g. My major findings were as follows: that writers prepare to write in different ways, the linear writing process of people on the job, they are usually aware of their reader.
   h. Focusing on the major problem, some workers are not following current safety regulations.
   i. By letting the student try different fields without declaring a major, there is a chance to find out which field proves most interesting.
   j. Like the surveys, the interviews with the three different groups were similar in terms of their feelings about the present lack of facilities.

2. If you can consciously do something wrong, you can usually do it right. Following this principle, try to make the following mistakes:
   a. Write two sentences, but make one a fragment.
   b. Write a sentence with a dangling introductory modifier.
   c. Write a sentence with parts that should be parallel but are not.
   d. Write a sentence that sounds awkward to your ear.

3. A number of sentence structure errors have purposefully been made in the letter to the right. Edit it carefully, correcting all sentence problems.

PUNCTUATION

Most people are confused and overwhelmed by our current system of punctuation. Its history explains why. The ancient Greeks invented punctuation as an oratorical aid, showing speakers when to pause at the end of a rhythmical unit to take a breath. By the Middle Ages and early Renaissance, writers were using punctuation marks more as a way of marking sense than rhythm. But because their use varied from writer to writer, most punctuation marks meant little to readers. Finally, with the development of printing, punctuation gradually became standardized. By the end of the nineteenth century, printing houses, grammarians, and schools had developed the system of prescriptive rules that our current practice is based on, except that we use fewer marks than people did a hundred years ago.

Given the complicated history of our punctuation system, it's no wonder that writers of today wonder when to use a particular mark. Occasionally, the *pause test* works—"Use a mark when you and your reader would naturally pause." More often, though, a rule, such as, "Use a comma to separate a long introductory adverb clause from its main clause," is needed as a guide. But printers, grammarians, and teachers of the nineteenth century did their job so well that there seems a rule for every occasion. Only writers, editors, and a few English teachers seem to remember them all.

And yet imagine trying to understand the following sentence without a system of punctuation:

```
If we didn't have a punctuation system to write might
not be any harder to read though would be a time
consuming difficult task better left to people who
like Rip Van Winkle had the time
```

A few punctuation marks, rightly distributed, clear up the confusion (although they don't help to straighten out the clumsy convolutions).

Mr. Julius M. Valdrighi
University of Milan
Milan, Italy

Dear Mr. Valdrighi:

Congratulations on your selection in the University of Maryland Foreign Exchange Program for the coming academic year.

The Office of Student Housing is pleased to provide you with the enclosed brochures describing on-campus housing opportunities available to you during your stay.

The University's mid-city location enables the on-campus student choice from a unique blend of available student housing. Styles ranging from traditional dormitory buildings to modern high-rise residence halls and apartment buildings. The University's on-campus student housing is fully furnished and equipped to provide you with a relaxed, safe, and conducive to learning atmosphere.

Consisting mainly of apartment buildings and privately owned residences, you will find also off-campus housing in a number of styles and price ranges. While the University has no control over private, off-campus housing. We can provide you with a list of reputable realtors registered with our office.

Please review the brochures and return your housing application as early as possible to reserve the housing of your choice. If you have any further questions, please write me at this office.

We look forward to having you here at the University of Maryland.

> If we didn't have a punctuation system, to write might not be any harder; to read, though, would be a time-consuming, difficult task, better left to people who, like Rip Van Winkle, had the time.

As this sentence indicates, the function of punctuation marks is to separate and relate elements in a sentence. Commas are used just to separate; other marks, such as semicolons, colons, and dashes, both separate and indicate relationships, showing that two elements are equal, that one is a summary of the other, or that one sharply interrupts another.

In the following paragraphs are eleven major punctuation rules. While they don't cover every punctuation situation that may arise, they will help you solve the majority of problems. If you already punctuate pretty well, reading over the rules will be a good review. If you have trouble punctuating, take the time to study the rules and their examples. Then practice applying them in the exercises that follow.

Comma

1. Use a comma to separate two main clauses from each other if they are connected by a coordinating conjunction. (A **main clause** has a subject and verb and will stand by itself. The most frequently used **coordinating conjunctions** are "and," "but," "for," and "so."

    > The company will provide you with enough chairs to seat your guests, and their groundskeeper will set them up before the ceremony and take them down afterward.

    > Exception: Don't use the comma if clauses are very short.

2. Use a comma to separate an introductory word, phrase, or clause from the rest of the sentence.

    > However, I don't think that this project is worth the extra trouble.

    > After examining the effectiveness and condition of the old warehouse, I agree that we need to requisition the funds to build a new one.

    > As you can see from my résumé, I have been working for the last four summers at King's Dominion Amusement Park.

Exception: Don't use the comma if the phrase or clause is short and if the sentence would be clear without it.

3. Use a comma to separate parenthetical elements, whether they are individual words, dates, phrases, or clauses, from the rest of the sentence. (A **parenthetical element** can be left out of the sentence without changing its basic meaning.) *Note:* If the parenthetical element comes in the middle of a sentence, be sure to put both commas in.

    He has, moreover, two other line items that are higher than usual.

    On October 15, 1985, we met with the full group to discuss the new procedures.

    Gone, or at least going, are the post-office, general store, and service station.

    We intend to explore the third option, which seems the most feasible.

    or

    We intend to explore the third option, which seems the most feasible, with all concerned.

    but not

    We intend to explore the option that seems the most feasible with all concerned. (Because the clause is now needed to identify which option and is therefore not parenthetical.)

4. Use a comma to separate items in a series.

    The pamphlet is a helpful guide to writing letters, memos, and reports.

    Exception: Some style guides, including those that journalists use, omit the comma before the "and."

5. Don't separate subjects and verbs or verbs and complements with commas.

    The length and type, of these documents, varies with the situation of their writer.

Semicolon

6. Use a semicolon to separate two main clauses that are close in meaning and not joined by a coordinating conjunction.

    The IBM 100 will cost a good deal more than we anticipated; for this reason, I recommend that we consider other machines.

    The IBM 100 will cost a good deal more than we anticipated; with its use we will quickly make up this extra expense.

    Note: Use the semicolon even if the sentence is also connected by a word like "however," "therefore," "moreover," etc.

7. Use a semicolon to separate phrases already separated by commas. In this situation, the semicolon functions as a kind of supercomma.

    Present at the conference were engineers, both mechanical and electrical; chemists, both physical and organic; and technicians from various fields.

8. Ordinarily, don't separate two unequal elements (such as a phrase and a clause or a subordinate and main clause) with a semicolon.

    Even though the report does not indicate that the variation is a critical one; it does recommend we monitor operation of the machine closely.

Colon

9. Use a colon to separate an explanation, summary, series, or quotation from rest of sentence. (Capitalize the first word in the second sentence if it is a formal statement.) Also use it after the salutation of a letter.

    These policies all have the same purpose: They protect employees from accidents.

    Our department recommends that you buy one of the following systems: IBM 3,000, Digital Vax, or Tandy 2,900.

Dash

10. Use a dash to separate parenthetical elements or a summary sharply divided from the rest of the sentence.

```
Current policies--especially those that pertain
to safety--must be followed carefully.
```

```
The most important people to reach are the ones
we met with yesterday--Jack Thomas, Jill
Baughan, and Ron Overton.
```

Quotation Marks

11. Use quotation marks to separate direct quotations and titles of works within larger works (chapters in a book or report, articles in magazines, parts of a training tape, etc.). Underline (Italicize) titles of works that are published separately.

```
In our survey, we discovered that the most
frequent question asked by supervisors was
the following: "What are the differences
between an independent contractor and an
employee?"
```

```
The "Operations Budget" section of that
report is the one we should examine most
closely.
```

Note: When using quotation marks with other marks, always put periods and commas inside quotation marks, even when they set off one word at the end of a sentence.

Put semicolons, colons, dashes, question marks, and exclamation points inside or outside quotation marks, depending on whether they apply to the whole sentence or just to the part within quotations.

If you need to review the use of other punctuation marks—parentheses, ellipses, etc.—consult a good handbook. But the rules above will cover the majority of situations you will encounter. If you can't justify using a mark by one of the rules above, don't use it unless you want your reader to pause for a special effect.

APPLICATIONS: PUNCTUATION

1. To practice applying rules for using commas, add or delete commas in the following sentences. Explain your correction by referring to the appropriate rule.
   a. The need for self-defense, in today's society is increasing at a rapid rate.
   b. Before concluding that the report is based on sound data I want to double-check some of the major collection techniques.
   c. He in turn expects that the position will be filled by the end of the month.

d. His illustrations which sometimes may be confusing, are crisp and clear this time.

e. This is educational to the public, and also much better for the companies in question.

f. When you consider a person for a position with this company you cannot discriminate because of gender, race, or religious preference.

g. You may have several views on the subject under discussion but you can't avoid making a decision in the near future.

h. Moreover the department will be expanded by adding two new positions.

i. I told him, that I didn't think our sales would be increased substantially unless we move into the new territory.

j. Soon we will be able to buy the copying machines as well as the other materials you ordered.

2. To practice applying other punctuation marks, add, delete, or change punctuation marks in the following sentences. Explain each change you make by referring to the number of the rule that applies.

a. In his testimony before the commission, the witness said: The new rates will not increase the average customer's bill more than 8%.

b. Hospital administration is an occupation that involves working with complex equipment, intricate systems and numbers of people, therefore, we think that any person interested in such a career should have a rich background in the humanities, the sciences, and in business administration.

c. It will be helpful if you list all three of the following items checkbook, ledger, and balance sheet.

d. At first the company progressed rapidly then it seemed to lose its position in the market.

e. While the information given to us on the twenty-fifth was very scant; we still feel that the system is a good buy.

f. We don't feel that you need to change current buying practices at this time: in the future, though, you may have to consider other alternatives.

g. It's going to be late this afternoon before we complete the run, I don't think we'll encounter any difficulty though.

h. It's not going to be long at least in my mind it's not before we find ourselves in a better position.

3. The following letter does not contain any punctuation marks except periods. Punctuate it appropriately.

Ms. Rene Hanna
Heritage Savings and Loan
Richmond, VA 23220

Dear Ms. Hanna:

After reading your advertisement for a position in the finance department I believe that I am fully qualified for the job. My academic work coupled with my summer experience in banking has prepared me well to perform all its duties.

Working for your company will require a wealth of knowledge in various aspects of finance. My major in finance which is supplemented by concentrations in accounting and economics has given me this knowledge. In addition my two years of liberal arts has given me the necessary breadth to work at an institution such as yours which conducts business both here and abroad.

For the past three summers I have worked in the finance department of Franklin Savings and Loan learning much about the operations of such a department. In this position I gained a practical awareness that I never could have gotten from school moreover I learned the invaluable skill of working well with a variety of people.

Both in school and on the job I have learned the skills needed to work for your bank. I will be calling you shortly for an interview so that I may demonstrate my abilities.

Sincerely

4. Explain why you punctuated the letter above as you did. To do this, consecutively number each punctuation mark you put in, list the numbers, and then beside each number write the number of the rule that applies.

AGREEMENT

If you have been dreading a long discussion of grammar rules, you can relax. As I said earlier, if you are a native speaker of English, you probably know almost all the grammar rules you need to speak and write effectively. (If you are a nonnative speaker, the best way to develop your skills is to read, speak, and write as much as possible.) There are, however, a few trouble spots for writers on the job. One of these is the area of agreement—agreement between subject and verb and pronoun and antecedent.

You already know that subjects and verbs should agree with each other. But don't let words that fall between the subject and verb throw you, as the writers of the following two sentences did:

> Attempts to identify a cure for AIDS has [have] been given major priority by researchers all over the world.

> The assessment of noncognitive skills, another national problem noted in the article, are [is] not as consistently made as it should be.

Words such as "an individual," "the person," "each," "everybody," and "everyone" also seem to throw writers, as the following mistakes indicate:

> If the person does not have all the experience required for the job, they [he or she] may be put on a probationary period.

> Each of the new employee training sessions are [is] being held at the Main Street branch.

> Everybody might feel that they [he or she] cannot solve this problem.

Remember that words with "a" and "the" in front of them, even though they may refer to more than one person, take singular verbs and pronouns. Also, words such as "each," "either," "one," and all the words that end in "one" (someone, anyone) and "body" (somebody, anybody) take singular verbs and pronouns.

Of course, the problem of agreement is more complicated now than it used to be because readers are sensitive to sex discrimination. Many readers now feel that the sentence, "Each of the employees will get his bonus in the next paycheck," is discriminatory. And the argument that masculine pronouns represent both sexes doesn't carry much weight with some of them. There is no perfect solution to the problem. Here are two suggestions; sometimes one works better, sometimes another.

1. Whenever you can, change the singular noun or pronoun to plural.

```
All employees will get their bonuses in their
next paycheck.
```

2. If you can't change the noun or pronoun, use both masculine and feminine pronouns (his or her, but not the awkward his/her).

```
Each employee will get his or her bonus in the
next paycheck.
```

APPLICATIONS: AGREEMENT

1. Correct the subject–verb and pronoun–antecedent agreement errors in the following sentences:
   a. It was expected that my understanding of statistical analysis and research design methods were sophisticated enough to handle this project with depth and clarity.
   b. Somebody in the department is bound to complain, even if we make sure that all their overtime is paid at the higher rate.
   c. The cost associated with the loss of productivity and increased medical expenses are estimated to be 38 billion dollars a year.
   d. Each person who is associated with the test are assured of the quickest possible turnaround time for results.
   e. Any individual may be considered for the position, but all their materials must be submitted before the 15th of the month.
   f. Both my social work internship and course work in rehabilitation services has prepared me well for such a position.

MECHANICS

Another set of writing conventions, often called mechanics, includes capitalization, abbreviations, and numbers. Although practice can vary from discipline to discipline and even company to company, there are some conventions that are generally accepted. If your organization has a style manual (a set of directions on what conventions to follow), it will help you answer particular questions.

Capitalization

Generally speaking, capitalize whenever you are referring to a particular member of a group. Following this principle, capitalize—

- names of people, languages, nationalities, and religions
- names of places, regions of the country, historical periods, or events

- names of organizations, institutions, companies, departments within particular companies, trademarks
- adjectives formed from proper nouns
- titles of people when they precede the name or substitute for it
- titles of books, articles, films, reports, computer programs—capitalize the first and last word and all other words except articles, prepositions, and conjunctions

When in doubt, check the dictionary or other reference manuals.

Abbreviations

Avoid abbreviations unless you are certain your readers will recognize them instantly. Generally speaking, complete words are easier to read and understand. Here are some common abbreviation conventions. Besides the obvious abbreviations of beginnings of sentences and titles, abbreviate—

- Well-known businesses and organizations, as well as countries
- Acronyms (words made from the first letters of long titles)
- Scientific terms; e.g., 45 mph, 375 rpm
- Commonly used Latin terms

  —e.g. (exempli gratia = for example)
  —i.e. (id est = that is)
  —et al. (et alii = and others)
  —etc. (et cetera = and so on, and so forth)
  —vs. (versus = against)

Numbers

You'll need to become familiar with the style of your discipline or organization. In general, you can follow these principles.

- Use words for numbers when the number begins a sentence and when the number is ten or less.
- Use figures for numbers for a number that is over ten and for dates, times, percentages, money, measurements, pages, and prices.

APPLICATIONS: MECHANICS

1. Correct the errors in capitalization, abbreviation, and numbers in the following sentences:

   a. Johnson and johnson company will hold its fall convention in salt lake city, home of the morman church, the morman tabernacle choir, and the university of utah.

b. To receive an associate's degree, you must take courses in liberal arts; eg, English, Mathematics, and History, as well as in Business and Economics.

c. We will have thirty three positions vacant this year If we fill all these, our staff will total over one hundred fifty people.

d. 203 cases of flu were reported for that district in one week last winter.

e. Our new word processing program will be known as *write well* and will be written by Stephen Jacobs etal.

f. We plan to relocate somewhere in the west, probably in the western part of Colorado or Wyoming, but will always retain the texan spirit with which we started.

g. They plan to make John Day president of the company at a salary of forty-five thousand dollars.

SPELLING

It may surprise you to see a section on spelling, although mercifully short, in a text such as this. There are two reasons why it's necessary to discuss spelling a little. First, correct spelling has become the mark of a cultured, intelligent person. One misspelled word ("alot," "recieve," or "becomming") could cost you a job or a promotion. But second, our modern spelling system is a thicket of rules, exceptions, and contradictions, inherited from English people of the Middle Ages and Renaissance who just didn't care about consistency in spelling. During those times, a person might spell a word one way one day and another the next.

If you are one of us many unfortunates who has trouble spelling, give up trying to memorize every word in the dictionary. Since you may still have to rely on your own abilities many times, follow these steps to learn the words that you will have trouble spelling.

1. Know these four rules well enough so you can refer to them when you need to. (*Warning*: most of these rules have exceptions. I've listed a few.)

   - *When spelling words with **ei** or **ie***:
     Put i before e, except after c and except when e sounds like a, as in neighbor or weigh.

     Examples: believe, field, yield, freight

     Exceptions: forfeit, foreign, height, heir, seize

- When adding suffixes such as **-ed, -er, -ness, -ing, -ful, -able, -ment**:
  If the word ends in a silent e, drop the e before suffixes beginning with a vowel.

  Examples: desirable, provable, writing; but careful, management, safety.

  If the word ends in y preceded by a consonant, change the y to i before adding the suffix, except for the suffix -ing.

  Examples: hurried, happiness, heavier; but hurrying, studying

  If the word ends in a consonant preceded by a vowel, if accent is on last syllable, and if suffix begins with a vowel, double the final consonant before adding the suffix.

  Examples: hidden, beginning, stunning; but benefit (stress on 1st syllable) and commitment.

2. Check the words on the two lists at the end of this chapter that you think you will have trouble spelling.

3. Memorize any other words that give you trouble.

Once you are aware of the words that you may misspell, proofread your document once, looking just for these words. One trick is to read it backwards so you will pay attention to spelling rather than to sound or meaning.

Remember, you won't always be able to rely on a secretary or spelling checker in a word processing program to spell for you. For example, a spelling checker won't catch a mistake like "its" if you mean "it's." Even if you do have such help, there will be times when you need to write someone a quick note; for example, your boss. If you don't want to run the risk of looking dumb, check closely for spelling errors.

SUMMARY

The theme of this chapter has been the need for careful proofreading. If you have studied it section by section, see whether you can apply the principles of paragraphing, sentence structure, punctuation, usage, mechanics, and spelling to correct all errors in the letter that opened the chapter.

Donald G. Hill
Personel Department
Johnson Controls
San Diego, CA 92101

Dear Mr. Hill:

After the converation we had a few days ago, about the office manager's position, I am convinced, I am qualified for the position. My strong asset is the experience I have recieved in training, and interacting with people on a consistent basis. Also, my experience in having to think through problems to reach a decision.

All the satistics I have read in weekly magazines and newspapers, indicate that companies are earning profits, but at the same time losing valuble employees. For the simple reason, they do not know how to work with their people.

I am convinced that I have the qualifications to do the job. To do the kind of job, not only to help Johnson controls make a profit, but help them to operate more eficiently.

I hope you contact me soon for an interview.

LIST 1: TROUBLESOME SPELLING WORDS

accommodate	desirable	mortgage
appearance	dilemma	occasionally
appreciated	dissatisfied	occurrence
arguing	efficient	omission
argument	eligible	personal
believe	embarrass	personnel
benefited	existence	preceding
calendar	feasible	privilege
cancellation	February	questionnaire
certain	foreign	receipt
changeable	grievance	receive
commitment	hindrance	repetition
committed	independent	secretary
concede	irrelevant	separate
congratulations	judgment	similar
conscientious	labeled	transferred
conscious	maintenance	unanimous
counseling	manageable	
controlled	manual	

LIST 2: TROUBLESOME PAIRS

Because the following pairs of words sound alike, they confuse writers sometimes. If you study the sample sentences closely, you will see how to use each word properly.

accept except	We will *accept* everyone *except* the three people who appplied after the deadline
access excess	You can gain *access* to the system through that code, but be sure that your characters are not in *excess* of those allowed.
advice advise	You'd better consult your attorney for *advice* on this matter; you'll probably be *advised* to sign the contract, though.
affect effect	Your decision will have no great *effect* on the outcome of the matter, but it may *affect* the way the two parties work out the details.
already all ready	If the supervisor has *already* made up her mind, I know that you are *all ready* to cooperate with her.
all together altogether	I am *altogether* sure that the companies are *all together* in their opposition to this matter.

allusion illusion	She was under the *illusion* that you had made an unkind *allusion* to her performance this morning.
assure ensure insure	I always *assure* the people I talk to that the proper accident policy will *insure* them against loss, even though it cannot *ensure* that an accident will never occur.
beside besides	*Besides* the three organizations I've already mentioned, there is one more that is located *beside* the river in question.
capital capitol	The *capitol* building is located in the *capital* of that state.
cite site	He *cited* the document in question again and again in the discussion of the best *site* for the new plant.
complement compliment	To say that my actions *complement* yours is quite a *compliment* to me.
continual continuous	The *continual* attacks of the media have been a *continuous* source of dissension between us.
council counsel	The local *council* failed to heed the *counsel* of their chairperson on the matter.
decease disease	The *deceased* person had been attacked by the fatal *disease* when only 55 years old.
eminent imminent	The *imminent* visit of that *eminent* politician was dreaded by most of the local population.
farther further	She *further* assured me that it was not much *farther* to our destination.
formally formerly	We have not been *formally* introduced, although we were slightly acquainted with each other *formerly*.
infer imply	I think I can *infer* from what you *implied* in your response that we are in agreement with each other.
ingenious ingenuous	It takes an *ingenious* person to operate that complex system; that person must also be *ingenuous* to admit when a mistake has been made.
its it's	*It's* a little hard to understand why an organization as large as this would destroy *its* own market.

later latter	You won't encounter the *latter* problem until *later* on this year.
less fewer	I earn *less* money than you do, but then I have *fewer* problems too.
loose lose	His *loose* tongue caused his company to *lose* the most important contract of the year.
moral morale	The *moral* of the story is that worker *morale* can only be increased by a bonus.
persecute prosecute	You must *prosecute* that case, but be sure that in the process you do not end up *persecuting* your opponent.
perspective prospective	Her new *perspective* on the problem enabled her to decide that the *prospective* solution was the best one.
proceed precede	We will *proceed* in our discussion, but make sure that the major points *precede* the minor ones.
principal principle	Although I refuse to violate my *principles* in the process, my *principal* interest is to win their approval.
quiet quite	I am *quite* sure that it will be a relatively *quiet* meeting.
stationary stationery	These two words sound exactly like, but *stationery* refers to envelopes and letters while *stationary* means a fixed position.
than then	*Then,* I can only conclude that he feels things much more deeply *than* she does.
to too two	*Two* weeks is way *too* little time *to* enjoy that trip *to* Europe.
their they're there	*They're* too concerned about safety to hide *their* keys *there.*
weather whether	Whatever the *weather*, we'll *weather* it, *whether* we like it or not.

INDEX

A 7
B 8
C 9
D 0
E 1
F 2
G 3
H 4
I 5
J 6